Who Is Jesus Christ for Us Today?

Who Is Jesus Christ
for Us Today?

Pathways to Contemporary Christology

EDITED BY

Andreas Schuele
Günter Thomas

WESTMINSTER
JOHN KNOX PRESS
LOUISVILLE · KENTUCKY

© 2009 Westminster John Knox Press
Chapter 14, "Personhood and Bodily Resurrection," © Christoph Schwöbel

First edition
Published by Westminster John Knox Press
Louisville, Kentucky

09 10 11 12 13 14 15 16 17 18—10 9 8 7 6 5 4 3 2 1

Book design by Sharon Adams
Cover design by Eric Walljasper, Minneapolis, MN

Library of Congress Cataloging-in-Publication Data

Who is Jesus Christ for us today? : pathways to contemporary christology / edited by Andreas Schuele, Günter Thomas.
    p. cm.
Includes index.
ISBN 978-0-664-23339-6 (alk. paper)
1. Jesus Christ—Person and offices.   I. Schuele, Andreas.   II. Thomas, Günter, 1960–
BT203.W479   2009
232—dc22

                                    2009001917

PRINTED IN THE UNITED STATES OF AMERICA

∞ The paper used in this publication meets the minimum requirements
of the American National Standard for Information Sciences—Permanence of Paper
for Printed Library Materials, ANSI Z39.48-1992.

Westminster John Knox Press advocates the responsible use of our natural resources.
The text paper of this book is made from at least 30% post-consumer waste.

In Honor of Michael Welker

Contents

Preface

This volume, together with its German sister publication "Gegenwart des leben-digen Christus" (G. Thomas, A. Schuele, eds., Leipzig: Evangelische Verlagsan-stalt, 2007), offers an interdisciplinary approach to a particular question: What is the task of a contemporary Christology that understands the biblical traditions and the many witnesses of the church as a constructive resource to address the complex character of the modern world? We are grateful to the contributors who have dedicated their essays to honor our distinguished colleague and friend Michael Welker on the occasion of his sixtieth birthday. Our special thanks go to Westminster John Knox Press and to Amanda C. Miller, PhD student at Union Theological Seminary and Presbyterian School of Christian Education.

Andreas Schuele, Richmond, Virginia
Günter Thomas, Bochum, Germany

Introduction

ANDREAS SCHUELE

In his prison letters from the last years of the Second World War, Dietrich Bonhoeffer outlined a future Christology that evolves around the question, "Who is Jesus Christ for us today?" Sadly, Bonhoeffer was not given the time to elaborate on this question and its possible answers, which left it for future generations to pick up the thread where he had left off. At first glance, this might appear a rather unspectacular approach to the task of Christology, for there was probably never a period in the history of Christianity in which Christians did not ponder the question of who Jesus Christ was for them at their particular time and in their particular place. Already the New Testament traditions themselves suggest that the presence of Christ among his people should be the starting point of any Christology: "For where two or three are gathered in my name, I am there among them" (Matt. 18:20). This famous sentence belongs to a collection of Jesus' words and sayings that characterize the life of the community. The way in which these words are presented suggests that they were not meant for Matthew's own community alone but for the church in all times and places. One might be tempted to understand this as a mainly spiritual presence of the community that assembles in Jesus' memory. Matthew, however, seems to hint at a much more comprehensive kind of presence that includes every aspect of the life of the community and its individual members. Different from most modern thinking that conceives of personhood and personal presence primarily in individualistic terms, the New Testament seeks to envision the corporate character of Christ's being with and among his people.

Nevertheless, the great promise in the words "I am there among them" remains vague unless it points to a concrete, identifiable, and nameable reality. The idea of "Christ existing as community," to use Bonhoeffer's own formula, does not already provide an answer but rather suggests a direction in christological thinking. Consequently, Bonhoeffer's Christology turns this promise into a question, "Who is he for us today?" and unpacking this question along the lines that Bonhoeffer suggests might give us a sense of what is at stake in contemporary Christology.

1. Bonhoeffer wrote at a time that had witnessed the rise and fall of the historical Jesus movement. As is well known, modern historical scholarship had a significant impact on Christology by introducing a categorical distinction between the historical Jesus and the Christ of the church. However, as became clear with the many "lives of Jesus" that attempted to go back behind the kerygma, the historical Jesus proved to be an elusive figure. There were just too many possible versions of Jesus' life, and all of them were unavoidably flavored by the theological backgrounds and interests of their authors, as Albert Schweizer demonstrated in his famous book *The Quest of the Historical Jesus* (1906). This, of course, raised the question of whether one had to simply give up on the historical Jesus altogether and settle for the later ecclesiastically influenced picture of Jesus that we find in the final version of the four Gospels.

Bonhoeffer belonged to a generation of theologians who sought to take the next step and move beyond the dichotomy between history and kerygma. If the quest of Jesus Christ was already initiated by the New Testament itself, this dichotomy appeared not only simplistic but also theologically questionable. The enigma about Jesus of Nazareth is not only a phenomenon of the historical distance between him and a contemporary audience. On the contrary, the question "Who is he?" is a leitmotif that runs through all four canonical Gospels. Jesus' identity beyond the sheer biographical data was not an open book at all—not to the political and religious authorities of his days, and not even to his own followers. There are only a few, and again elusive, moments where the evangelists lift the veil and let their readers in on who, in their view, Jesus Christ really was.

Thus, it seems safe to conclude that identifying Jesus required interpretative efforts "from the first day on," but as such is open to misunderstanding, doubt, spontaneous messianic enthusiasm, and disappointment. The fact that the Gospels make no attempt to eliminate the traces of these many efforts to come to grips with the person of Jesus of Nazareth suggests that Christology—at least one that is based on the New Testament traditions—cannot be done in a reductive way, sundering the historical Jesus from the Christ of the kerygma (or vice versa!). The fact that there is a plenitude of witnesses to Jesus Christ and that he cannot be separated from these witnesses puts the later readers of the Gospels in a position that is not categorically different from that of the first followers of Jesus. There is no Christ apart from the believing community; this is no less true today than it was in the early years of the first century CE.

2. Beyond the historical Jesus debate, the question "Who is he for us today?" implies that there may be many possible answers, and that no single one of them exhausts the fullness of Christ's presence in our day. This situation makes it imperative to realize that the task of Christology requires a willingness to listen to, and make an effort at understanding, other Christians' witness, even though this approach may lie beyond the horizon of one's own tradition, cul-

ture, or worldview. In this regard, Christology is not only a theological but also a hermeneutical and ethical task. It implies that there is no aspect of human life from which the christological perspective can be excluded. It is not only human nature and culture in their most sublime moments that give evidence to the presence of Christ but also the everyday, the mediocre, the trivial, even the ridiculous. Distancing himself from the high-culture Christologies of his teachers, Bonhoeffer was among the first to acknowledge that Christology must make a connection with human life in whatever form it may come. This does not mean that Christology would have to see the good in even the most corrupt, brutal, or disgraceful forms of human existence. It does mean, however, that Christology cannot ignore what seems unattractive, undesirable, or suspicious in favor of a nonexistent ideal of humanity when it defines the "us" in the question, "Who is Christ for us today?"

3. This leads us to another point where current Christology faces the challenge of a nonreductive approach to reality. Reflecting on the "Christ for us" not only has to relate to a variety of expressions of human life but also needs to be sensitive to the parameters that characterize us as natural and cultural persons, such as gender, age, race, and cultural and ethnic backgrounds—parameters that we cannot normally change, even if we wanted to. Being human means being stuck in a particular skin, which implies in turn that genuine appreciation of the other should be imperative in every interpersonal encounter.

In a postmodern world, this may sound like a commonplace. However, the impact of this commonplace on Christology has not always received proper attention. Despite the validity of the creeds' universal statements about Christ, the question of who he is for us should make one wary of a one-size-fits-all approach. Christology can no longer abstract from the fact that the Christ for an infant child is different from the Christ for a middle-aged white male, and it also cannot disregard the fact that high-Christology language such as "he died for our sins" has a very different impact on someone dying of AIDS in South Africa than on a mainline consumer of the Western world. Christology needs to be as sensitive to individual life contexts as possible, but without losing its contours. Therefore, any future Christology will have to be able to make sense of the phrase "Christ *for us*" in such a way that it comprises and combines both, "for each of us" and "for all of us."

4. Unpacking the key question of Bonhoeffer's Christology would not be complete without noticing its allusion to the "pro nobis" that, in the Reformation period, especially Luther and Melanchthon emphasized in what has been called their "experiential theology." How is the Christ "for us" a reality that affects our lives and transforms it in tangible ways? A Christology would be in danger of operating in a merely descriptive and potentially even ideological mode if it was limited to who *we think* Christ is and how we can relate our lives to his presence. The "pro nobis" that echoes in Bonhoeffer's "for us" accounts for the fact that the presence of Christ has its own momentum and its own thrust in the way it makes itself known in our lives.

Today we see a lot of experience language especially in popular religion, and the offerings of what Christ can and will do for us are endless, tailored to the needs of the consumer market: a happy life, success, health, being shielded from the evil world around us. And even if we encounter trials and tribulations, we are assured that nothing will happen to us that the gracious God did not intend for us. While it seems impossible to promise more and better things, the issue becomes what might be a more credible account of Christ's presence "for us." How does the reality of the living Christ make contact with our lives, if this reality makes a difference at all? The Reformers thematized this question in their work on soteriology. Bonhoeffer made it the central issue of his "Ethics," and today one notices that theologians develop eschatology as a framework for understanding human life—past, present, and future—as affected and transformed by Christ. As a matter of fact, it seems fair to say that a good number of key christological issues and concepts now find their place in an eschatological mind frame, which indicates in turn that eschatology is not limited anymore to questions about the "last things" but that it also includes what it means, to use Pauline language, that we are growing into the "body of Christ" or are transformed into "Christ's image."

The contributions to this volume in honor of Michael Welker's sixtieth birthday are dedicated to these four different areas outlined along the lines of Bonhoeffer's theology, which has been one of the major sources of inspiration for Welker's own work. Each of these sections brings together scholars from different disciplines—Bible, history of Christianity, constructive/systematic theology, practical theology, and ethics. For all the reasons given above, it seems not only impossible but also undesirable to limit the christological discourse of our day to dogmatics alone. Christology, more than ever, requires a thick description from which its systematic contours can emerge. Thus, Part I of this volume, which explores the New Testament portraits of Jesus of Nazareth and its reception history, includes contributions by Bible scholars, theologians, and ethicists.

Patrick Miller opens this section by tracing one of the most controversial titles applied to Jesus, namely, "king of the Jews." Miller demonstrates that, despite the polemical and strategic ways in which this title is used especially in the passion narrative, this title also provides key insight into how Jesus' contemporaries perceived his ministry. As Miller states,

> The rule of God embodied in and identified with the life and death as well as the teaching of this Jesus the king happens precisely in his identification with the poor and needy who are the king's subjects. The righteousness and justice reflected in care of the poor are not simply something to come or a matter of the ruler's decrees and acts. They are embodied in the acts of Jesus, his self-understanding, and his transformation of the image of ruler into the image of one who is with the poor, both in the way he lives and dies and in his identification with them in the church's ministry to the poor (Matt. 25).

Dirk Smit focuses on a related question. He investigates why the "suffering under Pilate" became a crucial element not only in the New Testament traditions but also in the creeds of the ancient church. Smit concludes that linking the suffering of Christ to a particular historical person, Pontius Pilate, plays a crucial role in the memory formation of early Christianity and also in the church of our own time:

> Keeping the words ". . . under Pontius Pilate" alive will remain attentive to new situations in which political power, institutions of justice, cultural practices, communal forms, moral systems, public opinion, and religious traditions collapse and fail—not only when they are evil, but precisely in their claims to be beneficial. Confessing Jesus Christ today—including his suffering and death under Pontius Pilate—may therefore indeed call for such confession in the face of contemporary realities, whether excessively evil or extremely self-righteous.

Thomas Gillespie draws attention to the significance of the "faith of Christ" in Paul's salvation theology. Although there may not be much debate over whether the historical Jesus had faith in God, the more intriguing question is whether it makes sense to say that Christ as the Son of God could have faith in God. Here in particular, the transformation of the early witnesses into the ecclesial picture of Jesus Christ becomes a crucial issue. Paul addresses the "faith of Christ" by referring to the justifying "faith of Abraham" in Genesis 15:6. As Gillespie writes:

> The God whom Paul calls "our Father" in Galatians (1:1, 4) is attested throughout the argument of chapter 3 to be an active agent—in initiating the promise to Abraham and his seed (3:8, 16), in reckoning faith "unto righteousness" (3:6), and in supplying the Spirit to and thus working wonders among the Galatians in the realization of the promised "blessing of Abraham" (3:5, 14). Central to Paul's argument, however, is his conviction that all of this turns on "the faith" that "has come" being the divine "Son" who was "sent" by God, "born of a woman, born under the law, in order to deliver those under the law, that we might receive adoption as a son" (Gal. 4:4–5).

The essays of Part II explore what the humanity of Christ means for humanity, and they also focus on the interpretative efforts that have been undertaken in Christian traditions to understand the central claim that Christ became human.

Peter Lampe analyzes the notion of hypostasis ("reality, concrete appearance") in the New Testament, and here in particular in Hebrews 1:3. Hypostasis was the term that eventually assumed doctrinal weight in the creeds of the ancient church to express both the divinity and the humanity of Christ. Nonetheless, as Lampe demonstrates, the semantic spectrum underlying the creedal use of hypostasis is quite diverse and accommodates a variety of ways of expressing the nature and purpose of Christ's becoming human.

Focusing on the next stage in the history of the ancient church, Sarah Coakley turns to Gregory of Nyssa, one of the three Cappadocian fathers whose influence on the language of the Chalcedonian creed has been subject to controversial debates. Coakley presents Gregory's Christology as one that makes a unique contribution to the presenting question: "The issue at stake is precisely how the divinity of Christ should be perceived as relating to the humanity, and so—by analogous implication—how our own humanity is capable of coming into 'union' with Christ and participating in his resurrection life, whether through the sacraments specifically, or through the accompanying life of prayer and service in the Spirit." Coakley interprets Gregory's concept of "mingling" as describing the process of "gradual purgation and transformation of the nature of the human in Christ, and its final restoration to an unsullied condition, as before the fall, in the resurrection. Here [Gregory] is describing that achieved transformation of the human in Christ's resurrected body, in which the human nature, while assuredly continuing in existence, operates now in its fully perfected mode, 'in the Godhead.'"

From a modern hermeneutical and ethical perspective, William Schweiker raises the question of what it means for our identity and our moral self-understanding that Christ himself became human. Focusing on traditions of Christian humanism from the Renaissance to the present, Schweiker advocates a position that does not limit itself to the metaphysical question of how God could become human but considers the implications of the incarnation for our own ways of being "creatures of dust":

> Unlike some religions where enlightenment or redemption entails an escape from or transcendence of finite, bodily existence, for the Christian humanist incarnate existence is treasured in its finitude as a place for a relation to the divine. . . . That God was incarnate in Christ means conceptually that one must conceive of matter and spirit in their union but without confusion. This is why Christian humanists insist on the distinctive drive, the aspiration and energy, of human life: to be human is to seek the overcoming, the transcendence, of our given condition toward the divine. However, self-overcoming is not against or beyond but rather in and through the "flesh."

In the final essay of Part II, John Polkinghorne draws attention to the fact that a christological account of humanity should not be based on an atomized understanding of human nature, if such an account is meant to be in keeping especially with the Pauline view of Christ as a corporate rather than a solitary entity. However, as Polkinghorne reminds us, the reality of the corporate Christ is more comprehensive and in a sense more radical than our understanding of "social beings":

> We should be prepared to acknowledge that there is a sense in which we are members of each other and that it is indeed the case that "no man is an island" (John Donne). Yet the degree of mutual association that this implies seems quite different from the New Testament understanding of the corporate character of Christ. Human incorporation into Christ is there portrayed as much more intensively constitutive of who we are intended to be, transcending all lesser distinctions of status, gender, or culture.

Polkinghorne further suggests that such a deep level of interconnectedness has intriguing parallels in the world of quantum physics: "These profound and revisionary discoveries in physics have totally transformed our conception of the nature of the physical world. It is constituted by a subtle web of inter-connections."

The essays of Part III concentrate on the consequences of the incarnation for our understanding of the variegated nature of humankind. What is the "body" into which Christ incarnated? Are we to understand incarnation only as the "prin-ciple" of Christ becoming human, or should the incarnation not in fact make the diversity of humanity in terms of gender, age, race, and other characteristics the necessary starting point for conceiving of the presence of Christ "in the flesh"?

Catherine Keller introduces this section by reflecting on divine love both as God's will and desire to immerse himself in the world of creatures and as the very essence of what becomes creaturely reality. Drawing on Beguine mysticism as well as process metaphysics, Keller characterizes incarnation as the key concept in which divine love materializes in an abundance of life that cannot be contained by one form or pattern alone: "The logos incarnate in the life of Jesus seeks materialization in all becoming creatures: nothing comes to be without it." This calls precisely for a nonreductive approach to the manifold forms of life not just as a "multiplicity of the same" but as an intended plurality in which divine love wants to take shape.

Piet Naudé shares a homily on Mark 8:29, where Jesus himself raises the crucial question about his identity: "Who do you say that I am?" Variations of this question form a leitmotif that we find throughout the Gospel of Mark. But whereas in other places this question captures the rumors around the appearance of Jesus, in Mark 8:29 it is posed to the disciples as the closest witnesses of Jesus' words and deeds. Naudé highlights the discrepancy between Peter's answer and the disciples' stunning inability to incorporate the insight about Jesus' messianic identity in their lives: "The problem does not lie in the words of the confession; Jesus is indeed the Christ. The problem—as we saw earlier—lies in the inter-pretation of this Christ, and the consequences it has for the practical choices made by the disciples. They were dogmatically correct, but were still standing in God's way: closing out others in a sectarian mind-set, struggling to be the most important, involved in a secret politicking for positions of glory, and clearly overestimating their own religious loyalties to Christ." Naudé reminds us that the truth about Jesus manifests itself on a variety of levels that comprises our entire personalities as thinking, desiring, and acting beings.

John Hoffmeyer, in an interpretation of Matthew 25:31–46 ("The Judgment of the Nations") turns to the ethical and diaconical implications of the incarnation. If one takes seriously the fact that Christ became human—and not just the person we like to surround ourselves with—service to and love of one's neighbor can-not be a matter of our own choosing. It is not for any human being to reevaluate the world in which he or she lives according to his or her preferences, standards, tastes, and so on. Hoffmeyer draws attention to one element in particular:

Matthew's story enjoins us to forget Christ for christological reasons. More precisely, Matthew enjoins an encounter with Christ in "the least of these" that entails a christological forgetfulness, which is both a forgetting of Christology and a christological forgetting. Following the example of the sheep in the story precludes looking beyond the concrete hungry person in search of Jesus. Such looking beyond smuggles in the assumption that Jesus is ultimately located elsewhere, that Jesus is just making an appearance in the person suffering from hunger.

The incarnate Christ *is* the other, which makes the love of one's neighbor a value in and of itself and not just as a passageway to finding Christ somewhere else.

Marcia Bunge shares reflections on one group of human beings that is seldom recognized when it comes to imagining the humanity into which Christ incarnated—namely, children. "While acknowledging that Jesus was a human being, theologians today and in the past sometimes neglect to affirm that Jesus was also an infant and grew up as a child or to draw implications of the incarnation for our attitudes and treatment of children. In other words, the 'heightened' worth and dignity of human beings, which is affirmed in the incarnation, is not always applied to children themselves." Bunge objects to a theological perception of children that regards them merely as not-yet adults. When Jesus places a child in the midst of adults this is not so much a symbol of protection but to symbolize that children are in fact full human beings with an openness to God and God's kingdom that is not missing anything but has its own irreducible value and its own dignity.

The authors of Part IV shift the emphasis from the incarnation to the impact of Christ's humanity for the transformation of the human world as it participates in the life of Christ and the coming of his kingdom.

Andreas Schuele points to the notion of forgiveness in the Lord's Prayer and in the Gospel of Matthew in general. One can show that forgiveness is intrinsically tied to Matthew's theology of the approaching "kingdom of heaven," which will re-create the world so that eventually the will of God will be done on earth as it already is in heaven:

It is not within the power of humans to eliminate sin und suffering from the world. What human beings can do, however, is what the Lord's Prayer suggests: ask God for forgiveness and forgive one's neighbor. The kingdom of God has its own momentum and dynamic to permeate the world beyond human influence. Nonetheless, forgiveness can be characterized as a form of acknowledging the nearness of this kingdom, as a way of reaching out for it, and also as the readiness to receive it. It is worth noticing that Matthew's ethic is not geared simply toward a top-down implementation of eschatological values. Rather, it is an ethic that captures and highlights how human value systems change when the kingdom of God is expected as an immanent reality.

In critical discussion with the Jesus Seminar, Paul Hanson proposes a model for Christology that does not divorce the historical question about Jesus from his significance for the life of his followers and, eventually, for the church. A purely historical approach to the New Testament traditions will limit their significance to what a contemporary audience deems historically plausible. Hanson charges the representatives of the Jesus Seminar with an inadequate fore-understanding (*Vorverständnis*) that needs to operate against the texts' own intentions: "First of all, the secular naturalism that underlies the historical-critical method is rejected as an inadequate basis for understanding the message of the New Testament and discerning the source of that message in the words and deeds of Jesus of Nazareth. Not only is its view of a closed universe unbiblical; it is also a view deemed to be impoverished and woefully inadequate conceptually in dealing with the most profound aspects of existence." Outlining a model that he calls "historical-theological," Hanson proposes a fore-understanding that does not bracket the theological and spiritual character of the New Testament traditions about the life, death, and resurrection of Jesus Christ: "In the case of the historical-theological approach fore-understanding includes the belief that the chain of tradition from Jesus of Nazareth to Paul to the Gospel writers to the present gathering of Christians around the bread and wine is a tradition guided by God through the abiding presence of the Spirit of Christ."

According to Christoph Schwöbel, the connection between personhood and the resurrection of Christ is "one of the central problems that occurs in the Christian doctrine of God, in Christology as well as in the Christian understanding of what it means to be human." Schwöbel characterizes the resurrection of Christ as a "disclosure event" and "disclosure experience" in which the meaning and destiny of our finite bodily existence is ultimately revealed:

> The disclosure experience reveals Christ in his spiritual body, which is the transformation of his natural body in the communion of God's eternal life to those whose experience is still bound to the capacities of their natural bodies. The body of the risen Christ is therefore the exemplification of the resurrection body Paul is at pains to describe in the dialectics of continuity and discontinuity: "The body that is sown is perishable, it is raised imperishable; it is sown in dishonor, it is raised in glory; it is sown in weakness, it is raised in power; it is sown a natural body, it is raised a spiritual body" (1 Cor. 15:42–44).

Evaluating the recent debate about the historicity or nonhistoricity of the resurrection and the plausibility of expecting a second coming of Christ, Ted Peters follows a similar train of thought as Schwöbel. Peters argues in favor of a close interconnection between the resurrection and the Parousia:

> Based upon the biblical witness to Jesus' resurrection, we can now anticipate our eschatological future in at least three ways. First, we can use our imaginations to construct a picture of what deliverance and salvation might look like. . . . Second, by imagining a new and better world, we can use this constructed picture to guide moral activity. Ethics begins with a vision of a better world, then seeks to actualize or realize that vision. Proleptic ethics

seeks to make real today what we expect God will deliver tomorrow. . . . Third, when celebrating the sacraments we expand our vision of reality to gain a foretaste of the feast that is yet to come. The final future is not here yet, so we cannot perceive it with our senses. Yet the sacraments can bridge the realm of present sense with anticipated future.

PART I
"WHO IS HE?"
Tradition, Doubt, and Misperception
as Keys to Understanding Christ

"The King of the Jews"

PATRICK D. MILLER

Among the many titles ascribed to Jesus in the New Testament, one of the more ambiguous is the epithet "king of the Jews" with its parallel form, "king of Israel."[1] Since Christology, both by its terminology and its history of tradition, centers on the ways in which the rule of God is manifest in Jesus of Nazareth, it is appropriate in this context to examine one of the terms by which that central christological feature is—or is not—characterized. While the phrase "king of the Jews" is by no means the only or most characteristic expression identifying Jesus as a royal figure, its very specific usage warrants a close look at its connotations not only in the immediate context in which the epithet appears but also in the larger gospel story, and in Scripture as a whole, specifically with regard to the way the Old Testament connects—or does not connect—with the understanding of Jesus' kingship in the New Testament.

THE KING OF THE JEWS/ISRAEL

Though there are important earlier references, the passion narrative is the primary context for the title "king of the Jews/Israel." There the term has two functions or plays two roles. In each Gospel, the question asked of Jesus by Pilate is: "Are you the King of the Jews?" (Matt. 27:11; Mark 15:2; Luke 23:3; John 18:33). The tradition is unanimous that this was the critical issue in the appearance before the Roman governor. There can be little doubt that the query was a political one and that the term was to be understood politically. The charges against Jesus, indicated in the quotations below from Luke 23 and John 19 make that clear. The political character of the matter is further indicated by Pilate's general lack of interest in pursuing the matter when he finds no evidence to support the accusation that Jesus is a political rebel, a part of the story that is also consistent throughout the Gospels (Matt. 27:33; Mark 15:14; Luke 23:4; John 18:38; 19:4, 6).[2] In fact, the Roman governor cannot find any criminal or rebellious activity on Jesus' part and realizes that the whole matter is a trumped-up job on the part of the jealous leaders of the Jews (Matt. 27:18; Mark 15:10). The title "king of the Jews" is ascribed to Jesus by the chief priests, elders, and so forth (John 19:12, 21) in order to have him executed by the Roman authorities for treason. The threat posed by Jesus seems to be to the religious leadership, not the political powers (Mark 15:1–11; Luke 23:5). The Roman governor sees no political danger and indeed no crime or threat at all in the person of Jesus. His sentencing Jesus to death is in order to keep the religious elements, and perhaps the people generally, satisfied enough so as not to create an uprising.[3] The irony is that the potential uprising would not be on the part of "the king of the Jews" but by those who rejected this view of Jesus and vowed their loyalty to the emperor:

> They began to accuse him, saying, "We found this man perverting our nation, forbidding us to pay taxes to the emperor, and saying that he himself is the Messiah, a king." (Luke 23:2)

> From then on Pilate tried to release him, but the Jews cried out, "If you release this man, you are no friend of the emperor. Everyone who claims to be a king sets himself against the emperor." (John 19:12)

> Pilate asked them, "Shall I crucify your King?" The chief priests answered, "We have no king but the emperor." (John 19:15)

After Pilate questions Jesus and hands him over to be executed, the expression "king of the Jews/Israel" continues to be applied to Jesus, now in a derisive manner. The title becomes a taunt, a means of mockery to demonstrate that in fact the claim inherent in the title is meaningless. It is inscribed on the cross over his head as an indication of the charge against him (Mark 15:26), and the cross itself is an instrument for execution of political rebels, a further piece of irony. Jesus is mocked by being dressed in royal colors, crowned (with thorns), given a stick for a scepter, and hailed as a king (Mark 15:17–19 // Matt. 27:27–30 // John 19:2). The mockery of the claim to royalty is emphasized when Jesus is then beaten with the royal scepter and stripped of the royal clothes (Mark 15:19–20; Matt.

27:30–31). It is probably no accident that the crown of thorns is not mentioned as being stripped, and indeed most of the crucifixion's artistic representations depict the crown of thorns on Jesus' head. More than anything it conveys the irony and the truth in the accusation that is made against him. The inappropriateness of the claim that Jesus could be king of the Jews seems to be reflected in his inability to save himself (Mark 15:31), to exercise a power presumed to belong to the messiah, God's king: "'Let the Messiah, the King of Israel, come down from the cross now, so that we may see and believe.' Those who were crucified with him also taunted him" (Mark 15:32 // Matt. 27:42–44).

Thus the narrative report of Pilate, the soldiers, the chief priests and elders, the crowd (stirred up by the chief priests—Mark 15:11), and those who passed him by sets the phrase "king of the Jews/Israel" as pure mockery, having no basis in reality, a trumped-up charge to get rid of someone who in fact was attracting the affections of the people in large ways. The response of Jesus to the charge when put before him by Pilate suggests, however, that there is an irony inherent in it, one that neither Pilate nor the Jewish leaders perceive. In all four Gospels, when Pilate asks Jesus, "Are you the king of the Jews?" the response is *su legeis*, "You say so" (Matt. 27:11; Mark 15:2; Luke 23:3; John 18:37). This is clearly the primary response, though in John that initial word is elaborated by Jesus. The force of Jesus' succinct response has been much debated. The pronoun at the beginning is emphatic, and thus, the meaning is something like "That is your way of putting it."[4] It is not a denial, as comparison with Luke 22:70–71 shows. Neither, however, is it clearly an affirmation in its immediate context. The answer remains ambiguous. Luke's narrative seems to point to the distinction between the Jewish hope of a messiah and the Roman concern for any threat to political rule, as represented by the term and the notion of "king" (Luke 23:2; see n. 2)

It would be a mistake, however, to assume that the term "king of the Jews/Israel" is only a Gentile expression.[5] In the passion narratives, such a formal royal title also occurs on the lips of Jewish leaders. They conjoin the terms "Messiah/Christ" and "king" in Luke 23:2, uncovering the difference and making the point. Further on in the Lukan narrative, the distinction is maintained as the soldiers are the ones who refer to Jesus as king of the Jews (Luke 23:36–38), while the "leaders" and the criminals who are crucified with Jesus use the term "Messiah" (Luke 23:35, 39). The Johannine account is the most detailed in portraying the Jewish leaders resisting the term "king of the Jews," refusing to have Jesus labeled by the term at all, and insisting on their loyalty to the emperor (John 19:12, 15, 21–22). Elsewhere in the narratives, however, the chief priests, scribes, and elders join in with the Gentile soldiers in mocking Jesus as "King of the Jews/Israel" (Matt. 27:42; Mark 15:31–32). And in Pilate's dialogue with the chief priests, he refers to Jesus as "the man you call the King of the Jews" (Mark 15:12). Throughout the narrative in all the Gospels, the use of the term is full of irony. Lamar Williamson has made the point succinctly with reference to the Gospel of John:

The religious authorities never acknowledge Jesus as their king, but they insist that Rome should execute him for claiming to be. Pilate apparently does not care whether or not Jesus claimed to be Messiah, so long as he is not a threat to Roman law and order, but he sees in the inscription another opportunity to needle the local authorities from whom he has extracted a pledge of allegiance to Caesar (v. 15) and to whom he now says imperiously, "What I have written, I have written" (v. 22). So the inscription stands as a witness to the whole world that Jesus is the Messiah, ironically contrary to the intention of the Jewish and Roman authorities alike, but contributing significantly to the purpose of the Fourth Gospel (20:30–31).[6]

The prominence of this ascription to Jesus in the passion narratives should not lead one to ignore other places where Jesus is called "king" or more specifically "King of the Jews/Israel." Of critical importance is the beginning of the Gospel of Matthew where the opening chapter specifically places Jesus in the royal lineage of David, several times explicitly using "Messiah" language: at the beginning of the genealogy and the Gospel (Matt. 1:1), at the end of the genealogy (Matt. 1:16), at the conclusion of the genealogical summary (Matt. 1:17), and at the beginning of the birth story (Matt. 1:18). Immediately after the birth story, we are told of the visit of the magi who inquire "Where is the child who has been born king of the Jews?" (Matt. 2:2). They have come to pay homage to this king (Matt. 2:2). When Herod hears of this word, he asks the chief priests and scribes where the "Messiah" is to be born. So the two terms come together in the story, one a Gentile ascription, the other the primary Jewish denomination. The story makes it clear that the first to acknowledge Jesus as king of the Jews and to bow down before him are the Gentiles (see Ps. 72). Whatever rationale may be proposed to account for the magi coming to pay homage to this Jewish baby as king, it is clear that they are representatives of the Gentiles, and that the babe is, by their homage, affirmed as king at the beginning of the story of Jesus. The story also makes it clear that the kingship of this child is perceived in political terms, again with all the ambiguity and irony carried by that connotation in the passion narrative.[7]

At the beginning of the Gospel of John, Nathaniel, "an Israelite in whom there is no guile/deceit," declares, "Rabbi, you are the Son of God. You are the King of Israel!" Here the acknowledgment of Jesus as king of the Jews/Israel at the beginning of one of the Gospels is by one whose sole identity is as (a) an Israelite and (b) one who speaks the truth. From Matthew to John, the beginning of these two Gospels frames the Gospel story with confessions from within Israel and from without that Jesus is the king of the Jews/Israel. It is an authentic title but also inflammatory.

Then, each of the Gospels tells of Jesus' climactic entry into Jerusalem as the procession of a king. As his death is an ambiguous and ironic word about his kingship, so also is his entry into the city on the way to the cross. Mark is the least explicit about this as the ceremonial entry of a king (Mark 11:1–11), and John is the most so:

So they took branches of palm trees and went out to meet him, shouting, "Hosanna! Blessed is the one who comes in the name of the Lord—the King of Israel!" Jesus found a young donkey and sat on it; as it is written: "Do not be afraid, daughter of Zion. Look, your king is coming, sitting on a donkey's colt!" (John 12:13–15).

In Matthew 21:5, the entry is also understood to be a fulfillment of the quotation from Zechariah 9:9 about "your king" coming on a donkey. Luke takes the quotation from Psalm 118:26—"Blessed is the one who comes in the name of the LORD"—and, like John, adds the word "king": "Blessed is the king who comes in the name of the Lord!" (Luke 19:38). Whether or not Psalm 118 is to be understood as a royal psalm or related to the entry of a king, the Gospel narratives have understood—and emphasized—Jesus' identity as king of Israel.

All of the uses of the term "king of the Jews/Israel" outside the passion narratives serve to confirm—on the part of outsiders, a disciple, and the people—that Jesus is the king of the Jews/Israel. And even as the passion story usage betrays a high degree of irony, so also does the repeated picture of this king on a donkey. The donkey imagery has associations with royalty in the Old Testament (Gen. 49:10–11; 2 Sam. 16:2; 1 Kgs. 1:33) and in the ancient Near East.[8] But the citation of Zechariah 9:9 with its reference to the king as "humble and riding on a donkey" clearly points to the humility of this king. The texts are explicit about his kingship and use political ("king" or "king of Israel/the Jews") as well as religious ("Messiah") terminology to express that fact. But the triumphal entry texts, like the other references to Jesus as king, serve to undergird the picture of this political-spiritual kingship as different from the common modes of rule by the symbols of kingship that appear: the manger, the donkey, the cross, the crown of thorns, and the stick scepter.

THE KING IN THE OLD TESTAMENT

Reference to these several Old Testament texts makes it clear that the Scriptures of Israel are very much in view in the various ascriptions of kingship to Jesus. A theological understanding of Jesus as "king of the Jews/Israel" needs, therefore, to give some accounting of how that role is understood in the Old Testament. Not everything can be said about the Old Testament picture of kingship in this context, but two or three aspects belong to any association of Jesus with the role and image of king. They are to be discerned less in the practice of kingship—with some exceptions—than in the prophetic critique and vision as well as in the royal psalms.

The King as God's Son

If the title "Son of God" becomes the defining christological title for Jesus, it does so primarily as another way of speaking about Jesus as king, or about the rule of God through the one called Son of God. That connection between divine sonship and human rule is not peculiar to the Old Testament, but it is clearly a part of the royal theology.[9] The classic expression of this association is in the adoption formula that seems to have belonged to royal enthronements and is now preserved in Psalm 2:7:

> He said to me, "You are my son;
>   today I have begotten you.
> Ask of me, and I will make the nations your heritage,
>   and the ends of the earth your possession."

The use of son and father language to speak of the one whom God has chosen to rule over God's people and, as the quotation from Psalm 2 indicates, the whole earth, occurs elsewhere as well (2 Sam. 7:12–14; 1 Chr. 28:6; Ps. 89:26–27). Further there are frequent associations of "Son of God" with "Messiah" (Matt. 16:16; 26:63; Mark 1:1; 14:16; Luke 4:41; 22:67–70; John 11:27; 20:31; Acts 9:20–22; 13:32–34) or "King of Israel" (Matt. 27:39–43; John 1:49) or "king" (Luke 1:31–33; 1 Cor. 1:9; 2 Cor. 1:19; Heb. 1:5–9) in the New Testament, reinforcing the close association of this language about sonship and the royal role. One of the most obvious instances is Nathaniel's response to Jesus' address: "Rabbi, you are the Son of God! You are the King of Israel!" (John 1:49). In one of the depictions of the crucifixion and the mockery of Jesus, the Matthean account reports that "those who passed by derided him" by saying, "You who would destroy the temple and build it in three days, save yourself! If you are the Son of God, come down from the cross" (Matt. 27:40), and then says, "In the same way the chief priests also, along with the scribes and elders, were mocking him, saying, 'He saved others; he cannot save himself. He is the King of Israel; let him come down from the cross now, and we will believe in him'" (Matt 27:41–42). Like Nathaniel's response, the report equates the ascriptions "Son of God" and "King of Israel."

The royal association does not exhaust the connotations of "Son of God," but that is the starting point. The royal language and the son language work in tandem with each other. The one who bears these titles is to be defined and understood primarily as ruler, and that rule is over all. The New Testament begins where it ends up with the homage of the nations before the king. The rule is to be understood as political, a point that is scored both in the use of the royal terminology and in its resistance. The son language both underscores the ruling work of Jesus and understands it as a divine assignment. That is, the rule of Israel and the nations is, as it has always been, under divine aegis, by divine choice, and to carry out the Lord's rule over all. The quotation from the royal Psalm 2—"You are my son" (or "This is my son")—is reiterated at or associated with key moments in the story: Jesus' baptism (Matt. 3:17 // Mark 1:11 // Luke 3:22), his transfiguration (Matt. 17:5 // Mark 9:7 // Luke 9:35; 2 Peter 1:17); and the resurrection (Acts 13:33; Rom. 1:3–4). James Mays has summarized the significance of these texts and the rootage of this terminology in the Old Testament words about the king:

> The declaration of God to the king, "You are my son," becomes the central assertion about the relation of Jesus to God. In the Old Testament "king" and "anointed" [messiah] are more frequent and important titles, but in the New Testament, "son" moves to the fore as the identification of the One whom God has chosen to represent his kingdom in the world. More than the other titles it emphasizes the correspondence between the heavenly sovereign and the person of his human regent. . . . The psalm insists that it is precisely this person, in his preaching and teaching and healing, and in his death and resurrection, who is God's sovereign response to every seat of power and use of power that is independent of God's rule.[10]

The son language points to the close association with the divine purpose and intent, the divine rule, while the king language points to the role and responsibility of the one so adopted and enthroned.

The King and the Poor

Throughout the Old Testament, the primary task of the king and the way in which true kingship is manifest is in the care of the poor and the needy. As in the notion of the king as divine son, it was not peculiar to Israel that the first and defining task of the king was the support and protection of the poor in his realm. To cite one example, fairly close to Israel's context, one of the major texts from Ugarit in ancient Syria, the Kirta epic, in a narrative context, sets attention to the plight of the poor as definitive of kingship. It seems to be "a legend about a royal hero [Kirta] whose specific identity is unknown."[11] Near the end of the epic, Kirta's son, Yassib, seeks to take over the throne from his father and says to him:

> Step down—and I'll be the king
>   From your rule—I'll sit on the throne.[12]

Prior to that demand Yassib twice gives the grounds on which he can call for such a radical action. The first two lines of his claim are very uncertain as to meaning. The rest of the critique is as follows:

> You've let your hand fall to vice.
> You don't pursue the widow's case,
> You don't expel the poor's oppressor,[13]
> You don't feed the orphan who faces you,
> Nor the widow who stands at your back.[14]

In effect, Yassib defines kingship and its proper administration essentially in terms of the maintenance of justice and righteousness with the primary criterion of that being the care of the weak and the poor, those without adequate support and vulnerable to the effects of economic oppression (taxation, foreclosure, etc.).

The continuity with the notion of kingship in the Old Testament is immediately evident. The most obvious connection is to the primary ideal of kingship in Psalms, that is, Psalm 72, possibly a coronation psalm, though that cannot be pinned down. There the petition opening the psalm is the prayer: "Give the king your justice, O God, and your righteousness to a king's son" (v. 1). What follows carries that forward and in more detail:

> May he judge your people with righteousness,
>   and your poor with justice.
> May the mountains yield prosperity for the people,
>   and the hills, in righteousness.
> May he defend the cause of the poor of the people,
>   give deliverance to the needy,
>   and crush the oppressor.
>   (Ps. 72:2–4)

Notable are the parallelism/equation of "people" and "poor" as the objects of the king's justice and righteousness. The whole people are, of course, in view, but those who specifically need the king's justice are the poor. This is then underscored in verse 4 with the cause of the poor and the needy as the king's primary agenda, which, as in the Kirta epic, means opposing those who oppress them economically. Not to be missed is the association in verse 3 of "prosperity" with "righteousness"—the substance of which is defined in the surrounding verses. The psalm then goes on at length with prayers of blessing for the king—long life,[15] dominion from sea to sea, his enemies and all the kings bowing down before him, the nations serving him, and tribute from many distant places (vv. 3–11).[16] The reason for all this blessing, tribute, and universal rule is then given in the following verses (12–14), explicitly connected to all the previous petitions by the particle *kî* = "for/because":

> For he delivers the needy when they call,
>   the poor and those who have no helper.
> He has pity on the weak and the needy,
>   and saves the lives of the needy.
> From oppression and violence he redeems their life;
>   and precious is their blood in his sight.

The psalm finishes with further large blessings similar to the first group prayed for the king by the people.

On the whole, it is clear that this ideal of kingship has one focus: the care and protection of the poor and needy. What is expected from God's son when he takes the throne? What will bring about a prosperous and long and peaceful reign under this king's rule? The answer to both questions is the same and emphasized. All will be well when God's son gives his full attention to maintaining justice and righteousness for the poor and needy. Indeed, such care and protection for the poor as the king's primary assignment is the substance or content of "justice and righteousness" not only here but generally in the Old Testament.[17]

An important connection between Psalm 2 with its divine appointment of the king as "my son" to rule the nations and Psalm 72 with its promise of good for the king and the kingdom as the ruler provides justice for the poor is to be found in Psalms 9–10, a pair of psalms that are clearly to be read together.[18] The character of the Lord's rule as on behalf of justice and righteousness—that is, attentive to the poor and the oppressed—is articulated in Psalm 9 and then reiterated in Psalm 10, which expresses this character in the context of a prayer for help that is probably the voice of the king.[19] The two psalms climax with the declaration that "the LORD is king forever and ever," confirming the intent of the psalms to point to and characterize God's rule over the nations. I have argued that in the Psalter "the prayer for the poor, the weak, the needy, and the oppressed first arises in Pss 9–10, and that happens with such vigor that it places *the protection and support of the poor and the needy as the fundamental content of the sovereignty of God* [italics in original]."[20] If that is the case, the task of the one who rules on earth on behalf of the Lord is the same. Psalm 2 sets the rule of the Lord's anointed, the Lord's "son," over the nations as one of the dominant themes of the Psalter. Psalms 9–10 carry that forward. The interaction of the two/three psalms as well as their resonance with Psalm 72 can be characterized in the following way: "If the focus of Ps 2 is on the human ruler, the derivative character of that rule is clear. If Ps(s) 9–10 focus on the Lord as king, the working out of that rule is implicit in the voice of the king as the one who prays and whose rule is defined in the same way as the rule of the Lord—the help and deliverance of the poor, the afflicted, and the oppressed."[21]

In another of the main texts setting forth the ideal of kingship, and one that looks forward to the coming of a king who will rule as God wills, the responsibility for righteousness—understood as justice for the poor—is again the main task of the king:

> His delight shall be in the fear of the LORD.
> He shall not judge by what his eyes see,
>   or decide by what his ears hear;
> but with righteousness he shall judge the poor,
>   and decide with equity for the meek of the earth;[22]
> he shall strike the earth with the rod of his mouth,
>   and with the breath of his lips he shall kill the wicked.
> Righteousness shall be the belt around his waist,
>   and faithfulness the belt around his loins.
>   (Isa. 11:3–5)

The whole of the king's responsibility is righteousness, explicitly marked by proper justice and equity for the poor and lowly.[23] The wicked are those who oppress and do in the poor and needy. The fear of the Lord covers many things. For the ruler under God's mandate, its central feature is the protection of and provision for the poor and maintaining justice for them in and out of the court-room. From another angle, the book of Isaiah reinforces the king's role as protector of the poor when it says of Zion, the royal citadel, "The LORD has founded Zion, and the needy among his people will find refuge in her."

One further passage should be brought into this picture. It is one of those texts that serve to define the role of the human ruler primarily in a negative way, that is, as critique of what actually is happening. The prophets in general speak often of the injustice pervading the land and call the people, especially the leaders, to a more righteous way. In Jeremiah 21:11–23:8, a sequence of prophetic oracles sets the maintenance of justice and righteousness as the defining task of the king. The unit begins with a positive call to "the house of the king of Judah" addressed as "O house of David" to "execute justice in the morning, and deliver from the hand of the oppressor anyone who has been robbed" (Jer. 21:12). That this exhortation is meant to be definitive is indicated by its reiteration in Jeremiah 22:3, again in address to the king: "Act with justice and righteousness, and deliver from the hand of the oppressor anyone who has been robbed. And do no wrong or violence to the alien, the orphan, and the widow, or shed innocent blood in this place." Then in direct words to King Jehoiakim, his rule is contrasted with that of his father Josiah in the following manner:

> Woe to him who builds his house by unrighteousness,
>   and his upper rooms by injustice;
> who makes his neighbors work for nothing,
>   and does not give them their wages;
> who says, "I will build myself a spacious house
>   with large upper rooms,"
> and who cuts out windows for it,
>   paneling it with cedar,
>   and painting it with vermilion.
> Are you a king
>   because you compete in cedar?
> Did not your father eat and drink
>   and do justice and righteousness?
>   Then it was well with him.
> He judged the cause of the poor and needy;
>   then it was well.
> Is not this to know me?
>   says the LORD.
> But your eyes and heart
>   are only on your dishonest gain,
> for shedding innocent blood,
>   and for practicing oppression and violence.
>   (Jer. 22:13–17)

The definition of the proper rule is defined here negatively (unrighteousness and injustice—v. 13) and positively (justice and righteouness—v. 15). The content of that is once again proper care of the poor and needy (vv. 13, 16) as over against economic oppression and appropriation at the expense of the poor.

Finally, at the end of this section of Jeremiah, the Lord promises Israel a ruler in days to come who will rule wisely or effectively "and shall execute justice and righteousness in the land" (Jer. 23:5). The continuity between this king's rule and the Lord's way is manifest in the name the future king shall bear: "The LORD is our righteousness" (Jer. 23:6).

In short, through these texts—and there are others—one may see that the care of the poor does not belong to a list of administrative duties of the kings of Israel. It was their primary job, their raison d'être. No other activity receives this kind of attention in the royal definition texts, and where the texts do speak of the king's responsibilities, they are virtually confined to this one area. Providing help for the poor and needy, securing their justice, and destroying their oppressors—these are not among the things the king does. They are what kingship is all about. This is what it means to be king according to those texts that seek to profile and characterize what is expected of the anointed of the Lord, the chosen son.[24]

The King as Keeper of Torah

There would seem to be one significant exception to the picture of kingship just described. In Deuteronomy 17 we find one of the primary texts defining kingship. Indeed in its context, one might argue that it is more definitive and more binding than any of the other texts considered above. It is what has come to be known as "the law of the king" (Deut. 17:14–20). As part of Deuteronomy, one may speak of it as in some sense constitutional, or at least, as Josephus first called it, the "polity" for Israel's life as a people.[25] In these verses, a particular qualification is given—that is, the king must be "one of your own community," not a foreigner (Deut. 17:15). Then a series of restrictions is set on what the king may not do, or better, acquire: horses, wives, and silver and gold. Finally, the king is given one responsibility:

> When he has taken the throne of his kingdom, he shall have a copy of this law written for him in the presence of the levitical priests. It shall remain with him and he shall read in it all the days of his life, so that he may learn to fear the LORD his God, diligently observing all the words of this law and these statutes. (Deut. 17:18–19)

The only royal task is regular reading and keeping of the Torah or law found in the book of Deuteronomy. Nothing is said about justice and righteousness or about the care of the poor. What becomes very clear, however, from even a superficial reading of the Deuteronomic Code (Deut. 12–26) is that the care of the poor, the proper treatment of the weak, the widow, and the orphan is at the heart of the law. The point of the Deuteronomic statute on the king is not to set up a long list of royal duties but to make it clear that the proper rule of God's people is effected by careful attending to all this law, with its large focus on the poor and the marginal.

JESUS AS THE KING OF ISRAEL/THE JEWS

The lines from the Old Testament portrayal of God's rule through the human ruler lead into the Gospels' depiction—and indeed the New Testament portrayal as a whole—of Jesus of Nazareth. It is as king that Jesus is the Son of God, the one appointed and anointed to enact the rule of God over Israel and the nations. It is as king/messiah that Jesus brings the law to fulfillment.[26] Donald Hagner, with reference to the work of Roland Deines, has summarized the matter cogently:

> The antecedent figure who prefigures Jesus is not so much Moses as it is David; it is *as Messiah* that Jesus brings the law to fruition, together with the inbreaking of the rule of God. . . . The essential factor in a correct understanding of Matthew and Matthew's view of the law is the evangelist's conviction that with the coming of Jesus, Son of David and Son of God, the promised rule of God arrives. . . . Righteousness is something that only Jesus can bring. Here again we see the crucial importance of Christology. Through Jesus, the promised Messiah and Son of God, the Torah is taken up and given new legitimacy. It becomes the Messianic Torah and is perpetuated in and through the teaching of Jesus.[27]

At the heart of that teaching and enactment of the Torah by the Messiah/Son/ king, of the righteousness that only Jesus can bring, is—as the Old Testament bears witness over and over—the care and protection of the poor, the weak, and the needy, a rule that stands against economic oppression and ensures the maintenance of justice for all and especially for those who lack the power and resources to ensure their right and their dignity and that their means to life are upheld and protected.

Jesus himself at key points in the Gospels makes this a part of his self-understanding.[28] So in the programmatic Lukan text where Jesus stands in the synagogue at Nazareth and reads from the Scriptures, his opening words from Isaiah are: "The Spirit of the Lord is upon me, because he has anointed me to bring good news to the poor" (Luke 4:18). When he finishes with his reading of Isaiah 61:1–2 and 58:6, he announces, "Today this scripture has been fulfilled in your hearing" (Luke 4:21). In other words, the good news to the poor and the release from oppression underscored in the rest of the quotation (see below) is what has now happened when Jesus comes on the scene. The anointed king is on the scene, and the work of God's rule to provide justice for the poor and release from bondage is now under way. That is what God is doing in Jesus the Messiah, the king of the Jews. The "gospel" is defined in Luke's Gospel as specifically good news to the poor.

Jesus' identification with this understanding of the divine rule through God's appointed and anointed son is underscored in Matthew's Gospel with his words in Matthew 25:31–46. It is a depiction of the coming of the "Son of Man" in his glory and in the role of king:

> "Then the king will say to those at his right hand, 'Come, you that are blessed by my Father, inherit the kingdom prepared for you from the foundation of the world; for I was hungry and you gave me food, I was thirsty and you gave me something to drink, I was a stranger and you welcomed me, I was naked and you gave me clothing, I was sick and you took care of me, I was in prison and you visited me.' Then the righteous will answer him, 'Lord, when was it that we saw you hungry and gave you food, or thirsty and gave you something to drink? And when was it that we saw you a stranger and welcomed you, or naked and gave you clothing? And when was it that we saw you sick or in prison and visited you?' And the king will answer them, 'Truly I tell you, just as you did it to one of the least of these who are members of my family, you did it to me.'" (Matt. 25:34–40)

In teaching and proclamation but also in Jesus' own being the promise to the poor is brought to its place and actualized as the definition and reality of the kingdom of God. What Jesus teaches, he also realizes. The ministry to the poor and naked and hungry, the prisoner and the sick is the service of Christ. Homage to this king now happens in a different sort of way: in acts of ministry to the poor and needy.

That this rule on behalf of the poor is a different sort of rule and centers significantly in Jesus' own identification with the poor and needy is underscored in a variety of ways. One is the degree to which the prayer for help of one in pain and suffering that we find in Psalm 22 becomes the interpretive key to understanding the passion, death, and resurrection of Jesus in the New Testament. The incarnation—that is, Jesus' commonality and identification with the human condition, and especially the human condition of oppression and suffering—is affirmed in its strongest form in the suffering and death of Jesus on the cross.[29] Yet this is, as we have noted, the death of the king of Israel/the Jews. Donald Senior delineates this association of Jesus' death with the claim about his rule as we find it in the Gospel of John:

> Thus each of the deadly details of the execution ritual are transformed and receive a new meaning: the crucifixion is the ascent of a throne; those crucified with Jesus are his retinue; the placing of the inscription becomes the proclamation of Jesus' royal status; the multiple languages of the inscription and the public site of the execution ensure the universal transmission of Jesus' message.[30]

The rule of God embodied in and identified with the life and death as well as the teaching of this Jesus the king happens precisely in his identification with the poor and needy who are the king's subjects. The righteousness and justice reflected in care of the poor are not simply something to come or a matter of the ruler's decrees and acts. They are embodied in the acts of Jesus, his self-understanding, and his transformation of the image of ruler into the image of one who is with the poor, both in the way he lives and dies and in his identification with them in the church's ministry to the poor (Matt. 25). That is indeed good news!

It also is a reminder to the church that its tendency to reduce the redemptive work of God in Christ to atonement and the forgiveness of sins is a diminishing of the Gospel story. Nowhere is that more evident than in the remainder of the quotation from Isaiah 61 and 58 (see above) that Jesus reads in the synagogue at Nazareth:

> The Spirit of the Lord is upon me,
>> because he has anointed me
>>> to bring good news to the poor.
> He has sent me to proclaim release to the captives
>> and recovery of sight to the blind,
>>> to let the oppressed go free,
> to proclaim the year of the Lord's favor.
>> (Luke 4:18)

The insertion from Isaiah 58:6 is the clause "to let the oppressed go free," which, by its addition to the text serves to underscore the word *aphesis*, the Greek of the Septuagint for both the "release" to the captives and the "let go free" for the oppressed. It is also the word for "forgiveness." The good news to the poor is release from *all* the chains that bind and oppress.[31] In and through Jesus Christ, that good news "has been fulfilled." Neither our Christology nor our preaching can let go of that claim.

NOTES

1. No one has exercised more influence on my thought and work in the last twenty years than Michael Welker. It is a joy to express my deep appreciation through this contribution to the volume in his honor.
2. As Robert Tannehill notes, the accusations against Jesus are most explicit and most dangerous for the Roman Empire in Luke, where Jesus is accused of "perverting" the people in two ways: forbidding paying taxes to the emperor— an accusation without basis (Luke 20:20–26)—and calling himself "messiah, king," a charge that has more plausibility in Luke but not in a direct assertion on Jesus' part (see below) (Robert Tannehill, *Luke,* Abingdon New Testament Commentaries [Nashville: Abingdon, 1996], 332). The emphasis in the second charge is on the word "king," which seems to be an intentional interpretation and conversion of the Jewish "messiah" language into terminology that would make Jesus more of a political threat to Roman rule (Joseph Fitzmyer, *The Gospel According to Luke X–XXIV,* Anchor Bible 28A [Garden City, N.Y.: Doubleday, 1985], 1475).
3. Note that Pilate is described as being afraid in John 19:8.
4. Tannehill, *Luke,* 338.
5. "King of the Jews" is the term used by Gentiles (the magi, Pilate, the soldiers), while "king of Israel" is the term used by Jews. Both expressions are political titles.
6. Lamar Williamson, Jr., *Preaching the Gospel of John* (Louisville, Ky.: Westminster John Knox, 2004), 263.

7. Cf. Beverly Roberts Gaventa, *Acts,* Abingdon New Testament Commentaries (Nashville: Abingdon, 2003), 245–46.
8. See David L. Petersen, *Zechariah 9–14 and Malachi,* Old Testament Library (Louisville, Ky.: Westminster John Knox, 1995), 58; and E. Lipinski, "Recherches sur le livre de Zacharie," *Vetus Testamentum* 20 (1970): 51–52.
9. For discussion of texts from the milieu as well as the connection between divine adoption as son and the king in Israel, see, e.g., Hans-Joachim Kraus, *Psalms 1–59: A Commentary,* trans. Hilton C. Oswald (Minneapolis: Augsburg, 1988), 130–32, and bibliography cited there.
10. James L. Mays, *Psalms,* Interpretation (Louisville, Ky.: John Knox Press, 1994), 49–50. Cf. P. Craigie (with 2004 supplement by Marvin E. Tate), *Psalms 1–50* (Nashville: Nelson Reference and Electronic, 2004), 68–69.
11. Edward Greenstein, "Kirta," in *Ugaritic Narrative Poetry,* ed. Simon B. Parker, Writings from the Ancient World 9 (Atlanta: Society of Biblical Literature, 1997), 9. See pp. 9–11 for summary of the epic story.
12. The translation is from ibid., 42.
13. In an essay to be published in *Ugarit Forschungen* ("Kirtu and the 'Yoke of the Poor': A New Interpretation of an Old Crux," KTU 1.16 VI 48), Christopher Hays proposes with good arguments that this line should be translated: "You did not drive out those who make heavy the yoke of the poor." The point is the same in either case, only Hays's reading of the text draws on a powerful image of oppression—found also in 1 Kgs. 12:4.
14. Greenstein, "Kirta," 41.
15. One line in this group of petitionary blessings says, "In his days may righteousness flourish" or, more likely according to the Hebrew, "may the righteous flourish." That is, may those who are innocent and in the right survive and do well under this ruler's dominion.
16. Erich Zenger has argued that "in the story of the adoration of the Magi from the East (Matt 2:1–12), the significance of Jesus as the saving king of the world of the nations is presented through the use of Psalm 72," in Frank-Lothar Hossfeld and Erich Zenger, *Psalms 2,* Hermeneia (Minneapolis: Fortress, 2005), 220.
17. On the king's responsibility for justice, see Walter J. Houston, *Contending for Justice: Ideologies and Theologies of Social Justice in the Old Testament,* Library of Hebrew Bible/Old Testament Studies 428 (London: T&T Clark, 2006), chap. 5.
18. For the arguments in that regard and for more detailed presentation of the psalm and the matters discussed here, see Patrick D. Miller, "The Ruler in Zion and the Hope of the Poor: Psalms 9–10 in the Context of the Psalter," in *David and Zion: Biblical Studies in Honor of J. J. M. Roberts,* ed. Bernard F. Batto and Kathryn Roberts (Winona Lake, Ind.: Eisenbrauns, 2004), 187–97. Reprinted in Miller, *The Way of the Lord: Essays in Old Testament Theology,* Forschungen zum Alten Testament 39 (Tübingen: Mohr Siebeck, 2004), 167–77.
19. Miller, *The Way of the Lord,* 170–71.
20. Ibid., 176.
21. Ibid., 177.
22. As Walter Houston has observed: "The parallel with *dallîm* in the first half of the verse shows that *le 'anewê' āreṣ* means not 'the meek of the earth' (NRSV) but the 'poor of the land'. . ." (Houston, *Contending for Justice,* 154n64).
23. Cf. Isa. 9:6–7. "In Isa 11.4 it becomes clear that his justice means especially his justice for the poor whom he defends if necessary by bringing about the death

of their exploiters, the 'tyrant' or 'violent' and 'unjust.' The understanding of justice and how it is achieved is identical to that in Psalm 72" (ibid., 154).

24. Note Walter Houston's concluding comment after taking up the texts discussed above and others: "What we said about Psalm 72 can also be said of these further texts, and on a broader front: that regardless of the intention with which they may have been written, they present or presume an ideal of the king's office as one which exists *primarily* for the poor . . ." (ibid., 152, italics added).

25. S. Dean McBride, "Polity of the People: The Book of Deuteronomy," Interpretation 41 (1987): 229–44 (reprinted in *Constituting the Community: Studies on the Polity of Ancient Israel in Honor of S. Dean McBride,* ed. John T. Strong and Steven S. Tuell [Winona Lake, Ind.: Eisenbrauns, 2005], 17–33).

26. On Jesus as embodiment of the Deuteronomic depiction of kingship, see Robin Gallaher Branch, "The Messianic Dimensions of Kingship in Dt. 17:14–20 as Fulfilled by Jesus in Matthew," *Verbum et Ecclesia* 25 (2004): 378–401.

27. Donald A. Hagner, "Review of Roland Deines, *Die Gerechtigkeit der Tora im Reich des Messias. Mt 5, 13–20 als Schlüssel der matthäischen Theologie.* Tübingen: Mohr Siebeck (2004), 704 S," *Theologische Literaturzeitung* 131 (2006): 1151. (Deines's book was unavailable to me.)

28. Reference to self-understanding is in terms of the Gospels' presentation, not an attempt to discern the specific words of the historical Jesus.

29. A less obvious narrative identification of Jesus with the poor is his execution as a result of false witness against him (Matt. 26:59; Mark 14:53–65). Justice for the poor is very much a part of the trajectory of the commandment against false witness as it is spelled out, specified, and illustrated in legal codes, prophetic oracles, psalms, and wise sayings. Not only does that involve ensuring justice for the poor, which is the most immediate implication of not bearing false witness against the neighbor; it goes further to provide for dignity and proper treatment of the poor, especially with regard to wages, loans, and provision of daily sustenance. A central feature of some of the statutes relating to false witness is concern for execution of the innocent as a result of lying testimony—as in Jesus' case.

30. Donald Senior, *The Passion of Jesus in the Gospel of John* (Collegeville, Minn.: Liturgical Press, 1991), 104–5.

31. For further elaboration, see Patrick D. Miller, "Luke 4:16–21," *Interpretation* 29 (1975): 417–21.

2

"... Under Pontius Pilate"

On Living Cultural Memory and Christian Confession

DIRK SMIT

> *This memory is a cultural power that transforms the world.*
> —Michael Welker[1]

PILATE IN THE CHRISTOLOGY OF THE CREED?

"He was crucified under Pontius Pilate," according to the Nicene-Constantinopolitan Creed. "He suffered under Pontius Pilate," according to the Apostles' Creed. In the heart of the Christian creed, the name of Pontius Pilate is recalled. In the heart of the christological section of the creed, of the ecumenical confession concerning Jesus Christ, the name of Pontius Pilate is remembered.[2] In the heart of the Christian liturgy, of regular Christian worship through the centuries and all over the world, again and again, the name of Pontius Pilate is reiterated. But why? And to what effect?

Through the centuries, the presence of Pontius Pilate in the church's Christology and creed has been a source of constant puzzlement and intrigue. Historically, he was an obscure, probably rather insignificant figure,[3] but through his presence in the creed his name became known all over the world, often leading to speculation, legend and myth, religious imagination and pious adoration, literature and drama.[4] But why? What did his memory, his presence in the creed, evoke, through the centuries until today?

The confession ". . . under Pontius Pilate" forms an integral part of the church's faith in Jesus Christ and its proclamation of Jesus Christ. In these words, something is hidden of the mystery of the person and work of Jesus Christ and therefore also of the identity and calling of the church itself, for the church finds its own identity and calling in the fact that it belongs to this Jesus, the One who suffered and was crucified "under Pontius Pilate." In fact, if the creed in its Trinitarian form is ultimately the church's confession about God, then these words also seem to claim something about the nature of Godself.

But what do these words say about Jesus Christ and therefore about the church, perhaps even about God? Why do these words belong in the christological creed? Why has it been so important for the church to retain the expression ". . . under Pontius Pilate" in its creedal tradition, in its christological confession?

". . . UNDER PONTIUS PILATE": HISTORICAL INDICATION?

Probably the most direct and common answer in the tradition of theological reflection has been that these words serve as reminder that the Christ event took place in history. It was historical in nature. It happened within human history and as part of human history. It was real, it was concrete, it truly happened, in a historical sense of the word. It happened publicly, for all witnesses to see. It happened at a specific time and in a specific place, and the historical figure of Pontius Pilate is explicitly mentioned to keep this crucially important memory alive.

In the authoritative exposition of the creed in the ecumenical movement called *Confessing the One Faith*, this historical and public identification is clearly given as reason for these words in the Nicene-Constantinopolitan Creed. "The phrase 'under Pontius Pilate' indicates that the death and suffering of Jesus Christ is a specific historical event in world history."[5]

Not only the ecumenical church, but many theologians also underline this historical and public aspect in their discussions of these words. Of course, for many of these commentators this fact in itself involves claims both about the nature of God, who is not unwilling to get involved in the realities of human history, and claims about the nature and calling of the church, who should not be unwilling to follow this God into these realities of human history. In other words, hidden in the conviction that these words serve as historical indication, one finds fundamental christological, and therefore theological, ecclesiological, and ethical implications. These words were and still are confessed over against contrary claims concerning Christ, and therefore the Triune God, the church, and the Christian life. Perhaps Karl Barth and Jan Milič Lochman may serve as well-known illustrations of this kind of interpretation.

In *Dogmatics in Outline*, Barth argues that Pilate's name in the creed "makes it unmistakably clear" that Christ's passion "did not take place in heaven or in some remote planet or even in some world of ideas; it took place in our time, in the center of the world-history in which our human life is played out."

> So we must not escape from this life. We must not take flight to a better land, or to some height or other unknown, nor to any spiritual Cloud-Cuckooland nor to a Christian fairyland. God has come into our life in its utter unloveliness and frightfulness. That the Word became flesh also means that it became temporal, historical. It assumes the form which belongs to the human creature, in which there are such folk as this very Pontius Pilate—the people we belong to and who are also ourselves. . . . We are not left alone in this frightful world. Into this alien land God has come to us.[6]

The fact that he gives these lectures in the historical reality of 1946 in Bonn, amid the rubble and ruin of societies, of a whole world caused by the "utter unloveliness and frightfulness" of a terrible war, makes the thrust of this interpretation only more radical.

In similar fashion, Lochman underlines the historical reference of these words from the creed in *The Faith We Confess*, again emphasizing the christological, theological, and ethical implications. Instead of history, however, he uses the expression "the complete humanity" of Jesus Christ to make the same point. "To sum up in a phrase the main theme of this clause, 'Suffered under Pontius Pilate,' I would say it is concerned with the complete humanity of Jesus Christ." Together with the complete divinity of Jesus Christ and the divine incarnation, this now forms "a third main Christological theme" in the creed. These three themes are inseparable, and without the divinity and the divine incarnation, the full effect of the historical reference and the complete humanity of Jesus can not be understood either. "The essential character of the history attested in the Creed, the integrity of the Christological article, depends on all three themes."[7]

He points out that confession of the complete humanity of Jesus was already controversial during the time of the early church, when these words became part of the creed. "Recognition of the complete humanity of Christ and confession of its significance for salvation were not something that could be taken for granted in the ancient church. Indeed, it was only through costly struggle that this recognition and this confession came to be clearly and unambiguously secured."[8] Docetism, watering down the historical and human reality of Jesus, became the most insidious temptation for Christology in the ancient church, a temptation that the creed "resolutely" and "unmistakably" rejects when it affirms the ". . . under Pontius Pilate" phrase. "This series of short staccato statements rules out all flight into mythology and symbolism. . . . What is attested here is . . . the harshest of harsh human realities—suffering, dying, and being dead. The living and dying of a suffering human being is the bitter horizon to which the apostolic faith in Christ refers."[9]

". . . UNDER PONTIUS PILATE":
POLITICAL IDENTIFICATION?

The historical indication, however, serves only as an initial and partial answer to the question, for the ecumenical church and for most of these theologians. The presence of Pilate in the creed calls even richer and more complex allusions to the fore. Widespread is the claim, for example, that this historical reference has a very deliberate political intention. Pilate should be seen as a political representative and the Christ event as a political event.[10] This phrase of identification in the ancient creed deliberately draws the christological confession and faith into a political framework and therefore also into contemporary political realities.

The ecumenical document *Confessing the One Faith* once again provides a very explicit illustration: it is not only a historical indication, but also a political identification with direct relevance for today, for political oppression, occupation of countries, violations of individual human rights, private-public distinctions, political misrepresentation of the message of the kingdom—in short, for contemporary church life and discipleship.

> Particularly significant in this creedal formulation is the phrase under Pontius Pilate which not only indicates that the death and suffering of the incarnate Son of God is a specific historical event, but today allows us to put it also in the wider context of world history and human political power. . . . Pilate represents in general terms political oppression over an occupied country. . . . The statement that Jesus was crucified under Pontius Pilate indicates that his life was not a private affair and that the end of his life was deeply interwoven with the political circumstances in Palestine at that time. . . . That Christ's life and death was in different ways intertwined with the social and political conditions of his native country is of significance for the life, commitment and death of his disciples today.[11]

Again, both Barth and Lochman follow exactly the same logic: ". . . under Pontius Pilate" is not only historical, but also political—like indeed many other commentators.[12]

Barth says that "it would not be right to stop here," seeing Pilate's presence in the creed only as "just the human being of this world in general." No, he is "not only that, but he is the statesperson and politician," and the meeting taking place here is not a general meeting between God and humanity, but "the meeting between God's Kingdom and the *polis*."

> Pilate . . . is the representative of the Emperor Tiberius. He represents world-history, so far as at all times it is ordered on State lines. That Jesus Christ suffered under Pontius Pilate therefore means also that He did subscribe to this State order. . . . He does not attack the authority of Pilate. He suffers, but he does not protest against Pilate having to utter the judgment upon Him. In other words the State order, the *polis*, is the area in which His action too, the action of the eternal God takes place. . . . By suffering under Pontius Pilate He too participates in this order, and so it is worth

while considering . . . how the whole Pontius Pilate reality looks from the standpoint of the suffering Lord.[13]

From this perspective of the suffering Lord, from the perspective of the ". . . under Pontius Pilate" in the creedal Christology, Barth especially stresses the perversion and the unrighteousness of the state, the failure of human politics to achieve what it claims to do.

> State order, State power, as represented by Pontius Pilate *vis-à-vis* Jesus, is made visible in its negative form, in all its human perversion and unrighteousness. . . . What does Pilate do? He does what politicians have more or less always done and what has belonged to the actual achievement of politics in all times: he attempts to rescue and maintain order . . . and thereby at the same time to preserve his own position of power, by surrendering the clear law for the protection of which he was actually installed.[14]

Barth's description of the political failure and disgrace taking place here is fierce:

> In surrendering Jesus, he is surrendering himself. By becoming the prototype of . . . the unrighteous State . . . it is the State as such that is disgraced. In the person of Pilate the State withdraws from the basis of its own existence and becomes a den of robbers, a gangster State, the ordering of an irresponsible clique. *That* is the *polis*, *that* is politics. . . . The passion of the Christ becomes the unmasking, the judging, the condemnation of this Beast, whose name is *polis*.[15]

For Lochman, too, the "underlying interest" behind the words in the creed "is not simply historical";[16] there is "a special reason" for the reference to Pilate, namely, the deliberate purpose to establish "the connection of faith with the field of politics."[17]

> Here we have the second basis for the permanent relevance of the reference to Pontius Pilate in the Apostles' Creed, a reference that at first sight seems almost scandalous. Indeed, this second aspect may be even more important than the first. . . . Our churches still have problems with the political dimensions of their faith. Our problem today is not so much historical Docetism as political Docetism. . . . The political dimension of church theory and practice still seems underdeveloped.[18]

Again, for Lochman this has crucially important implications for the Christian life today—such that concentrated theological study of the role of Pilate in the creed could bring the contemporary church closer to one of the fundamental concerns of the early church.

> What is long overdue and would really be helpful is a concentrated theological study of the foundations of the Christian faith—including, above all, the role of Pontius Pilate in the Creed—that would include intense reflection on its historical and political components. . . . By resisting any

reduction of the down-to-earth realism of the Christian faith, we would come closer than we might imagine to one of the fundamental concerns of the ancient church.[19]

Finally, the Yale historian Jaroslav Pelikan's detailed "historical and theological guide to creeds and confessions of faith in the Christian tradition," *Credo*, also offers an interesting argument for the (original and continuous) political function of the words ". . . under Pontius Pilate." He deals with this expression in his long chapter on "the formation of confessions and the politics of religion."[20]

He shows convincingly how important issues of political authority have always been in the history of Christian creeds and confessions, as integral elements of their very nature and function. Confessing was a political act.[21] Many confessions bear the designations of the political powers that be, whether in their references to nations, states, cities, or rulers;[22] many were addressed to political rulers, whether hostile or friendly;[23] many made seemingly innocent theological and christological claims but with far-reaching political implications;[24] many called for public, legal, social, and ethical embodiment, often involving political codification.[25] In short, the influence of the politics of religion on the formation of creeds and confessions and, vice versa, the influence of creeds and confessions on the formation of politics was all part of the various forms of political, economic, and social influence exerted by the church.[26]

According to Pelikan, it is therefore always necessary also to pay attention to the political context in any serious attempt to understand the creeds and confessions and their claims and expressions.

> What were the power relations between the central political authority and the patrons of the confession? Is it possible to discern the political strategies at work in the presentation of the confession, and perhaps even its composition? Does the confession espouse overtly political positions, and in what ways do its positions on questions of faith and morals carry political implications?[27]

In the case of the Nicene-Constantinopolitan Creed, accordingly, the orthodox and for us perhaps seemingly apolitical formulas confessing the one God to be the Father all powerful, maker of all things both seen and unseen and the Son to be one in being with the Father can therefore, according to him, "be taken to imply the radical subordination of all political authority, including even that of an orthodox Christian emperor, to the lordship of God the Father and of his coequal Son."[28]

In similar fashion, he argues, Christian confessors through the centuries, addressing hostile political authorities, and in their experiences of opposition and even of persecution, would remember the biblical precedent of "Christ Jesus who in his testimony before Pontius Pilate made the good confession."[29]

> These confessors were ever mindful that Christ not only made a confession *before* Pontius Pilate but, as both *The Niceno-Constantinopolitan Creed* and *The Apostles' Creed* affirm, also "suffered *under* Pontius Pilate." His

confession "before Pontius Pilate" and his suffering "under Pontius Pilate" went together, with Pilate representing both an imperial regime that would persecute the church during the following centuries and a Greco-Roman paganism over against which the church would, in those same centuries, begin to define itself in its creeds. Therefore, "as Jesus witnessed to the truth before Pontius Pilate, the representative of the Roman Empire, so we are called today to speak the truth to the rulers."[30]

"... UNDER PONTIUS PILATE": FAILURE OF JUSTICE?

For a widespread tradition of theological interpretation, however, the focus was even more specific. Pilate is regarded as not merely the representative of political power, but particularly of the legal system, of human justice. From this perspective, Pilate in the creed serves not merely to represent the failure and perversion of human politics, but very specifically the failure and perversion of human justice. According to this line of interpretation, Pilate is seen first and foremost as a judge, exercising the responsibilities of the legal system and representing human justice.[31]

In the Reformed tradition, this has probably been the dominant understanding. Already Calvin himself described Pilate's role primarily as that of a judge. We should learn to view this scene in the passion narrative as judgment, he says, as the unjust condemnation of the just by an official judge.[32] In Calvin's typical rhetorical style, the role of Pilate in the Gospels and in the creed is to teach us, when we see, read, perceive, remember, understand, when we are comforted and assured. What we have to see and remember is the soteriological function of this unjust judgment of the innocent, for us, by a judge who admits as judge that the one judged is innocent and the suffering therefore not for himself.

> One principal point in the narrative is his condemnation before Pontius Pilate . . . to teach us that the punishment to which we were liable was inflicted on that Just One. We could not escape the fearful judgment of God; and Christ, that he might rescue us from it, submitted to be condemned by a mortal, nay, by a wicked and profane man. . . . When he is placed as a criminal at the bar, where witnesses are brought to give evidence against him, and the mouth of the judge condemns him to die, we see him sustaining the character of an offender and evil-doer. . . . When we read that he was acquitted by the same lips that condemned him (for Pilate was forced once and again to bear public testimony to his innocence) . . . we perceive Christ representing the character of a sinner and a criminal, while, at the same time, his innocence shines forth, and it becomes manifest that he suffers for another's and not for his own crime. He therefore suffered under Pontius Pilate, being thus, by the formal sentence of a judge, ranked among criminals, and yet declared innocent by the same judge, when he affirms that he finds no cause of death in him. . . . We must specially remember this substitution in order that we not be all our lives in trepidation and anxiety, as if the just vengeance . . . were still impending over us.[33]

The Reformed Heidelberg Catechism makes this interpretation even more explicit, still seeing Pilate primarily as human judge. Question 38 asks very specifically: "Why did he suffer under Pontius Pilate, as judge?" The answer is brief but clear: "That he, being innocent, and yet condemned by a temporal judge, might thereby free us from the severe judgement of God to which we were exposed."

The Belgic Confession, another Reformed confessional document, similarly sees Pilate acting as judge, simultaneously condemning Jesus Christ as a criminal and declaring him to be innocent, thereby both fulfilling his role as human judge and failing his role as human judge.[34] In this tradition of interpretation many Reformed theologians would read the person and role of Pilate, including Dutch theologians Berkouwer, Noordmans, Van Ruler, and Ridderbos, but also Karl Barth himself, who would point out that there are in fact two legal systems at work here and two traditions and institutions of human justice at failure, namely, the justice of the Jewish nation and the justice of the Roman law.[35]

> Jesus dies the penal death of Roman justice, as one delivered up by Israel to the heathen. . . . The heathen world in the form of Pilate can for its part only accept this handing over. It executes the judgment which the Jews have pronounced. . . . The figure of the suffering Jesus is the figure of one condemned and punished. From the very start, what causes Jesus' suffering is the legal action of His nation, which finally becomes quite explicit. . . . Think of the attitude of the Pharisees, right up to the Sanhedrin: there you have the pronouncement of a verdict. This verdict is laid before the worldly judge and executed by Pilate. The Gospels have laid emphasis precisely upon this legal act. Jesus is the Person accused, condemned and punished. Here in this legal action is disclosed human rebellion against God.[36]

". . . UNDER PONTIUS PILATE": CULTURAL COLLAPSE?

According to the New Testament portrayals, of course, Pilate's role is even more complex and his failure much more ambiguous. Taking all New Testament references to Pontius Pilate together, the picture that emerges is one rich in plurality and ambiguity.[37] Only considering his person and role in the different accounts of the trial of Jesus according to the four Gospels, the readers' imagination is challenged by a complex portrayal, weaving many themes and indeed questions together.[38] In fact, just considering one specific account, like the one in chapters 18 and 19 of the Gospel of John, already leads to such an impression of complexity, plurality, and ambiguity.[39] Reading these chapters as integral part of the overall story of John, as chapters in which earlier motifs appear again and are further woven together in a dramatic account, recognized and understood by the listeners and readers who have been following the whole Gospel story, only strengthens such an impression.[40]

Over many years, Michael Welker has argued that theological scholarship should read the biblical accounts carefully, taking the complexities in the texts, the plurality of layers of authority and meaning, the fascinating variety of motifs woven together, the challenges of the ambiguities, and the seeming contradictions very seriously—doing what he has called biblical-realist theology.[41] In his own systematic-theological work, he has often demonstrated just how creative and imaginative and how rich in reward such procedures of close reading of the biblical narratives may be.

So, when John's story moves into this dramatic account of the night of betrayal and the trial of Jesus before the different authorities in Jerusalem, the readers of the Gospel have already been invited to consider many themes and questions of crucial importance.[42] Through the centuries, these motifs would capture the imagination of hearers. This is not the proper place to deal with these motifs in any serious manner, but all readers of this Gospel will recognize them immediately.

There is the question of humanity—yes, what it means to be human, whether the mystery of Jesus is indeed the human mystery, or whether there is more to him, whether he is different, perhaps somehow from above?

There is the question of power—yes, of authority and indeed of final authority, to whom does power ultimately belong, to whom has authority been given, who can lay claim to power, who is finally in control, who is king, and what kind of king?

There is the question of justice—yes, of the legal system of the people of God and of the imperial system of the world power Rome, what justice means, who represents true justice, who practices true justice, who administers true justice?

But there is also the question of peace, of the nature and the source of real peace, and of its absence; questions of the sword, violence, conflict; of murderers and violent people, how to deal with them, how to respond to them?

And there is the question of truth; questions of knowledge and wisdom, of certainty and assuredness, of culture and civilization, of meaning and happiness; questions of the true way of life, of words of truth, of people of truth, of embodiment of truth, where words of truth and life are to be found, what truth truly is?

And there is the question of community, of belonging and solidarity and love, questions of the masses, of the people, of nationhood and friendship and family life, of human bonds, what real belonging means, true community and true love?

There is the question of human morality, of ethics, of right and wrong, of who sinned and who not; questions of responsibility, guilt and innocence, when is someone responsible, or not, and does it help to wash your hands for all to see?

There is the question of the human ability to see, and human blindness; where does it come from, what causes blindness, and who are those who really see, and who are those who perhaps cannot?

There even is the question of public opinion and public choices, of human decisions and decision making, whether to leave or not, whom to follow or not, whom to set free, what freedom of choice means, being able to decide, standing before alternatives?

There is further the question of religion; of traditions, teachings, and discipleship; of whom ultimately to belong to, whom to serve, whom to trust, whom to obey, whom to fear, whom to call king—or emperor?

There is indeed the question of salvation, of ways to fulfillment and happiness, of ways to be fed and satisfied, how to be happy and full of joy, how not to fear but to trust?

All these motifs—every single one of them, but many others, too—have been present in the Gospel of John from the beginning, at work in the plot, sometimes hidden, sometimes explicit in the rich diversity of stories, incidents, confrontations, characters, words and teachings, signs and miracles, speeches and claims—motifs of humanity, power, justice, truth, culture, knowledge, light, darkness, bread, life, death, tradition, religion, and many more. Every person who has read the Gospel even superficially has already been made attentive to at least some of them, has already begun to listen for further clues, has become sensitive to further keys to help solve these teasing questions—until one hears this moving scene in the passion, carefully narrated to unfold dramatically around the person and the actions of Pontius Pilate.[43] Suddenly, all these motifs are woven together in this gripping picture, albeit in complex, even ambiguous and deeply ironic ways.

Perhaps one could therefore claim that it is not only human politics and justice, but human culture as such, humanity with all its ideals and achievements and claims, that comes to failure here. Pilate—both as one actor in the dramatic scene and as representative symbol for the whole trial—stands not merely as representative of politics and justice, but also as representative of human history and striving, of human culture and achievement, and of its collapse in the confrontation with Jesus. Against the background of the earlier chapters of the Gospel of John, almost every word in this description of the scene around Pilate becomes double-edged, ambiguous, ironic, tragic—words of total failure and collapse.

Political power and the representative of the state fail—yes, legal systems and their administration of justice fail—but this story is also about the failure of respect for human dignity and for humanity as such (behold, the human being! . . . while Jesus is wearing his crown of thorns and his robe of mockery); the failure of peace and dealing with violence (it is precisely during Passover that they cry "not this man, but Barabbas," Barabbas who was a robber!); the failure of human wisdom and knowledge (if the representative of the classical world does not know what truth is, who will?); the failure of the human sense of community, belonging, and loyalty (Jesus is being interrogated "about his disciples and his teaching" (18:19), with the scene surrounded by two brief incidents during which Peter is denying that he even vaguely knows this man!); the failure of human morality and responsibility (the bitter irony in the shocking words "take him yourselves and crucify him, for I find no crime in him!"); the failure to see what is at stake (are you? are you not? from where are you? will you not speak? do you not know?); the failure of public opinion and the will of the people (whom do you want, which son-of-the-father?); the failure even of religion (no one else but the chief priests themselves say that they have no king but Caesar!).

In short, this is a story about the total collapse of human culture and achievement in serving life, happiness, justice, peace, knowledge, truth—yes, serving fellow human beings and God. Many commentators have movingly articulated this total collapse.[44]

"... UNDER PONTIUS PILATE": HUMAN SIN?

Quite remarkably, when dealing with other theological themes—including, for example, the Holy Spirit, the Lord's Supper, human sinfulness, and the resurrection of Jesus Christ—Michael Welker has often painted similar scenarios in describing the events of what he prefers to call "the night of betrayal."[45]

Perhaps his descriptions in *What Happens in Holy Communion?* could be helpful as a point of entry into his views. One of his many answers to the question asked in his book's title is that Christ's cross and death are brought before our eyes in public proclamation as often as Holy Communion is celebrated.[46] The meaning—or rather, to put it in his own way, the rich and complex potentiality—of Christ's cross and death is being revealed to us.[47] What is this potentiality? It is the same complete cultural failure and collapse that readers encounter in John's account of the trial before Pilate.

> The cross stands for the fact that Jesus of Nazareth, who proclaimed the coming reign of God and who freed many people from sickness and possession, was apparently shown to be in the wrong, condemned, and exposed to contempt. . . . But the cross does not stand for just any process by which Jesus, the God whom he proclaimed and Jesus' communion with that God might be called into question. *The cross stands for the fact that Jesus of Nazareth was condemned to a shameful and torturous death and was executed in the name of religion, in the name of the ruling politics, in the name of two legal systems (Roman and Jewish), with the support of public opinion* ("All of them said, 'Let him be crucified!'") (my italics).[48]

Again and again, Welker uses this kind of description to make clear the potential (rather than "the meaning," which sounds too static) of the cross, the death, the night of betrayal.

> The cross confronts us with the hideous knowledge that religion, law, politics, morality, and public opinion—all of them institutions that are supposed to serve piety, public order, universal justice, and the promotion of human community and of what is good—can collaborate in driving the human beings who use these institutions into ongoing falsehood, injustice, mercilessness, disintegration, and distance from God. The abysmal power of the systemic masking and reinforcement of relations detrimental to life—the power that the biblical traditions call "sin"—becomes manifest "under the cross."[49]

Welker's crucial insight is that what is revealed here—whether in the account of the night of betrayal, in the death on the cross, in the celebration of the Lord's Supper, or in the creed's reminder during regular worship of the ". . . under Pontius Pilate"—is not mere historical fact, but present reality. We are confronted with "hideous knowledge" of what can still happen and what in fact is always happening anew. We are confronted with what "the biblical traditions call 'sin'"—and this knowledge is of extreme importance for living our lives today.

> The situation that becomes manifest is one that encounters us in an obvious way when we look back—or from the outside—at societies and epochs fundamentally corrupted by fascism, racism, ecological brutality, or in other ways. But it is a situation which, even in those times and places where it is not obvious in the world, is latent. It is a situation of systematic and systemic corruption, in which the religious, political, judicial, moral and other forces of reciprocal normative control and correction are absent as a whole. According to the testimony of the biblical traditions, natives and foreigners, the occupied and the forces of occupation, Jews and Romans, Jews and Gentiles collaborate in Jesus' crucifixion. That is, the entire representative world cooperates and conspires here against God's presence and against the powers of life. The "back-up controls" exercised by a global public, another judicial order, another religion, or even "the enemy" are absent here. Here it is not just the elites, but the gathered "crowd" (the concrete public), and even Jesus' most intimate circle, who collaborate together.[50]

Welker describes this ever-present reality of human sin, this pervasive, often very visible, but often also latent and deeply hidden power, as "the unsurpassable depths of the human power for destruction and self-destruction."

> The cross of Christ places before our eyes the unsurpassable depths of the human power for destruction and self-destruction. . . . It confronts us with the fact that religion and law, politics and morality, memory and public opinion are fundamentally corruptible and corrupt. It confronts human beings with our abysmal power to spread destruction, meaninglessness, and hopelessness. . . . On the cross, the failure of an entire world becomes manifest. Religion, law, politics, and public opinion—but also neighbours, friends, and disciples—turn against the one who proclaimed in word and deed God's presence, God's righteousness, and God's love. In part they turn against him with evil intent; in part they turn helplessly away.[51]

Instead of "the cross," "the Lord's death," or "the celebration of the Lord's Supper," Welker could just as well also have said "the regular liturgical reminder by the creedal expression '. . . under Pontius Pilate.'" They all serve the same purpose, namely, confronting us with the failure of our worlds, exposing human sin, warning against self-deception, destroying all illusion and pride—whether political, legal, scholarly, cultural, moral, or religious. "Under Pontius Pilate" is the church's way of summarizing what Welker calls "the night of betrayal."

> The night of God-forsakenness; hell on earth; the recognition that religion, law (Jewish and Roman!), politics, morality, and public opinion are misused; the recognition that even friendship and discipleship are not dependable—all this belongs to the "memory of Christ."[52]

The night of betrayal is, for him, a vivid memory of the reality and power of sin over us.

> The proclamation of Christ's cross, indeed of his death, pulls the rug from under all religious, legal, political, and moral self-righteousness of human beings. In the light of this proclamation, no one can boast, no one can point the finger at others, can separate oneself from others, can elevate and look down on others. All illusions are destroyed that human beings can by their own power deliver and liberate themselves from their own act of closing themselves off from God. The self-inflicted condition of being closed off from God, the self-encapsulation against the powers of Good, against justice, against what is creative, against life—this is what the biblical traditions call *sin*. The proclamation of Christ's cross brings before our eyes a situation of "the sin of the world" in which ... God alone can help.[53]

But can God help? And how can God help? The dark events of the night of betrayal and of the cross, of the utter collapse captured in the creedal " ... under Pontius Pilate" seem to end in questions of such utter hopelessness.

> Yet how can God help in this situation, if—and this is what is most terrifying about the cross of Christ—the entire representative world—all powers, all agents responsible for order—have conspired in "a will to be far from God"? How can God help, if the world so to speak hermetically seals itself off from God, if the world can completely cut itself loose from God and set itself in opposition to God? ... The cross confronts God with the death and sin of the world in a way that calls into question not only Jesus' life, but the divine life.[54]

If all of humanity, all our social, cultural, and institutional forms turn against God and against ourselves, can God then still help? How can God help?

"... UNDER PONTIUS PILATE": FOR US?

The most remarkable aspect of all these diverse interpretations of the "... under Pontius Pilate" in the creed has precisely been the conviction that in and through all of this God was in fact helping, that God was at work, that somehow these terrible events of the night of betrayal and Christ's death on the cross all served God's purposes of salvation.

The "... under Pontius Pilate" takes place "for us ... and our salvation," according to the christological confession of the Nicene-Constantinopolitan Creed.

The church is confessing a mystery in these words, the mystery of salvation. There are even deeper levels of meaning hidden in these chapters of the trial and death of Jesus—and therefore in the creedal statements and liturgical actions that the church employs to summarize them—than what superficially meets the eye. The responses given thus far to the question why Pontius Pilate is mentioned in the creed still completely fail to articulate the richer, more complex, deeply ambiguous potentialities, for example, already present in the account of John's Gospel.

John is not simply telling his readers how politics, law, morality, friendship, loyalty, religion, culture, and knowledge have all collapsed during that night of betrayal, when Jesus Christ suffered and died under Pontius Pilate, but he is actually telling them that in spite of all this—yes, mysteriously and ambiguously in and through all of this—God was present and at work to save and raise to new life. Several clues in the narrative are clearly intended to raise the readers' awareness for this divine presence and activity in and through what is happening. From the perspective from which John is seeing these events, they seem to appear in a different light.

There are, for example, the several explicit references that the events took place so that the Scriptures or Jesus' own words would be fulfilled (18:32; 19:24; 19:28; 19:36; 19:37). The events of the night and the trial may seem arbitrary, chaotic, out of control—but somehow hidden purposes and promises are being fulfilled. There is the very explicit key at the beginning of the narrative, when Jesus hands himself over to the band in the garden, that he knew all that was to befall him (18:4); he even knew by what death he was to die (18:32). There is the direct assurance of Jesus to Simon Peter that he is drinking the cup that his Father has given him (18:11). There is the crowing of the cock, for which the readers have already been prepared (18:27). There is the saying of Jesus that he was born for this and came into the world for this, to bear witness to the truth (18:37). There is the ambiguous inscription of Pilate on the cross that Jesus is the king of the Jews and his refusal to remove the title (19:19–22). There are the several striking references to the fact that all was finally finished, completed, fulfilled (19:28; 19:30). Two motifs are of special importance in this regard. There is the explicit exchange about the authority of Pilate and Jesus' straightforward claim that Pilate would have no power over him unless it had been given to him from above (19:10–11). There is also the highly loaded words that Pilate "handed Jesus over" to be crucified (19:16)—since the same expression is also used for the disciples, but also for God the Father, who in deeply mysterious ways are all together handing Jesus over. In short, these and other allusions leave readers without any doubt that something deeply mysterious and hidden, something divine and full of salvation, is taking place in and through these terrible acts and events.

The story of ". . . under Pontius Pilate" is not so much a story about human failure and cultural collapse, but a story about God, about salvation, and about new life. Sure, it is also a story about human failure, but precisely in the way that story is told, it becomes a story of salvation and new orientation. Almost all the documents and theologians already mentioned have known that.[55]

Those who argue that these words in the creed are first of all a historical indication thereby want to underline that this is a claim about the identity and nature of God and about the nature of our salvation and our life.

Those who emphasize that Pilate represents the state and political power thereby want to underline that precisely in his failure he is still being used by God as state and as political power—so that even in its most terrible forms politics still demands our respect, serious attention, and continuous involvement, if necessary in the form of resistance on behalf of the real state and true politics. That is indeed the thrust of Barth's extensive use of Pilate in his reflections on political abuse, responsibility, and resistance in 1938, but also in his later work, when he attempts to develop further the implications of his well-known christological foundation for the state and politics.[56]

Those who emphasize that Pilate represents human law and our systems and institutions of legal justice want to show that it is precisely as judge that Pilate plays his crucial role in the divine work of salvation. That is indeed the thrust of the argument in the Reformed tradition, since Calvin and the early confessional documents. God is achieving the divine purposes of salvation by using this human judge, even in his failure to administer justice justly he is still fulfilling his indispensable role.[57]

Those who argue—like Welker—that the night of betrayal and therefore the events "... under Pontius Pilate" represent the total collapse of human achievement and culture see in this narrative the real and saving presence of Jesus Christ, until today. It is perhaps even possible to see in Welker's views and logic an even more comprehensive version of the same logic underlying the Reformed and especially Barthian christological grounding of the state and of human justice. For Reformed faith and especially for Barth, the collapse of the state does not mean that the state becomes unimportant for salvation and that Christians should withdraw from participating in the affairs of the state and politics—on the contrary. In its failure, its crucial importance for human life and for the world is affirmed. Under circumstances, Christians may even be called to resist the Pilate-state in the name of and for the sake of the justice-state, precisely because it is so important.

In similar fashion, one could perhaps argue that the complete collapse of culture in the night of betrayal does not mean that all these human and cultural activities—exercising authority and power, administering justice, seeking truth and knowledge, living in friendship and community, serving peace, practicing forgiveness, contributing to public opinion, participating in public life—become unimportant in the light of salvation, meaningless, and something from which Christians should withdraw themselves—on the contrary.

Welker is deeply interested in all these activities and deeply concerned with their social and institutional forms in modern, complex, and pluralist societies. Their ultimate failure to provide human fulfillment and salvation—so dramatically illustrated ". . . under Pontius Pilate"—does not make them irrelevant—on the contrary. This memory only serves as a critical reminder of the importance to continuously discern between their constructive and life-giving potential and their destructive and life-endangering, even life-destroying powers. This memory should continuously orient and inspire the church—as a community seeking truth, justice, mercy, peace, and freedom—to discern between, perhaps to adapt Barth's words, Pilate-culture and life-giving culture, in order to recognize and resist destructive forms and to support and serve life-giving forms.

How does this become possible? Only if the church throughout history sees this narrative not merely as an account about a historical event, about the collapse of human achievements, but as something different, something more. Only if the church continues to hear in these words from the creed both a call and a promise, the call still to discern critically in the present between life-endangering and life-giving forms and the promise of the presence and power of Jesus who stood before Pilate "for us."[58] In other words, only if the church sees these events from the same perspective from which John saw them and from which he recounted his narrative, and the perspective from which the ancient church deliberately included these words in their confession of the Triune God—that is, from the perspective of the resurrected Jesus.

". . . UNDER PONTIUS PILATE": IN LIVING CULTURAL MEMORY?

The perspective of the Christology of the church is the perspective of the resurrection of Jesus Christ, the crucified. For the church, it is only from the perspective of the risen Christ that talk about the so-called historical Jesus and about his so-called real presence today becomes meaningful and coherent. The Gospels are indeed narratives about a risen crucified One, and the rest of the New Testament documents indeed offer us testimonies to the activities, the presence, and the future of this risen crucified One. In recent years, Michael Welker has argued on many occasions, in diverse contexts and in discussion with many different figures and audiences, that the Christology of the church, of Scripture and tradition, is ultimately about the real presence of the risen Christ.[59]

Key in this approach to Christology have been distinctions between "communicative memory," "cultural memory," and "canonic memory."[60] Communicative memory always remains fluid; it is continuously being changed, transformed, and enriched, but it is also continuously disappearing and being lost. Cultural memory is more formed, organized, and stabilized, and it provides enduring content, bases for orientation, and directions for new learning to any particular community. When such cultural memory "is codified in a plurality of different interpretations," argues Welker, it "potentiates itself and becomes a canonic memory." This means, for him, that "*a structured and bounded pluralism of interpretations leads to necessarily restless memory that continually calls forth new interpretations without losing its centering.*"[61] Canonic memory can therefore also be called "living cultural memory."[62]

Expressed in typically Welkerian language, this could be taken as helpful commentary on the role of the creed in the history and life of the church. Important aspects of the nature and role of the creeds in the ongoing life of the church could be understood in this way.

> The Christian faith affirms the vitality and inexhaustibility of the canonic memory of the risen Christ by desiring to cultivate this memory until Christ's *parousia*. Living canonic memory is oriented toward a future that remains beyond its control, because it moves toward that future out of many contexts that are all concentrated on it. An anti-ideological and anti-triumphalistic power lies in this canonic memory as it grows ever anew out of many testimonies. It is communicative, critical, and self-critical memory. . . . Truth-seeking communities . . . should work to bring canonic memory into play to such an extent that Jesus' earthly life before and beyond his death shines forth in a multiform provision of testimony.[63]

Christian faith should not lose its centering—which is also given in the full Trinitarian confession of the ancient creeds, as "compressed narratives," as concentrated summaries of the rich and complex, pluralist and ambiguous, fragmented and multiform biblical witnesses and testimonies. The words ". . . under Pontius Pilate" find their proper place only within the framework of this living cultural memory, as an integral moment in the earthly life of the Jesus who was crucified and then raised by the Living God.

". . . UNDER PONTIUS PILATE": STILL TRANSFORMING THE WORLD?

The "vitality and inexhaustibility" of this living cultural memory calls for multiform new witnesses, many new testimonies, moving toward the future but out of many contexts. As integral part of the Christology of the church, the words ". . . under Pontius Pilate" therefore also call forth new applications, new relevance, new voices, new witnesses, new testimonies, new power—in many new situations throughout history.[64] These new testimonies can be given in word and in deed, in theology and ethics, in search of truth, justice, and mercy.

The typical Reformed understanding of confessions may serve as one such possible illustration of this function of living cultural memory, in addition to many others. Bernd Oberdorfer has correctly pointed out that Welker holds such a Reformed view of confession[65]—or, again in his own expressions, "the communicative, critical, and self-critical memory of truth-seeking communities, always striving to bring the canonic memory into play in order that Jesus' life before and beyond his death can shine forth in a multiform testimony."[66] In fragmentary ways, ever anew, ever provisional, the vitality and inexhaustibility of the living cultural memory of Jesus Christ—and therefore, whenever necessary, also of the words ". . . under Pontius Pilate"—can be appropriated anew under changed historical circumstances, leading to new acts of confessions, in word and deed.

Welker has always been attentive to the concrete forms and disciplines in and through which the potential of such a living cultural memory is released and embodied. His characteristic stress on the pluralistic nature of contemporary societies,[67] on the complexity and multiformity of publics and public audiences,[68] on the legitimate diversity of important institutional forms of the real church[69]—liturgy and worship, congregations, denominations, the ecumenical church, believers cooperating freely in associations, theological work, leadership, diverse networks, public discourses—serves to demonstrate his deep awareness of the many different ways in which the living cultural memory of the church is kept alive, proclaimed, and practiced. In comparison to many other systematic theologians, he has consistently shown a remarkable sensitivity for the importance of the practical and ethical embodiment of the Christian faith and confession. Christology, finally, also has to do with being the church and with concrete discipleship.

> One can imagine a multitude of further events that set the canonical memory in motion—from graciously turning attention to children and to sick, suffering, or possessed human beings, on the one hand, to the meal community's acceptance of the excluded.[70]

In particular, the "necessarily restless memory" keeping the words ". . . under Pontius Pilate" alive will remain attentive to new situations in which political power, institutions of justice, cultural practices, communal forms, moral systems, public opinion, and religious traditions collapse and fail—not only when they are evil, but precisely in their claims to be beneficial. Confessing Jesus Christ today—including his suffering and death under Pontius Pilate—may therefore indeed call for such confession in the face of contemporary realities, whether excessively evil or extremely self-righteous.[71] Pelikan describes this ever-present possibility that the church may feel called to confess anew, for example, "against colonialism, racism, and idolatrous nationalism."

> The twentieth century, which saw the rise of both Nazi and Communist totalitarian regimes that were inimical to Christianity, also therefore produced several such confessions that were political acts in this special sense. Preeminent amongst these, both in its own time and in its subsequent role as a normative confession adopted by several Protestant churches in Germany and well beyond, was *The Barmen Declaration* of May 1934, as Christian confessional response to a twentieth-century revival both of polytheism and of Caesar-worship no less virulent (though sometimes less overt) in its opposition to the Christian gospel. Particularly in the fifth of its sixth theses, protesting against the teaching that the church is "an organ of the state" and that the state is "a total ordering of life," *The Bar-*

men Declaration became the rallying point, across confessional lines, for the Christian rejection of National Socialism and of other ideologies of racial purity. It has performed this function also for churches engaged in the subsequent political-theological struggles of developing "Third World" societies against colonialism, racism, and idolatrous nationalism.[72]

The ecumenical church comes to the same conclusion.

> Christians believe that human beings—individually and collectively—live in bondage to sin and death. . . . The NT understanding of death . . . also comprises everything that surrounds death like the powers of evil, decay and corruption in individual and social life. This perception of the human condition is reflected in general human experience, where human self-centeredness, egoism and striving for power over others manifests itself in the attitudes of groups of people and in many contemporary social, political and economic structures: unjust and oppressive forms and conditions of life, hunger, imposed poverty, exploitation, discrimination, anxiety in the face of armed conflicts. . . . These consequences of sin cause hatred, suffering, despair and death among human beings, and lead humankind to disrupt the natural order and to threaten the very existence of our world. . . . In which way is the gospel of the suffering and death of Christ the Good News for all people? *In the light of his resurrection we see in Christ's suffering and death God's action*, the fulfilment of God's saving purpose for all people, by which he destroyed the power of death. He took away the guilt of humanity and he created the prototype of new life for those who follow Jesus. *This is the Good News which is paradoxically bound up with the scandalous character of Jesus' cross which judges the securities and claims for the world. Therefore the Church must never cease to preach Christ crucified. It encourages Christians in their life and mission to follow the example of Christ.*[73]

And Welker himself writes in similar fashion:

> The risen Christ becomes present in a way that retains the multidimensionality of his person and influence, as well as the multidimensionality of access to his person and influence. The powers of love, the powers of forgiveness, the powers of healing, the powers of special attention to children, to the weak, to the rejected, to the sick, and to the suffering are communicated with the presence of the risen Christ. *The powers of struggle with the so-called "principalities and powers" for example, with political and religious powers in the search for justice and truth also take shape in the presence of the risen Christ. The person and life of Jesus Christ thus make a multiplicity of powers for transformation and renewal available.* These powers "in the Spirit" should by no means be belittled as mere subjectivist impressions and wishful thinking.[74]

And elsewhere:

> Many events that would initiate canonical memory are also possible from Jesus' "symbolic political conflicts" with the temple cult and the Roman Empire, as well as from analogous conflicts in historically analogous constellations.[75]

Indeed, the Christology of the church is about much more, but somewhere within this multidimensionality of the risen Christ and the multidimensional ways of remembering, experiencing, and following this Christ today is also the claim that he suffered and was crucified for us ". . . under Pontius Pilate." These words, in the heart of the Christian creed and worship and therefore of Christology, ecclesiology, and discipleship remain part of this living cultural memory, and thus indeed constitute a cultural power that continues to transform the world.

NOTES

1. Michael Welker, *What Happens in Holy Communion?* (Grand Rapids: Eerdmans, 2000), 132.
2. Luke Timothy Johnson, *The Creed: What Christians Believe and Why It Matters* (New York: Doubleday, 2003), 9–39, provides a helpful overview of the origins and development of the ancient creeds in the West and the East. Already during the second century there are glimpses of short professions of faith, showing a steady movement toward an increasingly standard creed, but at the same time showing diversity, reflecting local concerns and rhetorical circumstances. Although the early Christians felt, for various reasons, impulses to develop a creed, they were not concerned with uniformity of expression. Both aspects are quite remarkable, also concerning the words ". . . under Pontius Pilate." It is remarkable that the expressions appear in so many of these early professions and eventually in both Western and Eastern creeds. It is just as remarkable that these words are used differently in the creeds, and that there is no concern with uniformity of expression.

   Johnson refers to Ignatius, bishop of Antioch, as the first example. Journeying across Asia Minor on his way to a martyr's death in Rome, in about 115, he wrote a series of pastoral letters to local churches. He was especially concerned about the threat to the faith coming from Donatists, who denied that Jesus fully and physically shared in the human condition. Johnson writes, "In his *Letter to the Trallians 9:1–2*, Ignatius exhorts his readers, 'Be deaf, therefore, whenever anyone speaks to you apart from Jesus Christ, who is of the stock of David, who is of Mary, who was truly born, ate and drank, was truly persecuted under Pontius Pilate, was truly crucified and died . . . , who was also truly raised from the dead. . . .' His providing historical details from the Jesus story (naming David, Mary, and Pontius Pilate) and his emphasizing on Jesus' 'truly' being born, eating and drinking, being persecuted, and dying show his concern that Jesus be known to have shared fully in the human condition." He also refers to Justin Martyr's *First Apology 61*. Before 165 he is defending the Christian movement to the Roman emperor, by describing the manner of Christian baptism. During the washing, the "name of Jesus Christ, who was crucified under Pontius Pilate," was evoked.

   Toward the end of second and into the third century, among other reasons because Christianity was increasingly becoming an ecumenical or worldwide church with a desire to establish more coherence among its local communities, and also because of the increasing challenge posed by dualistic versions of the faith, proclaiming saving knowledge and an escape from matter, he argues, there is a more definite growth toward a norm by which to measure orthodoxy. He discusses Irenaeus, Tertullian, and Origen, showing how these impulses increasingly led toward a creed or a so-called rule of faith, meeting the challenges to the Christian story and identity, at the same time serving antiquity and stability and being compatible with flexibility in formulation. In the West, the earliest set form of a creed is found in the *Apostolic Tradition* of Hippolytus (around 215), already including the words "... under Pontius Pilate." During the fourth and fifth centuries, this so-called Roman Symbol appears in many places at once with only minor variations, e.g., in an explanation by Ambrose of Milan, in several sermons of Augustine of Hippo in North Africa, in sermons of the bishop of Ravenna, and especially in the *Commentary on the Apostles' Creed* by Rufinus of Aquileia (404), where it receives this name for the first time. Local variations appear for centuries, until a final, standard form is attested in the seventh century, according to which Jesus "suffered under Pontius Pilate."

In the East, there is less evidence of development, according to Johnson, although examples of local creedal formulations are found in Eusebius of Caesarea, Cyril of Jerusalem, Epiphanius of Salamis, and Theodore of Mopsuestia. During the first ecumenical council of Nicaea in 325, a creed was formulated, intended to serve as a measure of orthodoxy for the entire Christian community, and after a long period of instability in the empire, Theodosius I called another synod in Constantinople in 381, anew to unite the church, by adapting and reaffirming the earlier creed. The pneumatological section on the dignity and role of the Holy Spirit was elaborated, in response to the challenge from radical Arians, and the christological section was formulated much more explicitly than the earlier Nicene Creed in the narrative style of earlier creedal traditions, summarizing the biblical events in storylike form. As a result of this, the words "crucified for us under Pontius Pilate" became part of the Nicene-Constantinopolitan Creed.

3. We actually know very little about the historical person Pontius Pilate. He was governor of the Roman Judea Province from AD 26 to 36. On the one inscribed stone that has been found referring to him (discovered in 1961 at Caesarea Palaestina, the then capital of Judea) he is described as prefect, while Tacitus (in one factual sentence looking back from the time of Hadrian, *Annals* 15.44) calls him the procurator of the province, but this is easy to explain and it does not make any historical difference. Until 44 someone in his position was called prefect, but after that, without any difference in rank or function, they were called procurator. Tacitus simply anachronistically used the title from his later period. Pilate was from the equestrian order, a lower rank of governors, with primarily military functions, as well as responsibility for the collection of taxes. There are a few paragraphs about Pilate in works by the first-century Jewish historian Josephus (*Antiquities of the Jews* and *The Wars of the Jews*) dating from about forty years after Pilate had been recalled from Judea. There is finally also reference to Pilate in the work of the contemporary Jewish writer Philo of Alexandria (*Embassy to Gaius* 38) and on a few small coins. The New Testament, of course, often refers to Pilate, and he plays a crucial role in the Gospels.

4. There has been much speculation about his person, his character, and therefore his attitude toward Jesus and during the trial. Already the early Christian apocryphal writers began to embroider his personality and conduct before, during, and after the trial (very influential was the fourth-century apocryphal document the *Acts of Pilate*, available in different versions in Greek, Coptic, Armenian, and Latin, and still regularly printed during the fifteenth and sixteenth centuries, but there have been many other legends as well). Many

stories claimed that he later felt sympathies for Christianity and even converted to the faith. Inspired by that, medieval writers invented a diversity of origins for him, describing in detail his childhood and youth, albeit in many different ways, and created elaborate myths accounting for the last, missing years of his life—about which nothing is actually known—and about miraculous appearances in many places after his death; some of these mountains, rivers, and lakes remain named after him until today. This speculative mythology even provided a name and reputation for his wife (Claudia Procula, canonized as saint in Orthodox Christianity). Generally speaking, one could claim that Western traditions mainly regarded Pilate as responsible and guilty because of his actions during the trial, but Eastern Orthodoxy argued that he was exonerated and did everything in his power to release Jesus, or that he committed suicide out of remorse. The Ethiopian Church recognized Pilate as a saint during the sixth century, based on the account in the *Acts of Pilate*. Art and literature remain fascinated by the figure of Pilate, and paintings, sculptures, poems, plays, fiction, films, and music keep appearing in this imaginative tradition. A well-known example is Mikhail Bulgakov's *The Master and Margarita*, in which Pilate plays a central role in the lives of leading characters—but there are many more.

5. *Confessing the One Faith: An Ecumenical Explication of the Apostolic Faith as It Is Confessed in the Nicene-Constantinopolitan Creed (381),* Faith and Order 153 (Geneva: World Council of Churches, 1991), 55 (paragraph 131).

6. Karl Barth, *Dogmatics in Outline* (New York: Harper and Row, 1959), 109.

7. Jan Milič Lochman, *The Faith We Confess: An Ecumenical Dogmatics*, trans. David Lewis (Philadelphia: Fortress, 1984), 115.

8. Ibid.

9. Ibid., 116.

10. Ann Wroe, American editor of *The Economist,* published a fascinating study, *Pilate: The Biography of an Invented Man* (London: Vintage, 2000). She describes how for the early Christians the phrase ". . . under Pontius Pilate" often carried overtones of power and of the struggle against and the victory over powers. Already Justin Martyr claimed that devils trembled not merely at the mention of Christ, but when Christ and Pilate were mentioned together. "The reason why he is in the Creed . . . is not merely to set Christ's death in time. Pilate represented not simply his age, but the full power-structure of his age and the worst that it could do. He sat on the judgment seat of Caesar transplanted to Judea. . . . The trial of Jesus before the imperial judge was the moment when he challenged overweening power and appeared to lose; but, as the faithful knew, he burst out of the tomb and threw that power over. It was essential not merely to express faith in Christ but in 'Christ crucified under Pontius Pilate,' brutally murdered but not—ha! killed at all. Among the early Christians the phrase *sub Pontio Pilato* was used almost as an incantation, an invocation, a magic spell. In one apocryphal gospel St. Peter commanded a camel 'in the name of Jesus Christ crucified under Pontius Pilate' through the eye of the famous needle; the tiny needle, glinting in the sand, opened 'like a gate,' and the camel lurched through. Demoniacs were exorcised 'by the name of Christ crucified under Pontius Pilate,' and converts were plunged three times in the baptismal water while Pilate's name, as well as Christ's, washed over them. The purged demoniacs immediately began to cure the sick, where other charm-wavers had been unable to cure them. The name made devils tremble; and Justin Martyr makes it clear that they did not fall down merely at the mention of Christ, but at the name of 'Pontius Pilate

the governor of Judea,' who had administered his death 'by dispensation' and had been trumped, utterly" (164–65).

11. *Confessing the One Faith*, 61.

12. Timothy Luke Johnson, for example, sees these words as a reminder that "the worldly authorities actively oppose this power at work through the crucified Messiah Jesus. The words 'under Pontius Pilate' remind us that the imperial authorities hate challenges to their absolute power to order the world as they wish. Jesus died a violent but also a legal death. The reminder has two sharp edges. The first is the memory that when Christians have most followed the pattern of Jesus' life, they have also come most clearly and painfully into conflict with political rulers and have often followed Jesus not only in manner of life but also in manner of death. The second edge is the memory that when Christians have relied on the power of the state to advance their own goals, or, even worse, imitated in the life of the church the values and practices of the state, they have lost their distinctive identity and have become oppressors of others" (*Creed*, 167–68).

A well-known representative of such a political reading is Wolfhart Pannenberg, e.g., in *The Apostles' Creed in the Light of Today's Questions,* trans. Margaret Kohl (Philadelphia: Westminster, 1972): "The cross sheds a similar light on Pilate's involvement in the death of Jesus—and consequently the involvement both of Rome itself and the interest of political rule in general, which were embodied by Rome in the world of the day. The background here is the conflict between Jesus' message and the claims of political rule. . . . Jesus' proclamation of the coming rule of God and its exclusive authority for human beings undermined the spiritual foundations of the Roman imperium. . . . In the light of the divine proof of lordship in the resurrection of Jesus . . . the act of his condemnation appears as that very crime of lèse-majesté, the crime against the ruler, for which the Roman procurator had Jesus, the supposed or ostensible rebel, executed, though of course the majesty which is violated here is the majesty of God, no longer that of the Roman emperor. Thus the cross of Jesus demonstrates the tendency of political rule to violate the majesty of God, a tendency which operates everywhere where political rule usurps absolute binding force. At the same time it is clear in the light of the raising of the crucified Jesus that human beings are not bound in conscience to obey such claims, as the first Christians also showed later, through their resistance to the emperor cult. Through the raising of the one who was crucified, the individual is freed from the absolutely binding force of everything that counts in society. But political rule is not merely condemned, either. It is certainly humbled by the higher authority of God, who turned its judgment upside down by raising the crucified Jesus; but it is also pardoned on condition that it accepts this humiliation" (85–86).

An interesting example of a politician reflecting on Pilate as a paradigmatic political figure comes from an interview with former British prime minister Tony Blair. "The intriguing thing about Pilate is the degree to which he tried to do the good thing rather than the bad. He commands our moral attention not because he was a bad man, but because he was so nearly a good man. . . . It is a timeless parable of political life. It is possible to view Pilate as the archetypal politician, caught on the horns of an age-old dilemma. We know he did wrong, yet his is the struggle between what is right and what is expedient that has occurred throughout history. . . . And it is not always clear, even in retrospect, what is, in truth, right. Should we do what appears principled or what is politically expedient? Do you apply a utilitarian test or what is morally absolute? . . . Christianity is optimistic about the human condition, but not naive. It can identify what is good, but knows the capacity to do evil. I believe that the endless striving to do the one and avoid the other is the purpose of human existence" (*Sunday Telegraph*, April 7, 1996).

13. Barth, *Dogmatics in Outline*, 110. Although his brief discussion of the creed is not the right place, according to Barth, to develop a Christian doctrine of the state, he briefly refers to his well-known views on the state—perhaps one should say on "how the whole Pontius Pilate reality looks from the standpoint of the suffering Lord." Already in 1938, in his famous essay called "Rechtfertigung und Recht," later translated as "Church and State" and published in Karl Barth, *Community, State, and Church: Three Essays*, with an introduction by Will Herberg (Garden City, N.Y.: Doubleday, 1960), he used the figure of Pilate to develop his views on the relationship between church and state, in particular the right of resistance. After the war, he further developed his views in his equally famous, albeit controversial, essay "Christengemeinde und Bürgergemeinde" (translated as "The Christian Community and the Civil Community" in the same volume). For a helpful introduction to Barth's thought regarding resistance, see Wolf Krötke, "Theologie und Widerstand bei Karl Barth. Problemmarkierungen aus systematisch-theologischer Sicht," in *Karl Barth in Deutschland (1921–1935): Aufbruch—Klärung—Widerstand*, ed. Michael Beintker, Christian Link, and Michael Trowitzsch (Zürich: TVZ, 2005): 121–39.

14. Barth, *Dogmatics in Outline*, 111.
15. Ibid.
16. Lochman, *Faith We Confess*, 116.
17. Ibid., 121ff.
18. Ibid., 122–23.
19. Ibid. The same kind of claim is made in very interesting ways in an essay by N. T. Wright, "The New Testament and the 'State,'" *Themelios* 16, no. 1 (1990): 11–17, also with reference to Pilate: "What then might Jesus have meant by those words, 'my kingdom is not of this world' (John 18:36)? . . . The claim before Pilate is that the kingdom Jesus is inaugurating is not worldly in its methods. . . . Kingdoms of the world fight; physical power, strategic, revolutionary or military power is the rule of the game. Jesus' kingdom has a different *modus operandi*. The sentence should not be read as referring to an other-worldly, Platonic, non-physical kingdom. It designates Jesus' kingdom as the breaking into the worldly order of a rule which comes from elsewhere, from Israel's God, the creator God. It does not mean the abandonment of the created order and the escape into a private or 'spiritual' sphere. On to the scene of worldly power—precisely there, or it is meaningless!—has come a new order of sovereignty, which wins its victories by a new method" (13, 15, 16).
20. Jaroslav Pelikan and Valerie Hotchkiss, eds., *Credo: Historical and Theological Guide to Creeds and Confessions of Faith in the Christian Tradition* (New Haven, Conn.: Yale University Press, 2003), 216–44.
21. Ibid., 218–25.
22. Ibid., 218ff.
23. Ibid., 220–25.
24. Ibid., 222ff.
25. Ibid., 225–28.
26. Ibid., 229–41.
27. Ibid., 217–18.

28. Ibid., 217.
29. Ibid., 222, referring to 1 Tim. 6:13.
30. Ibid., 222.
31. Historically, his position of procurator only involved limited judicial responsibilities. Civil administration lay in the hands of local government, municipal councils, or ethnic governments such as the Sanhedrin and the high priest, as in the case of Judea and Jerusalem. During Pilate's time he (or the even more influential Roman legate of Syria) would have the power of appointment of the high priest. Normally, he would have lived in Caesarea the capital, but during the Passover, a festival of deep national and religious significance, he would have visited Jerusalem to keep order. As the accounts in the Gospels indicate, it is only because the Jews needed his permission for the death penalty (John 19:31) that he was involved in the judicial proceedings. The Gospels accordingly stress his role as judge in this particular episode.
32. This is his view in the *Institutes*, but also in his *Genevan Catechism* (1541/1545), where exactly the same logic is followed, portraying Pilate in his necessary role as human judge: "Question 56: Why do you not simply say in one word that he died instead of adding also the name of the governor under whom he suffered? Answer: This has reference not only to our credence of the story, but that we may know his death to have been connected with his condemnation. Question 57: Explain this more clearly. Answer: He died so that the penalty owed by us might be discharged, and he might exempt us from it. But since we all, because we are sinners, were offensive to the judgment of God, in order to stand in our stead, he desired to be arraigned before an earthly judge, and to be condemned by his mouth, so that we might be acquitted before the heavenly tribunal of God. Question 58: But Pilate pronounces him innocent (Matt. 27:23; Luke 23:14), and hence does not condemn him as malefactor. Answer: Both things must be considered. For the judge bears testimony to his innocence, so that there may be evidence that he suffered not for his own misdeeds but for ours. Nevertheless, at the same time he is formally condemned by the same judge to make it plain that he suffered as our surety the judgment which we deserved, that thus he might free us from guilt. Question 59: Well said. For if he were a sinner, he would not be a fit surety to pay the penalty of another's sin. Nevertheless, that his condemnation might secure our acquittal, it was requisite that he be reckoned among the malefactors (Isa. 53:12). Answer: So I understand it."
33. John Calvin, *Institutes* 2.16.5. See also the discussion by Stephen Edmondson, situating this discussion of Pilate's role in the larger context of Calvin's soteriology and Christology of the threefold office of priest, king, and prophet (Stephen Edmondson, *Calvin's Christology* [Cambridge: Cambridge University Press, 2004], 99ff.).
34. "It is written that the chastisement of our peace was placed on the Son of God and that we are healed by his wounds. He was led to death as a lamb. He was numbered among sinners and condemned as a criminal by Pontius Pilate, though Pilate had declared that he was innocent" (Belgic Confession, Article 21).
35. See, e.g., G. C. Berkouwer, *The Work of Christ* (Grand Rapids: Eerdmans, 1965); Oepke Noordmans and J. M. Hasselaar, *Verzamelde werken* (Kampen: Kok, 1990), 55–57; A. A. van Ruler, *Ik Geloof. De twaalf artikelen van het geloof in morgenwijdingen* (Nijkerk: G. F. Callenbach, 1969); Herman N. Ridderbos, *Het Evangelie naar Johannes*, deel I, deel II (Kampen: Kok, 1987, 1992).

36. Barth, *Dogmatics in Outline*, 104–6.

37. This is indeed part of the fascination of Wroe's *Biography of an Invented Man*. Every chapter represents, as it were, a totally new attempt, from a new starting point, pursuing a new motif through the history of interpretation and imagination.

38. For separate treatments of Pilate in the different Gospels, see, e.g., the published doctoral dissertation by Helen K. Bond, *Pontius Pilate in History and Interpretation*, SNTS Monograph Series 100 (Cambridge: Cambridge University Press, 1998), with ample literature and detailed analyses. Her purpose is to understand how various Jewish and Christian authors of the first century used Pilate as a literary character in their writings. She therefore looks at the ways in which both Philo and Josephus as well as the four Gospels portray Pilate and at the rhetorical concerns that shaped their different interpretations of his person and role. She is particularly interested in the question dominating this kind of scholarship for so long, namely, whether their respective views of the Romans have influenced their portrayals of Pilate. She argues that it would be a mistake to distinguish between so-called historical and theological portrayals, since all the theological accounts also reflect rhetorical and ultimately political views and concerns. Although the focus of her question, namely, the background of the first-century documents, falls outside the scope of these reflections on the ancient creeds and the history of their reception, her approach is very valuable, since it also applies to the later period during which the words were included in the ancient creeds, and of course also to the diverse interpretations that these words received during the centuries, until today. Ecclesial and theological interpretations are always also political, social, and rhetorical interpretations. Their continuing power to influence, orientate, move, and motivate lies precisely in this fact.

39. For detailed discussions of the historical background, see the many monographs and commentaries, for example, Raymond E. Brown, *The Gospel According to John* (London: Geoffrey Chapman, 1978); also Brown, *The Death of the Messiah: From Gethsemane to the Grave: A Commentary on the Passion Narratives in the Four Gospels,* Anchor Bible Reference Library (New York: Doubleday, 1994), especially 1:665–877.

40. See the helpful contribution in a volume dedicated to Michael Welker on the occasion of his fiftieth birthday, by Ralf Frisch, "'Was ist Wahrheit?' Ein biblisch-theologischer Versuch über die Johannespassion," in *Resonanzen: theologische Beiträge: Michael Welker zum 50 Geburtstag,* ed. Michael Welker, Sigrid Brandt, and Bernd Oberdorfer (Wuppertal: Foedus-Verlag, 1997), 12–25.

41. He has often explained what he means theoretically by biblical theology and by biblical realism, he has often written about his own Protestant views of *sola scriptura* and the authority and interpretation of Scripture, and he has most of all often practiced such an approach concretely, in dealing with diverse doctrinal and theological themes, regularly with surprising and challenging results. See, e.g., his own "Biblische Theologie: Fundamentaltheologisch," *Religion in Geschichte und Gegenwart: Hand wörterbuch für Theologie und Religionswissenschaft,* vol. 1 A–B, ed. Hans Dieter Betz, Don S. Browning, Bernd Janowski, and Eberhard Jüngel (Tübingen: Mohr Siebeck, 1998), 1549–53; his "Sola Scriptura? The Authority of the Bible in Pluralistic Environments," in *A God So Near: Essays on Old Testament Theology in Honor of Patrick D. Miller,* ed. Brent A. Strawn and Nancy R. Bowen (Winona Lake, Ind.: Eisenbrauns, 2003), 375–91; and his "The Tasks of Biblical Theology

and the Authority of Scripture," in *Theology in the Service of the Church: Essays in Honor of Thomas W. Gillespie*, ed. Wallace M. Alston Jr. (Grand Rapids: Eerdmans, 2000), 232–41. For a considered discussion of the promises, the challenges, and the legitimacy of such a realistic biblical theology under the conditions of modernity critical of the authority and use of Scripture, see Bernd Oberdorfer, "Biblisch-realistische Theologie. Methodologische Über-legungen zu einem dogmatischen Programm," in *Resonanzen*, ed. Welker, Brandt, and Oberdorfer, 63–83. One major implication is that Welker is not interested in a single authoritative interpretation, whether based on the intention of the author or on the methodological superiority of the exegetical approach; see Oberdorfer, "Biblisch-realistische," 74ff. He rather delights in the rich potential of multiple and even ambiguous readings.

42. For a more detailed exegetical treatment, see, e.g., "Johannine Themes Cul-minating in the Trial before Pilate," in Bond, *Pontius Pilate in History and Interpretation*, 166–74; also several contributions of mine in B. A. Müller, C. W. Burger, and D. J. Smit, eds., *Riglyne vir prediking oor regverdiging en reg*, Woord teen die lig III/3 (Kaapstad: Lux Verbi, 1992), 1–14, 27–88, 127–34, 236–50.

43. Raymond Brown has convincingly shown how the narrative of the trial devel-ops through seven scenes, linked together by Pilate as character, who con-tinuously moves outside to the Jews and back inside to Jesus. In the first scene he is outside, with the Jews, asking them about their accusation against Jesus (18:28–32). In the second scene he is back inside with Jesus asking him whether he is king of the Jews and finally what truth is (18:33–38a). In the third scene he is back outside, asking the Jews whom he should release for them (18:38b–40). In the fourth and central scene, Pilate is back inside with Jesus, allowing the soldiers to strike and ridicule him as king of the Jews (19:1–3). In the fifth scene, he is outside, taking Jesus with him, and telling the Jews to see this human being, in whom he finds no crime (19:4–7). In the sixth scene, Pilate takes Jesus back inside, asking whether Jesus knows that he has power even to crucify him (19:8–11). In the seventh and final scene, he goes outside again, to sit on his judgment seat and to hand Jesus over in response to the claim by the Jews that they have no king but Caesar (19:12–16); see his commentary on *The Gospel According to John* and *The Death of the Messiah*; also Bond, *Pontius Pilate in History and Interpretation*, 175–93.

44. In Wroe's words, "The Pilate of the gospel is not just a Roman judge whose character must be softened for political reasons. That is almost the least of the roles he plays. He is also a symbol of the state, the secular power, the mate-rial world, ignorance, and darkness. He is all men facing, considering and ultimately rejecting Truth. That is why . . . people cling to Pilate as the great equivocator. Like an audience at a show, they love to watch him teeter, strug-gle, almost save himself, and fall. In some sense, they feel they are watching themselves" (in *Pontius Pilate in History and Interpretation*, 217–18). The Dutch ethicist E. L. Smelik wrote moving meditations on Pilate, powerfully portraying his role as such a total collapse of culture and civilization. He speaks of "de culturele vermoeidheid van de mens," and describes it as the skepticism of a whole culture, "Het is het sceptisisme van een gehele cultuur, dat zich ontlaadt in deze retorische vraag. Een overbeschaving, die aan haar uitholling op den duur te gronde gaan, staart ons hier met glanslose ogen aan; een rijk, dat twijfelt aan zijn opdracht; een samenleving, die wanhoopt aan haar zin; een organisatie, waar de spanning uit is van het ideaal," in *Gevraagde Postille* (Den Haag: Daamen, 1956), 79–82; also *Het Evangelie*

naar Johannes. De weg van het Woord, De Prediking van het Nieuwe Testament (Nijkerk: Callenbach, 1973).

45. E.g., Welker, *What Happens in Holy Communion?* 43–54, but also many other places.
46. Ibid., 101ff. He gives twelve different answers to the question, of which this is the sixth.
47. The translation of *What Happens in Holy Communion?* uses "potentiation," but it is probably also possible to use "potential" or "potentiality" for what Welker wants to convey, namely, the reservoir of possible meaning and power at work in common memories.
48. Ibid., 104–5.
49. Ibid., 105.
50. Ibid., 105–6.
51. Ibid., 106. For similar descriptions, see also Welker, *God the Spirit* (Minneapolis: Fortress Press, 1994), 303ff. ("The perception of the dominant forms in which the world is endangering itself is constantly shifting"); and Sigrid Brandt, Marjorie Suchocki, Michael Welker, and Klaus Verger, eds., *Sünde. Ein unverständlich gewordenes Thema* (Neukirchen-Vluyn: Neukirchener Verlag, 1997).
52. Welker, *What Happens in Holy Communion?* 171.
53. Ibid., 106–7. Welker is often very critical of theologians and church documents that fail to take this night of betrayal seriously, and therefore fail to account for the reality and power of sin from which we need to be saved; see, e.g., his critique in this regard of the *Baptism, Eucharist and Ministry* document of Faith and Order ("fruit of ecumenical understanding in a global context in which the word 'sin' has become an incomprehensible or even laughable expression," 151–54); internal developments within Protestantism ("a striking uncertainty concerning the place . . . of forgiveness," 154); the influence of dialectical theology (powerless against "the moralization of the biblical concept of sin," 155); several bilateral dialogues (including the 1983 *Helsinki Report,* 156–57); and leading ecumenical theologians, like Lehmann and Pannenberg ("still . . . a blindness in its theology of sin," 158–60).
54. Ibid., 107.
55. Wroe dedicates a key chapter in *Biography of an Invented Man* to Pilate as "God's secret agent"—discussing these many claims that somehow behind the historical detail a divine purpose was being achieved (109–60).
56. See especially Barth, "Church and State," 111: "Gerade der dämonisierte Staat kann wohl das Böse wollen, um dann doch in eminenter Weise das Gute tun zu müssen. Er kann seinem Dienst nicht entlaufen."
57. A quotation from Berkouwer (*Work of Christ*) illustrates this Reformed logic: Mysteriously, Pilate is serving God's purposes; *exousia* has been given to him. Berkouwer uses the word *ondoorgrondelijk,* "unfathomable," to refer to this mystery of salvation at work in Pilate's failure: "For this reason we are interested only in that interpretation of *sub Pontio Pilato* which sees this history in the light of God's activity and consequently in the soteriological light, as is so evidently done in the Heidelberg Catechism. . . . Scripture clearly states that Christ himself acknowledged Pilate's authority. Given from above—that is the reason why Christ acknowledges the authority (*exousia*) of Pilate on whom he is now dependent: dependent in the hour of decision. This authority has been thus explained: Pilate can decide to crucify Jesus only by God's permission. The mystery of the crucifixion cannot, however, be approached in this way. This would make God a passive spectator in the suffering of

the cross instead of the One who is *doing* something; remember the prayer after Pentecost! It is true, Pilate is doing something, but therein he is but the medium of God's sovereign, omnipotent activity. . . . God's action manifests itself in and through the judge Pilate even after he has declared Jesus innocent and before the final verdict. Pilate acts here as *persona publica* and thus he passes judicial sentence on the Son of man. That is the biblical background of the Catechism's explanation, which fully recognizes the arbitrariness in this verdict (he, being innocent, and yet condemned); nevertheless it does not detach this sentence from the given *exousia*. This reveals again—as in Caiaphas' prophecy—God's *crossing* the activity of man *in* the historical identity between Pilate's act in his capacity of a judge and God's act. That is why the Church always emphasizes the substitution, the aspect 'for us' in the condemnation of the innocent Christ. . . . There is a divine 'must' also in the fact that not his own people but a temporal judge condemned him. . . . And so the Church confesses: 'who suffered under Pontius Pilate.' There is an *unfathomable* relationship between this verdict, this judgement, and the grace of God, the deliverance from judgement" (Berkouwer, *Work of Christ*, 156–59).

58. In his pneumatology, Welker movingly describes this real presence and power as the public person of the Holy Spirit; see *God the Spirit*, especially 279ff., but also in earlier chapters on Christ and the Spirit and the church and the Spirit. It is, however, also possible to describe this presence and power in different theological terminology from a Trinitarian perspective, and most certainly using christological language.

59. See, e.g., his essays "Resurrection and the Reign of God," in *Hope for the Kingdom and Responsibility for the World: The 1993 Frederick Neumann Symposium on the Theological Interpretation of Scripture*, ed. Daniel L. Migliore, *Princeton Seminary Bulletin* 15 (1994): 3–16; "Auferstehung," *Glauben und Lernen* 9 (1994): 39–49; "Die Gegenwart des auferstandenen Christus als das Wesentliche des Christentums," in *Das ist christlich: Nachdenken über das Wesen des Christentums*, ed. Wilfred Härle, Heinz Schmidt, and Michael Welker (Gütersloh: Chr. Kaiser, 2000), 91–103; "Die biblische Auferstehungsberichte und das kanonische Gedächtnis," in *Wie wirklich ist der Auferstehung?* ed. Hans-Joachim Eckstein and Michael Welker (Neukirchen: Neukirchen Verlag, 2000), 311–32; "Resurrection and Eternal Life: The Canonic Memory of the Resurrected Christ, His Reality, and His Glory," in *The End of the World and the Ends of God: Science and Theology on Eschatology*, ed. John C. Polkinghorne and Michael Welker (Harrisburg, Pa.: Trinity Press, 2000), 279–90; "Theological Realism and Eschatological Symbol Systems," in *Resurrection: Theological and Scientific Assessments*, ed. Ted Peters, Robert John Russels, and Michael Welker (Grand Rapids: Eerdmans, 2002), 31–42; "Wright on the Resurrection," *Scottish Journal of Theology* 60, no. 4 (2007): 458–75.

60. In this regard, he often acknowledges the contributions of his Heidelberg colleague in Egyptology, Jan Assmann, referring particularly to *Das kulturelle Gedächtnis* (Münich: Beck, 1992), and "Was ist das 'kulturelle Gedächtnis'?" in *Religion und kulturelles Gedächtnis* (Münich: Beck, 2000), 11–44.

61. Welker, "'Who is Jesus Christ for us today?'" *Harvard Theological Review* 95, no. 2 (Apr 2002): 145–46 (italics added).

62. Sometimes he follows Assmann (who followed Lévi-Strauss) in distinguishing between "cold" and "hot" forms of memory. The cold elements no longer serve as potential for active and living retrieval and new appropriation, while the hot elements continue to orient, move, and inspire: see Welker, *What Happens in Holy Communion?* 127–29. Perhaps one could argue that

the immense corpus of legend, myth, speculation, and interpretations that grew around Pontius Pilate throughout the centuries demonstrates both the importance and the difficulty of the distinction between cold and hot elements. Much of this is today merely of historical interest, leading to curiosity and amusement, but at the heart of the tradition, as embedded in the canonical Gospels and in the ancient creeds and Christology of the church, there lives a powerful cultural memory that has continued to inspire, not only to produce art and literature, but in fact to resist oppressive regimes and to risk lives. Sometimes, however, what is not important or inspiring to one part of the community and tradition may be very powerful to another, under different circumstances.

63. Welker, "'Who is Jesus Christ for us today?'" 146.

64. It remains very interesting that Welker chose the four pneumatological themes of the Nicene-Constantinopolitan Creed for the final chapter of his *God the Spirit*, 279–342.

65. Oberdorfer, "Biblisch-realistische Theologie," 81. For Reformed confession, see my "Social Transformation and Confessing the Faith? Karl Barth's Views on Confession Revisited," *Scriptura* 72 (2000): 67–84.

66. It is important that the ongoing process of reception and confession should be self-critical, and the history of interpretation of Pilate may demonstrate this necessity. In many ways, it was used over centuries to propagate and justify anti-Semitism. "These fantasies could be laughable if they did not carry a dark undercurrent: the determination of early Christian writers in every branch of the church, whether Greek, Coptic or western, to shift the blame for the crucifixion from Pilate to the Jews. . . . This could reach grotesque levels, as when Origen . . . simply pronounces Pilate innocent, and ascribes to the Jews all the cruelties that were inflicted on Christ by the Romans. . . . The reason for these inventions, at least at first, was not simply to hurt the Jews. For at least three centuries after Christ's death, as the new religion struggled to establish itself, it was vital to have a Roman official who would say, repeatedly, that Jesus posed no threat to the empire. Pilate had to be Christ's advocate, even his friend, and this made the Jews the villains. . . . Nonetheless, medieval anti-Semitism was still based squarely on the notion that the Jews had killed Christ. Pilate . . . became a witness to their . . . capacity to sow evil in the world. . . . Even the most tyrannical Pilate put the Jews in a bad light. In invented story after invented story he complained that they had misled him, made him do what he had never wanted to do. He had tried every subterfuge to save Jesus, but they had insisted on his death. Even twentieth-century anti-Semitism, which had its roots in all kinds of prejudice both political and economic, was not free from that lingering image" (Wroe, *Biography of an Invented Man*, 315–16).

67. See, e.g., "Christentum und strukturierter Pluralismus," in *Konstruktiver Toleranz—gelebter Pluralismus*, ed. Andreas Feldtkeller (Frankfurt: Lembeck, 2001), 108–19; also "Warum brauchen pluralistische Gesellschaften christliche Theologie?" in *Christentum und Spätmoderne: ein internationaler Diskurs über Praktische Tehologie und Ethik*, ed. Wilhelm Gräb and Denise Ackerman (Stuttgart: Kohlhammer, 2000), 10–26.

68. See, e.g., "Theology in Public Discourse Outside Communities of Faith?" in *Religion, Pluralism, and Public Life: Abraham Kuyper's Legacy for the Twenty-First Century*, ed. Luis E. Lugo (Grand Rapids: Eerdmans, 2000), 110–22.

69. See, e.g., *Kirche im Pluralismus* (Gütersloh: Kaiser, 1995), but also many other writings about different social forms of the church, from local congre-

gations to the ecumenical church, from serious reflection on what happens in worship and liturgy to direct involvement in studies about the future of the denomination.

70. Welker, *What Happens in Holy Communion?* 129–30.

71. Welker often warns not only against obvious forms of evil, but especially against the influence of pervasive but seemingly innocent systems, institutions, and powers, especially media, market, and morality.

72. Pelikan and Hotchkiss, *Credo*, 223. They suggest that such confessions are attempts to draw the implications of the early church's confession that Jesus is the Lord. This is also the case with the South African Confession of Belhar (1986). Originating during apartheid, it confesses the compassionate justice of God, claiming "that the church, belonging to God, should stand where God stands, namely against injustice and with the wronged (and) that in following Christ the Church must witness against all the powerful and privileged who selfishly seek their own interests and thus control and harm others," and closes, "We believe that, in obedience to Jesus Christ, its only Head, the Church is called to confess and to do all these things, even though the authorities and human laws might forbid them and punishment and suffering be the consequence. Jesus is Lord."

73. *Confessing the One Faith*, 142–43 (italics added).

74. Welker, "Wright on the Resurrection," 472–73 (italics added).

75. Welker, *What Happens in Holy Communion?* 17; cf. 130, with reference to Gerd Theissen, "Jesus und die symbolpolitischen Konflikte seiner Zeit: Sozialgeschichtliche Aspekte der Jesusforschung," *Evangelische Theologie* 57 (1997): 378–400.

3

"Faith" as a Christological Title in Paul

THOMAS W. GILLESPIE

I

No less an eminent New Testament scholar than C. E. B. Cranfield concludes his essay, "On the Πίστις Χριστοῦ Question," with the suggestion that "we should be wise to hesitate about trying to construct a theology in which Jesus Christ's faith has an important place."[1] The thesis of this essay, written in honor of Professor Michael Welker, contravenes the wisdom of such counsel, contending to the contrary that such a move is exegetically warranted and theologically necessary. Specifically, it argues that in Galatians 3:23–26 (and elsewhere) Paul uses the term "faith" (πίστις) with the definite article in an absolute sense as an epithet, and that this usage is a titular reference to Jesus.[2] We begin with the literary context of these provocative verses.

Whether or not the apostle composed his letter to the Galatians with a handbook on Greco-Roman rhetoric open before him for compositional guidance, the third chapter represents at least the initial arguments he develops or the proofs he offers in support of his "law free" gospel as attested in 2:14–21. It is thus designated as the *probatio* or *confirmatio* by those who view the letter as an example of judicial[3] or deliberative[4] rhetoric, or a mixture of the two,[5] and among others who doubt the dependence of the letter upon any ideal rhetorical type, it is simply identified as the "Main Argument."[6] The significance is the reasonable inference that here if anywhere in the letter Paul expresses himself with as much linguistic and theological precision as he can muster.

In Galatians 3:15–26, the apostle argues on the analogy of the inviolability of legally enacted human testaments that the giving of the Mosaic legislation[7] 430 years *after* God's promise to Abraham that he would bless the nations through him (Gal. 3:8; citing Gen. 12:3) and his "seed" (Gal. 3:16, citing Gen. 12:7; cf. 13:15; 17:7; 24:7), cannot be viewed as an annulment of that initial covenant promise or as an added codicil that makes its fulfillment conditional upon human obedience evidenced by "works of the law," however that might be construed. For the Abrahamic promise is "graciously bestowed" (κεχάρισται) by God, and to base the promised "inheritance" (κληρονομία) upon law observance would effectively destroy its grace character (v. 18).[8] The answer to the question of why then the legislation was introduced at all is that it was "added" temporarily because of transgressions "until the time when the seed should come (ἄχρις οὗ ἔλθῃ τὸ σπέρμα)" to whom the inheritance was promised (v. 19). This does not imply that the law code is "against the promises of God," only that it is powerless to give life in terms of righteousness (v. 21). What it can and does do as "Scripture" is imprison everyone under sin "in order that the promise might be given ἐκ πίστεως Ἰησοῦ Χριστοῦ to those who believe" (v. 22). We leave the phrase untranslated for the moment because of the debate among scholars over whether here and elsewhere in Paul *faith* as a *nomen actionis* in this genitive construction is directed to Jesus Christ as its *object* ("faith *in* Jesus Christ") or Jesus Christ is the *subject* of this action ("faith *of* Jesus Christ").[9]

II

It is at this point in the argument (vv. 23–25) that we encounter the use of "the faith" three times in what can be called at best "an odd way to speak."[10] For here Paul states that "before the faith came (πρὸ τοῦ δὲ ἐλθεῖν τὴν πίστιν) we were imprisoned under the law, being confined until the coming faith should be revealed (εἰς τὴν μέλλουσαν πίστιν ἀποκαλυφθῆναι)" (v. 23). During this period of time the Mosaic legislation functioned as a pedagogue "unto Christ (εἰς Χριστόν)," in order that we might be justified "by faith (ἐκ πίστεως)" (v. 24). But now that "the faith has come (ἐλθούσης δὲ τῆς πίστεως)," we are no longer under a disciplinarian (v. 25).

The oddity of these expressions lies not only in the particularity assigned to "faith" here by the deictic use of the definite article, but equally in the fact that only in verses 23 and 25 among his genuine letters does the apostle use the noun πίστις, with or without the article, as the subject of an active verb: "the faith" acts as a personal agent in that it "came." Also, it is designated as "the *coming* (μέλλουσαν) faith," suggesting that its arrival was expected. Further, its advent is termed a relevatory event (ἀποκαλυφθῆναι: note the divine passive), a term previously used in the letter to identify the incident in which God revealed to Paul that the risen Jesus is his son (1:16) and thus became the source of his gospel (1:12). Finally, it is attested that "the faith having come (ἐλθούσης)" effects liberation from the imprisonment, confinement, and discipline imposed by the Mosaic legislation. This much is clear, but what is the sense and reference of "the faith" that has come as revelation to effect redemption? Two antecedent texts address this question.

The first identifies the reference. In verse 19 the apostle specifies that the Mosaic code was added to the Abrahamic promise for a limited period of time, namely, "until the seed should come to whom it was promised (ἄχρις οὗ ἔλθη τὸ σπέρμα ᾧ ἐπήγγελται)." Clearly, the three references to *the anticipated faith having come* (vv. 23–25) have this promissory *coming of the seed* as their textual antecedent and material referent. This connection is secured by the statement that since the coming of "the faith" the services of the pedagogue have been terminated (3:25). Thus, the two arrivals have the same identity; the promised "seed" of Abraham is "the faith" that has now come in fulfillment of the promise. Because Paul identifies "the seed" as "Christ" (3:16), the arrival of "the faith" attested in verses 23–25 quite evidently has in view the revelatory and redemptive advent of Jesus.

The second and more immediate textual antecedent is verse 22, where the focus is upon the contested expression ἐκ πίστεως Ἰησοῦ Χριστοῦ. On the basis of proximity, commentators tend to read the definite article (τὴν πίστιν) in the immediately succeeding verse as an instance of anaphora, meaning "this faith," that is, the faith just mentioned.[11] But in what sense is that to be understood? Is it the confessional faith that finds its object *in* the Jesus who has come or is it the faith *of* the Jesus who, having come, is so confessed? Put otherwise, is πίστις Χριστοῦ an anthropological or christological formula?

III

Given that the ambiguity is occasioned by the semantic range of the Greek genitive case, it is not surprising that arguments for both options have revolved, at least initially, around issues of grammar and syntax.[12] The details of this discussion need not be repeated here, however, for there is general agreement among the disputants that the grammatical and syntactical evidence alone is insufficient to command a broad consensus.[13] More promising, however, are exegetical observations from the immediate context.

Surprisingly overlooked in the discussion are the implications of the apostle's affirmation that "Abraham believed God (Ἀβραὰμ ἐπίστευσεν τῷ θεῷ)" (Gal. 3:6, citing Gen. 15:6). The faith of Abraham was not a generic belief in God, but a response to the divine promise. In its Genesis setting, the text cited is the sequel to God's pledge that his descendants will be as innumerable as the stars above (15:5). Because this feature of the patriarchal promise tradition applies singularly to Abraham, Paul conflates it with the universal promise that "all the nations shall be blessed in you" (Gal. 3:8, citing Gen. 12:3; 18:18). Moreover, he claims that this promise was made in the Scripture's foreknowledge of God's intention to justify the Gentiles ἐκ πίστεως. As such it was an anticipatory proclamation of the gospel to Abraham (προευηγγελίσατο τῷ Ἀβραάμ) (3:8), implying that he responded in faith to the gospel in its proleptic form. Most significant of all is Paul's insistence that these promises of God were spoken (ἐρρέθησαν) not only to Abraham but also to his seed (καὶ τῷ σπέρματί σου). Specifically, they were addressed to the individual seed who is the heir of the promise, that is, to Christ (3:16, citing Gen. 13:15; 17:8; 24:7). For emphasis the apostle adds that this seed is the heir "to whom [the inheritance] was promised (τὸ σπέρμα ᾧ ἐπήγγελται)" (3:19).

While it is true that nowhere in his extant letters does the apostle use the verb πιστεύειν with Jesus (Christ) as the subject and God as the object,[14] it strains credulity to infer from this that the divine promise required no response from the seed of Abraham to whom it was equally addressed or that the nature of this answer was for Paul a matter of adiaphora. Having twice made the point that God spoke the promise to Christ the seed as well as to Abraham (3:16, 19), Paul is clearly inviting the inference that Christ also, like his ancestral father, "believed God."[15] For this reason Jesus is to be numbered among "those who are ἐκ πίστεως" and thereby identified as one of "the sons of Abraham" (3:7). It is the apostle's view that his Lord was not faith-less, and he expressed this conviction by the ἐκ πίστεως Ἰησοῦ Χριστοῦ formula in the sense of the "faith of Jesus Christ," a phrase that parallels precisely the "faith of Abraham (ἐκ πίστεως Ἀβραάμ)" (Rom. 4:16) both formally and materially.[16] This christological reading of the πίστις Χριστοῦ formula in Galatians 3:22 identifies the one who has come as a revelatory event to effect redemption from the jurisdiction and curse of the law as the promise-believing Jesus Christ.

IV

But in what sense is "faith" attributed to Jesus? The noun πίστις ranges semantically from "trust" to "fidelity" in social relationships (its context here) and to "belief" in epistemological settings. Because of Paul's express language of the "obedience of faith (ὑπακοὴ πίστεως)" (Rom. 1:5; 16:26) and his focus upon the soteriological obedience of Christ (Rom. 5:19), even unto death upon a cross (Phil. 2:8), proponents of the christological reading of πίστις Χριστοῦ tend to emphasize the fidelity nuance and thus speak of "the faith(fulness)" of Jesus Christ.[17] But the validity of this emphasis should not cause Christ's faith as trust to be ignored or minimized. For obedience predicated upon a promise presupposes trust in the promisor. In making a promise, the speaker commits to doing something in the future in behalf of the one(s) addressed. By its very nature a promise seeks to establish a relationship of trust on the basis of this commit-ment. For a promise to be successful as a speech-act it must first be recognized for what it is and then acknowledged as dependable by "an act of consent to another's self-commitment."[18] This being the nature of promise making and believing, the response of Christ to God's promise addressed to him as the elect seed of Abraham must be considered equally an act of trust.

Whatever difference there may be between the faith of Abraham and of Christ is located not in the formal structure of believing, therefore, but in their respective vocations in the giving and keeping of God's promise to bless "all the nations." Through Abraham, God made the promise; in Christ, he fulfilled it. This is what makes Jesus an object of faith and not merely its exemplar like Abraham. For Christ is the "enabler" of the promise, the one who "delivered us from the curse of the law" by "becoming a curse" in his death on the "tree" and thereby allowing the "blessing of Abraham (ἡ εὐλογία τοῦ ᾿Αβραὰμ)" to "flow freely" to all people (Gal. 3:13–14).[19] It is this vocational difference between Christ and Abraham that shaped the particularity of their otherwise shared faith.

Paul reflects upon the dynamics peculiar to Abraham's faith in Romans 4:16–25 where the issue is oriented to the promise of countless progeny (v. 17, citing Gen. 17:5, and v. 18, citing Gen. 15:5) and Abraham's struggle to believe that promise when in fact he and his wife Sarah remained childless. This struggle is located, according to the apostle, in the context of death. Abraham "hoped against hope" that the promise would be kept, despite his recognition that his own body, nearing its centennial year, was "as good as dead (νενεκρωμένου)" and that Sarah's womb was equally "dead" (τὴν νέκρωσιν τῆς μήτρας Σάρ-ρας) (v. 19). Implied is the fact that keeping the promise to Abraham under these conditions would require nothing less than a demonstration of resurrec-tion power. According to Paul, however, the God whom Abraham believed is precisely "the one who gives life to the dead and calls into existence the things that do not exist" (v. 17). Indeed, it was because Abraham believed that "God was able to do what he promised" (v. 21), which is trust at its highest (and blind-est) level, that his faith was "reckoned to him as righteousness" (v. 22).

When Paul goes on to say that these words "were written not for his sake alone, but for ours also" (vv. 23–24), he is pointing up the prototypical nature of Abraham's faith, which is to say that it is destined to be repeated by and among those who with Abraham believe the promise of God.[20] It is repeated in those who believed prospectively in the God of the promise who "gives life to the dead and calls into existence the things that do not exist" (v. 17) as well as in those who believe retrospectively in the same God "that raised from the dead Jesus our Lord" (v. 24). The crucial point is that this circle of belief includes Christ, who, like Abraham, believed in the promise as yet unfulfilled. Only the trust issue for Christ the seed was not the threat posed by aging reproductive organs, as with Abraham, but rather the menace of death itself to the heir of the promised blessing of the nations. His was an obedience unto death, to be sure, but it was predicated upon a trust that the God who called him to bear the curse on the tree would vindicate his sacrificial act. As with Abraham, so with Christ: "No distrust (ἀπιστία) made him waver concerning the promise of God, but he grew strong in his faith as he gave glory to God, fully convinced that God was able to do what he had promised" (Rom. 4:20–21). "The faith" that has come is the believing Jesus Christ who trusted and obeyed the God of the promise.

V

Paul's affirmation that Christ, with Abraham, "believed God" entails also his faith being "reckoned to him unto righteousness (καὶ ἐλογίσθη αὐτῷ εἰς δικαιοσύνην)." For as one who "believed God," Christ is not only numbered among οἱ ἐκ πίστεως who are "the sons of Abraham" (3:7), but also included with those (again οἱ ἐκ πίστεως) who are "blessed with the faithful Abraham" (3:9). To be blessed "with" (σύν) Abraham is to be blessed as he himself was blessed—that is, reckoned righteous ἐκ πίστεως (3:8).[21] "Righteousness" in Paul's semantic domain is basically a *relational* concept expressed in *forensic* language about an *eschatological* hope of salvation.[22] When God "reckons righteousness" to the "ungodly" (Rom. 4:5), it is a performative act that creates a new reality—a relational reality based on promise and faith—between pledger and recipient that is itself promissory. This is the redemptive reality that God promised through Abraham to all the nations, and it is this reality that God effects through the promise-believing Christ whose faith was "reckoned to him as righteousness."

The primary objection to this view is Paul's claim that Jesus was sinless and thus not in need of justification ἐκ πίστεως.[23] Yet the one verse that explicitly attests to the sinlessness of Christ also declares that it was this very sinless one whom "God made sin for us, in order that we might become the righteousness of God in him" (2 Cor. 5:21).[24] Here it is important to note the formal and material parallel to this text in Galatians 3:13–14 where the phrase "God made sin for us (ὑπὲρ ἡμῶν ἁμαρτίαν ἐποίησεν)" has its semantic equivalent in Christ "becoming a curse for us (γενόμενος ὑπὲρ ἡμῶν κατάρα)." Both the "making" and the "becoming" are acts of the same divine "reckoning" (λογίζεσθαι) that effects "righteousness" in those who believe the promise of God (Gal. 3:6). For Paul these are real states, not ethical fictions. Christ actually became sin and a curse "for us." Yet his sinlessness is preserved when his obedience unto death on the cross is understood not moralistically as conformity to some abstract ideal of ethical perfection (such as complete observance of the Mosaic legislation) but vocationally in terms of his willingness to be "made sin" or to become "a curse."[25]

In so doing Christ acts as an agent of redemption, as the concluding purpose clauses of these two texts underscore. According to 2 Corinthians 5:21, God made Christ sin for us "in order that we might become the righteousness of God in him." The same thing is said differently in Galatians 3:13–14, where Christ became a curse "in order that the blessing of Abraham might be given in Christ" to the nations, that is to say, "in order that we might receive the promise of the Spirit through the faith." The second clause here is in apposition to the first and therefore is explanatory. When viewed schematically the interpretative points become evident:

ἵνα εἰς τὰ ἔθνη (1) ἡ εὐλογία τοῦ Ἀβραὰμ (2) γένηται (3) ἐν
   (4) Χριστῷ Ἰησοῦ,
ἵνα (1) τὴν ἐπαγγελίαν τοῦ πνεύματος (2) λάβωμεν (3) διὰ
   (4) τῆς πίστεως.

In (1) "the blessing of Abraham" (being reckoned righteous) is interpreted as "the promise of the Spirit," indicating that it is the Spirit that effects the reality of a "right" relationship with God. (Terminologically, it may also be noted that "promise" replaces "blessing," thus setting the stage for the ensuing discussion in 3:15–25.) In (2) the verb "receive" (λάβωμεν) suggests that γένηται be understood in terms of an act of "becoming" or "originating" that entails "giving," thereby underscoring the grace character of the fulfilled promise. In (3) the preposition "through" (διὰ) requires that its counterpart (ἐν) be understood instrumentally, "by means of," rather than locally. Most important for our thesis is the introduction in (4) of "the faith"[26] as a metonym for "Christ Jesus."[27] Thus, the way is prepared for the titular use of ἡ πίστις in 3:23–25 where it refers to the coming of the promise-believing Christ whose faith was "reckoned unto him as righteousness" because of his trusting obedience and obedient faithfulness.

VI

Paul's use of "the faith" as a christological title qualifies Jesus for the classical creedal category of "very human." Indeed, a faith-less Christ would be docetic.[28] The question is now whether this epithet entails more than Ebionite categories.

The God whom Paul calls "our Father" in Galatians (1:1, 4) is attested throughout the argument of chapter 3 to be an active agent—in initiating the promise to Abraham and his seed (3:8, 16), in reckoning faith "unto righteousness" (3:6), and in supplying the Spirit to and thus working wonders among the Galatians in the realization of the promised "blessing of Abraham" (3:5, 14). Central to Paul's argument, however, is his conviction that all of this turns on "the faith" that "has come" being the divine "Son" who was "sent (ἐξαπέστειλεν)" by God, "born of a woman, born under the law, in order to deliver (ἐξαγοράσῃ) those under the law, that we might receive adoption as a son" (Gal. 4:4–5).[29] Here at the conclusion of his argument, even as earlier, Paul understands the advent of Jesus that eventuated in his sacrificial death as a redemptive event that delivers us from the law and its curse (cf. 3:13, ἐξηγόρασεν). Thus, the time of the Mosaic legislation has expired because in Christ the Abrahamic promise has been ful-filled by God. In brief, God's faithfulness to his promise and the human response of trusting obedience meet in Jesus Christ.[30] This "meeting" encourages such paraphrases of the πίστις Χριστοῦ formula as "the faith that is God's deed in Christ," or "God's rectifying act in Christ," or even "God's eschatological act,"[31] the point being that God himself is involved with Jesus Christ in his advent, trust, and obedience unto death on the cross. How that is to be understood is the theological task of christological reflection.

This meeting of Jesus the Son and God the Father explains why Paul views Christ as the object of Christian faith, but not exclusively. Although the apostle frequently uses the verb πιστεύειν without identifying its object (Rom. 13:11; 15:13; 1 Cor. 3:5; 14:22; 2 Cor. 4:13; 1 Thess. 1:7; 2:10), he twice identifies Christ specifically as the one to whom believing is directed (Gal. 2:16; Phil. 1:29) and implies the same thing in several others (Rom. 3:22; 10:4; Gal. 3:22). In certain texts from Romans, however, the focus shifts to God. In 3:22 the implied object of believing is "the righteousness of God" (3:22) and in 4:5 it is specified as "the one who justifies the ungodly" (4:5). The latter citation in particular points in this direction by calling attention to "the faith of Abraham" (4:16), who "believed God" (4:3), and whose faith is prototypical of "those who believe in the One who raised Jesus our Lord from the dead" (4:23–24). Thus, Paul can say that Abraham is the ancestor of "all who believe" (Rom. 4:11), which is the context of the statements in Galatians that it is οἱ ἐκ πίστεως who are "the sons of Abraham" (3:7) and thus "blessed with the faithful Abraham" (3:9). Clearly, then, neither the christological reading of the πίστις Χριστοῦ formula nor the titular understanding of ἡ πίστις that "has come" threaten the traditional view that the object of Christian belief is Christ. But the conjoining of the faith of Christ with the faithfulness of God does require that the object of this believing be seen as this bi-focal reality called "the faith."

The argument in Galatians 3:22–26 is capped off with the assurance that "you are all sons of God through the faith in Christ Jesus (διὰ τῆς πίστεως ἐν Χριστῷ Ἰησοῦ)" (v. 26). In what follows there is an interpretive gloss on this text in the assertion that "you are all one in Christ Jesus (ἐν Χριστῷ Ἰησοῦ)" (v. 28), indicating that the phrase "in Christ Jesus" qualifies "sons of God" rather than "the faith" in verse 26 and thereby identifies the locale of sonship rather than the means by which it is attained. The instrumentality of this status falls then to "through the faith," the preposition διά having the same sense of "by means of" here as it has in the parallel phrase διὰ πίστεως Ἰησοῦ Χριστοῦ (Gal. 3:16; Rom. 3:22). It is "through" the trusting obedience and obedient trust of Jesus Christ in his atoning death that the gift of a right relationship with God (righteousness) is given by God to those who believe. This relationship (which includes other believers so related) is the reality that Paul often expresses by his "in Christ" phrase, a concept that is better understood as a relational rather than a "mystical" (Schweitzer) or "participationist" (Sanders) notion. Through "the faith" we are related rightly to God "in Christ Jesus."[32]

VII

Recognition of the titular character of ἡ πίστις illumines its usage in the only other two texts in Galatians in which it appears. In 1:23 the apostle acknowledges the word about him circulating among the Judean churches that "he who once persecuted us now proclaims the faith (εὐαγγελίζεται τὴν πίστιν) which once he destroyed." The commentaries vacillate between reading "the faith" in terms of *fides qua creditur* and *fides quae creditur*, neither of which represents typical Pauline emphases. According to his own testimony, he did not preach a body of doctrine or even believing itself but rather the person of Jesus Christ (1 Cor. 1:23; 2 Cor. 4:5). When "the faith" is understood here as a christological title, however, it corresponds nicely to the singular masculine pronoun in the apostle's previous statement that it had pleased God "to reveal his Son to me in order that I might preach *him* (εὐαγγελίζωμαι αὐτόν) among the nations" (1:16, emphasis added).

Among his concluding exhortations, Paul appeals to the Galatians to "do good to all people," especially to those who are of "the household of the faith (τοὺς οἰκείους τῆς πίστεως)" (6:10). The text is usually interpreted in terms of "the household of fellow believers." While this has a certain egalitarian appeal to modern sensibilities, it is wholly unrealistic in view of first-century Hellenistic vertical social structures where households were identified by "the head of the house" (i.e., "the household of Stephanus," 1 Cor. 1:16; 16:15–16; cf. "the household of God," Eph. 2:19).[33] If "the faith" is a title referring to Jesus, however, then the exhortation makes sense in its assumed social milieu: "Let us do good to all people, and especially those who are of the household of *Christ*."

All seven instances of πίστις with the definite article in Galatians either require a titular understanding of the term or make better sense when it is so interpreted. Limitations of space prohibit the needed extension of this study to other pieces of Pauline correspondence, especially the Letter to the Romans, but the evidence of Galatians is sufficiently strong that a prima facie case may be claimed for reading "the faith" in its absolute sense as a christological title in Paul.

NOTES

1. C. E. B. Cranfield, *On Romans and Other New Testament Essays* (Edinburgh: T&T Clark, 1998), 97.
2. Larry W. Hurtado, *Lord Jesus Christ* (Grand Rapids: Eerdmans, 2003), 98, focuses his exposition of Pauline christological language upon "the key honorific terms and themes that constitute the ways Paul expresses Christian beliefs about Jesus." Our thesis is that "the faith" belongs among these terms and themes.
3. Hans Dieter Betz, *Galatians* (Philadelphia: Fortress, 1979), 126.
4. Joop Smit, "The Letter of Paul to the Galatians: A Deliberative Speech," *New Testament Studies* 35 (1989): 13.

5. Richard Longenecker, *Galatians* (Dallas: Word Books, 1990), 97.

6. J. D. G. Dunn, *The Epistle to the Galatians* (Peabody, Mass.: Hendrickson, 1993), 20.

7. The term "legislation" (νομοθεσία) is Paul's and is used to distinguish the Mosaic law from the other contents of the Torah, such as the sonship, the glory, the covenants, the worship, and the promises (Rom. 9:4).

8. Cf. Rom. 11:6, εἰ δὲ χάριτι, οὐκέτι ἐξ ἔργων, ἐπεὶ ἡ χάρις οὐκέτι γίνεται χάρις.

9. The debate focuses on the variations on the full prepositional phrases διὰ πίστεως Ἰησοῦ Χριστοῦ and ἐκ πίστεως Ἰησοῦ Χριστοῦ that occur in Paul's letters at Rom. 3:22; Gal. 2:16; Phil. 3:9; and at Rom. 3:26; Gal. 2:16; 3:22, respectively. A different but related formulation occurs in Gal. 2:20. For a brief history of the discussion, see Richard B. Hays, *The Faith of Jesus Christ*, 2nd ed. (Grand Rapids: Eerdmans, 2002), 142–48.

10. Ben Witherington III, *Grace in Galatia: A Commentary on St. Paul's Letter to the Galatians* (Edinburgh: T&T Clark, 1998), 267.

11. In addition to the standard commentaries, see Bruce W. Longenecker, *The Triumph of Abraham's God* (Nashville: Abingdon, 1998), 103.

12. See, especially, George Howard, "On 'the Faith of Christ,'" *Harvard Theological Review* 60 (1967): 459–65; Howard, "The Faith of Christ," *Expository Times* 85 (1974): 212–15; Arland J. Hultgren, "The Pistis Christou Formulation in Paul," *Novum Testamentum* 22 (1980): 248–63; Luke Timothy Johnson, "Romans 3:21–26 and the Faith of Jesus Christ," *Catholic Biblical Quarterly* 44 (1982): 77–90; and Sam K. Williams, "Again *Pistis Christou*," *Catholic Biblical Quarterly* 49 (1987): 431–47.

13. Thus Hays, *Faith of Jesus Christ*, 276: "Little is to be gained by rehearsing the familiar arguments about syntax. I stand by my earlier judgment that the balance of grammatical evidence strongly favors the subjective genitive interpretation and that the arguments for an objective genitive are relatively weak. Such syntactical arguments are, however, finally inconclusive."

14. Cranfield, *On Romans and Other New Testament Essays*, 82–84, enlarges this objection to include the entire New Testament.

15. Morna D. Hooker, "ΠΙΣΤΙΣ ΧΡΙΣΤΟΥ," *New Testament Studies* 35 (1989): 329: "Now the promise was made to Abraham *and his seed* (v. 16), but it was made on the basis of Abraham's faith; it is fulfilled in Christ, who is Abraham's seed and therefore shares his faith" (italics in original).

16. With this exegetical confirmation of the christological reading of Gal. 3:22, the grammatical, syntactical, and translation issues are resolved: (1) the πίστις Χριστοῦ formula is a subjective genitive; (2) this phrase modifies the verb δοθῇ rather than the noun ἡ ἐπαγγελία; (3) the redundancy of the concluding phrase τοῖς πιστεύουσιν, when the genitive construction is read objectively, is eliminated; and (4) the translation is "in order that the promise might be given, on the basis of the faith of Jesus Christ, to those who believe."

17. Thus Hays, *Faith of Jesus Christ*, 152: "If Paul can speak so compellingly in Rom 5:19 of the soteriological consequences of Christ's ὑπακοή, there is no a priori reason to deny that Paul could intend the expression πίστις Ἰησοῦ Χριστοῦ to refer to Christ's soteriologically efficacious faith(fulness)."

18. Francis Watson, *Paul and the Hermeneutics of Faith* (London: T&T Clark, 2004), 179.

19. J. Christiaan Beker, *Paul the Apostle* (Philadelphia: Fortress, 1980), 50.

20. Ernst Käsemann, *Perspectives on Paul* (Philadelphia: Fortress, 1971), 97, views Paul's typology in Rom. 4 as a "correspondence," a "correlation," or a

"repetition" of events based on "a deep-lying stratum" of history understood teleologically.

21. Watson, *Paul and the Hermeneutics of Faith*, 188: "For Paul, the blessing of Abraham cannot be something extrinsic to the God who blesses; the blessing of Abraham is to be found in his relationship with God."

22. Karl Kertelge, "Zur Deutung des Rechtfertigungsbegriffs im Galaterbrief," *Biblische Zeitschrift* 12 (1968): 211–22.

23. A variation on this objection is the view that "faith" in its Pauline usage "carries with it what may be called a 'negative' or 'excluding' or indeed a 'sinfulness-admitting' sense." Thus Cranfield, *On Romans and Other New Testament Essays*, 96.

24. Rudolf Bultmann, *The Second Letter to the Corinthians* (Minneapolis: Augsburg, 1985), 165: "The meaning is, just as believers are 'just' because God regards ('reckons') and treats them as such, though they are sinners, so Christ is regarded and treated by God as a sinner . . . though he is sinless."

25. Ivor Davidson, in an unpublished paper on "The Sinlessness of Jesus" presented at the Center of Theological Inquiry in Princeton, New Jersey, on October 4, 2006, argues that at "the most elementary level" the sinlessness of Jesus consists in his being "set apart by and for a particular vocation of service to God's will" (14).

26. Frank J. Matera, *Galatians* (Collegeville, Minn.: Liturgical Press, 1992), 124–25: "This awkward expression indicates that Paul has more in mind than the act of believing. The Spirit comes through 'the faith,' that is, the faith of Christ on the basis of which both Gentile and Jew believe."

27. G. B. Caird, *The Language and Imagery of the Bible* (Philadelphia: Westminster, 1980), 136–37, defines metonymy as "calling a thing by the name of something typically associated with it."

28. Douglas A. Campbell, *The Quest for Paul's Gospel* (London: T&T Clark, 2005), 193.

29. On Paul's belief "that Jesus had really come from God," see Hurtado, *Lord Jesus Christ*, 118–26.

30. Ian G. Wallis, *The Faith of Jesus Christ in Early Christian Traditions* (Cambridge: Cambridge University Press, 1995), 118.

31. Thus J. Louis Martyn, *Galatians* (New York: Doubleday, 1997), 270–71, 362.

32. The same point is scored in Gal. 2 where Paul, contending publicly with Peter, notes that they have believed in Christ Jesus "in order that we might be justified on the basis of the faith of Christ (ἐκ πίστεως Χριστοῦ)" (v. 16), and then speaks of their "seeking to be justified in Christ (ἐν Χριστῷ)" (v. 17). The preposition ἐκ denotes the basis of the right relationship; the ἐν denotes the relationship itself.

33. Wayne A. Meeks, *The First Urban Christians* (New Haven, Conn.: Yale University Press, 1983), 29–31, 75–77.

PART II
SINKING INTO
THE HUMAN
Christology and the Disclosure
of the Human Condition

4

Hypostasis as a Component of New Testament Christology (Hebrews 1:3)

PETER LAMPE

1. In the ancient church's discussion regarding the divine Trinity—particularly in the works of Gregory of Nyssa and Gregory of Nazianzus[1]—hypostasis characterized that which is particular to each of the three elements of the Trinity, in contrast to their unity (*ousia*). Hypostasis is connected with the concept of person (*prosopon*). Accordingly, the Council of Constantinople in 553 CE spoke of one essence (*ousia*) and three hypostases, and the Council of Chalcedon in 451 CE recognized Christ as one hypostasis or person who united two natures (*physeis*) within himself. Influenced by this language, modern religious science often uses the concept of hypostases to describe the different concrete ways in which a divinity acts.

However, these semantics have only very little in common with the prior scientific and everyday use of these words in the ancient world. In general usage, hypostasis referred to that which stood behind (the Greeks would say "under") the appearances, which could mean many things. Courageous determinism, for example, stands behind a visible display of strength and dynamic actions.[2] The moment is the basic building block of time and thus stands, in this way, behind or "under" time.[3] But above all, the term constantly appears (even in the Septuagint) with the meaning of plan, design, or project. A plan underlies an action or a concrete phenomenon as its most important element. While at first it exists only

63

in the mental imagination, it does not need to be reduced to it; in certain circumstances, it is (or will be) visibly implemented as well. The English word "project" is capable of comprising these two aspects. Hypostasis is the plan for a book ("book project"),[4] the floor plan for a huge almost-completed temple, the blueprint for a partly constructed monumental mausoleum,[5] a political or military plan (an attack plan, for example),[6] or the Egyptians' plan ("concept") for the year to always have 365 days, without leap days.[7] In the Septuagint, one finds "plan" or "project" in Deuteronomy 1:12 (directed against God, in parallel to *antilogiai*) and Ezekiel 19:5[8] and 43:11 (plan or layout of the temple). God has a hidden plan for every person's life (Ps. 138:15), and finally, God's council, the place where God's plans are made, in Jeremiah 23:21–22, is derived from "plan."[9]

In the context of ancient natural sciences, hypostasis (as that which stands behind or underneath something) characterized the basis or foundation of a fluid: that which remained behind after the fluid has evaporated—for example, white salt in the case of saltwater. Thus, "basis" or "foundation" marks out the primary meaning of hypostasis for the natural sciences: that which has a lasting and tangible existence is deposited on the bottom when its associated solution evaporates (thus also "residue" or "accumulation").

Some examples include the following: the residue in a jug of wine (Menander in Socrates, *Hist. eccles.* 3.7), curd as the residue of milk (Hippocrates, *de mulierum affectibus* 242: γάλακτος ὑπόστασις), the muddy bed of a standing body of water (Aristotle, *Hist. an.* 551b 28–29), the standing body of water itself as the residue or accumulation of rain (Aristotle, *Mete.* 353b 23), or the residue from smelting iron ore (Polybius, *Hist.* 34.9.10–11). Additionally, one finds it occasionally used in the sense of support, as a derivation from the concept of basis or foundation: the forelegs of an animal serve to support or act as a basis for its weight (Aristotle, *Part. an.* 659a 24: ὑπόστασις τοῦ βάρους). In the same way, an injured hip joint can still serve as support (Hippocrates, *Artic.* 55).

In ancient philosophy,[10] which followed the usage of the natural sciences, hypostasis often meant tangible and lasting existence:[11] being, existence, reality, in contrast to that which is imagined.[12] Posidonius,[13] natural scientist and Stoic philosopher, defined ὑπόστασις τῆς οὐσίας as that being that is realized in the existence of individual things and thus has come into existence; οὐσία, on the other hand, is infinite being without form or quality—that is, the primary matter that manifests itself as ὑπόστασις in empirically perceptible matter. Existence emerges out of the depths of being—for the Stoic, who thought in materialistic terms, this represented a physical process, the result of which he termed ὑπόστασις. The primary matter is deposited in existence (just as salt is deposited as crystals on the sides of a bowl once the saltwater has evaporated). Nonetheless, even Posidonius was able to distinguish between the primary matter and its reified existence only in theory. The primary matter is only existent in "things"; ὑπόστασις is the οὐσία in its reality.[14]

At the same time, however, for the Stoics, the οὐσία cannot be found in all visible phenomena, which is why ὑπόστασις is not used simply to refer to any empirically perceptible phenomenon. A distinction was made between phenomena lacking substance (κατ' ἔμφασιν)—for example, a rainbow—and those with substance, those that reify the primary nature (καθ' ὑπόστασιν)—for example, hail or lightning.[15]

For both Posidonius and the middle-Platonic Albinus (*Epit.* 25.1), a ὑπόστασις reifies and objectifies the infinite primal being. However, for the middle Platonist, this ὑπόστασις or reality was not material, but mental and spiritual. On this middle-Platonic plane we also find Philo, *De somniis* 1.188 (a text that might have been interpolated): the world of mental reality (νοητῆς ὑποστάσεως κόσμος) is set apart from that which can be experienced empirically.[16]

In Plotinus's work, which also broke away from the Stoic program to connect ὑπόστασις to matter, hypostasis referred to the subordinate realization—the outflow or the product (ποιησαμένης)—of a higher level of being; the latter would, however, remain undiminished despite the outflow. For Plotinus, ὑπόστασις, as a derived and subordinate yet entirely valid reality of being, was synonymous with οὐσία. It manifested the "one" on lower levels.[17]

With an eye upon the philosophical usage of the word ("reality"), New Testament research has been in the habit of translating the characterization of God's Son in Hebrews 1:3 as χαρακτὴρ τῆς ὑποστάσεως αὐτοῦ as "imprint/impression" of the "invisible, other-worldly reality" of God. The scholarly translation proposals have included "Ausprägung" der "unsichtbaren, jenseitigen Wirklichkeit" Gottes (H. Köster),[18] "Ausprägung/Abdruck seines Wesens" (H.-J. Eckstein),[19] "Abbild seines Wesens" (Einheitsübersetzung, 1980), "Ebenbild seines Wesens" (Revised Luther Bible, 1984), "exact imprint of his nature" (English Standard Version, 2001), "exact imprint of God's very being" (New Revised Standard Version, 1989), and "effigie de sa substance" (French Bible Jerusalem). Much earlier, the Vulgate proposed "figura substantiae eius."

2. As for Hebrews 1:3a, the following brief argument will call into question the philosophical tendency to equate hypostasis with "reality" or "essence/substance," raising its objections on the basis of micro- and macro-contexts within the Letter to the Hebrews, the New Testament as a whole, and the Septuagint. The solution is much simpler than previously thought.

In the entirety of extant Greek literature predating Origen,[20] who was clearly dependent upon Hebrews 1:3a, the expression χαρακτὴρ ὑποστάσεως is unique; not even Philo offers any explanation.[21] Primarily, a χαρακτήρ (coming from χαράσσω, to scratch or engrave) is active—the minter (of coins), the engraver, or the instrument that he or she uses[22]—and secondarily, it also became the product of this work—that is, that which is imprinted (which derives from the primary sense). Translators should test the active sense of the term before hastily adopting the translation "impression/imprint" without any discussion.

Already in 1:2, the author of Hebrews characterizes the "Son" as the mediator of God's creation (δι' οὗ καὶ ἐποίησεν τοὺς αἰῶνας). The next lines (1:3ab) elaborate further upon this role before 1:3c raises the issue of soteriology (καθαρισμὸν τῶν ἁμαρτιῶν ποιησάμενος) and 1.3d; 1:4ff. raise the topos of the Son's exaltation (ἐκάθισεν ἐν δεξιᾷ τῆς μεγαλωσύνης ἐν ὑψηλοῖς) to a position higher than the angels (1:5ff.). Since the author of Hebrews purposefully progresses toward this exalted status as his argumentative goal (cf. 1:4ff.), ἐκάθισεν operates as the predicate of the relative clause, while the Son's mediatory role in creation and his work of salvation in 1:3a–c are pushed into the role of subordinate participles. Yet it is these participles that interest us.

The mediatory role in creation (1:2) is paired in 1:3b with that of sustaining creation (present participle: φέρων τε τὰ πάντα τῷ ῥήματι τῆς δυνάμεως αὐτοῦ; also Col. 1:17b). Sandwiched between these roles as creation's mediator and sustainer we find χαρακτὴρ τῆς ὑποστάσεως, which in this micro-context is easily understood in the active sense, along the lines of "minter or engraver of his plan"—active in just the same way as φέρων. "Plan" refers to God's plan/project of creation, which the Son then implements, as both mediator and sustainer: he "imprints." The Son carries out God's blueprint for the universe (τοὺς αἰῶνας, τὰ πάντα) and sustains this work "with the word of his power."

God's power is intended here: it is God who figures as the superordinate subject of the entire sentence complex that begins in 1:1. The three relative clauses (1:2b f.) depend upon the main clause in 1:1–2a. Therefore, as with the parallel αὐτοῦ in 1:3a, the αὐτοῦ here refers to God. "The word of God's power" (the word charged with divine power) is the instrument with which the Son sustains God's creation. The Son himself is being distinguished here from the word of God, as the dative in 1:3b demonstrates. Thus, the popular equations of the Son with the Word of God, or the mediator of creation with the Word of God, do not come into play here.

If the word serves the Son as an instrument for sustaining creation, then one cannot consider the second interpretive possibility for χαρακτήρ in 1:3a—that is, "instrument of the engraver"—because the role of "instrument" is already occupied by the word. The Son, then, is not the mediator of creation in the sense that God uses him as an "engraving tool" (χαρακτήρ) for his creative work,[23] but rather it is the Son himself who carves out the work of creation. God's role is in delivering the plan, the blueprint, for this piece of work.

This places the Son in an extraordinary position between God and creation. He is ἀπαύγασμα, radiance/effulgence, of God's glory (1:3a), a reflector who makes the divine glory clearly visible for the creation. Αὐγή refers to dawn or sunrise, when earthly objects become clearly recognizable; correspondingly, αὐγάζειν means to see absolutely clearly or, in an intransitive sense, to shine. Αὔγασμα refers to brightness (Lev. 13:38), and ἀπαύγασμα to bright radiance.

As we have seen, ὑπόστασις is not a christological term in Hebrews 1:3. Rather the word simply represents one component of the compound christological expression χαρακτὴρ τῆς ὑποστάσεως, "the engraver/executor of God's creative plan," an expression coined by the Letter to the Hebrews to express the mediation and sustaining of creation. That mediation and sustaining belong together is conveyed by the particle τε in 1:3b, which connects sentences or phrases that are closely related. In contrast, the participle for the work of salvation in 1:3c is connected asyndetically and thus positioned closer to the exaltation: ". . . who, because he is the radiance of glory and the executor of his plan (of creation) and sustains everything with the word of divine power, sat down to the right . . . , after he had accomplished the cleansing from sins" (1:3).

The advantage of such a translation over against the more traditional "imprint of his (i.e., God's) reality" is that it takes the immediate context frame (the end of 1:2 and 1:3b) more seriously. Why should Christ as an "imprint of God's reality" be the mediator and sustainer of creation? This would only be clarified with the help of further interpretative explanations not found in the text, because the formula "imprint of God's reality" itself is only a piece of information about the inner-Trinitarian relationship. In contrast, "executor of God's plan" in the creation context of 1:2–3 immediately makes the connection to creation clear.

One might object that "radiance of God's glory" is no better than "imprint of God's reality" in linking directly to the work of creation. However, ἀπαύγασμα expresses more activity than the purely passive "imprint." "Reflecting radiation of God's glory" immediately raises the question of where this radiance is being directed; it is precisely as the (active) mediator and sustainer of creation, as the executor of God's creative plan, that the Son passes the radiation of God's glory on to the universe. Such a reading highlights (just as well as the alternative reading "imprint of God's reality") the parallelism between ἀπαύγασμα τῆς δόξης and χαρακτὴρ τῆς ὑποστάσεως.

3. Despite conventional opinion, ὑπόστασις can also be understood in the other four New Testament passages in the sense of plan, project, or intention. This would lead to a uniform usage of the term within the New Testament.

3.1. *Pistis* (faith, reliance, trust) means planning of, i.e. expecting of, counting on (ὑπόστασις) things hoped for. It is because of such *pistis* that the people of old received approval (Heb. 11:1–2).

In this future-oriented sense, the author of Hebrews interprets *pistis* as relying on eschatological goods; "hypostasis" means to plan and assume their arrival in the future, to count on them in one's life, even though they lack any empirical tangibility in the present and are merely anticipated. Planning and counting on them means allowing the present to be determined by a future perspective that has become certain in one's mind and heart. It does not mean bringing about these eschatological goods by oneself; that is for God to do. Luther's rendering here of ὑπόστασις as "firm confidence" perfectly addresses the meaning behind it, but does not "translate" it; it only interprets.

It was Melanchthon who suggested this solution to Luther, who had been undecided about it for some time. As a Protestant alternative to the patristic and medieval interpretation of this verse (in the sense of *ousia* or *substantia*), Luther's rendering is by no means totally "untenable" as Köster declared in the

Theologisches Wörterbuch.[24] Luther's alternative hits the mark—at least in respect to the theological gist of this verse.

3.2. As a parenthetical remark within its context, Hebrews 3:14 represents an interjection provoked by the formulation "every day, as long as it is called 'today'" (3:13)—that is, as long as our history still runs and the eschaton is long in coming. The interjection (3:14) then reads, "We have become and are Christ's partners[25] (γεγόναμεν, perfect tense), if only we firmly hold on until the end to the beginning of the planning/counting on (the announced eschaton)" (Heb. 3:14)—that is, if only we continue to count as steadfastly on God's eschaton as we did at the beginning of our Christian life.[26]

As a parallel we have an earlier passage in Hebrews 3:5–6, which is also formulated in a conditional sense: we are God's house, over which Christ is set as a reliable son, "if only we . . . hold firmly to the boasting in hope" (ἐάν[περ] . . . τὸ καύχημα τῆς ἐλπίδος κατάσχωμεν). The Christians' "planning" (ὑπόστασις) is essentially identical to their eschatological hope. However, we should not forget that when we read "confidence" for ὑπόστασις (as in the English Standard Version of 2001, in the Revised Luther Translation or the so-called Einheitsübersetzung), we are dealing, strictly speaking, with a paraphrase rather than a translation.

3.3. In 2 Corinthians 9:4, ὑπόστασις designates Paul's still incompletely implemented plan/project to collect offerings. Though he is currently working on this plan, Paul fears it will run aground. If the project were to fail, it would disgrace the apostle.

A similar formulation is found in 2 Corinthians 11:17, in the "fool's speech": "What I am saying now, I say not in accordance with the Lord, but rather as a fool within the framework of this plan/project/undertaking to brag about myself," which I am currently putting into action in this fool's speech that is not even finished yet; more foolish bragging is still to come (11:18 ff.; cf. above, e.g., the only incompletely implemented construction plan of a temple).

Conclusion: (a) We see a uniform use of ὑπόστασις (as plan/project) throughout the New Testament, which picks up a prominent semantic line from the Septuagint and from everyday pagan language. No other interpretative solution of Hebrews 1:3a can claim the same. (b) The Son of God as χαρακτὴρ τῆς ὑποστάσεως αὐτοῦ in Hebrews 1:3a is the "shaper/executor of God's plan of creation," both in his function as mediator (1:2) and sustainer (1:3b) of creation.

NOTES

1. E.g., Gregory of Nazianzus, *Or. Bas.* 20 (*de dogmate et constitutione episcoporum*), 35.1072 at the end (χρὴ καὶ τὸν ἕνα Θεὸν τηρεῖν, καὶ τὰς τρεῖς ὑποστάσεις ὁμολογεῖν, εἴτ' οὖν τρία πρόσωπα, καὶ ἑκάστην μετὰ

τῆς ἰδιότητος); Gregory of Nyssa, *ad Graecos ex communibus notionibus* 26 (φυλάττουσα δὲ μᾶλλον ταυτότητα θεότητος ἐν ἰδιότητι ὑποστάσεων ἤγουν προσώπων τριῶν).

2. Polybius, *Historiae* 6.55.2.4–6.55.3.1; similarly 4.50.10. In the example quoted, the concept of cause is amalgamated, as in Sextus Empiricus, *Math.* 10.266, where "hypostasis" is parallel, if not synonymous, to "genesis": "The *genesis* of illness is the cessation of health, the *genesis* of health is the cessation of illness, and the *hypostasis* of motion is the end of immobility, while the *genesis* of immobility is the cessation of motion."

3. Pseudo-Galen, *De victus ratione in morbis acutis ex Hippocratis sententia liber* 19.188 (τῆς στιγμιαίας τῶν καιρῶν ὑποστάσεως): the "nuclear basis of time," i.e., "hours," "days," "months," etc., is a moment, e.g., "the early morning of the day" (19.187).

4. Ibid. 4.2.1; Diodorus Siculus, *Bibliotheca historica* 1.3.7. In 1.3.2.11, the pleonastic combination ὑπόστασις τῆς ἐπιβολῆς can be found.

5. Diodorus Siculus, *Bibliotheca historica* 13.82.2–3; 1.66.6.1–4.

6. Ibid. 16.32.4–16.33.1; 15.70.2.6; 1.28.7.3; Claudius Aelianus, *Fragm.* 59.1–3.

7. Geminus, *Elementa astronomiae* 8.16.4.

8. Ὑπόστασις is not the subject of ἀπῶσται here, but the lion cub dragged off to Egypt in v. 4.

9. "I did not send the (false) prophets . . . , I did not speak to them. . . . If they had stood (ἔστησαν) in my plan/council and had listened to my words, they would have turned my people away from their evil ways." "Plan" or "council" is also best in Wis. 16:21. Other meanings within the Septuagint (cf. Helmut Köster, "ὑπόστασις," *Theologisches Wörterbuch zum Neuen Testament* VIII/9, ed. Gerhard Kittel and Gerhard Friedrich [Stuttgart: Kohlhammer Verlag, 1968], 571–88, here 579–81): "ground," which gives a foothold, Ps. 68:3; "wealth" as a foundation, support or basis for life in Deut. 11:6; Job 22:20; Judg. 6:4; the basis of life, Pss. 88:48; 38:6; also 38:8 (used in the latter for the Hebrew "hope"); "basis of power" (ὑπόστασίν σου τῆς ἰσχύος) in Ezek. 26:11; the "physical possibility/substance/basis for bearing children" (in Hebrew "hope") in Ruth 1:12.

10. Cf., e.g., Jürgen Hammerstaedt, "Das Aufkommen der philosophischen Hypostasisbedeutung," *Jahrbuch Für Antike Und Christentum* 35 (1992): 7–11; Hammerstaedt, "Hypostase," *Reallexikon für Antike und Christentum*, vol. 16, ed. Theodor Klauser (Stuttgart: Hiersemann, 1994), 986–1035; Ubaldo Ramón Pérez Paoli, *Der plotinische Begriff von Hypostasis und die augustinische Bestimmung Gottes als Subiectum* (Würzburg: Augustinus-Verlag, 1990); M. Erler, "Hypostase," in *Religion in Geschichte und Gegenwart: Hand wörterbuch für Theologie und Religionswissenschaft*, vol. 3, ed. Hans Dieter Betz, Don S. Browning, Bernd Janowski, and Eberhard Jüngel (Tübingen: Mohr Siebeck, 4th ed., 2000), 1980–81; Köster, "ὑπόστασις," 574–76; Heinrich Dörrie, *Hypostasis: Wort- und Bedeutungsgeschichte* (Göttingen: Vandenhoeck & Ruprecht, 1955), 35–92.

11. This meaning is probably also true for Lucian, *Par.* 27: The art of being a parasite can be distinguished from philosophy, if we look at its tangible existence (κατὰ τὴν ὑπόστασιν): it exists as a precisely identifiable and definable entity (ὑφέστηκεν)—which cannot be said about philosophy, because it is unclear what philosophy is supposed to be. The latter has unraveled into many self-contradictory schools. Köster, "ὑπόστασις," 578, lines 30–31, mistakenly interprets ὑφέστηκεν as "allowing for a truly good life," which is

certainly not the point of this comparison between the art of being a parasite and philosophy, as the context shows.

12. Artemidorus, *Onir.* 3.14.9–10: *Phantasia* versus *Hypostasis*. The same in Diogenes Laertes, *Vit.* 9.91.6–8: That something really "is" and persists contrasts with mere appearance and pretense (φαίνεται).

13. See esp. *Fragmenta* 268 (*Arius Did.* 27.462.13–463,4); *Fragmenta* 267 (*Arius Did.* 20.458.8–11).

14. The Peripatetics also distinguished ὑπόστασις from that which is only theoretical; Themistius, *In Aristotelis physica paraphrasis* 5.2.4.26–27.

15. *Aetius de placitis reliquiae* 371.28–372.3; Ps. Aristotle, *De mundo* 395a 29–31. Cf. also Philo, *Aet.* 88.3; 92.2.

16. The Peripatetics, of course, could not share in this development of meaning. As far as they were concerned, reality exists only in individual things, not beyond them. Only individual things can possess reality within themselves. Generic concepts, on the other hand, do not exist within themselves (Alexander, *Comm. Top.* 355.13–14). Cf. also Themistius, *In Aristotelis physica paraphrasis* 5.2.4.26–27.

17. See, e.g., Plotinus, *Enn.* 3.5.3.1; 3.6.7.13. For Plotinus's concept of hypostasis, cf. Christoph Horn, *Plotin über Sein, Zahl und Einheit: Eine Studie zu den systematischen Grundlagen der Enneaden*, Beiträge zur Altertumskunde, vol. 62 (Stuttgart: Teubner, 1995), 15ff.

18. Köster, "ὑπόστασις," 584.

19. Hans-Joachim Eckstein, "Die Anfänge trinitarischer Rede von Gott im Neuen Testament," in *Der lebendige Gott. Auf den Spuren neueren trinitarischen Denkens*, ed. Rudolf Weth (Neukirchen-Vluyn: Neukirchener 2005), 37.

20. E.g., *Cels.* 8.14.

21. Contra Köster, whose corresponding remark ("ὑπόστασις," 584, lines 15–16) refers to διαχαραχθέντι in the Philonic text *Somn.* 1.188. This text claims that the mental/spiritual world, which is named ὑπόστασις (see above), is molded according to the archetype. If Heb. 1:3 is read as "imprint or impression of the reality (ὑπόστασις)" of God, then the imprint is subordinated to the ὑπόστασις, whereas in the Philonic text ὑπόστασις and the imprint are ranked on the same level under the archetype. Thus, no parallels can be drawn between these two texts.

22. Euryphamus, *Fragm.* 86.6 (ed. Thesleff); *Inscriptiones Orae Septentrionalis Ponti Euxini* (IPE) I² (1916), 16 A 14. Cf. Henry George Liddell and Robert Scott, *A Greek-English Lexicon*, rev. and avg. Henry Stuart Jones (Oxford: Clarendon, 1958), 1977–78.

23. A similar concept can be found in a traditional formulation (cf. 1 Cor. 8:6d; John 1:3; Heb. 2:10) at the end of Heb. 1:2.

24. See p. 585. Köster's own translation ("ὑπόστασις," 586) reads: "Faith is the reality of what is hoped for." He himself recognizes how poorly such a predicative noun goes with "faith" as its subject, and therefore actually praises this "paradoxical" formulation in Hebrews for its "unequaled boldness." Thus, he remodels his problem into a virtue. However, the problem only arises if one fails to test what is philologically more obvious. Köster's prohibition—"Therefore one may not ask: To what degree is faith ὑπόστασις?" (586n141)—while admittedly coherent from his perspective, is unnecessary philologically and even a slap in the face to the text (ἔστιν δὲ πίστις). Faith is not "the reality of what is hoped for"; rather, having faith means *assuming* or (*pre*)*supposing* the reality of what is hoped for, as we might formulate in view of the above analysis.

25. The possible adjectival alternative, "sharing in Christ," is less convincing.
26. Hebrews offers a parallel to these beginnings in 5:12, but not in 2:3 (contra Köster), where "beginning" does not refer to the start of the Christian life of the Hebrews, but rather to Jesus' teaching, which the disciples once heard.

5

"Mingling" in Gregory of Nyssa's Christology

A Reconsideration

SARAH COAKLEY

In his recent *What Happens in Holy Communion?*[1] Michael Welker has given us an attractive and cogent rethinking of the contemporary ecumenical problems of the Eucharist, and has sketched out—albeit briefly—the Christology that must necessarily support his proposed solution to those problems.[2] A developed version of his Christology is still in the making, and expectantly awaited by the theological community. In this grateful *Laudatio* to Michael, I should like to explore a small, but significant, detail in the history of patristic Christology that may be of interest to him as he continues to forge his own systematic work on the doctrine of Christ. If I am right, it is an unjustly neglected strand of patristic thought, which nonetheless was to prove important—in an influence that reached via several later Greek authors to John of Damascus, and thence to Luther—for later debates about the metaphysical workings of the *communicatio idiomatum*, and thus too about the contested nature of Christ's presence at the Eucharist.[3] The issue at stake is precisely how the divinity of Christ should be perceived as relating to the humanity, and so—by analogous implication—how our own humanity is capable of coming into "union" with Christ and participating in his resurrection life, whether through the sacraments specifically, or through the accompanying life of prayer and service in the Spirit. Of these last matters Michael Welker has of course already written with verve and insight.[4] What I offer him here is a reflection on a distinctive and radical reading of this christological union found in Gregory of Nyssa (ca. 330–ca. 395), a reading indeed so radical as to suffer later misapprehension by those retrospectively fearful of the dangers of unorthodoxy. My claim is that this strand of tradition is now worthy of positive review and reinterpretation. To essay this reinterpretation, however, we have to attend closely to the relation of biblical exegesis and philosophical allusion in Gregory's argument. We also have to take account of the distinctive and subtle entanglement of doctrinal exposition, narrative substructure, and implied ascetical demand in his christological approach.[5] As we shall see, this is a rich nexus that has some surprising implications. It even brings technical christological debate into relation with what we would now call "sex" and "gender," suggesting an intrinsic connection between various levels and types of intimate relationship—between the divine/human in Christ, the divine/human in contemplation, and the human/human in sexual union.[6]

OUTLINE OF THE THESIS: THE MISUNDERSTANDING OF GREGORY OF NYSSA'S CHRISTOLOGICAL USE OF "MIXTURE" TERMS

The precise christological question at stake in this discussion concerns the evocations of the language of "mixture" or "mingling" (μίξις, κρᾶσις, and related cognate terms) in Nyssen's understanding of the divine and human in Christ. The "mingling" language of Cappadocian Christology later came, of course, to be besmirched by association with the very Apollinarianism that Gregory was countering at the time,[7] since after the Apollinarian crisis Chalcedon was to shun the language of mingling for fear of docetic or monophysite overtones. Gregory's persistent use of such language has thus been a crucial factor in the sidelining of his Christology by a tradition of modern Western *Dogmengeschichte* bent primarily on recounting foreshadowings of later Chalcedonian orthodoxy. (One thinks here not only of earlier twentieth-century commentators such as Tixeront, but of more recent, and equally damning, assessments in the work of Grillmeier and Pannenberg.[8]) Much hangs, then—at least for the dogmatician—on the precise meaning of "mingling" for Gregory, and whether its overtones would fall foul of the "without confusion" and "without change" of the later Chalcedonian definition. But even if we avoid such anachronistic judgments, Gregory's own notable unwillingness to use the new normative Trinitarian language of ὑπόστασις (person) in the context of his Christology[9] makes the precise exploration of his favored "mingling" metaphor the more pressing. What exactly does Gregory mean by the mingling of the human and divine in Christ? Does the humanity dissolve into the divinity here, as many have charged?

Almost all the previous modern discussions of this problem, we should note at the outset, have proceeded as if the only issue to consider is one of philosophical allusion—to the various technical discussions of different sorts of "mixture" in Aristotle and the Stoic writers with which Gregory was certainly familiar. But it is precisely this initial presumption that I wish to contest. More is at stake, I believe, than an artful set of allusions to philosophical debates about "mixture" (although they are certainly there); a primary sense of biblical authority is more fundamentally in play, as too are certain underlying presumptions about divine power and intimacy, and human analogues thereto, which come into question for Gregory when union or mingling in Christ is discussed. My own exegetical argument on this issue of mingling has in fact two prongs, which may be described succinctly at the outset. I shall then go on to spell out the two sides of the argument in some greater detail, and bring their combined force to some systematic conclusions in closing.

First, in relation to the different philosophical meanings of "mingling" discussed in Greek pagan philosophy (to which Nyssen is clearly alluding), I want to argue that it is extremely misleading to say that the Aristotelian category of the "mingling of predominance" fits Nyssen's christological use with exactitude. This latter position, however, is precisely the view of H. A. Wolfson, in an analysis whose influence has proved wide-ranging.[10] Such an interpretation, as we shall see, would have Christ's divine power effectively obliterate his human nature. But this I cannot find to be Gregory's intention: he is certainly not so foolish as to fall foul of the dangers of the very Apollinarianism that he is combating. On the contrary, it seems that Nyssen is doing something much more subtle. For a start, he is primarily engaged here in a complex negotiation of relevant biblical texts (in particular, as we shall see, of 1 Cor. 15), which factor modern writers of *Dogmengeschichte* have curiously ignored, but which gives the lie—as we shall show—to Wolfson's and others' conclusion that Gregory simply succumbs to an unconscious Apollinarianism. But in addition, it seems he is also summoning out of his notable philosophical armory suggestions of Stoic, as well as Aristotelian, categorizations of "mixture,"[11] and deliberately setting them into a mutually destabilizing conjunction, while simultaneously overlaying them both with an allusion to a medical mixture appropriate to Christ's healing power.[12] If I am right, this playful strategy of utilizing overlapping (but mutually corrective) philosophical evocations, while also implicitly trumping them by appeal to a relevant scriptural text, is entirely deliberate on Gregory's part. It may cause us to question Wolfson's verdict in a way that has important implications for revisiting the charges of covert Apollinarianism or proto-Monophysitism in Gregory, but also for better comprehending his christological intentions, *tout court*. As elsewhere in his theology (his theory of universals and his doctrine of the soul immediately come to mind), Gregory deliberately sets off allusions to various competing possibilities from ancient philosophy, and then resolutely refuses to be boxed into any of them.[13] Scriptural authority, we might say, finally triumphs, rendering even paradoxically related philosophical tags sublated and overcome.

But this is not even yet the whole picture, for—second—we must also take account, in our full assessment of Gregory's christological repertoire, his use of the same language of mingling with the completely different evocations of sexual union. As far as I know, no one has previously charted the christological significance in Gregory of such an erotic allusion, perhaps because his biblical commentaries have been underused sources for textbook accounts of his doctrinal contribution. But in a highly revealing passage in his fourth homily on *The Song of Songs*,[14] utilizing again the language of "mingling" (but this time with its sexual meaning), Gregory ranges side by side, in analogical relation, three levels of such intimacy: first, the divinity and humanity in Christ; second, the nuptial love of Christ for the individual soul; and third, the sexual love of husband and wife. Commenting here on *The Song of Songs* 1:16 (where, in the LXX version, the male lover "overshadow[s] [the] bed"),[15] Gregory presents us, as we shall see, with another bundle of superimposed and mutually bombarding allusions, both biblical and philosophical, on the crucial issue of mingling. He cites, or makes allusion, to Philippians 2:5–11, for the kenotic act of incarnation; to Ephesians 5:22–33, for the analogy between married love and Christ's love for the church; and then finally— by way of philosophical polemic—to the Plotinian view of the soul as besmirched by contamination with the body, a view that, for Gregory, Christ's incarnation decisively refutes. But we shall see here once more that it is not only philosophical debates about mixture that Gregory is alluding to in his chosen christological form of speech; overarching questions of scriptural exegesis, and—with that—issues of power intimacy, and gender are also in play in intriguing ways.

Let me now turn to a slightly more detailed textual exposition of each of the two prongs of this argument, before drawing some final systematic conclusions about the wider implications of this analysis for contemporary Christology.

"MIXTURE" REVISITED: NYSSEN'S STRATEGIES FOR DESCRIBING THE INDESCRIBABLE IN CHRIST

For the first prong of my argument, I shall take as representative one of the important passages (in the letter to Theophilus; there are two other parallel ones, in the *Contra Eunomium* and *Antirrhetikos*, respectively[16]), where Gregory famously specifies the type of mingling of the human and the divine involved in Christ's incarnate life to be akin to a drop of vinegar dissolved in the ocean. Since it is here—and in the parallel passages—that nervous commentators fear an actual loss of the human nature of Christ, the text presents an especially important test case; we must first attend to its details, in both Greek and English, before assessing its full significance. The language is indeed startling.

Text 1: *Ad Theophilum* (*GNO* III.1: 126–27)

But death has been swallowed up by life [1 Cor. 15:54; 2 Cor. 5:4], the Crucified has been restored to life by power from weakness, and the curse has been turned into blessing. And everything that was weak and perishable in our nature, mingled with the Godhead, has become that which the God-head is. How then would anyone suppose there to be a duality of Sons, when of necessity one is led to such a rejoinder as this by the [Son's] "econ-omy" in the flesh? For he is always in the Father, and always has the Father in him, and is one with him, as it was in the beginning and is now and always will be; and there never was any other Son beside him, nor is there, nor will there be. The first-fruits [1 Cor. 15:20] of the human nature which he has taken up—absorbed, one might say figuratively—by the omnipo-tent divinity like a drop of vinegar mingled in the boundless sea, exist in the Godhead, but not in their own [viz. human] distinctive characteristics. For a duality of Sons might consistently be presumed, if a nature of a dif-ferent kind could be recognized by its own proper signs within the ineffable Godhead of the Son—as being weak or small or perishable or temporary, as opposed to powerful and great and imperishable and eternal. But since all the traits we recognize in the mortal [person] we see transformed by the characteristics of the Godhead, and since no difference of any kind can be perceived—for whatever one sees in the Son *is* Godhead: wisdom, power, holiness, *apatheia*—how could one divide what is one into double signifi-cance, since no difference divides him numerically?[17]

Read on its own, and in isolation from a proper understanding of the distinc-tively progressivist logic of Gregory's Christology,[18] this passage might indeed seem to imply that the humanity of Christ is completely subsumed into his divinity. There is none of the cautious emphasis on a consistent and continuing duality that we would expect from an earlier Latin writer such as Tertullian, for instance, or from the later Tome of Leo: that must be readily acknowledged at the outset. Gregory's entire christological project assumes that the task of the incarnation is the gradual purgation and transformation of the nature of the human in Christ, and its final restoration to an unsullied condition, as before the fall, in the resurrection. Here he is describing that achieved transformation of the human in Christ's resurrected body, in which the human nature, while assuredly continuing in existence, operates now in its fully perfected mode, "in the Godhead." And the language of "mingling" here is made to do some very interesting work, which we must now explore in detail.

What Gregory is doing, it seems, is superimposing on the metaphor of min-gling as utilized in pagan philosophy another, biblical, metaphor (firstfruits) that helps him explicate with exactitude the precise sort of mingling he has in mind. By doing things this way he is indicating how the unique christological mingling of human and divine falls out, or rather *fails to fall out with exactitude*, in the range of availalable philosophical meanings of mingling with which his educated readers would be familiar. Two such philosophical views of mingling might immediately come into mind, out of about five different possibilities explicated in Aristotelian and Stoic thought.[19] According to the different cat-egories of "mixture" or physical union discussed in Aristotle's *De generatione et corruptione* Book 1, first, it is surely right to say, with Wolfson, that Aristotle's so-called union of predominance is quite deliberately being alluded to by Greg-ory here.[20] If that were the full picture, in fact, then Wolfson would be right to conclude that "the weaker has changed into the stronger,"[21] and the charge of proto-"Monophysitism" would stand.

But artfully and deliberately, it seems, Gregory has changed the classic Aristotelian example of wine and water to *vinegar* and water. He must surely have done this for a reason—or perhaps, I would suggest, for two reasons. Not only does this change set off another sort of philosophical allusion, this time to one of the Stoic types of "mixture" discussed by Stobaeus, in which vinegar significantly features (with notably different allusions of mutual interaction rather than near obliteration);[22] but it also introduces a well-known medical allusion, since a mixture of seawater and vinegar is discussed more than once by Hippocrates as alleviating all kinds of chronic aches and pains.[23] Since Gregory is regularly wont to describe Christ as the ultimate "physician," and often uses the metaphor of different sorts of divine "prescriptions" required for different souls,[24] this final evocation makes clear the soteriological impact of this unique christological mixture. Once we see this, we can better understand the decisive, and undergirding, layer of biblical meaning created by the appeal in this same passage to the firstfruits of 1 Corinthians 15:20. This particular mingling of divine and human in Christ that is being discussed is one in which we are also destined to participate: it is the firstfruits of "them that slept," and hence the union (or mingling) of human and divine that occurs in Christ that enables *our* final union with Christ—a mysterious eschatological change to the body/soul "in the twinkling of an eye." It cannot therefore be an *obliteration* of the human that is implied by this mingling (which would make nonsense of Paul's entire argument in 1 Cor. 15). Rather, it is its unique transformation.

All in all, an artful reading of this dense and crucial passage shows us that Gregory refuses to allow just one metaphor, or philosophical category, to dominate. The clear and primary allusion to the Aristotelian mixture of predominance illustrates his insistence on the indescribably greater power of divinity over humanity, its capacity to transform it, and the unity of what is achieved. But the simultaneous hint of the Stoic example of vinegar and water refuses the possibility of the total loss of existence or identity by the lesser element: there is neither a *tertium quid* created here, nor a simple obliteration of the weaker element by the stronger. A "suffusion" is perhaps the happiest English translation of this kind of mixture of the divine with the human in Christ,[25] and accords best with the meaning implied by the appeal to 1 Corinthians 15.

Let us now compare the lessons from this first passage with those of the apparently quite different, erotic overtones of "mingling" in the fourth *Homily on the Song*. We may be surprised at how consistent with our first example is the overall impact.

Text 2: *In Cant.* IV (*GNO* VI: 108–9)

For unless you shaded yourself over with "the form of a servant" [Phil. 2:7] while unveiling the pure rays of your divinity, who could stand your appearance [Mal. 3:2]? "For no one can see God's face and live" [Exod. 33:20]. You have now come as the one who is "beautiful" [Song 1:16], but as one we are capable of receiving. You came, having shadowed over [Luke 1:35] the rays of your divinity with the covering of a body. How could a mortal, perishable nature be capable of union with an imperishable, inaccessible nature unless the shadow of the body acted as a mediator of the light for us who live in darkness? The bride uses the term "bed" to interpret in a figurative sense the mingling of human nature with the divine. In the same way, the great Apostle Paul joins us as virgins to Christ and acts as an escort for the bride. He says that the affixing together of two persons in the union of one body is a great mystery of Christ's union with the church. For he said, "The two shall be one flesh," and then added, "This is a great mystery with reference to Christ and his church" [Eph. 5:31–32]. Because of this mystery, the virgin soul names the union with the divine a "bed." This could not have happened at all unless the Lord had appeared "overshadowed" to us in a human body.[26]

This passage in Gregory's fourth *Homily* is discussing Song 1:16, read, as in the LXX, as the male lover "overshadowing [the] bed." The first reading Gregory makes of this is to see it as a figurative way of talking of the mingling of the human nature with the divine in the incarnation. The reference to Philippians 2:7 (with the phrase "the form of a servant") summons up all the overtones of the highly distinctive way that Gregory interprets "kenosis" elsewhere in his work—not as a mere assumption of humanity, but as a veritable pouring out of divinity into it, here effected by the bridegroom.[27] It is this outpouring that causes the need for overshadowing, as is well brought out in a recent discussion of this passage in Gregory's *Commentary* by Alessandro Cortesi.[28] "Shadow" does not have here for Gregory the connection to sin that darkness can often symbolize in Song, but rather indicates the apophatic mysteriousness that necessarily attends the effusive revelation of the divine when it comes into the human incarnationally (as in the annunciation in Luke 1:35). Yet even as Gregory alludes to the biblical text in Luke, there is almost certainly a polemic implied here against Plotinus's well-known discussion in *Enneads* 1 of the "mingling" (μίξις and κρᾶσις) of soul with body that inevitably involves a besmirchment of the soul and a darkening of its light.[29] For Gregory, in contrast to Plotinus, the divine Logos's effusion into a human body/soul is "shadowed" only because of its ineffable greatness.

Now as Christ's fructifying divinity is represented as the bridegroom here, so it follows that the human nature of Christ is figured as feminine, as the bride. But it is by no means clear from this that she (the humanity in Christ) is simply passive: as Bernadette Brooten has noted, the verb μείγνυμι of sexual intercourse is one of the few in Greek that allows a sense of genunine mutuality;[30] and, as we have seen above, ἀνάκρασις and μίξις are inexorably linked for Gregory in the christological sphere. Finally, not the least significant aspect of this passage is the way that the ἀνάκρασις, ἕνωσις, and συζυγία of the incarnation are then seen as the primary exemplification and enablement of the other two levels of interaction. There is what we might call an erotic sliding-scale here that moves downward: first the primary mingling between the divine and the human in Christ, then the union between Christ and each human soul in the church, then sexual union between husband and wife. It is an interesting hermeneutical expansion on the way that merely the latter two levels are linked in Ephesians 5:21–33; and the whole passage differs markedly from Origen's reading of the same passage in his second *Homily on the Song*, in which the "overshadowed" body is not about what we might call the proto-erotic incarnate body of Christ, but about the sinful and unhealed state of the human body in general, represented here for Origen by the paralytic of Mark 2:1–12 and parallels.[31] For Gregory, in contrast, human sexual union in the Christian context is precisely one of the outworkings of the primary mingling of the divine and human in Christ; and thus—when rightly understood—it can be seen as a proper, albeit finally mysterious, metaphor for the workings of the incarnate life.

CONCLUSIONS: CHRISTOLOGY, SOTERIOLOGY, AND THE ASCETIC TASK IN GREGORY OF NYSSA

What then do we conclude from this exploration of the many different overtones of μίξις, κρᾶσις, and other cognate nouns in Gregory's Christology? A full search of this cluster of terms in Nyssen—following Bouchet's excellent lead[32]—produces an enormous, even chaotic, range of other and different contexts in which these terms are applied, and we have only been able to explore some of these. But in the specifically christological application, I think that through the two rich and revealing examples discussed here I have indicated the main points of allusion, showing that in Gregory's ingenious and consciously anti-Apollinarian uses of the terms, we must attend at all times to the cat's cradle of biblical symbolism that he weaves around his theme of mingling, and hence as much to evocations of divine power, resurrection, and the ascetical training of desire, as to philosophical and medical niceties and distinctions.

It has been said of late (by Brian Daley) that Gregory is more interested in "narrative" soteriology than metaphysical Christology; and maybe—Daley avers—this explains why his language of "mingling" is less precise or clear than we might like it to be.[33] But this little investigation has led me to a slightly differently nuanced conclusion. While it is certainly true, as we have indicated, that the soteriological theory of suffusing deification sustains Gregory's whole christological undertaking, and gives it its narrative substructure, I would prefer to say that Gregory has deployed a particular, and very subtle, form of apophatic speech in expressing his Christology, rather than that he is metaphysically imprecise, defective, or sloppy. By adopting a policy of mutually bombarding (and thus mutually correcting) metaphorical allusions in his key christological passages, Gregory has utilized the key metaphor of mingling in ways that never claim finally to explain the mystery of the incarnation (which must always remain shadowed to the sinful human eye), but which indicate with unusual precision what he does and does not want to say.[34] There are striking anticipations in this regard of the linguistic strategies of the later negative theology of the pseudo-Denys, here applied explicitly to the christological sphere. Once we read Nyssen in this way, I see no reason to dub his Christology as either covertly Apollinarian or, for that matter, naively proto-"Nestorian" (as Tixeront charged). While the jury may be still out on the final coherence or consistency of Gregory's Christology *tout court*,[35] his theory of "mingling" seems to me remarkably rich and strange, not happily acceptable to those bred on the clarificatory dualisms of Leo's Tome, to be sure, but continuing a tradition of participatory deification that goes back to Athanasius and then stretches forward (with huge and conscious debts to Nyssen) to Leontius, Maximus, and John Damascene.[36] From here it was ultimately to leave its contentious mark on Luther's eucharistic theology, a tradition with which, of course, the Calvinist tradition of Michael Welker has always been in tension.[37] But in Nyssen's own treatment, as we have seen, there was a remarkable integration of biblical witness, philosophical insight, and implied ascetic demand, albeit always without abrogating an essential aspect of apophatic mystery. A rich heritage of ingenious biblical exegesis could itself be mingled with, but ultimately trump, sophisticated philosophical analysis and allusion. The mingling found in Christ's person could thus become, through prayerful living of the Christian life, a derivative mingling equally available now to the blessed: Christology could erotically guide spirituality, and even—by implication—cause a certain rethinking of faithful sexual practice. Such an integrative approach to Christology, asceticism, and sexuality seems, at the very least, worthy of reconsideration in our current era of the renegotiation of the systematic theological task, in which Michael Welker has himself played such a notable role.[38]

NOTES

1. Michael Welker, *What Happens in Holy Communion?* (Grand Rapids: Eerdmans, 2000).
2. See ibid., chaps. 5–6.
3. The rendition of the *communicatio idiomatum* in this line of tradition is one in which the characteristics of the divine nature are not simply linguistically attributed to the human nature, but the divine nature actually ontologically transforms the capacities of the human as a result of the incarnation. A useful (albeit somewhat oversimplified) typological account of different classic understandings of the *communicatio* is provided in Wolfhart Pannenberg, *Jesus—God and Man* (London: SCM Press, 1970), chap. 8, in which Luther's dependence on this "Alexandrian" tradition is highlighted. See also my *Powers and Submissions: Spirituality, Philosophy and Gender* (Oxford: Blackwell, 2001), chap. 1, for a brief critical account of this history in relation to the emergence of Chalcedonian "orthodoxy." In *Powers and Submissions,* I point out (16–19) that Luther's own position on the *communicatio* was seemingly not completely consistent; and—in contrast to the "Alexandrian" reading to

which he was heir—allowed at times for a two-way interaction, such that the human could affect the divine, as well as vice versa. This feature was what caused various nervous counterreactions among subsequent Lutheran scholastics.

4. See Michael Welker, *God the Spirit* (Minneapolis: Fortress, 1994); note also the attention to the work of the Spirit in Welker, *What Happens in Holy Communion?* esp. chaps. 8, 12.

5. Few secondary authors have achieved a balanced assessment of these different dimensions of Nyssen's Christology. The best recent study, in my view, is that now supplied by John Behr, *The Nicene Faith: The Formation of Christian Theology,* 2 vols. (Crestwood, N.Y.: St. Vladimir's Seminary Press, 2004), vol. 2, chap. 8, in a volume that appeared a year after I had originally presented this current paper at the Oxford Patristics Conference, 2003. I am very grateful to John Behr for subsequent conversations that have helped me refine my argument. In broad terms we agree that Nyssen should not be read as endangering the obliteration of the human in Christ, and that most twentieth-century commentators have failed to appreciate the distinctively narrative propulsion of his christological approach. On this latter point, however, we are both indebted to Brian E. Daley, "Divine Transcendence and Human Transformation: Gregory of Nyssa's Anti-Apollinarian Christology," in *Re-Thinking Gregory of Nyssa,* ed. Sarah Coakley (Oxford: Blackwell, 2003), 67–76. This current essay may be read as complementing Behr's recent analysis (a) by providing a detailed analysis, and new interpretation, of Gregory's use of the various meanings of "mingling" in Greek philosophical discussion; and (b) by drawing attention to the material in Gregory's *Commentary on the Song,* which links "mingling" to erotic themes.

    Earlier work on Gregory's Christology that I have consulted should be mentioned here. The invaluable word studies by Jean-René Bouchet, "A propos d'une image christologique de Grégoire de Nysse," *Revue Thomiste* 67 (1967): 584–88, and "Le vocabulaire de l'union et du rapport des natures chez sainte Grégoire de Nysse," *Revue Thomiste* 68 (1968): 533–82, are necessary starting points in any assessment of Gregory's complex Christology, and especially of the theme of mingling. One should also note: Elias D. Moutsoulas, *The Incarnation of the Word and the Theosis of Man According to the Teaching of Gregory of Nyssa* (Athens: Eptalophos, 2000); George D. Dragas, "The Anti-Apollinarist Christology of St. Gregory of Nyssa: A First Analysis," *The Greek Orthodox Theological Review* 42 (1997): 299–314; Bernard Pottier, *Dieu et le Christ selon Grégoire de Nysse* (Namur: Culture et Vérité, 1994); Reinhard M. Hübner, *Die Einheit des Leibes Christi bei Gregor von Nyssa: Untersuchungen zum Ursprung der "physischen" Erlösungslehre* (Leiden: Brill, 1974); and the still-valuable Karl Holl, *Amphilochius von Ikoniumin seinem Verhältnis zu dem grossen Kappadoziern* (1904; repr. Darmstadt: Wissenschaftliche Buchgesellschaft, 1969), 220–35.

6. In my "Introduction: Gender, Trinitarian Analogies, and the Pedagogy of *The Song,*" in *Re-Thinking Gregory of Nyssa,* 1–13, I argue that Gregory is ill-served by interpretations that force a disjunction between his writings on doctrine and spirituality, respectively. The latter category is an (early-) modern one, and its retrospective imposition on Gregory's oeuvre is misleading.

7. This problem has been most recently discussed and illuminated by Brian E. Daley, in "'Heavenly Man' and 'Eternal Christ': Apollinarius and Gregory of Nyssa on the Personal Identity of the Savior," *Journal of Early Christian Studies* 10 (2002): 469–88.

8. See Joseph Tixeront, *Histoire des dogmes dans l'antiquité chrétienne,* vol. 2 (Paris: J. Gabalda, 1912), 128–30; A. Grillmeier, *Christ in Christian Tradition,* vol. 1 (London: Mowbray, 1975), 370–72; Pannenberg, *Jesus—God and Man,* 297.
9. This feature is remarked upon in Daley, "Divine Transcendence and Human Transformation," 72.
10. H. A. Wolfson, *The Philosophy of the Church Fathers,* vol. 1, *Faith, Trinity, Incarnation* (Cambridge, Mass.: Harvard University Press, 1970), 372–86 (for "Five Types of Physical Union" in pagan philosophy), and 396–99 (for the analysis of Gregory of Nyssa on the "union of predominance").
11. Wolfson (ibid., 379–87, esp. 385 for his typology) does discuss the Stoic views, but—as we shall see—he slightly distorts his account of one of them (that expressed by Stobaeus), which is peculiarly applicable to Gregory's case.
12. This last point was already noted by Bouchet, in "A propos d'une image," 587–88.
13. On this point, see again my Introduction in *Re-Thinking Gregory of Nyssa,* 7–8.
14. *In Cant.* IV (*GNO* VI: 108–9), discussed in detail below. In this essay I follow the usual convention of citing Gregory of Nyssa's works by reference, where applicable, to the critical edition: *Gregorii Nysseni Opera* (*GNO*) (Leiden: Brill, 1958–).
15. This reading of Song 1.16b in the LXX is seemingly the result of an interpretative rendition or misunderstanding of the Hebrew word for "green" or "luxuriant," which applies in the Hebrew to the bed; in the LXX it is taken to apply to the lover who "shades" or "overshadows" the bed.
16. *Ad Theophilum* (*GNO* III: 126), discussed in detail here; cf. *C. Eun.* 3.3.68–69 (*GNO* II.2: 132–33); *Antirrh.* (*GNO* III.1: 201).
17. The translation of this passage is by Brian Daley ("'Heavenly Man' and 'Eternal Christ,'" 483), slightly adjusted and expanded.
18. As Behr's analysis (*Nicene Faith,* 2:435–51) well emphasizes, it is vital to understand that Gregory's talk of the human nature of Christ being "swallowed up" refers to a process only completed in the resurrection and exaltation. For Gregory, it is in the earthly sojourn of the Son, and especially through the events of the Passion, that the purgation and transformation of the human is effected.
19. The two relevant ones are the Aristotelian "union of predominance" (in which one component virtually disappears, as, e.g., a drop of wine in gallons of water); and a Stoic understanding of "mingling" in which the substances and qualities of the two elements remain, even as the two interpenetrate each other. See Wolfson, *Philosophy of the Church Fathers,* 1:385, for his list of the full five such types of union or mingling; but note that his account has been challenged on his representation of the crucial third (Stoic) one: see Richard Sorabji, *Matter, Space and Time: Theories in Antiquity and Their Sequel* (Ithaca, N.Y.: Cornell University Press, 1988), chaps. 5–6; and more recently, Richard Cross, "Perichoresis, Deification, and Christological Predication in John of Damascus," *Medieval Studies* 62 (2000): 69–124, esp. 72, 86–97. My own account here differs from Cross's in that, unlike him (see Cross, "Perichoresis," 86), I precisely disagree that "the Cappadocians" used the language of "mixture" in "a way that suggested a complete obliteration of the human nature" (a conclusion that Cross simply takes on from Wolfson). On the contrary, I am arguing that the complex Stoic background that Cross highlights for John of Damascus's use was already in play in Gregory of Nyssa's christological use.

20. See Aristotle, *Gen. corr.* 1.10 (328a, 27–29). Arguably this allusion is even more strongly enunciated in the other two passages in which Gregory uses this analogy: *C. Eun.* 3.3.68–69 (*GNO* II.2: 132–33); *Antirrh.* (*GNO* III.1: 201).

21. Wolfson, *Philosophy of the Church Fathers,* 1:397.

22. Wolfson misrepresents this type (see Cross, "Perichoresis," 89, 93). Wolfson mentions Stobaeus (*Ecl.* 1.17; see *Philosophy of the Church Fathers,* 1:379), but fails to point out that an allusion to this particular Stoic type would involve contesting his reading of "the mixture of predominance" as alone applicable to Gregory of Nyssa's Christology.

23. See Émile Littré, ed., *Oeuvres Complètes d'Hippocrate* (Paris : J. B. Ballière, 1846), 5:240–41, 434–35.

24. He does so, in fact, in the *ad Theophilum* (*GNO* III.1: 124) just before the passage here under discussion, making the point that the incarnation allowed the cure for those of a more fleshly minded disposition. For a more complete account of Nyssen's fondness for medical metaphors, see Mary E. Keenan, "St. Gregory of Nyssa and the Medical Profession," *Bulletin of the History of Medicine* 15 (1944): 150–61.

25. Daley fleetingly uses this term in "Divine Transcendence and Human Transformation," 71. I make greater use of it in my recent analysis of Gregory's unique reading of Philippians 2, in which Christ's "emptying" is seen neither as a loss of divinity, nor as a mere "assumption" of humanity, but as a suffusing outpouring of divinity into the human; see Sarah Coakley, "Does Kenosis Rest on a Mistake? Three Kenotic Models in Patristic Exegesis," in *Exploring Kenotic Christology: The Self-Emptying of God,* ed. C. Stephen Evans (Oxford: Oxford University Press, 2006), 246–64.

26. This translation is a modified version of that by Casimir McCambley, OCSO, Gregory of Nyssa, *Commentary on the Song of Songs* (Brookline, Mass.: Hellenic College Press, 1987), 94.

27. See again Coakley, "Does Kenosis Rest on a Mistake?" esp. 256–59.

28. Alessandro Cortesi, *Le Omelie sul Cantico dei Cantici di Gregario di Nissa: proposta di un itinerario di vita battesimale* (Rome: Augustinianum, 2000), esp. 81–87. Cortesi provides an elegant analysis of this section of Gregory's Song commentary, noting some of Gregory's allusions to pagan philosophy as well as comparing Gregory's exegesis to that of Origen.

29. *Enn.* 1.6.5: "the soul becomes ugly by mixture and dilution and inclination towards the body and matter," ed. and trans. A. H. A. Armstrong, *Plotinus* (Cambridge, Mass.: Harvard University Press, 1966–88), 1:248–49.

30. See Bernadette J. Brooten, *Love between Women: Early Christian Responses to Female Homoeroticism* (Chicago: University of Chicago Press, 1996), 246: "The specific verbs for sexual intercourse are usually active when they refer to men and passive when they refer to women. . . . Some verbs, such as 'to mingle' . . . do occur in the active for both women and men, but the more common pattern is to use an active verb for the male and a passive one for the female."

31. Origen in fact exegetes Song 1:16 twice, in illuminatingly different ways. In his second *Homily on the Song,* the bed is first understood as the human body in its unhealed state, as "the feeble body of [the paralytic's] limbs," awaiting Christ's healing (see trans. R. P. Lawson, *Origen: The Song of Songs—Commentary and Homilies* (New York: Newman Press, 1956), 291. But in his *Commentary,* which (see Lawson's introduction, 16–19) is written for those of greater spiritual maturity, the interpretation is closer to that of Gregory's (and indeed probably influenced Gregory). Here the bed/body has become fit for Christ as bridegroom, suitably spiritualized: "Such a soul as this rightly shares

her bed—that is, her body, with the Word" (174); and the "shady" bed is read as "a thicket of good works" (172).

32. See again Bouchet, "Le vocabulaire de l'union," passim, who covers most, if not all, of the necessary christological ground. A wider search in the *TLG* for "mixture" terms in Gregory provides a veritable maze of interconnected associations and patterns, too complicated to chart here.

33. Daley, "Divine Transcendence and Human Transformation," 72–73.

34. We should not forget that Gregory is ever wont to stress the final incomprehensibility of the mingling of the incarnation. See his *Oratio Catechetica* 11 (*GNO* III.4:39), trans. Cyril G. Richardson, in *The Christology of the Later Fathers*, ed. E. R. Hardy (London: SCM Press, 1954), 288: "We are unable to detect how the divine is mingled with the human. Yet we have no doubt, from the recorded miracles, that God underwent birth in human nature. But *how* this happened we decline to investigate as a matter beyond the scope of reason."

35. There are certainly remaining difficulties, which cannot be addressed in this context, but they indicate where my assessment of Gregory's Christology might still differ somewhat from that of John Behr (see n. 5, above). Thus, the problem of how, *exactly*, the "human Jesus" relates to the Word in the incarnation, and what happens to "the human" after the resurrection/exaltation, are both issues in need of further probing and critical explication.

36. Gregory's interest in the transforming humanity of Christ, including his human soul, arguably owes more to Origen than to Athanasius (a topic worthy of further research); but otherwise his presumptions about the pattern of participatory deification in Christ are strongly indebted to Athanasius. On this Eastern tradition of "deification," and its subvariants, see Norman Russell, *The Doctrine of Deification in the Greek Patristic Tradition* (Oxford: Oxford University Press, 2004).

37. Cross, "Perichoresis," 70, 123, briefly clarifies the extent and nature of John of Damascus's influence on Luther's eucharistic theology and on the later Lutheran christological category, the *genus maiestaticum*. It has been the burden of this short paper to suggest that some of the subtle moves made by John of Damascus on the *communicatio idiomatum* are already suggested by Gregory of Nyssa. If this is correct, then it would be interesting to explore how the Calvinist tradition, in contrast to the Lutheran, assimilated the Greek patristic theme of participation (both christologically and Trinitarianly), even as it took a polemically different approach to eucharistic theology. For a new assessment of the theme of "participation" in the theology of Calvin, see Todd Billings, *Calvin, Participation and the Gift: The Activity of Believers in Union with Christ* (Oxford: Oxford University Press, 2007).

38. I wish here to record my special gratitude to a former Harvard pupil and research assistant, Philip McCosker (who also studied with Michael Welker during Welker's visiting appointment at Harvard Divinity School, 2001–2). McCosker took a "reading and research" course with me in spring 2003 on Gregory's Christology, during which time the research for this current paper was undertaken, and McCosker's bibliographic flair was fully in evidence. I am much indebted to him, not only for his gathering of arcane resources, but for numerous subsequent discussions that have helped me to clarify my views.

6

Flesh and Folly

The Christ of Christian Humanism

WILLIAM SCHWEIKER

In the long career of the Christian tradition there have always been individuals who with care and deliberation have sought to inhabit the borders, who have lived at the intersections between biblical faith and nonbiblical patterns of thought and life. Their lives were crisscrossed with multiple identities woven into an integral form of life. Sometimes called "apologists," like the great ancient Christian thinkers Justin Martyr and Clement of Alexandria, by the time of the Reformation and Renaissance they often took the name "humanist," partly because they sought to link the simplicity of the gospel with the best of ancient learning. In our own time, the same aspiration has been called the reality of the "third man." Neither dominated by forms of Greek thought, to which the Christian message was proclaimed, nor the circle of Hebraic life, from which the gospel arose, this "'third man,'" Paul Ricoeur once noted, "this cultivated Christian, this believing Greek, is ourselves."[1] The reflections that follow stand squarely within this long, if now often neglected, strand of Christian thought and life. They aim at a form of life, an identity and way of being, that is internally complex and yet integrated by devotion to what respects and enhances the integrity of life before the living God.

This essay is dedicated to Michael Welker with deep friendship and lasting appreciation. I met Welker years ago when we were fellow participants in a seminar at the Institute for the Advanced Study of Religion (now called the Martin Marty Center) of the Divinity School of the University of Chicago. That year was a hubbub of conversation, delight in hearing Buddy Guy's soaring blues guitar work at the famous Checkerboard Lounge, and, along with Ulrike Welker, also much, much laughter. The talk and the laughter have continued. The friendship has deepened to include family and the rough-and-tumble of our human lot. Michael's joy in life, his constant probing of Christian faith in and through the complexity of social existence, and his unflinching demand that theology make good on its claims to truth have always inspired and instructed me. Aristotle put it too simply when he said that a friend is another self; we actually find in a genuine friend a singular individual whose life and mind and heart are truly beyond our own and who yet inspires and delights us. For the grace of Michael's steadfast friendship, I am profoundly thankful. I am also quite sure that he raises an eyebrow at my picking up the banner of Christian humanism. Still, I hope he sees in these pages a kindred spirit dedicated to thought and life at the intersection of the biblical witness and the lived structure of contemporary reality.

Let me now explain the task of this essay.

THE POINT OF REFLECTION

Beginning in the fourteenth century in Italy, especially with certain forms of neo-Platonism, and then spreading to northern Europe, leading humanist thinkers helped to shape theology, education, rhetoric, and classical studies. The heart of the humanist agenda was the humanities, and so a vision of education coupled with the concern to reclaim classic texts—including the Bible—on the perfectibility of human life rooted in human potentialities.[2] It would be delightful to trace the work of various humanists (Petrarch, Erasmus, Pico, Melanchthon, Colet, More, Leonardo Bruni, and others) and their engagement with classical sources (Plato, Cicero, Lucian, etc.). It would also be important in a more extended essay to explore the immense impact of these thinkers on a wide array of literary forms and scholarly disciplines. That is not possible in this essay, even if I were able to do so.

I mention these historical details at the outset in order to note that I am trying to grasp basic ideas and develop leading concepts rather than to provide a historical account of Christian humanist thinking about Christ. I would like my argument to be judged on its theological and ethical merit rather than in terms of historical depth or accuracy. I am more anxious to persuade my reader to adopt a specific outlook now possible and needed within the Christian community than to contribute to historical research. And in this way I am also trying to show the energy and progressive force of ideas buried deep within this tradition in a time when, it must be said, we suffer from cultural and religious exhaustion. I am using historical sources not to recover the past but, rather, to release potential for the future orienting of life.

Further, if truth be told I am not too concerned in the pages that follow to advance christological reflection in any technical sense of the word. Following one of Welker's own dicta, a theologian should not enter into the thicket of a specific doctrine or topic until he or she has some clarity about what might be said. To do otherwise is to risk falling unwittingly into false abstractions. (That is, for Welker, the theologian's original sin!) Of course, work in Christology is without doubt important for Christian theology. Yet it is one task among many, usually the domain of the dogmatic theologian, and it does not necessarily specify the point of theological inquiry. My hope is to avoid the theologian's sin while also trying to further the legacy of Christian humanism in our troubled age. Insofar as a Christian humanist is a Christian, what can and must and may one say about Christ? That is the question that I intend to address in this essay.

The nondogmatic and practical tenor of this essay enacts the stance of most Christian humanists. Our worry is that doctrinal considerations too easily degenerate into scholastic gamesmanship and thereby create invidious divisions among Christians. Likewise, the drive to doctrine is all too often motivated by a quest for certainty that denies the goodness of humility about human capacities to know the truth, a kind of humility, even skepticism, that ought to characterize followers of Christ. The sin of a theologian from this perspective is not only to revel in false abstractions, but also to formulate Christian convictions in ways that thwart the purpose and point of the Christian life. Put differently, Christian humanists see faith more as a way of life than a set of beliefs. The point of thinking is to aid in the lifelong task of conforming existence to Christ's love rather than to fashion new christological formulations.

Theology is not an end in itself. It is a means. The aim or point or purpose of thought is to understand and orient Christian life. As a recent account of Christian humanism has put it, three themes have usually dominated this outlook on life and faith, themes that arise from the belief "that God in Christ has visited the habitation of the human race."[3] The themes include: first, the fact that in Christ the individual is saved from isolation and made the body of a living community; second, the awareness, basic to my argument below, that faith in the incarnation means that all finite existence—the earth, our bodies, daily objects of human use—can be the means for the work of the divine spirit among us; and, third, the idea, also important here, that true human freedom and perfection are found in faithful love toward Christ and the neighbor.[4] Taken together, these themes, and others as well, are why Christian humanists have always been drawn to politics and ethics and education or, as it is sometimes called, practical Christianity.

The specific purpose of this essay is to reflect on the Christ of Christian humanism in and through interlocking levels of inquiry, levels already anticipated. First, I set the problem of my reflection in terms of the reluctance of Christian humanists to engage in heavy dogmatic reflection given their practical conception of Christian faith. What then can be said about Christ by a Christian humanist? In order to answer that question, the second level of my reflections isolates important depictions or images of Christ found in classical Christian humanist discourse. One image is the fully incarnate, fleshly Christ. Because of the flesh of Christ, human bodiliness, comic or grotesque, falls within theological consideration. Here the Christ of Christian humanism is a response to mortality inscribed in human life, that we are creatures of dust. Yet, second, we also find Christ as fool who confounds the wisdom of the world. Humility, we must say, is a profound good for Christian humanists, because whatever we mean by "sin," it must entail a denial of our creaturehood, a denial of our dust, in ways that pit life against life, human beings against each other and against the living God. To reflect on flesh and folly as attributes of Christ is, therefore, to explore the bonds of death and sin that plague human existence. The wisdom that can and ought to guide life upends and disturbs our usual standards of thought even as it exposes the limits of human insight and knowledge and heals the wound of existence—our bondage to sin and death.

In the third level of reflection, I hope to reconstruct classical claims about Christ for the sake of a contemporary expression of Christian humanism. This account must make good sense of Christian faith, but it must also be practically viable within our world where life is endangered and conflict, often violent, rages among ideologies and religions. The cornerstone of reconstruction centers on how one understands the formation and importance of Christian identity. The force of Christian humanism, I contend, is to claim that one's identity as an incarnate but fallible creature exceeds any one description, and, further, must be oriented beyond itself toward life with and for others.[5] The very idea of Christian humanism, and Christ as the Word in flesh that is folly, means that one cannot pit Christian identity against other blocklike descriptions of human beings, like "pagan" or "Muslim" or "sinner." Any actual human existence is a complex relation among identities, some exceedingly broad (I am a human being who laughs, bleeds, and will die) and some more specific (I am a member of this congregation of the United Methodist Church in the U.S.A., a father to my son, a friend to Michael Welker). In our time, Christian humanism wants to show that Christians can and may and must decide in specific situations which identity ought to have priority in order thereby to respect and enhance the integrity of life. In some contexts, it is shared humanity that must take pride of place; in other situations, more particular ecclesial, social, linguistic, gendered, and racial identities can and ought to come to the fore. St. Paul grasped the same insight, it seems to me.

> For though I am free with respect to all, I have made myself a slave to all, so that I might win more of them. To the Jews I became as a Jew, in order to win Jews. To those under the law I became as one under the law (though I myself am not under the law) so that I might win those under the law. (1 Cor. 9: 19–20)

Paul goes on to insist that he became outside of the law for those outside the law, became weak for the weak, and so became "all things to all people" that some might be saved. If the aim or point of Christian existence is the labor of love for others in conformity to Christ, then, Paul suggests, it is possible to stress or emphasize some of one's identity (Jew, Gentile, weak, free—Paul was all of these) in specific situations. Christian existence is not monodimensional, defined by just one description—even the description "Christian"—because it is oriented beyond self. And that is just the point of Christian humanism. We will see that this means seeing Christ as the conscience of God. The labor of human conscience, the call to faithful labor on our moral identities for orienting life, is thus the focal point for the Christian humanist because of who Christ is and what he does.

I begin now with the reluctance of Christian humanists to formulate crisp doctrines.

INCARNATION, HIGH AND LOW

The connection between Christ and humanity in Christian faith is of course neither new nor surprising. It is not surprising since Christians have always confessed Christ to be savior, and, accordingly, that he must be truly human. "What he has not assumed," Athanasius, the so-called father of Orthodoxy, insisted, "he cannot save." That is also why the connection between Christ and humanity is not new in Christian theology. It is, in some way, at the very origin and core of the Christian witness.

Of course, how Christians *ought* to think about Christ's relation to our fallible and fault-ridden humanity is constantly debated. For some the incarnation of the eternal Word is the focus of attention; other thinkers center their inquiry on the crucified and risen Christ. One can explore the presence of Christ in the Eucharist or concentrate theological inquiry on the eschatological, coming Christ. For theologians, especially classical Protestants, interested in moral and political questions, the various titles for Christ—prophet, priest, king—have been used to understand Christian existence. Others have linked Christ to the development of the so-called theological virtues, among Roman Catholic thinkers, or, more recently, to Christ and liberation from various forms of oppression. Through it all, the complex connection between a doctrine of Christ and an account of salvation, a soteriology, has been important. It is hardly surprising, then, that the renowned church historian Jaroslov Pelikan could write a book titled *Jesus through the Centuries* in which he traces the many different ways Christ has been understood and imagined: rabbi, King of Kings, cosmic Christ, bridegroom of the soul, Prince of Peace, and so on.[6] There appears to be no end to the reflection, especially as Christian communities around the world seek to understand and inhabit their faith in new and distinctive ways outside the dominance of European modes of thought. We witness an endless proliferation of forms of christological thinking. Christ as the one who is believed, the object of deepest trust and loyalty, is also the one whose identity and work constantly spark thought and imagination about the God of faith and the meaning of our existence.

Obviously, the relation of Christ to humanity, that Christ is "true man" as well as "true God" (to use the creedal formulation), is important for any form of properly Christian humanism. Not surprisingly, for a long time there have been within Eastern and Western Christianity ways to speak of the "humanity of God." This language arises within the Christian tradition when the incarnation of God in Christ, the event of God becoming human, is taken as central to Christian thought and life. As Thomas Merton once wrote, "True Christian humanism is the full flowering of the theology of the Incarnation." Even Karl Barth, late in his career, spoke of the "humanity of God," the decision of God to be God for us in Christ. In the revival of Orthodox theology in the twentieth century, especially among Russians, *bogochelovechestvo*, or Godmanhood, has been central. It was a way to rethink and reclaim the Orthodox idea of *theosis*.[7] Similar ideas are found elsewhere. Classic Greek religion sought to humanize the gods, often portraying the deities in all-too-human ways but with the message that human excellence is the point of life. In Buddhism, Hinduism, and other religions there have always been personifications of deities and their relations to human beings.

Without entering comparative theology, it must be admitted that there is a difference between, say, Barth's formulation of "the humanity of God" and Merton's kind of "Christian humanism." For Barth and many Orthodox theologians, what matters is that God *became* human in Christ; a theological, and not humanistic, point is at stake, even if it carries profound human import. The Christian humanist, it seems to me, hardly denies the theological claim but wants to attend to the human import. As an outlook and orientation in life, a Christian humanist uses the distinctive claims and speculative resources of a tradition in order to articulate a specific way of life. Yet she or he also hopes to find points of contact with other people who share similar aspirations and convictions. So while one draws from the Christian tradition, one does not write only for Christians. Of course, some Christians find this a betrayal of what is uniquely Christian, and many humanists will hardly see the relevance of theological claims for human existence. Part of the argument of this essay is to stave off charges of betrayal and irrelevance while holding fast to the main concern to present the Christ of Christian humanism.

Here then is the first question any Christian humanist must answer. Why the reluctance to insist on doctrinal uniformity about what is obviously the core of Christian faith? Why insist on the unending task of interpreting Christian claims about Christ rather than seeking to achieve creedal clarity? The question is long-standing. In one of the most famous disputes over Christian humanism,

Luther attacked Erasmus for seeming unwilling to make "assertions." In "The Bondage of the Will," Luther muses that it is Erasmus's charitable bent of mind and love of peace that keeps him from making assertions. But, Luther continues, "To take no pleasure in assertions is not the mark of a Christian heart; indeed one must delight in assertions to be a Christian at all. . . . Away, now, with Sceptics and Academics from the company of us Christians; let us have men who will assert, men twice as inflexible as very Stoics!"[8] Luther's charge is that Erasmus is finally a skeptic who fails to see that Christian faith requires clarity of conviction and confession. One must draw a boundary around Christian existence in and through the confession of the gospel. Of course, the core of Luther's treatise is the question of the freedom or bondage of the will, the point (no doubt) of greatest dispute between him and Erasmus. We return to the question of freedom later in these reflections. At this juncture what emerges is precisely the reason for suspicion of "assertions" among Christian humanists.

The clue to an answer lies in Luther's grasp of a specific bent of mind and also the good of peace for a Christian humanist. If one understands the Christian confession of Christ, that is, God's identification with the human lot, then precisely because of that confession and because of the nature of the human lot it is neither proper nor possible to circumscribe Christian identity within one description. What prohibits a Christian in the full freedom of her or his faith from learning along with the Academics (Thomas Aquinas did)? Why not find common ground between Stoic insights and Christian faith (many of the church fathers did)? If God is flexible with us, why not be flexible with others? In other words, the Christian humanist's reticence to use the clarity of "assertions" to draw unbridgeable boundaries between human beings arises from the belief that in those cases "assertions" are contrary to Christ's way and word. The astonishing claim of Christian faith is that the God of all reality is related to—identified with—human flesh and folly, and, therefore, all things human and all things divine must be included in the embrace of Christian faith. In this respect, it is the scope of the divine embrace and the bond of shared humanity that are the point of Christian assertions rather than those assertions defining the boundary marker that sets Christians over against others.

One way to understand Christian humanism's reluctance to insist on doctrinal uniformity is to see that the point of faith is not clarity but charity; the tenets of faith find their perfection in the life of love. Yet nestled in that idea, I am suggesting, are also some claims about the very nature of Christian identity deeply rooted in beliefs about God's action in Christ and also the nature of human existence itself. If we are to understand the "Christ" of Christian humanism, we must then turn from debates within dogmatic theology to the actual picture of Christ developed among Christian humanists. I want to focus the next step of my inquiry on ideas or images or metaphors (variously used by different thinkers) found among classical Christian humanists, namely, those of "flesh" and "folly."

FLESH AND FOLLY

The use of the ideas of flesh and folly in order to think about who Christ is and what he does is drawn from a wide array of Christian humanist discourses. These ideas are, by no means, the only terms used to speak of Christ. Yet they do capture something basic to the Christian humanist mind-set. Because of Christ's incarnation, human mortal existence—our existence as embodied spirits—can bear the infinite. The matter of our being as living flesh is endorsed by and oriented toward the divine. Of course, each of these ideas (embodied spirit oriented toward the divine; finite existence can bear the infinite) needs careful elucidation. But the main idea is clear enough. Unlike some religions where enlightenment or redemption entails an escape from or transcendence of finite, bodily existence, for the Christian humanist incarnate existence is treasured in its finitude as a place for a relation to the divine. This does not mean a wholesale materialism, where matter and matter alone provides an adequate framework for understanding human existence. That God was incarnate in Christ means conceptually that one must conceive of matter and spirit in their union but without confusion.[9] This is why Christian humanists insist on the distinctive drive, the aspiration and energy, of human life: to be human is to seek the overcoming, the transcendence, of our given condition toward the divine. However, self-overcoming is not against or beyond but rather in and through the "flesh."

Now it is the aspiring drive of human life that calls forth the other idea used to speak of Christ, and preciously in its connection to flesh. To say that Christ is folly is to signal that most of the time most of us aspire to what is deemed wise or powerful or prestigious or honorable, not in relation to the love of God and one's neighbor, but in reference to ourselves and the gaze of others. We treasure the appearance of our own identities. We prefer, as the Gospels have it, to pray in public where others see us, rather than in secret where God alone searches the heart; we prefer to give our wealth in public places rather than conceal our generosity in order to give glory to God. Instead of living temporal existence as a medium of love for God and others, it is seen as end in itself. Here is the root of human folly, namely, the all-too-human denial of humanity in the aspiration to deify temporal existence. Folly arises within our fleshliness and then turns against itself. It indeed wishes to connect flesh and divinity, but in such a way that our finitude is our god. As some modern thinkers, like Martin Heidegger, might put it, our own most possibility for authentic being is found only through an encounter with our own being-toward-death such that our mortality, and not the needs of others or the living God, is the pathway to truth.[10] For the Christian humanist, the folly in this thought is the presumption of the self answers its own most question, and, accordingly, is precisely a denial of its finitude, its flesh. The folly of Christ, or, better, Christ as folly, is one who pours out life with and for others in love of God and yet appears inauthentic, fallen, and abject, but redeems flesh in its finitude.

It is the co-implication of flesh and folly that we must briefly explore, or so I believe. We can do so via a detour through two instances of these ideas in the writing of classical Christian humanists. While often associated with Roman Catholic rather than Protestant thought, Rabelais and Erasmus explore the connection of flesh and folly. Engaging their texts is meant to stress that one can give priority to a shared Christian identity rather than focusing on confessional differences that have divided the church. At the far end of this detour we will reach the constructive claims I think Christian humanists must make about Christ in our time.

Erasmus supposedly wrote *Praise of Folly* during one week in 1509 and dedicated it to Thomas More—whose name is the foil, a double entendre in the title (*Moriae Encomion*). Further, the text draws inspiration from the satire of Lucian of Samasota, a Syrian Roman author, whose works are often called "serio-comic," treating serious topics comically. More and Erasmus had been translating Lucian, and *Praise of Folly* as well as More's *Utopia* are in this tradition. Technically speaking, the work is an "encomium." That is, rhetorically, it is high-sounding or formal praise and derives its name from the Greek *komos,* for revelry. In this case, Folly praises herself as the source of human happiness. We know that the text was fabulously successful and also condemned from the first but ran many editions in many languages. While Erasmus hardly thought it his best work—his work in translation being that—it is a good introduction to the man's mind. And like Rabelais, it is clear that three basic constants of human existence (birth, sex, death) are the forces of our highest aspirations and also our deepest folly.

The text seems to move in and through four movements in which Folly takes on different voices. Chapters 1 to 30 are straightforward and gleeful comedy in which Folly tries to show that she is the source of all good that comes to human beings. In chapters 31 to 47 there is a shift to parody in which Folly exposes the vices of virtually the entire range of the social order and people in various groups and professions. By chapters 48 to 61 we arrive at what is, for some scholars, the heart of the work. In pure satire there is an attack on the presumption and stupidity of many, especially theologians, and even Erasmus himself. There is, in chapters 62 to 68, a final reversal and disclosure. Christ himself is Folly—the one who, although foolishness to the world, brings human felicity.

Erasmus as a Christian humanist found himself at odds with two other forces in Christianity. First, there were the scholastics with a rigid orthodoxy that held that what was needed for salvation was acceptance of norms of belief and practices of the sacraments. They gave little attention to the human mind's need to understand its experience or individual moral aspiration. Then, second, there was Luther and the Reformers for whom the very idea of moral perfectibility and aspiration was dangerous. The Evangelical reformers joined Erasmus in the criticism of scholastic forms and also the humanist bent to reclaim the original Christian texts, to get good versions and translations of the Bible. Against these options, Erasmus, as Terence Martin has written, outlines "an ethics of discourse crafted from both classical and scriptural resources, centered on irenic dialogue, and modeled on the love of God in Christ."[11] The Christian life opposes coercion with persuasion, force with love, and unbending belief with reasoned conviction.

Erasmus and other Christian humanists, including (importantly) John Calvin, called this outlook the "philosophy of Christ." Wherever truth is found, wherever insight into just and virtuous life is gleaned, it can and ought to be interwoven with the Christian message. In this respect, it is not too easy or too glib to repeat the ancient maxim that nothing human is foreign to one.

But of course it is no small thing to decide what counts as human. Erasmus probed the folly of human beings and in the *Praise of Folly* insisted on skepticism vis-à-vis human knowledge while lampooning presumption to truth. This is serious laughter. Rabelais agrees. In his "advice to readers" he begins *Gargantua* thusly: "When I see grief consume and rot / You, mirth's my theme and tears are not / For laughter is man's proper lot."[12] Of course, Rabelais has been interpreted in various ways: a teller of bawdy tales; a hermetic, even cabalistic writer; an atheist and proto-Marxist critic of medieval society; and also some kind of Christian, liberal but orthodox in some way.[13] As Florence Weinberg has noted, "Rabelais's entire approach, his *serio ludere*, the grotesque mask, is deeply justified by his conviction that true wisdom often disguises itself as foolishness (the converse is not always true, not all fools are wise)."[14] Indeed, the book, from its opening to end, claims to be a tale with no deep meaning at all. It seeks to disguise the wisdom it hopes to convey. Many a reader has failed to grasp the indirection in Rabelais's communication of the gospel. Only those with ears to hear and eyes to see will learn the true in the hidden.

While Erasmus, at least in *Praise of Folly*, makes this point by exposing the prideful foolishness of those who believe themselves to be wise, Rabelais focuses on flesh. Tracing the birth and education of the giant Gargantua, he explores the presence of divine spirit under the bawdiness of boozing, sex, flatulence, and the carnival. About his conception, Rabelais writes that Gargantua's father and his mother, "a fine, good-looking piece," "often play the two-backed beast, joyfully rubbing their bacon together, to such effect that she became pregnant of a fine boy and carried him into the eleventh month." Musing on the length of the pregnancy and the ways in which women try to avoid that consequence, he concludes "if the deuce doesn't want their bellies to swell, he must twist the spigot and close the hole."[15] With similar honesty, Rabelais traces the boy's education and his many adventures.

In celebration of his hero and his praise of fellow boozers, Rabelais conceals within a Dionysian festival a drunken wisdom, the wisdom of the Christ. Here the scope of salvation is extended to everyone. Weinberg continues, "We end as we began, with the knowledge that all things are revealed to the true seeker. All mankind . . . can be saved in the end."[16] The bonds and desires of the flesh can lead to death, of course. Some will be drunk with their own wisdom; some will not see that earthly desires need to be purified. This is not to deny "flesh" in order to escape folly. Salvation is not a denial or negation of human existence in all of its bawdy and broken ways. The human adventure, portrayed through Gargantua in its most gigantic and outlandish form, can reveal divine grace. God has not scorned our lot.

A good deal of modern Christian theology is less skeptical than Erasmus and certainly more prudish than Rabelais's celebration with his fellow Pantagruelists. That is, I imagine, just what Rabelais and Erasmus would expect of theologians. In our time, there is obsession over God's identification with human existence without, apparently, much reflection on what that could actually mean in human terms, how one would communicate such an outlandish message, or the ludic character of the confession itself. We read about God's solidarity with the outcast, God and erotic power, and the suffering of God, but these claims remain mainly at the level of abstractions. While Erasmus and Rabelais could practice the ancient art of "serious play," *serio ludere*, as well as use the classic tactic of serious comedy (*serio comic*) found in Lucian and others, contemporary theologians—for all their delight in postmodern "play"— are rarely found laughing over human foibles or divine wisdom.[17] Maybe the legacy of Dante's *Divine Comedy* and Milton's *Paradise Lost* clinch the reach and depth of Christian laughter despite the writings of Erasmus, Rabelais, and others. Of course, there are many kinds of laughter, some of them destructive as well as violent. Still, if Christianity is the "philosophy of Christ," then, in M. A. Screech's words, it "teaches men and women how to spiritualize their souls and to 'animate' their bodies."[18] This philosophy enables one to confront death and life mindful of folly and flesh but also the difference between the laughter of the "world" and the Folly of God—the Christ.

The question that provoked this essay now returns: what is the "Christ" of Christian humanism for our day? This is especially pressing in a culture where little is now seen as bawdy, where the domain of the profane expands daily to choke off the human spirit, and so nothing much shocks about the fate of human existence. How might this grand legacy of thought about the human condition in the light of the philosophy of Christ be revised and carried forward in a world of global dynamics? Without doubt, we need to train our gaze on our most treasured possession—our carefully wrought and dearly bought identities. For where your treasure is, there too will be your heart.

CHRIST AND CHRISTIAN IDENTITY

The pathway of reflection I have undertaken in this essay was to begin by noting that the point of theological reflection for the Christian humanist is the Christian life. It is, to use classic terms, to articulate the philosophy of Christ for the orientation of human existence. And I also noted that in our time people's identities are too often circumscribed within one description, and, we can now say, sipped as holy wine the treasure of heaven. Within the whirl of global dynamics there are powerful forces at work seeking carefully to demarcate people's identity in order to provide solid boundaries between communities and so to enshrine it as the Holy of Holies. There are also forces working to persuade us of our sovereign power to shape at will and whim who we are and what we will become.

The highest good, apparently, is the freedom to fashion and morph one's identity. These strategies of identity formation usually fail precisely because of the reflexive interaction among peoples on the global field. No community is free from interaction with others that shape the context of life; no one is sovereign over all of the forces, natural and social, that shape existence. Yet the failures to control the formation of identity lead to harsher and even more violent means to retain the boundaries or to reassert the right of self-formation.[19] What is needed, I believe, is a vision of the internal complexity of identities and the various ways one can and ought to live with them in oneself, one's community, and the world. The sovereignty a human being actually has over self is more limited, more deliberate, and yet more important than often thought. The sovereignty we ought to seek is to orient the dear self beyond itself for a life of love of responsibility with and for others. These facts show one promise, for Christians, of Christian humanism in our time.

In our current situation we need to articulate the complexity of any person's or community's identity in order to find noncoercive points of contact among people without loss of distinctiveness. And we must admit that much of who we are, much of what we cannot escape, has been given us, like it or not. The worry, to say it again, is that once an identity is defined through just one description, anyone who has a different identity will be seen in opposition. Identity then becomes, as Sen put it, an "illusion of destiny," something which cannot or will not be escaped or changed, that pits people against each other. With that horrific possibility in mind, I explored briefly in the second step of this essay some central ideas about Christ found among the great Christian humanists of the Renaissance and Reformation period. They explored the meaning of Christ in relation to what would seem to be features of any human life, namely, fleshliness and also foolishness. Yet it is not at all clear what their claims, much less their skepticism and even hermeticism, could mean in our global context. Revisions are again needed in how Christian humanists think about Christ and the Christian life.

Actually, I have already hinted at what I believe needs critical revision in the legacy of Christian humanism in order to carry that legacy forward into our own day. It is a subtle but important shift from the priority of confession to the problem of identity. Insofar as early Christian humanists could assume the stability of a wider Christian culture, their challenge was how to navigate between the clashes of confessions that plunged Europe into thirty years of war.[20] Even more recent Christian humanists, ones we have not been able to explore, confronted the modern challenge to the plausibility of religious faith in terms of a conflict of confessions, a scientific versus religious outlook.[21] That debate usually assumed a good measure of social stability and coherence. In our age, the question of the conflict of cognitive claims, the clash of confessions, is more deeply situated in the social and cultural proliferation of identities and the claim to sovereignty of those identities. The connection between these two concerns is obvious, of course. An identity without confession is empty. A confession without an identity is formless. The connection between confession and identity enables one to remain a Christian humanist and yet also requires revisions in that orientation to faith and life. How so?

If conflict among peoples is to be lessened and managed, then it must become possible to decide in specific situations which of several identities provides contact with others and directions for cooperative action. And that means—shockingly—that one's identities can and ought to serve a good beyond themselves. This is not a facile optimism or naive idealism. Genuine realism about possibilities for action acknowledges that in a particular situation human differences might not be overcome, and conflict then ensues. Yet even then violence can be blunted, if not escaped, if some bond of commonality places a limit on the use of force. But, again, this means that none of my specific identities, including my Christian identity, can trump my whole existence and claim exclusive right to orient action. In some contexts I need to see myself as a human being who faces death, who loves his family, and who bleeds *just like, in principle, every other human being*. In this case, my more distinct identities (say, United Methodist Protestant Christian or friend of Michael and Ulrike Welker) are set in the background and seen as supportive of shared humanity. That commonality can and must delimit the scope and extent of violence, because, as we know, unending conflict requires the dehumanization of the other. Of course, there will be other situations where I must stress more particular identities, say, in the midst of theological debate with fellow Christians or among theists of various kinds or talking and laughing with friends. Yet even in those cases, something shared is the condition for cooperation and persuasion and also limit to forms of coercive interaction.

Notice two things about my argument. It actually entails a practical rule and, more importantly, a specific stance toward oneself, one's community, and the identities of others. Together, these are important features of a viable form of contemporary Christian humanism. First, at each point of encounter with others the task is to find the relevant commonality that is the condition for cooperation or the limit on coercive interaction. This is, I will call it, a humanistic procedural rule for decisions about what priority to give to one's various identities in specific situations. It requires that no specific identity be deified as the singular description of one's existence because, as St. Paul knew, one's life can and ought to be dedicated toward right relations with and for others. Thus, second, this rule implies and enacts a more basic stance possible in our time. The various "confessions" (the cognitive, linguistic, traditional, and practical contents) that shape one's identities are subsumed under a more general project of fashioning a life dedicated to what respects and enhances the integrity of life with and for others before God.[22] This stance, I suppose, arises out of the deep humanistic longing for peace within self, among others, and with God. Whatever its origin, it is important to see that the rule for decision making implies the deeper moral and religious stance. Someone who accepts the stance ought also to abide by this rule. Anyone who can grasp the intelligibility of the practical rule thereby endorses, at least implicitly, the coordinate stance in life. Both the rule and the stance would seem to apply not only to individuals but also to communities insofar as the idea of "identity" is analogically applied to persons and communities.

This strategy for orienting life is deeply embedded in the very idea of Christian humanism insofar as it signals the complexity of a life: one is Christian (of some sort) and a humanist (of some sort) and has other identities, too. Yet the conditions of that outlook are also found at the crossing point of the predicates applied to Christ. Human beings are bound together in their mortality, their fleshliness, and also their presumption to wisdom, their folly. Because of our penchant to folly, one ought to be properly skeptical about one's grasp of the truth; because of one's mortality the plight of other human beings, even given their folly, can be recognized. These facts warrant both the rule and the stance just noted. And Christ, as we have seen, inhabits this human realm to heal and redeem it. The Christian humanist thereby undertakes the labor of life for both human and Christian reasons. There is no justification for the charge made by current Christian particularists that if a situation demands priority of one's humanity (or one's Christian identity), that is somehow a betrayal of the Christian confession (or humanistic convictions). Confessions, like identities, find their point in a way of life. One can and must treasure a life dedicated to love and responsibility rather than the particularities of our identities and the convictions we embody.

Now to affirm the right and responsibility of people to make decisions of priority about their identities actually reclaims another aspect of Christian humanism mentioned before but hardly explained. It is a distinctive form of freedom. Of course, this was a point that divided Protestants and Roman Catholics; it put Luther against Erasmus, and even today can raise the hackles of Christian particularists who wish to see Christian identity constituted through conformity to churchly authority. For those theologians, identity can and ought and must become one's destiny. Freedom is understood by them as little more than license and so the sad and troubled legacy of modern individualism.[23] That is not the idea of freedom advocated here. Rather, freedom is the capacity to labor responsibly for the integrity of life in oneself and in others. It is the ability to give priority to and reasons for orienting life in specific situations. It means that one's identity is neither an undeniable destiny nor, in more theological terms, a foreordained election. Whatever our ultimate end, in this life and at this time human beings can and may and must responsibly orient life in ways that foster life and delimit destruction. In Christian terms, freedom is made perfect in love rooted in Christ's flesh and divine folly.

How then is one to speak of freedom as intrinsically linked to the joys and demands of responsibility? That is, how is one to avoid the idea that freedom is just license and thereby unconstrained by Christian or humane purposes? Can one avoid the rush to authority and the seductive destiny of identity? Stated still otherwise, how is freedom linked to the aspiration to the integrity of life? This is not the time or the place to enter into an extended discussion of freedom and responsibility. Ideas of freedom are legion and so too conceptions of responsibility. Yet to my mind, the best way to think about this is to conceive of conscience as the claim of responsibility on freedom. More precisely, the claim of responsibility is that in our actions and relations we are to respect and enhance the integrity of life before God.

"Conscience" is a term for the most basic mode of our being in which the capacity for action (our freedom) is infused with a sense of responsibility. It names the distinctive human ability to make decisions and choices about how to orient and conduct one's life. Conscience is that power to make decisions and choices about the relative priority one can and ought to give to identities in relation to others. It is the call to orient the self beyond its several identities toward actions and relations that respect and enhance the integrity of life. For precisely this reason, a basic right of human beings is freedom of conscience. No human beings can rightfully be coerced to conform their identities and life to any power—no matter how seemingly legitimate or how divinely authorized—that denies the capacity of conscience as the labor of one's life. This right, Christian humanists claim, is rooted in God's way with us in Christ. Indeed, we might say that for a Christian humanist, Christ is the conscience of God. That is, Christ is the freedom of God oriented toward what respects and enhances the integrity of finite life made manifest in flesh and folly. We are neither coerced nor elected in faith, but bidden by Christ to a life of fidelity, responsibility, and love.

The Christian humanist is less anxious about being a Christian over against the "world" than many other contemporary theologians counted among the ranks of Christian particularists. The high priests of much current theology seem so certain that the Christian story offers peace to a fallen world that they hardly notice the goodwill of their "pagan" neighbors. A Christian humanist is also less worried about the supposed uniqueness of the gospel than most traditional confessions would insist. Christ said that only God was good, and yet so many Christian denominations log the one and true path to the divine within the lines of their prayer books. To be sure, the Christian life is a distinctive way of living the human adventure, but it is still a way of being human. The anxiety of the Christian humanist in our time is different. It is the fear that religious and cultural and social forces will stunt conscience and demand unity rather than integrity of identity. More profoundly, the anxiety is about human freedom, the failure of conscience, or a weakness of will (to put it in different ways) so that our commitments and responsibilities with and to others become constricted by our petty identities. The law of sin and death, the abyss of existence, continually enslaves our lives and shackles the conscience to pit us against ourselves, people against people, and the human heart against the love of God, all in the name of our dear selves. Our folly ever remains with us inscribed in the mortality and pain of flesh. The laughter we can muster at this folly is always and necessarily and sadly serious.

When the will fails and conscience is stunted, the Christian humanist with simple faith in the power of God must wield the only weapons she or he has consistent with that faith, the weapons of education, irony, satire, and forms of resistance to human fault and wretchedness that are once comic and serious. What can be more foolish and more dangerous than to believe that Christian convictions should stunt the scope of love in the name of Christian truth? Truth so sure and certain and proclaimed and lived without love is its own folly. But it is not the folly of God that finds habitation in love with our mortal lot. It is not the folly of faith that finds hidden in the flesh and folly of Christ the power to revoke the law of sin and death.

There is, perhaps, nothing deep or profound in that thought. It discloses nothing new or radical about our plight or the Christian convictions. Christian humanism is only a practical thing, after all. It leaves the deepest mysteries of faith to those who toil among the doctrines. It is the outlook of the "third man," the believing outsider, the one whose life is crisscrossed with multiple convictions about how to orient life humanely and faithfully. A Christian humanist does not know that much about God and God's ways. She or he just wants to find a way to orient life freed from the grip of the law, the destiny, which makes convictions and identities the motor of death among peoples. That way is the philosophy of Christ.

GRATITUDE

I suppose by now, dear reader, you have surmised that I have no intention or even ability of making good on the promise above to deliver to you neatly packaged in crisp doctrine the Christ of Christian humanism. I have been able neither to ascend to the godhead in order to glimpse the Logos made incarnate nor to descend to the depths of his suffering that breaks the law of sin and death. And I certainly have not been able to revel in the presence of his spirit made real under the fragility of human language, the turmoil of community, or the baser elements of life, bread and wine. All that I have been able to do, quite frankly, is to meditate on existence as one who, for reasons not completely obvious to me, found something right and even blessed in those seminars long ago when laughter and theology commingled with friendship. Yet if those experiences and many others like them have helped to fashion an outlook that I now identify as Christian and humanistic, it is because in ways that escape easy formulation Christ was present there, too. That is the meaning, I suppose, of the Christ of Christian humanism—that life in its terror and joy, ignorance and aspiration, its sorrow and laughter, flesh and folly, nevertheless evokes gratitude before God.

NOTES

1. Paul Ricoeur, "Faith and Culture," in *Political and Social Essays,* ed. David Stewart and Joseph Bein (Athens: Ohio University Press, 1974), 126.
2. On this, see Craig W. Kallendorf, ed. and trans., *Humanist Educational Treatises* (Cambridge, Mass.: Harvard University Press, 2002).
3. R. William Franklin and Joseph M. Shaw, *The Case for Christian Humanism* (Grand Rapids: Eerdmans, 1991), 11.

4. For a profound meditation on the material mediation of the divine, see David E. Klemm, "Material Grace: The Paradox of Property and Possession," in *Having: Property and Possession in Social and Religious Life,* ed. William Schweiker and Charles Mathewes (Grand Rapids: Eerdmans, 2004), 222–48.

5. Importantly, similar arguments have been made by prominent intellectuals in various traditions. See the Palestinian American literary critic Edward W. Said, *Humanism and Democratic Criticism* (New York: Columbia University Press, 2004); the Indian American economist Amartya Sen, *Identity and Violence: The Illusion of Destiny* (New York: Norton, 2006); the chief rabbi of the United Hebrew Congregations of the British Commonwealth, Jonathan Sachs, *The Dignity of Difference: How to Avoid the Clash of Civilizations* (New York: Continuum, 2002); and John W. de Gruchy, *Confessions of a Christian Humanist* (Minneapolis: Fortress Press, 2006). Also see *Humanity before God: Contemporary Faces of Jewish, Christian, and Islamic Ethics,* ed. Michael A. Johnson, William Schweiker, and Kevin Jung (Minneapolis: Fortress Press, 2006). I have developed some of these ideas in previous and current writing. See William Schweiker, *Theological Ethics and Global Dynamics: In the Time of Many Worlds* (Oxford: Blackwell Publishing, 2004), and William Schweiker and David E. Klemm, *Religion and the Human Future: An Essay on Theological Humanism* (Oxford: Blackwell Publishing, 2008).

6. Jaroslav Pelikan, *Jesus through the Centuries: His Place in the History of Culture* (New Haven, Conn.: Yale University Press, 1985). For a fine discussion of the issues in ethics, see James M. Gustafson, *Christ and the Moral Life* (Chicago: University of Chicago Press, 1979).

7. Thomas Merton, "Virginity and Humanism in the Western Fathers," in *Mystics and Zen Masters* (New York: Farrar, Straus & Giroux, 1967), 114. For a statement of this outlook in Protestant theology, see Karl Barth, *The Humanity of God,* trans. John Newton Thomas and Thomas Wieser (Richmond, Va.: John Knox Press, 1960), and in Russian theology see Paul Valliere, *Modern Russian Theology: Bukharev, Soloviev, Bulgakov: Orthodox Theology in a New Key* (Grand Rapids: Eerdmans, 2000).

8. Martin Luther, "The Bondage of the Will," in *Martin Luther: A Selection from His Writings,* ed. John Dillenberger (Garden City, N.Y.: Anchor Books, 1961), 167–68.

9. Within the science and theology discussion that Michael Welker has helped to foster, this is often conceived through ideas about "dual aspect monism" or emergence. I cannot enter those conceptual discussions in this essay, but, clearly, my own argument finds resonance, as Welker might put it, with those arguments.

10. This is the argument famously made by Martin Heidegger in his work *Being and Time.* It is crucial that some prominent post-Heideggerian thinkers have looked to the encounter with the other, and not only the fact of death, to understand human existence. On this, see, for instance, Emmanuel Levinas, *Humanism of the Other,* trans. Nidra Poller, with an introduction by Richard A. Cohen (Urbana: University of Illinois Press, 2003), and Paul Ricoeur, *The Just,* trans. David Pellauer (Chicago: University of Chicago Press, 2003).

11. On this, see Terence J. Martin, *Living Words: Studies in Dialogues about Religion* (Atlanta: Scholars Press, 1998), 251.

12. François Rabelais, *Gargantua and Pantagruel,* trans. J. M. Cohen (New York: Penguin Books, 1974).

13. For a helpful discussion, see Florence M. Weinberg, *The Wine and the Will: Rabelais's Bacchic Christianity* (Detroit, Mich.: Wayne State University Press,

1972). Also see Mikhail M. Bakhtin, *Rabelais and His World,* trans. Helene Iswolsky (Bloomington: Indiana University Press, 1984).

14. Ibid., 149.
15. Rabelais, *Gargantua and Pantagruel,* 46–47.
16. Ibid., 151.
17. For an excellent study, see M. A. Screech, *Laughter at the Foot of the Cross* (Boulder, Colo.: Westview Press, 1999). On the use of inhumane, cruel laughter, see Jonathan Glover, *Humanity: A Moral History of the Twentieth Century* (New Haven, Conn.: Yale University Press, 1991). Also see Schweiker, *Theological Ethics and Global Dynamics,* esp. 153–71.
18. Screech, *Laughter at the Foot of the Cross,* 255.
19. For postcolonial and feminist perspectives on these issues, see Arjun Appadurai, *Modernity at Large: Cultural Dimensions of Globalization* (Minneapolis: University of Minnesota Press, 1996), and Saskia Sassen, *Globalization and Its Discontents* (New York: New Press, 1998).
20. For a fine discussion, see Stephen Toulmin, *Cosmopolis: The Hidden Agenda of Modernity* (New York: Free Press, 1999).
21. I am thinking here of theologians ranging from Friedrich Schleiermacher and Ernst Troeltsch to twentieth-century thinkers like Karl Rahner, Paul Tillich, Robert Scharlemann, Wolfhart Pannenberg, James Gustafson, David Tracy, and others.
22. On the elaboration of this imperative of responsibility, see William Schweiker, *Responsibility and Christian Ethics* (Cambridge: Cambridge University Press, 1995).
23. This argument is usually associated with communitarian and postliberal theologians like Stanley Hauerwas, Paul Griffiths, Sam Wells, Stephen Long, George Lindbeck, and others in the United States.

7

The Corporate Christ

JOHN POLKINGHORNE

Michael Welker and I share a common conviction of the importance of the work of truth-seeking communities. We see such activity as present as much in theology as in science. Over a wide span of human inquiry—indeed ranging from the natural sciences to theology—the intellectual endeavor of these communities is driven by the desire to understand and to do justice to the way that things actually are. The richness of reality, in all its subtle complexity, implies the need to pursue a multidimensional approach, hence the importance of the interdisciplinary working groups that Michael Welker has done so much to encourage and in which he has participated with so much vigor and effectiveness.

The quest for truthful understanding resists attempts to impose upon it the kind of reduction that, while it might give the appearance of quickly allowing one to reach a universal and logically entailed conclusion, can in fact lead only to an illusory result induced by Procrustean oversimplification. In consequence of the need to encounter reality on terms that are respectful of its complexity, the character of truthful discourse is not one that will often be characterized by the achievement of indisputable proof, reaching conclusions that none but a fool could venture to deny. Rather, its realistic aim has to be the more modest goal of fulfilling the quest for inference to the best explanation, the attainment of

an understanding that is persuasive and intellectually satisfying but not logically coercive. This implies that the need for a degree of intellectual daring cannot altogether be avoided in pursuing the search for truth. Natural science is
not exempt from this element of rational venture, a point made eloquently by
Michael Polanyi in his emphasis on science's necessary character of involving
"personal knowledge," depending for its fruitfulness on unspecifiable tacit skills,
even when engaged in a pursuit with universal intent.[1]

While reductionist impoverishment is to be resisted, attempting to cope with the
bewildering multiplicity of experience requires that some kind of focused principle
of inquiry is necessary if the seeker for understanding is not to be overwhelmed by
the sheer complexity of phenomena. Heuristic strategies have to be formulated and
pursued that are not the result of a curtailment of the richness of reality, but they
are derived from a successful identification of those questions that it is really fruitful to ask, together with a judicious selection of the particular phenomena that are
likely to give the most transparent access to their answering. In the natural sciences,
triggers of insight of this kind arise either from the investigation of specific regimes
which through some extremity of circumstance yield simplicity of interpretation
(critical experiments), or through posing novel questions that arise from looking at
common experience from a new point of view. A remarkable example of the latter
was the question posed by the nineteenth-century German astronomer Wilhelm
Olbers, when he asked, "Why is the sky dark at night?" Olbers had realized that if
the universe were infinite in extent and age, as many then supposed to be the case,
every line of sight must eventually end on the surface of a star. This implied that
the night sky should be as bright as the Sun. One of the greatest gifts that a scientist
can possess is that of being able to ask truly penetrating questions.

For the Christian theologian, the New Testament testimony to Jesus Christ
is the record of that essential critical regime through which the nature and purposes of God have been most fully and transparently revealed—hence, the central significance of Christology for the whole endeavor of Christian theology. In
relation to the search for an understanding of the divine derived from a christological perspective, I believe that there are three questions whose answering will
critically shape the conclusions that are reached. They are:

1. Was Jesus indeed resurrected on the third day, and if so, why was
   Jesus, alone among all humanity, raised from the dead within history
   to live an everlasting life of glory beyond history?
2. Why did the first Christians feel driven to use divine-sounding language about Jesus?
3. What was the basis for the assurance felt by those first Christians that
   through the risen Christ they had been given a power that was transforming their lives in a new and unprecedented way?[2]

I have frequently discussed the resurrection in my writings.[3] I do not have
anything new to add, and I shall not repeat old material here. I have also sought

previously to pay attention to the remarkable way in which the New Testament writers feel that they cannot do without using divine phraseology in relation to Jesus, even to the point of applying to him texts from the Old Testament that clearly originally referred to the God of Israel, while holding this tendency in an unresolved tension with their Jewish conviction that "the Lord our God is one."[4] In this case also I shall not attempt to go over old ground. Instead, in this essay I want to concentrate on the third question, deepened by including within it an inquiry into how we can understand that the death and resurrection of Christ constitute a salvific event through which human sins are forgiven and a right relationship between God and humanity is established. I believe that an adequate account of soteriology is a necessary controlling criterion of an adequate account of Christology generally. We shall only understand the nature of Christ aright if that enables us to understand the work of Christ aright.

It seems clear that a Christology that sees the significance of Jesus principally in inspirational or functional terms, so that he simply affords a uniquely transparent "window into God"[5] through his unique closeness to his heavenly Father, leaves the central soteriological question inadequately addressed. The human condition is such that what we need is not just a clearer vision, or a more inspiriting example, valuable though these are, but an empowering that goes beyond them. What is required is not simply information but transformation. Many other holy lives can also be said to point us in the right direction, but humanity's problem lies in finding the grace and power actually to follow the examples given. A similar critique applies to subjective accounts of the atonement. The Christian heart is certainly moved by the thought of Jesus' willing acceptance of death on the cross, but some additionally effective degree of empowerment is surely also necessary if this attitude is to bear fruit in individual lives. To understand how this might be calls for the exploration of an objective dimension present in the salvific work of Christ.

No doubt all the different accounts that have been given of the work of Christ contain some element of truth and insight within them, but the reality exceeds each one of these individual understandings. Different perspectives will illuminate different aspects of the profound reality of salvation. Theologians discussing soteriology are like scientists discussing some complex phenomenon. A portfolio of models, none sufficient on its own, and often such that if anyone is pushed too far it will prove contradictory to the others, is often the best way of exploring a rich reality. It is sometimes helpful for a nuclear physicist to think of a nucleus as if it were a cloudy crystal ball, while at other times a liquid drop model will be more appropriate. Of course, the nucleus is neither of these things, but it shares in some of their properties.

There are three models through which one might gain some further insight into how the death and resurrection of Jesus liberated a new power of divine grace and forgiveness, active in the salvation of humanity. The first one sees the cross and resurrection as a great victory won in the ultimate battle against the cosmic powers that oppose God and the divine purposes. A classic expression of this idea in the New Testament is given in Colossians (2:15) by the assertion that Christ on his cross "disarmed the rulers and authorities and made a public example of them." A modern account of this concept is contained in the influential book by Gustav Aulén, *Christus Victor*.[6] The "deceiver deceived" theory of the atonement—the belief that the devil was decoyed into the disastrous error of attempting to claim illegitimate rights over the sinless Christ—was an early, but inadequate, endeavor to identify a mechanism by which this defeat of evil was achieved. The powerful mythic image of the cosmic warfare of light and darkness certainly moves the imagination and strengthens resolve. Yet for the modern mind it leaves much in need of further elucidation of how this great divine victory was actually achieved.

A second broad category of insight into the saving work of Christ is expressed in a variety of transactional accounts, such as theories of penal substitution or the Anselmian idea of a necessary "satisfaction" made to the offended Feudal Lord of the universe. What accounts of this nature do is to place a surely necessary stress on the costliness of salvation, and so they keep before us the New Testament understanding that there is a sacrificial character to Christ's dying for our sins, however difficult the concept of sacrifice is for many contemporary Christians. Yet once again, the particular details of these traditional insights are highly problematic for the modern mind.

I want to explore a third kind of strategy for seeking soteriological understanding, one that is relational in its character. Speaking of God's predestined act of salvific fulfillment, Robert Jensen says that "the one sole object of eternal election is Jesus with his people, the *totus Christus*."[7] This corporate concept of the *totus Christus* draws our attention to the striking way in which the New Testament not only refers to Christ as a known individual of recent history, but it also speaks of him in remarkably incorporative terms. This theme has been carefully explored by the New Testament scholar Charlie Moule.[8]

He summarizes his detailed survey of the Pauline writings by saying that, in part at least, they "reflect an experience of Christ as a 'corporate person,' to be joined to whom is to become part of an organic whole." While Moule goes on to acknowledge that this kind of corporate discourse was readily used by pantheists in the ancient world to speak of the cosmos or of society, he also sees it as being an entirely different matter when it is employed by a Jewish theist like Paul, referring to a known person of recent history: "in this form, it represents a religious experience which is new, and which drives us to ask, Who is this; who can be understood in much the same terms as a theist understands God himself—as personal indeed, but more than individual."[9]

A somewhat similar concept is to be found expressed in the Johannine writings, where the image used is that of mutual indwelling. There are some subtle differences of emphasis, however, in comparison to the Pauline statements. The latter frequently speak of believers as being "in Christ," a phrase that is often associated with the Christian community rather than with the individual.[10] The Johannine statements lay a greater emphasis on a reciprocal coinherence between Christ and the individual Christian, as in the great figure of the true vine and the branches (John 15:1–7) and in the high priestly prayer for the disciples in John 17.

A number of other considerations serve to reinforce Moule's emphasis on the corporate character of much New Testament thinking. He discerns a universalizing significance in the pervasive use of the preposition *huper* (for the sake of), in preference to *anti* (instead of) as expressing the relationship of Christ's death to the whole of humanity.[11] Many have noted Paul's liking for using verbs compounded with the prefix *sun* (a preposition expressing association, fellowship, inclusion), as for example in Romans 6:4–6 and 8:17, used as expressions of an intimately shared participation in a common experience. Moule is somewhat reserved about appealing to the Pauline concept of the body of Christ in support of his corporate thesis.[12] Yet, surely Paul's statement, "For just as the body is one and has many members, and all the members of the body, though many, are one body, so it is with Christ" (1 Cor. 12:12), carries more significance than its simply being a picturesque metaphor used to make a general point. The whole argument that follows seems to depend for its force on some sort of ontological undergirding of a counterintuitive nature.

Much more positively presented by Moule is an argument that is based on a careful analysis of the way in which New Testament writers appeal to testimonial culled from the Hebrew Scriptures. He believes that they are not just relying on a questionable concept of the fulfillment of an arbitrary selection of prophecies, but rather their concern is to express the conviction that the hopes and expectations of divine rescue and enoblement that had been assigned to the faithful remnant of Israel ultimately had come to be focused solely on a single individual, Jesus of Nazareth.[13] He was seen as carrying in his person the collective significance of fulfilling the destiny of God's people, in connection with which Moule emphasizes how frequently the verb *pleroun* (complete, accomplish) occurs in the New Testament. I believe that this more than individual role was expressed by Jesus himself in his lifetime on those particular occasions when his use of the phrase "Son of man" was made, as I believe, in reference to the figure of Daniel 7, who is identified with the coming of that kingdom which is to be the ultimate possession of "the holy ones of the Most High" (Dan. 7:14, 22).[14]

This brief survey of what in the original is a very detailed and scrupulous discussion may serve to indicate in outline why Moule concludes that

> Paul does seem to conceive of the living Christ as more than the individual, while still knowing him vividly and distinctly as fully personal. He speaks of the Christian life as lived in an area which is Christ; he thinks of the Christian community as (ideally) a harmoniously coordinated living organism like a body, and, on occasions, thinks of Christ as himself the living body of which Christians are limbs. . . . This means, in effect, that Paul was led to conceive of Christ as any theist conceives of God: personal, indeed, but transcending the individual category.[15]

Moule further believes that this corporate conception of Christ is implicitly present in other principal New Testament writers, though less expressed than in Paul.[16]

The New Testament theme of the corporate nature of Christ carries with it theological implications that were not explored at the time of the original writings, but whose consideration had soon to find a place on the agenda of Christian thinking. One of these issues is clearly expressed in the last quotation cited from Charlie Moule. In Christ the "individual category" is indeed seen to be transcended in a manner more consonant with divinity than with simple humanity. Some delicacy of discussion is required here. To make the point being considered it is not necessary to make the contrast too stark, as if one had to assert that human beings are just individual monads, wholly distinct and isolated from each other. In fact, I shall go on shortly to question such an atomized view of human nature, even though it is uncritically accepted in so much of Western society today. Rather, we should be prepared to acknowledge that there is a sense in which we are members of each other and that it is indeed the case that "no man is an island" (John Donne). Yet the degree of mutual association that this implies seems quite different from the New Testament understanding of the corporate character of Christ. Human incorporation into Christ is there portrayed as much more intensively constitutive of who we are intended to be, transcending all lesser distinctions of status, gender, or culture. "As many of you as were baptized into Christ have clothed yourselves with Christ. There is no longer Jew or Greek, there is no longer slave or free, there is no longer male and female; for all of you are one in Christ Jesus" (Gal. 3:27–28). Here the word "Christ" is not being used as a mere cipher for the commonplace groupings of social or religious life, but he is presented as the unique focus and location of a new form of human solidarity. Yet the one spoken of in these terms of potentially universal significance and consequence—and therefore, as Moule says, as one whose character is more than simply personal—is nevertheless also Jesus of Nazareth, a particular person who lived and died at a particular time and in a particular place. In this dialectical tension between the individual and the universal present in New Testament thinking about Jesus, we encounter experiential testimony that would eventually lead the church, after centuries of theological debate and struggle, to affirm the Chalcedonian understanding of the two natures of Christ. Justice could indeed not be done to what Christians had come to know of Jesus without employing about him both the language of humanity and the language of divinity.

An understanding of the corporate character of Christ also serves to cast some light on the soteriological issues that we considered earlier when seeking to understand the effectiveness of the work of Christ. It implies that human beings are not simply passive spectators of the drama of salvation, but they are intimate participants in it because of their intimate union with Jesus Christ, the true Savior. "If we have been united with him in a death like his, we will certainly be united with him in a resurrection like his. . . . If we have died with Christ, we believe that we will also live with him" (Rom. 6:5, 8). Subjectively, we are moved by the spectacle of Jesus' willing acceptance of death for our sake, not just because we have been told this as a touching story, but because, by incorporation, we have been made a part of that story. Objectively, Christ's victory over the powers of sin and death is also our victory precisely because we participate in him. The costly transaction of redemption, whatever its true character may be, is not an episode that took place somewhere else, but it is a salvific process in which we truly have our share. And conversely, if it were not true that Christians are part of the *totus Christus,* then the effectiveness of salvation would seem to be problematic, because it could then only be conceived in external formal terms and not in intimately internal terms.

Therefore, there is great theological coherence in understanding salvation in the relational terms that the New Testament encourages us to use by its emphasis on human solidarity in Christ. The corporate character of Christ is an essential element in christological thinking. When this story is told within the community of the church, it makes persuasive sense of many Christian convictions and experiences, not least those of the gathered worshiping community, united in the Eucharist with its risen Lord. But is it also persuasive when told outside the ecclesial enclave? Of course, the kind of detailed argument we have been attempting to explore must, if it is to have any fullness of content, make appeal to the testimony, given in the New Testament and by the church, to the story of Jesus and his first followers and to what is claimed to be the continuing illuminating presence and activity of the Holy Spirit. A stubborn refusal to countenance the possibility of this material having any authenticity is simply to have arbitrarily decided to settle the matter a priori. Yet one may also legitimately inquire whether there are not also any collateral considerations of a more general kind that might at least encourage taking seriously a claim that relationality should be a key concept in forming an adequate worldview, including a just estimate of the significance of Jesus Christ. If, on further consideration, it were to seem that an atomistic individualism ought really to be preferred, then theological exploration of the concept of the corporate Christ would have become distinctly problematic.

I do not think that the insights of tribal communities into a much greater degree of mutuality than is congenial to the Western mind are simply to be dismissed as primitive notions that we have rightly outgrown. Nor do I think that we should ignore the fact that at least some depth psychologists continue to explore the Jungian idea of a collective unconscious, a reservoir of powerful archetypal symbols to which all human beings have some degree of common access. But it is to modern science that I wish to turn for what I believe to be the most helpful source of encouraging support for the importance of relational ideas. One could write the history of physical science in the last two hundred years as being the tale of an unfolding discovery of the significance of relationality.

The first idea to be revised was that of a purely atomistic picture of the nature of the universe. The discovery of the importance of the field concept, made in the nineteenth century and enabled by the deep insights of Michael Faraday and James Clerk Maxwell, implied the demise of a simplistic Democritean picture of the world as composed of hard particles moving in the void. In the twentieth century, the quantum mechanical discovery of the duality of fields and particles further modified the picture. What we seem to encounter as individual electrons are in fact excitations in a single universal electron field, an insight that gives a corporate character to the physicists' thinking about corpuscles. The behavior of electrons is mutually constrained by the Pauli exclusion principle, decreeing that the presence of an electron in a state prohibits any other electron from occupying the same state. How an electron behaves depends upon how other electrons are behaving.

Newtonian physics had treated space as the container within which atoms moved around in the course of the inexorable unfolding of absolute universal time. Albert Einstein's great discoveries of special and general relativity produced an altogether more integrated and relational account, in which space, time, and matter are intimately interconnected in a single physical theory. Matter curves space-time, and the curvature of space-time bends the paths of matter—a delicate and beautiful synthesis involving mutual influence.

In 1935, Einstein, with two young collaborators Boris Podolosky and Nathan Rosen, showed that quantum theory implied that two quantum entities that had interacted with each other would thereafter be mutually entangled, so that any measurement made on one of them would have an immediate consequence for the other, however far away it might then have become. In a real sense the two entities now formed a single system.[17] Einstein himself thought that this result was so "spooky" that it must show that there was something incomplete in conventional quantum theory. He resolutely believed in strict physical separability and rejected the idea that there could be a counterintuitive nonlocality (a relation of "togetherness-in-separation") present in nature. Einstein supposed that a more complete theory would show that apparent entanglement was simply an artifact of incomplete knowledge. In fact, long after his death, beautifully precise experiments showed this supposition to be mistaken. There is indeed an intrinsic entanglement—a deep relationality—present in nature. Even the subatomic world, it has transpired, cannot properly be treated atomistically.

These profound and revisionary discoveries in physics have totally transformed our conception of the nature of the physical world. It is constituted by a subtle web of interconnections. Of course, in themselves these physical discoveries do not demonstrate that there must be an irreducible degree of relationality between human beings, and even less do they imply the truth of the theological concept of the corporate Christ. Yet there is a degree of consonance between these ideas, which means that one can say that the theological concept is not one that a scientist should find totally uncongenial, nor assert to be wholly inconceivable.

NOTES

1. Michael Polanyi, *Personal Knowledge: Towards a Post-Critical Philosophy* (Chicago: University of Chicago Press, 1958).
2. John C. Polkinghorne, *Quantum Physics and Theology: An Unexpected Kinship* (New Haven, Conn.: Yale University Press, 2007).
3. John C. Polkinghorne, *The Faith of a Physicist: Reflections of a Bottom-Up Thinker,* Theology and the Sciences (Minneapolis: Fortress, 1996), chap. 6; Polkinghorne, *The God of Hope and the End of the World* (New Haven, Conn.: Yale University Press, 2002), chap. 6. See also the essays in Ted Peters, Robert John Russell, and Michael Welker, eds., *Resurrection: Theological and Scientific Assessments* (Grand Rapids: Eerdmans, 2002).
4. Polkinghorne, *Faith of a Physicist,* chap. 7; Polkinghorne, *Belief in God in an Age of Science* (New Haven, Conn.: Yale University Press, 1998), chap. 2.
5. See John A. T. Robinson, *The Human Face of God* (London: SCM Press, 1972).
6. Gustav Aulén, *Christus Victor: An Historical Study of the Three Main Types of the Idea of the Atonement* (London: SPCK, 1931).
7. Robert Jensen, *Systematic Theology 2: The Works of God* (Oxford: Oxford University Press, 1999), 175.
8. C. F. D. Moule, *The Origin of Christology* (Cambridge: Cambridge University Press, 1977).
9. Ibid., 86–87.
10. Ibid., 54–63.
11. Ibid., 118–20.
12. Ibid., 69–89.
13. Ibid., 121–41.
14. See Polkinghorne, *Faith of a Physicist,* 98–100.
15. Moule, *Origin of Christology,* 95.
16. Ibid., 97–106.
17. See, for example, John C. Polkinghorne, *Quantum Theory: A Very Short Introduction* (Oxford: Oxford University Press, 2002), chap. 5.

PART III
WHOSE FLESH, WHOSE BLOOD?
Christology and the Politics
of Gender, Race, Age,
and Social Status

8

Forces of Love

The Christopoetics of Desire

CATHERINE KELLER

My distress is great and unknown to men. They are cruel to me, for they wish to dissuade me from all that the forces of Love urge me to. They do not understand it, and I cannot explain it to them. I must then live out what I am; What Love counsels my spirit, in this is my being: for this reason I will do my best.

—Hadewijch[1]

In the power of the Spirit this love, both experienced and given, experiences a powerful strengthening, because the fear of powerlessness and of the boundaries of one's own love and of others' love is taken away.

—Michael Welker[2]

RISKY LOVE

We begin with an already charged presumption—and perhaps in theology any presumption that is not innocuous comes charged by too many prior disputes: the alternative to the standard version of divine omnipotence is the power of love.[3] Omnipotence has classically signified that nothing happens without the will of God. That signification had implied a total control that may or may not be exercised in any instance, or that in the Calvinist extreme is eternally exercised as an all-determining providence. Hence the argument with Calvin's interpretation of God's care for the sparrow as an all-controlling determinism is crucial to the present presumption.[4] On jointly hermeneutical and constructive theological grounds I am insisting that the divinity revealed in Jesus as the

Christ, and precisely the power of that God, works not through control but through care. This intricate sparrow-by-sparrow, hair-by-hair care would be no less than the love that the Johannine epistle identifies by way of Christology as God. "Too sweet," some might say. How will the mere power of love, even of Love, resist the forces of destruction, empower the powerless, and embolden the meek? Love is too weak a force!

Not according to an intriguing Christian teacher from the early thirteenth century named Hadewijch, a leader and poet among the Beguines, the medieval movement of women who formed ascetic communities while refusing the veil, seclusion, and ecclesial supervision. "All that the forces of Love urge me to": What are these forces that do not force but urge and counsel—so strongly that this medieval mystic took great risks in relation to the church patriarchs of her age? What is this "counsel" in which she finds her "being," her sense of existence and self? "Love," the one counseling, translates the grammatically feminine term *Minne*, her favored name for God.[5] Whoever, she writes, "dares the wilderness of Love / Shall understand Love: / Her coming, her going." This Love shatters the Sunday school and Hallmark idols of a safe and sentimental love. It can seem elusive, withdrawn, even cruel at times, making us "stray in a wild desert." Hadewijch counsels an untamed courage: "*O soul, creature, And noble image, Risk the adventure!*"[6] This may be an unprecedented moment in theological anthropology: in the name of our humanity in *imago Dei*, we are empowered not to lord it over others but to "risk the adventure." In the name of our humanity in *imago Dei*, the same poem urges us to persist in this journey—"ever keep on to the end / In love." Only in Love do we actualize our potentiality as humans: only in the wilds of Love do we truly come to be.

Intriguingly, in none of her theopoetic writings does she oppose this Love to any other kind of love. She does not prosaically draw lines between the Love that is divine, indeed that is God, and the lower loves that urge, shake, and devastate us. It is Love itself somehow there calling to us in and through all of our loving; in and through all that hope, heartbreak, and high-risk vulnerability of human loves. To persist in Love is to learn that it can never be restricted to a relationship between two humans—though it may start and even dwell there. For Hadewijch this Love is truly God, truly Christ, and truly human. Yet she writes as a poet and not as a theologian; she does not offer dogmatic definitions. Anyone who has loved anyone passionately could be lured into her poetry. This or that belief is not presupposed. This is not a faith of formulae, of dogmatic shibboleths, but of adventurous becoming.

In this essay Christology may sneak up on us through such Love. If it does, it will happen with the help on the one hand of the systematic reasoning of process theology—a process that manages to remain an adventure; and on the other hand the theopoetics emitted not only by a mystic poet or two but by certain parables of Jesus.

IN CONTROL OR IN POWER?

If all of this talk of love and its attractions is a great analogy for God, it is also understood as the very medium of God—who *is* this Love. So the question still presses: what kind of "force" is love? Is it weak? Certainly love is weak as a doctrine of divine power—if the standard is control. In that case, one would have to admit that a tyrant's power is vastly greater than that of a loving partner or a caring parent. Is this the biblical standard? So then is love to be measured by power? Or is power to be measured by love? When it comes to the God standard, the answer is rather clear. The New Testament never says, "God is power." It does say, "God is love" (1 John 4:8). Therefore, the power we attribute to God must meet the standard of love—even the high standard of what we call "Christian love." Not vice versa. It is not that power needs love to balance it out, that the stern lordly power of divine domination is softened and complemented by the gospel of love. It would rather be that love is the power of God.

God in this view does not cause tsunamis with one hand and then tenderly comfort the survivors with the other. Contrary to the insurance companies, earthquakes and hurricanes are not "acts of God." They would be side effects of the complex self-organizing systems of the creation that God has—with great and risky adventurousness—lured forth. A God who is infinite, who is everywhere—even in Sheol—is also present in the tsunami. But being within is not the same as causing it. God's will cannot be read off the surface of events. The divine love-force can at one level be discerned in the continuing capacity of the earth—tectonic plates and all—to nurture life. At another, it can be discerned in the extraordinary postdisaster moments of human care for strangers. But such positive activities express at the same time the self-organizing complexity of the creaturely systems (contrary to the pious arbitrariness of crediting God just for the good and blaming nature or humans for the bad!). God is not hands-on or hands-off for a relational theology. In a relational theology we become God's hands.

What is the difference, then, in the way God is in destruction and in creation? Perhaps this: we can recognize in some events a positive response to the divine call. We recognize the atmosphere of love, justice, and mercy. This love is rarely sweetness and light. It may seem wild and risky—like the whirlwind spirit of Job. But it bears the marks of care. "Those who are beloved," writes Welker, "are to develop beyond their own conceptions." There may be great stress and pain in the growing. "Their surroundings are to be friendly and beneficial to them," adds Welker, riffing on Whitehead's reading of the "divine adventure" in a universe that we may embrace passionately as good, as "a friendly universe."[7] It invites creatures to the fullness of life. It is infinite in its intimacies: "the Love that moves the sun and all the other stars . . ." (Dante, *Divina Commedia, Paradiso*, XXXIII). If it does not, if you think this is just projection, if you just cannot feel any analogy to love outside of our own species, then you may prefer more purely naturalist explanations for the universe. They can be internally consistent and honest. But the resort to divine all-controlling force is not. How did a God of "power and might" get identified with "the God of Jesus Christ"? We should call him by his true names: Jupiter, or Wotan, or Fate.

Frankly it is easy to lose this rather delicate intuition: that love could have anything to do with the explosive, impersonal forces that form a universe, that drive its tempestuous evolution and effect all the reckless, unfathomable, irreversible losses of life—those losses that we cannot even blame on fellow humans. The sentimentality of Christian love, the Victorian Jesus of flowing auburn locks and moist eyes, seems to dissociate God from the wilderness patches, the *tohuvabohu* and *leviathan* of things. Hadewijch's love mysticism is alluring because it invokes that flooding, fiery force of nature that we can indeed link with erotic love. These "forces of Love" do not directly cause this or that disaster, or for that matter, this or that bit of good luck. She hints instead at a force that urges and counsels. This power of attraction will help us to articulate an alternative kind of force, one that does not send us back into the arms of an incredible omnipotence.

Let us get clear here then: of course love—as much as power—is an utterly and intensively human notion. Human notions, human finite images, concepts, analogies, metaphors, are what humans have. Some human notions are granted by their human communities the status of revelation: they are the especially inspired notions. The question is: what is the best possible, the most inspired and inspiring, human notion for living a better human life? For the community of Christian interpreters, love is understood (if somewhat begrudgingly) to provide the best analogy for the divine life. Love God with all your capacities—and your neighbor as yourself. This double love commandment emanates from what the followers of Jesus would call Love itself. Its counsel addresses human demeanor: we are the ones created, oh so creatively, in its image. It is our life for which we are first of all responsible. And therefore, because who we are is inextricably interdependent with the others who constitute our world, we are responsible for our relation to all the other beings. To love ourselves is to love the others. The ocean, the atmosphere, the earth, and all its populations included, we must now add. On the endangered planet of the third Christian millennium, in a peril almost inconceivable two millennia ago, except perhaps to the apocalyptic prophets, our rendition of Love can no longer ignore God's love of every creature.

In the Christian imaginary an amorous God invites us to our best possible response to the neighbor, to the fellow creature—regardless of whether those others will be able to give back. To love in the image of God is to stream like the sun and the rain (Matt. 5:45). This text advocates no domesticated virtue but an elemental adventure. It is to flow out into the unknown, the unpredictable, the unfriendly. Our love—our attentive care—for each other makes the life of the community, and now of the planetary community of all creatures, possible. So the analogy of Love makes it possible for us to relate to unknowable Mystery. Its infinite, impersonal creativity gets personal—in relation to persons. In spirit and in truth: we find ourselves in Love. The strange spatiality of the Spirit dis/closes itself here at a panentheistic pitch. Are we in Love? Or is Love in us—inviting, drawing, desiring?

Yet it would seem that for the most part we humans are more or less dead to the attraction, deaf to the invitation. The space dis/closure shuts down again. How well we know this closure, this loss of possibilities once briefly so very tangible, beginning to be actualized: the possibilities for intimacy between lovers, for joy within a family, for esteem between friends, for respect between competitors, for justice between peoples, for balance between species. It seems that we are often stirred beyond the greedier and needier stages of love—but rarely able to stay in love. We do not readily sustain the passion of love's larger challenge. No wonder. It always wants more from us—nothing less than the delicate, long-term work of reorganizing our worlds for more transnationally peaceful, more economically just, more sexually equitable, more ecologically sustainable becoming.

There remains, however, in the midst of the systemic socialized sin, the strange problem of the hardened heart. A numbness comes from too much habit, too much hardship, or, paradoxically, too much privilege. This heart may satisfy its craving for adventure through cruelty, perhaps even terror—in a movie or a war—to feel really alive. For these the good news is a bit of a yawn, unless perhaps it comes drenched in the bloody special effects of Mel Gibson's *The Passion of the Christ,* or the apocalyptic massacres of *Glorious Appearing.*[8] Among the more sensitive, the resistance is not hardness but to the contrary, fragility, a sense of woundedness that will not let us "risk the adventure." A systemic love blockage seems to beset the heart of our species. This causes us great suffering, inner turmoil, and dividedness—what in Korea is called *han.*[9] And we tend to pass that *han* on to others, as the violated tend to violate. We call this violence "sin," because it is never just between humans—as conversely, love is never just between us either. We even call it "original"—however tediously unoriginal are its stereotyped habits of violation, its loveless cycles of heterosexism, racism, greed. . . . The *han*/sin pattern begins to imprint us individually and collectively from the very origins of our lives, before we are conscious, before we are able to respond.

Nonetheless I am responsible for myself: "I must then live out what I am." Love, Hadewijch sings, never ceases to counsel "my spirit."[10] But she was a mystic of love, who threw her life into the God relation. In an ever more distracted, drugged, digitalized, overfed, and info-tainted culture, the amorous invitations may be lost on me.

We return to our nagging question, then: what kind of divine force is operative? What kind of power or efficacy does the divine have in the world? It is in attempting to answer this question with both honesty and faithfulness that the tradition of process theology becomes indispensable. It challenges a God concept that many Christians have confused with the biblical witness; it deconstructs, in other words, the classical tradition of an omnipotent, impassive God, an unmoved mover who causes suffering but does not suffer, who causes joy but does not enjoy.

PASSION AND COM/PASSION

Process theology speaks of two aspects of divine action in the world: the "creative love of God" and the "responsive love of God."[11] In a supplementary move, we might call this creative love "desire," or the divine "passion." Alfred North Whitehead, the philosopher of process, had much earlier called it "the Eros of the Universe." The divine eros is felt in each creature, according to process theology, as the "initial aim"—or sometimes, the "lure." The responsive love, by contrast, can be called "compassion," or the divine *agapē*. The eros attracts, it calls: it is the invitation. The *agapē* welcomes, responds: it is the reception. They are distinct gestures of divine relationality—yet their motions are in spirit inseparable, in constant oscillation.

Thus we will consider this dual love concept as a systematic alternative to omnipotence—an alternative I do not argue here on theological technicalities, but as the ground of a scriptural theopoetics of becoming. For neither the passion nor the compassion, neither the call nor the reception force us. In this essay, let us focus especially on the lure—the experience of a divine desire that, sweetly or dangerously, attracts us. Given the complementarity of these two divine motions, it is helpful to imagine them together, as the oscillation or juxtaposition of a single Love, from the start.

Let us then graph them onto a single moment of our becoming. For this is what is actual, what matters: this inter-becoming moment now. Its past and its future are ways that you collect yourself—in re-collecting past becomings and in anticipation of future ones. But for process theology the "actual entity" is key to the cosmos: the individual creature here/now, emerging out of the matrix of all creaturely relations.

Locate yourself as though in a guided meditation: you are feeling yourself here now, reading now within a ring of relations more or less chosen, edgy or warm, heavy with past, born in a dense collective of nature and nurture, turbulent with future anxieties and hopes, but still, here, now, feeling lungs opening, drawing breath, air shared by all the breathers near and far, breathing the same air as those near you, those whose feelings you sense, breathing together with all creatures, sealed in an ozone layer enveloping our rich atmosphere, swirling gracefully amid the choreography of the planets, turning amid the liturgy of the galaxies. . . . Here you are. The magnitudes of relation, the force fields of creation, shoot through this moment so tangibly that they can almost be felt connecting you to me. Imagine this moment as a wave of the bottomless waters of creation: a wave of the becoming that is at one and the same time my becoming myself and the collective emergence of our shared creaturely life.

That infinite depth is not the same as Love, or God. Yet the infinity, we have earlier imagined, is the depth of Godself, the creative womb of all that is: what is called traditionally the "father" or first person of the Trinity. That infinity enters into relations with the finite beings surfacing on the face of the deep: we creatures, called forth amid the swirling choreography of it All. Called forth, born—natured, nurtured, in our natality—at every moment. That call, that invitation, is the divine Eros: the amorous desire of God for life, and more life, life not for the sake of life alone but for the sake of ever more involvement, ever richer relationship.

That Love is revealed in and as the "second person" of the traditional Trinity, the Logos that seeks incarnation in the world. Not just once, but once-for-all, as the revelation of the divine desire "for all" creatures: the embodiment of God's eros in every wave of becoming. This is the love emitted from the "heart" of the universe, by which relationship itself takes place: in this Logos, this wisdom, this love. This is God-in-love: willing in the original sense of the word—wanting, desiring. It is what Whitehead called "God the poet of the world, with tender patience leading it" in a "vision of truth, beauty, and goodness."[12] These values are pure possibilities, only actualized in the creation. The possible is the content of the divine aim for the particular creature at a particular moment; thus God's desire calls in each of us, whether or not we share that desire as our own. In this sense the aim is like the ancient concept of prevenient grace. Amid the mess of our past stuff, God calls. Our mess becomes our potential. And we creatures come forth—in response. You this moment come forth, a wave freshly breaking on the face of the primal chaos of the deep, the *tehom* of Genesis 1:2.[13]

Here is the question, perhaps finally the only question that matters—though it can be paraphrased in endless ways: how do you materialize the possibility? Do you in some sense, consciously or not, actualize God's will? The call, the invitation, would not be a memo micromanaging our every move, dictating the next best action. We are called to improvise. We are invited to risk the adventure. For our adventure is inseparable from God's creativity: the unfolding world is not a preprogrammed drama predictable to God. How dreary that would be for the divinity. Yet neither are we quite on our own with these choices, these risks.

Like a wave cresting, turning, might you sense the wisdom for this moment? Do you begin, however minutely, to embody the love that is possible—in this moment, this time, this place? In the array of relations from which and toward which you are becoming, do you sense the magnetism of possibility? In your "heart's desire," is there a hint or echo of the larger life of the world? Perhaps this is the divine lure: that we "arise and come away" with the lover. In the mystical allegories this lover is also Love. We might meet her in any of her creaturely embodiments. For this it is to "do the will": to meet desire with a desire that combusts, that creatively enacts, that materializes in actions of care, of justice, of celebration.

How little this love atmosphere has to do with some grimly pious obedience. It is not a matter of following some top-down dictum, even of a good liberation or feminist or ecological variety. But if the scriptural symbols of command can move you, they too are available. The torah, the law, is not—as Welker has brilliantly argued—reducible to legalism or exclusivism, but the bearer of the "struggle for justice and mercy."[14] After all the law, the ethics of "should and should not" may also encode, if bluntly, the divine lure. But as Paul made clear, mere ethics will never motivate its own fulfillment. ("Love does no wrong to a neighbor; therefore, love is the fulfilling of the law" [Rom, 13:10].) Ethics becomes itself part of the love blockage, part of the *han*/sin pattern, when it stirs no spontaneous desire.

The initial aim from God cannot be identified with the demand of an abstract justice, nor with the voice of the vague moral stirrings amid the "moral markets." It signifies a call for this moment, here now, situated on the map of an ancient struggle. It is the way the all-pervading divine desire meets each individual becoming. It does not force; love does not, cannot, operate as a merely external cause. It invites always from a certain within—for God is already within us, before we quite exist. This "still, small voice" calls to our little margin of freedom—badly compromised by the habits of fear, greed, and dominance we call "sin," painfully constrained by the multitude of biological and social forces that limit our potential (1 Kgs. 19:12). Without strong, supportive structures of open-system community, society, liturgy, theology, the chances are minute that we can individually or collectively sense the initial aim: "the drawing of this Love and the voice of this calling."[15] For the interiority in which the lure is felt is not the inside of a bounded and autonomous subjectivity but of a social individual, emergent within the reciprocities of the open systems.

Every creature in a creature's own way is called. Persons personally, animals bestially, plants vegetably . . . Among persons, a tinge of consciousness of this lure is possible—a choice to grasp a fresh possibility, to actually actualize it. "For this reason I will do my best," wrote Hadewijch. Sometimes we do, to some extent, accept the invitation. It is not either/or, for the most part, but more or less. What then? Then we are received. This is what John B. Cobb Jr. and David Ray Griffin call "the responsive love of God."[16] This would be the divine hospitality: we are invited; we come as we are; and we are received, as we have become.

Yet the parable of the host's displeasure at those who come clad too casually for celebration should not be ignored.[17] To come "as we are" may not get us where we want to be. How we are probably needs a lot of work. The reception is not necessarily a happy homecoming. If this love is not coercive, it is nonetheless demanding—hence, perhaps, such a dark trope as "many are called, but few are chosen" (Matt. 22:14). The calling is pervasive—but only, it seems, some of us, some of the time can realize the call; most of us, most of the time, ignore it altogether—and so cannot be "chosen." Does this "chosenness" not seem to contradict the divine love? Certainly, if it means a cruel predestination of some for salvation, some for damnation (the Calvinist logic of omnipotence). But we may hear it very differently, and in less dissonance with the gospel of love: it realistically suggests that our habits of violation, of sin, are entrenched indeed, built right into the most normalized social conventions, economic bottom lines and political inevitabilities. They cramp our style of spirit. So despite God's prodigal welcome of the sinner, humans only occasionally accept the hospitality. That is, we can hardly receive our own reception. How many of us really want to be part of this banquet, full of strangers, aliens, outcasts, inferiors, and enemies? Few are chosen means, at the same time, few are choosing!

Remember, however, that in this model we are talking of something going on always, at the edge of every event of becoming, not just the end of a life or of time. Here is the heart of the co-creative process: the becoming/genesis of every creature from the ocean of potentiality, called by God's word, met by God's love. The love is a cosmic com/passion that will feel like judgment when we are out of sync with it. Creation and redemption are inseparable in this model, two moments of the same ongoing, open-ended process.

God's passion flows into us—and our response, responsible or not, is met by God's com/passion. And in these two gestures of the love that is God, there is intimate interaction, there is an empowerment of the creature to return and redistribute love. But there is no divine coercion. God takes us in in such a way that we become part of the divine experience, part of Godself. Here we might situate the third person of the traditional Trinity, for here we enter into the internal relatedness of God known as the Holy Spirit. We do not experience it in God but only as it "floods back again into the world" in the next moment.[18] This is the "pouring out of the Spirit." And we encounter that elemental flow embodied and preached in the most human of forms. Thus, Welker, interpreting the Suffering Servant motif of Isaiah 42:2, asks how the messianically promised righteousness of God can comprise any kind of "rule" at all. "The answer is that the bearer of the Spirit rules not by the use of force or by public relations strategies, but by powerlessness."[19] John Caputo, in a similar move, invokes "the weak force" as the only possible metaphor of a God of loving justice, "whose power is made perfect in weakness."[20]

This spirited powerlessness is precisely the loving means of empowerment; this holy weakness is what makes it possible—not inevitable—that we will find the strength to once again risk loving. And every time we do, the world alters just a bit for the good. For in our interconnectedness lie both our vulnerability and our power; we can exercise great influence by the butterfly effect of the "extreme sensitivity of initial conditions." For good or for ill. In love or out of it. I would rather not call it powerless or weak, even in the most acute christological moment of the cross: even there, great influence is being exercised. It is rather the power that is indistinguishable from love. The power of love is not a choice of self-sacrifice but an embrace of the risk of love—even at the cost of self-sacrifice.

To the extent that we are able, amid the turbulent waters of our churning lives, to accept our acceptance, to embrace the embrace, to coalesce with the complex potentialities of creation of which we are a part—to that extent we experience a certain satisfaction. It may allow a greater risk, a wider vulnerability, a more adventurous love, in the subsequent moments. The pouring out of the spirit, the in-spiration—consolation or judgment, depending on our relation to it—is not a disembodied ecstasy but the movement of life itself. Nicholas of Cusa, a fourteenth-century philosophical mystic, called the Holy Spirit "the infinite connection," in which all finite life unfolds. It reconnects us to our own process of becoming, inseparable from all becoming.

Out of the womb of the depths arises a passion for creation, calling forth creatures in love. And in their wild, limited freedom they respond one way or another. And like waves having crested, "return into the sea," which feels them as a trembling, a pulse, a bar of music; only to surge forward more or less differently in the next moment.[21] This rhythm, this pulsation, echoes in every beginning—in every struggle both for life against the evolutionary odds and, then, for just, sustainable, and joyful life against the human odds. Amid the whirlwinds of our conditions, there breathes a word of love. Divine love in the biblical tradition is not a Christian invention: dozens of psalms address "your steadfast love." In the Gospels we see Jesus citing the dual love commandment (Deut. 6:5; Lev. 19:18) as his hermeneutical key to the tradition, and after his death love is inscribed as the very incarnation of God and thus as the most apt characterization of what God is. In the foregoing triune account of passion and compassion connected and poured out in the spirit of love, I have suggested a model that we are invited to embody, to materialize, in all that matters.

THE MATTER OF JESUS

We are now at the heart of Christology, though (for Christ's sake) I am not waving the banner of Christ. Nothing has kept me a Christian more than my conviction that a horrified Jesus would demand to be liberated from the "Jesus Christ" shibboleths that control passage into so much of Christendom. The Jewish Jesus I encounter in the Gospels would never abide the fixation upon his person—in almost pure defiance of his message and mission for and to "the least of these." Nor would he stomach the worship of himself rather than the God to whom he prayed as Abba. At least for the historical Nazarene glimpsed in the first three Gospels, this would be an intolerable idolatry: "Get behind me, Satan" (Matt. 16:23; Mark 8:33). Imagine how this radical Jewish monotheist would feel about the Christian use of "Christ" to make him into God—or indeed into the only son of God. Even in the higher Christology of the fourth Gospel, Jesus' messianic leadership intends for others to become sons and daughters of God. His power, like that of the God he embodies, is not about control but empowerment: to his followers ". . . he gave power to become children of God" (John 1:12). A truly christocentric theology will decenter Christology so that we may again catch glimpses of what Jesus embodied and taught, hints and flashes for us to embody now. It will become *christopoetics*.

He offered his words and his deeds not to display himself as God, but to share his relationship to God. That relationship was so intimate that—in spirit—he experienced himself as child of God, as inseparable from God, perhaps in some sense even as embodying God. As process theology puts it, Jesus so fully identified with the divine aim that he was "at one" with it.[22] In this sense, he was one with God: with the creative love of God that Christians call "Christ." And so we say Jesus *is* the Christ, the Messiah: a witness and a truth that loses its dis/closive power amid all the glib "Jesus Christ" talk, all the closures of truth. This fusion of Jesus/Christ/God—where Jesus is good old Mr. Christ—is a theological confusion. The relational inseparability of Jesus as the Christ from God too early was turned into a Hellenistic kind of metaphysical identity. Indeed it is around the identity of "the Son" with "the Father" that the Hellenistic substance metaphysics took over rather confusingly. Substance, or essence, *"ousia,"* was defined by its independence and separation from other substances. Because the substances of Jesus and of God somehow were felt to fuse into one essence, this ousiology simply led to rather unedifying paradoxes—like the proposition that Jesus was made of two substances, human and divine, with one will; or that the Trinity was three substances that were nonetheless one. Jesus and his earlier followers, the Gospels indicate, did not think ousiologically, but relationally.

If the divine invitation to each becoming can be called the Logos, it is confessed by Christians to be Christ, the Logos as incarnate. This is the cosmic logos by which the universe is brought forth in every beginning. Classical Christianity developed a strong panentheistic account of God's presence in all things, and all present in God's logos.[23] John of Damascus, for example, offers a radically widened sense of the incarnation: reflecting on the God who "accepted to dwell in matter and through matter worked my salvation," he announces that he therefore will "reverence the rest of matter and hold in respect that through which my salvation came, because it is filled with divine energy and grace."[24] The logos incarnate in the life of Jesus seeks materialization in all becoming creatures: nothing comes to be without it.

The divine energy and grace permeate all bodies. But the bodily Jesus, we say, was distinctively the incarnation of this Love that he taught. The point of the early New Testament symbols is precisely not that his own body was exclusively this incarnation. How else shall we take seriously the metaphor of "the body of Christ"? If we think of the Johannine logos together with the Corinthian metaphor, we can only infer that the becoming-flesh of the logos in Jesus as the Christ meant the growth and inclusion of as many as possible in this very "body."[25] Concretely this interdependent embodiment—I want to call it an "inter-carnation"—emerged in the structural forms of the church, a new sort of institution in the ancient world. But even in the complex and open-ended struggles of its visible and invisible forms, the church can never encompass or exhaust the amorous dynamism at work in the world.

We have been suggesting a christic element, called by many names, invoking different facets of our God-relation: Logos, Word, Wisdom, Sophia. It calls every becoming toward its fullest actualization. Jesus embodies this Christ with unique fullness; in this sense he *is* this Christ. By an extension of the incarnational logic we can say that Christ is *in us*. And by this we mean that God is in us in a Christlike way. Symeon the New Theologian captured this in an exquisite poem over a thousand years old:

I move my hand, and wonderfully
My hand becomes Christ, becomes all of Him
(for God is indivisibly
whole, seamless in His Godhood).

I move my foot, and at once
He appears like a flash of lightning.
Do my words seem blasphemous?—then
Open your heart to Him.[26]

But this is not an ousiological transmutation, nor a miraculous exception—
but a transfiguration of and within the ordinary world: where we learn to move
our hands and feet in love. This opening of the heart, if we can ever release it
from centuries of sabotage by sentimentality, means precisely the dis/closure of
love at the heart of things, the unlocking of its gift and of its possibility.

Of course our attempts, creative as they may be, come into constant tension
with the formative patterns, the sin/*han* complex, of our past. Cobb and Griffin
put this relation very precisely: "There is a tension between oneself and one's
experience of what ideally would be, between what one is and the rightness in
things that one dimly discerns. Hence the divine presence is experienced as an
other, sometimes recognized as gracious, often felt as judge."[27] In the story of
Jesus, however, another relationship comes to light. He does not seem to have
felt the divine as over and against him. Instead, in the language of process theology, "His selfhood seems to be constituted as much by the divine agency within
him as by his own personal past. . . . Whereas Christ is incarnate in everyone,
Jesus is Christ because the incarnation is constitutive of his very selfhood."[28]
Cobb and Griffin note that the affinity of this view with the Chalcedonian creed
does "not prove its truth," but such affinity does enhance its interest. Thus process theology retains continuity with the classical creedal tradition without slav-
ishly replicating its nonbiblical background.

Finding such an alternative to the Greco-Roman metaphysics of change-
less, bounded substances helps us set the historical Jesus back into his earthly
context, his materiality. Otherwise how shall he matter? His significance as
"Christ," as "Messiah," may then be freed from the metaphysical ether, liberated to work for justice and mercy on the earth, indeed now also for the earth.
Thus we may also avoid the great Christian temptation of Christolatry. This
temptation, akin to what the fathers called the heresy of Docetism (that Jesus
only appears to be human and fleshly), besets every form and phase of Christianity. When the symbol "Christ" becomes little more than a synonym for God
it loses its particular messianic history and meaning. Sliding with dogmatically greased speed from the whole incarnate pre-Easter life to the post-Easter
Christ, we collapse the Gospel narrative into a mere cruciform transition into
resurrection.[29]

How continually do the actual life and message of Jesus get eclipsed by the
Christ of faith? This conventional eclipse is summarized in the creed, which—

amazingly!—skips right over the entire life, activity and teaching of Jesus: "He was . . . born of the Virgin Mary . . . was crucified, died. . . ." This summation focuses on the beginning and end of the life: the parts with which Jesus had the absolute least involvement! It is like preferring a frame to the portrait within it (of course, frames can be valuable works themselves). Thus, the church displayed its preference for origins and endings rather than life itself—rather than for the actual relationships of teaching, healing, care, and prayer modeled in the life of the pre-Easter Jesus.[30] The pre-Easter life is reduced to nothing but disempowered moments of birth and death, thus effectively eliminating the whole agency and point of Jesus' life. Thus abstracted from that life, bursting with his demanding love force, the cross and the resurrection shrink into shibboleths of absolutism rather than events of transforming relationship. The truth space closes down around the very sites of its narrative dis/closure.

"Well," one might say, "creeds had to compress." Indeed, and every compression is an abstraction and interpretation. Nothing wrong with either, as long as they are acknowledged as such. This theology, as an exercise in biblical hermeneutics, returns (in its own abstractions and interpretations) to another form of compression, a form preferred by Jesus himself: that of the parables. The parables of Jesus, more than lordly lordship talk about Jesus, structure the rest of this essay's christopoetics of desire.

IN JOY

Consider that the kingdom of heaven is like a person who finds a treasure in a field, and in joy goes and sells everything he has, to buy that field. . . .

What is this "kingdom," this *basileia*? "Kingdom" suggests the social field organized around a dominant power—that of a *basileus,* a king or emperor, the primary form of governance in the ancient world. Yet this parable—and most of the parables—seem to empty out every expectation of a kinglike intervention. What kind of power operates in the parable? The parable deliberately scuttles any simplistic "God did this" sort of logic. The very form of the parable, and the locution of the *basileia tou theou,* or *ton ouranon,* of the kingdom of God or of heaven, deflects interest from a divine Person or substance. It shifts focus to the metaphoric field, a space in which truth might take place. Let us consider the *basileia* not as a metaphor of hierarchical force, but rather as a force field of relations: the matrix of what Hadewijch calls the "forces of love."

If there is a power operating, would it not be precisely the power of desire? Not a casual fleeting desire, but what the mystics call "the heart's desire," the desire for the treasure. Not the kind that is good for buying other things, but rather the thing most treasured. The reality for which we are willing to give everything—not out of a grim spirit of self-denial, not as a self-sacrifice, but, as the parable says, "in joy." Let *joy* be your guide. Discern what you really want—and go for it!

Really? This joy is tougher than it seems. First of all, we may not know what we really want. And then if we do, we have choices to make, and they hurt. For example, the parable says to me: give up what you can give up in order to find enough time to write. In writing I find treasure. But it is a costly joy. It means giving up activities that I enjoy, which nurture my institution, my friendships, my spouse, my family. I don't take it to mean give up the things I have to do (since I have to do them). It does mean give up things that I don't really have to do—and that I don't really want to do. Hard choices—and not usually either/or once-for-all choices—but negotiations along a way of risk and adventure.

This "joy"—whose is it precisely? How do I tell the difference between my desire and the divine desire? Not readily! The *basileia* is not any established community, yet it demands our deepest and widest communing; it is not already realized, and yet it calls us to realize it now, here, together. It is never identifiable with an institution, and yet it draws us into rich and difficult relations of structural, social involvement. It comprises a complex interplay of relations, requiring an endless process of discernment. John Cobb translates the *basileia* as "the commonwealth of God," not only to lose the patriarchal and monarchical metaphor but also to emphasize its concrete political and economic potentiality, its messianic claim upon our collective future.

The dis/closive space of the spirit becomes actual as the *basileia*. And what is this *basileia* if not the hospitable space of Godself—the responsive love of God? The space that opens if we open into it? The *basileia* is always becoming: the not-yet and the already, within you and among us: a between time, a between space of becoming. The *basileia* is the Christic structure of becoming, the force field in which the "body of Christ" can heal, thrive, and reach beyond itself.

So then God's desire for this event—this immediate moment of your becoming—involves you in the sociality of interrelated becomings making up the ongoing creation. But God's will for the occasion expresses itself through attraction.

INVISIBLE ATTRACTIONS

"How does this unforcing force work?" we have been asking. By sparking your desire: desire ignites desire. Of course, our own desires are larded with every manner of addictive need and violative greed. This sparking process takes place largely beneath and before our consciousness. Sometimes glimpsed in a dream, in a stranger's face, in a flow of grief, a surge of music, a private illumination, a public act of truth, a movement for the earth. It is what we hope for in prayer, meditation, worship. We infer it—and can make no certain claims about it: "God told me this or that; God wills this or that for me." Anything so conscious would be already coated in our own subjectivity, in the aims of our own socialized desire.

For this reason a theology of relation returns always to the event and the flow of truth, to the mysterious Johannine spatiality of "in spirit and in truth," resisting absolute forms as much as dissolute formlessness. If the lure is the "initial aim from God," it becomes—before consciousness—the "subjective aim" of each individual moment. That is technical process language. But it helps us to unpack the power, the risk, and the joy disclosed in the parable. And this energy of discovery, of dis/closure, in turn helps transmute the paradigm of the omnipotent into the omni-amorous.

If God's creative love of the world works as a call, not as a coercion, it offers an invitation rather than a compulsion. Grace is attractive—but not irresistible. Or in Wesleyan terms, the initial aim is the "initiating grace." It seeks our free response. Wesley also knew that grace is indispensable to salvation—but likewise resistible: thus, "God does not continue to act upon the soul unless the soul re-acts upon God."[31] For grace, which for him is precisely Love, indistinguishable from the work of the Spirit in Christ, is not a power over us, but an empowerment of us: "We can do all things in the light and power of that love, through Christ which strengtheneth us."[32] We begin to sense—as we get free of the projection of a dominator-God—a divine desire for a thriving, adventurous, beautiful world. For God also and everywhere inhabits the matter of the world.

The question is always: what do we do with this lure? What do we make of it? It is like a magnetic force of possibility, drawing upon the multiple fibers of all that makes us up. It is not just an abstract possibility from above, presented for my actualization: "Here, do this"—a "Father knows best" who can reappear even in noncoercive process guise. Rather it is the possibility for something surprising. For the event of newness itself, of renewal: "Let us sing a new song."[33] "Behold, I do a new thing!"[34] The Hebrews had a genius for novelty, thus for history as the scene of the new, the irreversible, the "acts of God." But we can, in relation to the divine desire manifest in the Christ and in the doctrine of the creation, lose our sense of the new. Or we can absolutize that novelty. Biblically, however, the new comes not *ex nihilo*—out of nothing. It offers rather the newness of what I have elsewhere called *creatio ex profundis*: genesis from the relational complexity, the bottomless and irreducible past influence, the fluency of the very waters of creation, in our con/fusing historical lives. The suffering we inflict on each other in our aborted loving is inversely proportional to the mutual vulnerability of our fluid, interdependent becomings. In process thought, you and I are comprised not of skin-encapsulated subjectivities, not of atoms or of substances, nor of any fixed natures, sexual or otherwise. We are events of relationship, members of multiple incomplete collectives, human and nonhuman. All of the relations in which I come to be are at once both repeating themselves and shifting constantly, sometimes subtly, sometimes dramatically. No wonder it is hard to collect ourselves!

Wesley also recognized that faith does not subsist in a one-to-one intimacy with God: "By strong though invisible attractions, [God] draws some souls through their intercourse with others. The sympathies formed by grace far surpass those formed by nature."[35] The multiple attractions that lure us toward one another may be manifestations of the divine lure. By sympathies that are formed by grace rather than nature, Wesley is indicating the loves that exceed familial givens, the intimacies in which we experience spiritual growth. These

sym-pathies—pathos-with, fellow feeling—connect us into new patterns of relation, new collectives of grace.

The lure is a wisdom available to the creature, a word uttered in every beginning. The logos is not given in dictation but in invitation: to collect ourselves.
To re-collect the love in our lives. To re-member the one in whose body we are
members one of another. Thus, for instance, the Eucharist—if it takes place in
spirit and not merely in form—tunes us to the lure from God that tunes us back
to our relationships. We become differently embodied in this shared body, in
this event of inter-carnation, so then we might also feel our interdependence as
creatures of a carefully woven creation. We might have a Shug-like sense that "if
I cut the tree, my arm will bleed."[36] On the same principle, Jesus has inserted
himself in the Christian collective thus: "Just as you did it to one of the least
of these . . . you did it to me"; "I am the vine, you are the branches. . . ."[37] In
the dense sense of relatedness that Scripture brings to bear upon our flighty
spirits, creative newness is not disconnection, but new connection. Its transcendence is not a lone spirit soaring free of the creation and its limited, chaotic
creatureliness, but a flow of spirit within and through the open-ended creation.
Transcendence is the transformation inherent in the process of creative interrela-
tion. God calls in and through our most intimate and our most planetary contexts, luring us to liberation from what deadens, violates, or exploits any of us.

In the parables, the divine lure is not a unilateral donation, let alone an
omnipotent determination. It works at once from without and within, planted,
seeded, buried, and discovered—precisely a newness dis/closing what is, what I
am—as a becoming-other. Not the same old self, and so not the same "within."
Something in the field of my experience comes to light—and everything looks
different. All the relationships composing our memory, body, family, community, ecology, and world form the material, largely unconscious, of our
becoming. These relationships can close in on us, close us down, suffocating
that possibility, that talent, that promise. As Hadewijch hints, they routinely
try "to dissuade me [f]rom all that the forces of Love urge me to." For my own
good—for the countercultural counsels of this Love may expose me, or indeed
my community, to risk, to turbulence, to breakups and breakouts. Yet these
relationships also constitute the material through which spirit matters. Only in
and through these relations can I "live out what I am"—even in resistance to
structures that have formed and deformed relationship itself. The lure of God,
like a mustard seed, plants the possible—which can, if accepted and nurtured,
grow into a hospitable, communal actualization. For this flash or twist of the
new: this is the incalculable, not to be extrapolated from all those relations that
flow into who I have become.

In this grace we are accepted if we accept the grace. "'The kingdom of heaven
is like yeast that a woman took and mixed in with three measures of flour until
all of it was leavened'" (Matt. 13:33). It leavens us as we knead it through our
lives. Where is omnipotence here, in these parables, the favored form of Jesus'
teaching? This yeast again suggests the utter subtlety of the lure. How homey

is the image—and transgressive for his hearers. Yeast was understood to be profane, however commonly used it was outside of Passover with its great symbol of unleavened bread. Jesus is a bit of a trickster in his choice of metaphors, an ironist, ever working from the down under, from the chaotic ground. Doubly transgressive: if there is a God figure, it is a woman: the bakerwoman God.[38] But the parables do not identify any figure, except by uncertain analogy, with God. The parables of Jesus capture an elliptical glimpse of the *basileia*. The *basileic* becoming is never just an event already or in the future, never a smooth, linear process, never just private, never just political. It is a body of relationships that takes off, grows, expands exponentially from some small and unlikely beginnings.

The lure of the possible must be actualized, the yeast mixed through, or life stays flat. The desire sparks desire—or in Wesley's language we return God's love with our love—or nothing rises. That actualization, in process theology, is not something that God controls: the power that the parables so elliptically depict is itself elliptical—weak, indeed powerless, if compared to the phantasmagoria of omnipotence. But it is anything but impotent. It is another kind of power, a force like love, an inhuman love force. God does not do it to us but empowers us to do. So it is also nothing that we as autonomous subjects accomplish. We become in that actualization—as a member of open networks of relations. The mix of the yeast through all that flour is like the working of the lure upon the gritty pile of our stuff: our histories, capacities, contexts. We come to be—in this moment, afresh—only through that "mixing." Each of us is a complex mix indeed. I am not a mere unit in a collective, a grain of ground flour. Something new comes to be, in this impure mixing, this struggling, kneading, at once subtle and powerful leavening process: a becoming subject, the subject of a *basileic* becoming. In its becoming, we become not containers, pots, or pieces, but rather a rising body of life.

In a discussion of the parable of the bakerwoman last week with a favorite adult education forum, Margaret pronounced: "The leavening is the enlivening!"[39] Does this mysterious life, in its kneading and struggling, its fermenting, fecundating, and ultimately uplifting fullness, hint at a very present possibility? One cannot in truth separate between the divine input and the human response, the lover and the beloved, between the possible and its delicate first actualization. The dividing line between the wild love that is God and the love by which we love that love is forever blurred in Christ; it lies before and beyond our consciousness. But if a divine desire seeds our ground and leavens our lump, why not risk the adventure?

NOTES

1. Paul Mommaers, *Hadewijch: The Complete Works* (Mahwah, N.J.: Paulist, 1980), 185.
2. Michael Welker, *God the Spirit,* trans. John Hoffmeyer (Minneapolis: Fortress, 1994), 226.

3. Another form of this essay appeared as a chapter in Catherine Keller, *On the Mystery: Theology as Process* (Minneapolis: Fortress, 2007), a text for seminary students and pastors.

4. "Are not two sparrows sold for a penny? Yet not one of them will fall to the ground apart from your Father. And even the hairs of your head are all counted. So do not be afraid; you are of more value than many sparrows" (Matt. 10:29–31); and "Are not five sparrows sold for two pennies? Yet not one of them is forgotten in God's sight. But even the hairs of your head are all counted. Do not be afraid; you are of more value than many sparrows" (Luke 12:6–7). My argument is that Luke should be used to interpret the ambiguity of Mark, such that "apart from your Father" does not mean apart from "his will" but apart from his knowing, his remembering.

5. Hadewijch, a Flemish Beguine of the thirteenth century, is arguably the most important exponent of the love mysticism that sprang up during the second half of the twelfth century, in the area roughly corresponding to present-day Belgium. It is a preeminently female phenomenon. As the term "love" (*minne*) suggests, it envisions that "union with God is lived here on earth as a love relationship: God lets himself be experinced as Love (*Minne*) by the person who goes out to meet him with love (*minne*)" (Mommaers, *Hadewijch*, xiii).

6. Welker, *God the Spirit*, 231.

7. Ibid., 226.

8. Mel Gibson's *The Passion of the Christ*, from New Market Films, Icon Distribution, Inc., released in 2004. *Glorious Appearing: The End of Days* is the twelfth book in the Left Behind series, Tim La Haye and Jerry B. Jenkins (Wheaton, Ill.: Tyndale House, 2004).

9. Andrew Sang Park, *The Wounded Heart of God: The Asian Concept of Han and the Christian Doctrine of Sin* (Nashville: Abingdon, 1993).

10. Mommaers, *Hadewijch*, 185.

11. John B. Cobb Jr. and David Ray Griffin, *Process Theology: An Introductory Exposition* (Louisville, Ky.: Westminster John Knox, 1996).

12. Alfred North Whitehead, *Process and Reality* (New York: Free Press, 1978), 346.

13. A prior chapter in *On the Mystery* elaborates a theology of creation from the *tehom*, the "deep" or primal waters of chaos in Gen. 1:2, in a reprise of my *Face of the Deep: A Theology of Becoming* (London: Routledge, 2004).

14. Welker, *God the Spirit*, 124.

15. T. S. Eliot, "Little Gidding," *Four Quartets*.

16. See Cobb and Griffin, *Process Theology* (chap. 3).

17. "'But when the king came in to see the guests, he noticed a man there who was not wearing a wedding robe, and he said to him, "Friend, how did you get in here without a wedding robe?" And he was speechless. Then the king said to the attendant, "Bind him hand and foot, and throw him into the outer darkness, where there will be weeping and gnashing of teeth." For many are called, but few are chosen'" (Matt. 22:11–14).

18. Whitehead, *Process and Reality*, 351.

19. Welker, *God the Spirit*, 128.

20. John D. Caputo, *The Weakness of God: A Theology of the Event* (Bloomington: Indiana University Press, 2006).

21. I'm thinking of a trope important to John Wesley: "The sea is an excellent figure of the fullness of God, and that of the blessed Spirit. For as the rivers all return into the sea, so the bodies, the souls, and the good works of the righteous return into God, to live there in [God's] eternal repose," in "A Plain

Account of Christian Perfection." Cf. my "Salvation Flows: Eschatology for a Feminist Wesleyanism," *Quarterly Review* 23, no. 4 (2003): 412–24.

22. See Cobb and Griffin, *Process Theology*.

23. Athanasius: "Rather, but thing most marvelous, Word as he was, so far from being contained by anything, he rather contained all things himself; and just as while present in the whole of creation, he is at once distinct in being from the universe, and present in all things by his own power . . ." (Athanasius, *Christology of the Later Fathers*, Library of Christian Classics 3, ed. E. R. Hardy [Philadelphia: Westminster, 1954], 71).

24. John of Damascus, *Three Treatises on the Divine Images*, trans. Andrew Louth (Crestwood, N.Y.: St. Vladimir's Seminary Press, 2003), 29.

25. 1 Cor. 12:1–31.

26. Symeon the New Theologian, in *The Enlightened Heart: An Anthology of Sacred Poetry*, ed. and trans. Stephen Mitchell (New York: Harper, 1989), 38.

27. See Cobb and Griffin, *Process Theology*.

28. Ibid., 105.

29. For an accessible account of the tension of the pre- and post-Easter perspectives, see Marcus J. Borg, *Meeting Jesus Again for the First Time: The Historical Jesus and the Heart of Contemporary Faith* (San Francisco: HarperSanFrancisco, 1995), especially 80–99.

30. Kelly Brown Douglas, *The Black Christ* (Maryknoll, N.Y.: Orbis, 1994), who shows how this loss of the historical Jesus has devastating implications for race relations.

31. "Farther Appeal to Men of Reason and Religion," Part I, §I.3, in *The Works of John Wesley*, vol. 11, *The Appeals to Men of Reason and Religion and Certain Related Open Letters*, ed. Albert C. Outler (Nashville: Abingdon, 1986), 11:106; and Sermon 91, "On Charity," §III.12, *Works*, vol. 3, Sermons III, 71–114 (Nashville: Abingdon, 1986), 3:306.

32. John B. Cobb Jr., *Grace and Responsibility: A Wesleyan Theology for Today* (Nashville: Abingdon, 1995), 43.

33. "Praise the LORD with the lyre; make melody to him with the harp of ten strings. Sing to him a new song . . ." (Ps. 33:2–3); "O sing to the LORD a new song; sing to the LORD, all the earth" (Ps. 96:1); "O sing to the LORD a new song, for he has done marvelous things . . ." (Ps. 98:1).

34. "I am about to do a new thing; now it springs forth, do you not perceive it? I will make a way in the wilderness and rivers in the desert" (Isa. 43:19).

35. Cobb, *Grace and Responsibility*, 437.

36. Alice Walker, *The Color Purple* (New York: Harcourt, 1992).

37. See Matt. 25:40 and John 15:5, respectively.

38. Elisabeth Schüssler Fiorenza, "Bakerwoman God," in *Bread Not Stone: The Challenge of Feminist Biblical Interpretation* (Boston: Beacon, 1995).

39. Margaret Calloway's enlightening and en-leavened response emerged in conversation at the UMC Demarest under the leadership of Rev. Stu Dangler.

9

"But you, who do you say I am?"

A Homily on Ideological Faith from the Gospel of Mark

PIET J. NAUDÉ

MICHAEL WELKER AS BIBLICAL THEOLOGIAN

The growing oeuvre of systematic theologian Michael Welker accomplishes—among other things—restoring the intrinsic link between systematic theology and biblical scholarship. He understands his own work among the new approaches toward a biblical theology that have developed in interdisciplinary and interconfessional collaboration since the 1980s in Germany and North America,[1] and he has restated classical debates about authority of Scripture in terms of the differentiated "weight" of Scripture.[2]

The actual value of Welker's contribution is that he does not spend all his energy on a methodological defense of a new systematic program of biblical theology. His reflections on the task of biblical theology today[3] are accompanied and demonstrated by engaging in creative exegetical work, reflecting his enormous skill in this area and his fundamental respect for the plurality of voices embedded in the variety of biblical traditions in both Testaments. Without listing all these publications, Welker's works on creation, Holy Communion, resurrection, eschatology, and pneumatology are all testimonies to a systematic theology fundamentally shaped by Scripture, interdisciplinary debate, and ecumenical orientation.

Why does he choose such a biblical-theological approach? The reasons are varied and in themselves complex. To highly simplify, one could reconstruct three concomitant motifs behind Welker's biblical theology, or what he calls a "Reforming orientation."[4]

The first, external motif is the crisis of the Word that has lost its formative power to shape events in the world (from political conflicts to ecology) in the face of the powerful mass media and the lure of scientific/technological achievements.[5] The second, internal motif is to restore the orienting power of key theological concepts and biblical terms to overcome their dulling due to "multiple accommodations to prevailing habits of thought."[6] The third motif relates to the urge behind Welker's work to establish a credible link between creative biblical and theological exposition on the one hand, and the structured pluralism of reality on the other. Search for the knowledge of God must show that it is worth it, and has "positive repercussions for self-knowledge and for orientation in the world."[7] This explains Welker's insistence on a biblical-realistic theology that must be constantly submitted to the test of interdisciplinary work and ecumenical openness.[8]

In the spirit of this specific focus, and in line with the christological theme of this volume, a contextual reading of the Markan Gospel is offered below. Welker himself states that "God's word" encounters us in threefold form: as revelation, as Scripture, and as proclamation. Written by a systematic theologian, ethicist, and preacher, the proclamation or homily below does not meet all the demands of technical New Testament exegesis, nor reflect the status of current scholarship on Mark. It is sincerely hoped, though, that what follows reflects the kind of theology so eminently displayed by Michael Welker himself, while at the same time introducing contextual creativity from a South African perspective.[9]

SEEKING THE GROUNDS OF AN IDEOLOGICAL FAITH

One perennial question faced those of us who were born under apartheid and later studied theology during the time that South Africa struggled to liberate herself from her past: How was it possible not only to give Christian legitimacy to an inhuman, racist system, but also to actually co-design such a system with a direct and pious appeal to God and the Scriptures?

Many books and articles were written to analyze the ideologizing of the gospel by white Reformed churches. It slowly emerged that what was at stake was a deadly combination of nationalistic power and an enabling religious hermeneutics, resulting in an Afrikaner civil religion.[10] The rise of Afrikaners after the defeat in the Anglo-Boer War (1899–1902) and formation of the Union of South Africa (1910) was the engine that fueled a fervent nationalism that upheld itself with strong in-group (Afrikaners) and out-group (English, blacks, and communists) boundaries. Coupled with this was the appropriation of Scripture by some who identified Afrikaners as God's people,[11] with a mission in Africa, based on a differentiated pluralism assuming that God, from creation, assigned to each people (*Volk*) its own land and development potential.

It is possible—and has been done—to show the complex pro- and counter-theological currents in the years between 1935 and 1990. The roots of an apartheid theology lie in an interesting combination of neo-Calvinist Kuyperianism, the missiological thought of Gustav Warneck, and Scottish Pietism and German Romanticism, combined with a naive hermeneutics that shielded itself from critical scholarship.[12] The countercurrents were *inter alia* inspired by Barth's critique of religion,[13] Bonhoeffer's notion of a confessing church,[14] historical-critical exegesis,[15] and the rise of a critically minded, indigenous, black Reformed theology[16] that presented a credible alternative to what was accepted as "Reformed" at that stage.

We knew that all these intricate and important analyses were crucial to a theological interpretation of the situation, but this was not enough. What was needed was to use these theological insights to preach differently. Proclamation is the form of God's word that reaches ordinary people—black and white. You do not try to win a political or moral argument. You just allow the Word to take its course, believing that that Word will not return empty, but in fact will "succeed in the thing for which I sent it" (Isa. 55:10–11).

What follows is one such example. It is reconstructed from a real sermon, but expanded with some theological comments, and adapted to speak beyond one situation only.

"BUT YOU, WHO DO YOU SAY I AM?" A READING OF MARK[17]

It has been argued by both narrative and structural analyses that Mark 8:27–30 (the confession of Peter) is a turning point in the Gospel narrative. This passage is the "hinge" of the Gospel story that tells of Jesus' ministry up to that point (the road to Caesarea Philippi), and then recounts his journey to the cross (the road to Jerusalem).[18] Mark lays out his goal quite clearly in 1:1: Ἀρχὴ τοῦ εὐαγγελίου Ἰησοῦ Χριστοῦ [υἱοῦ θεοῦ],[19] and what follows is a narrative in which the true identity of this Jesus Christ is at stake.

In this regard, the group of disciples—those closest to Jesus—are of particular interest. At this point of Jesus' question to them in the narrative, they have been in his presence for quite some time (1:17–20; 2:13–14; 3:13–19; 6:7–13). They have heard his remarkable teaching—from reinterpreting the Jewish law in general (7:1–23) and more specifically on fasting and the Sabbath (2:18–28) to explaining with parables his mission and the nature of God's kingdom.[20] The disciples also witnessed many of Jesus' miracles, including many examples of physical healing, exorcism of devils, as well as the resurrection of Jairus's daughter from death (5:21–43). They witnessed Jesus' power over nature by his stilling of the storm (4:35–41) and walking on the sea (6:45–52), and were intimately involved in the two events narrated as the miraculous multiplication of the bread (6:30–44; 8:1–21).

A recurring theme in the Gospel up to the confession pericope is the vexing question of understanding who Jesus really is. There are numerous clues to this in the text:

The authority of his teaching and power over unclean spirits in Capernaum led those present to the question: "What is this? A new teaching! With authority (κατ᾽ ἐξουσίαν) he commands even the unclean spirits, and they obey him" (1:27). The exorcised demons are not permitted to speak on that occasion, "because they did not know him" (1:34), leaving Jesus' true identity open for now.

After declaring the lame man's sins forgiven, the question arose: "Who can forgive sins but God alone?" (2:7), attesting to some divine power at work in this man from Nazareth.

Despite Jesus' remark that to the disciples is given to know τὸ μυστήριον (the secret) of the kingdom of God (4:11), they are unable to interpret his parables (4:13) and are taught separately from the public at a level that they would understand (4:33–34). The fact that this is a great struggle emerges after the disciples' question about Jesus' teaching on traditions and inner cleanliness (7:1ff.): "Are you also then without understanding?" he asks (7:18), before explaining again that impurity comes from inside, from the heart, and not through what you eat, that is, "from outside."

After the stilling of the storm, the disciples are overwhelmed by a great fear, and they ask: τίς ἄρα οὗτός ἐστιν . . . ("Who is He then . . . that even the wind and the sea are subject to him?") (4:41). Jesus' walking on the sea later in the narrative is situated in the same "identity question" context. The disciples think they see a ghost, scream loudly, and are clearly upset. He identifies himself (6:50), gets into the boat, and stills the winds. This leaves the disciples "extremely astonished and perplexed" (6:51), and the narrator inserts the clue that the real issue is understanding who Jesus is. The disciples are astonished now, it is explained, "because they did not understand about the bread, as their heart was hardened" (6:52).[21]

This is reinforced after the second multiplication of the bread:[22] They do not understand Jesus' reference to the leaven of the Pharisees and Herod, and interpret his words as a rebuke that they forgot to bring bread into the boat, resulting in a quarrel among themselves. Jesus then asks: "Why do you argue that you have no bread? οὔπω νοεῖτε οὐδὲ συνίετε;[23] Are your hearts hardened? Having eyes do you not see, and having ears do you not hear?" He reminds them of the earlier multiplication of bread, and ends the conversation, "Do you still not understand?" (see 8:17–21).

In his hometown, the question of Jesus' true identity is posed with even greater perplexity as they obviously "know" him: "Is he not the carpenter, the son of Mary, and the brother of James . . . ?" they ask in 6:3. But where does he get these ideas and what wisdom is given to him? Whence the power that acts through his hands (6:2)? Mark is clear: they do not recognize Jesus and rather consider him a shame, a scandal: καὶ ἐσκανδαλίζοντο ἐν αὐτῷ (6:3).

The other actor in this drama of identifying Jesus is King Herod. He is reported to have heard about the healings in Jesus' ministry (6:14). Whereas some identify Jesus as Elijah, or one prophet or another, Herod himself is convinced that Jesus is the resurrection of John the Baptist (6:16).[24]

"Who do the people say I am?" in 8:27 is therefore no question out of the blue. The various audiences—the disciples, the Pharisees and teachers of the law, the crowds in different locations, King Herod, and the impure spirits—all struggled to pin down the identity of Jesus.

It is ironic that up to that point, the only replies close to the truth came from the least likely sources: The man with the unclean spirit explicitly confesses, "I know who you are: the Holy One of God" (1:24)[25] On two other occasions the demons see Jesus, and it is reported that they call out, "You are the Son of God!" (3:11), and "Son of the Most High God" (5:7), echoing the very first verse (1:1), which serves as superscript for the whole Gospel.

Jesus' self-identification before this question to the disciples is twofold: he calls himself "the Son of Man," able to forgive sins (2:10); "Kurios" the Lord of the Sabbath (2:28) and the Lord who healed the demon-possessed man from Gerasene (5:19).

The disciples' answer about the people's perceptions link Jesus to John the Baptist, Elijah, or one of the prophets (8:28). The crucial question, perhaps expecting a more informed reply from insiders than outsiders,[26] is then raised: ὑμεῖς δὲ τίνα με λέγετε εἶναι; (8:29: "But who do you say that I am?")

Peter's[27] answer, σὺ εἶ ὁ χριστός, does—in the context of the narrative—for the first time repeat the announcement at the beginning (1:1). Jesus is identified as the Messiah, the eschatological king who was promised from the Old Testament times (Jer. 23:5). Judged purely on its orthodoxy, its theological correctness, the reader is relieved to find that all Jesus' struggles to lead the disciples to a deeper understanding of himself bear good fruit. At last they got it right, we think. Is he not, indeed, the Messiah?

At this point, the narrative takes a more dramatic turn. Jesus begins his final journey to Jerusalem and makes three passion announcements in 8:31–33; 9:30–32; and 10:32–34 that have roughly the same structure; each of these announcements (varying slightly in content) is then followed by a reaction from the disciples (showing yet again their profound misunderstanding of Jesus' person and mission), and a counterreaction from Jesus (as an attempt to open the disciples' minds).

Jesus does not confirm or deny Peter's confession. He starts to teach them that the Son of Man[28] (not the Christ) must suffer and will be rejected by the elders, that he will be killed, and will rise after three days (8:31). Peter's reaction is one of total disbelief: he takes Jesus aside and rebukes him. Jesus, for his part, turns around and rebukes Peter in the presence of the disciples: "Go away behind me, Satan!" (ὅτι οὐ φρονεῖς τὰ τοῦ θεοῦ ἀλλὰ τὰ τῶν ἀνθρώπων). This may be translated as "Because you do not think about the things of God, but those of the people" or more aptly (but less literally), "You are thinking not as God thinks, but as human beings do" (8:33). This is immediately followed by the call to cross-bearing: "Whoever wants to follow me must deny himself, take up his cross, and follow me" (8:34).

In Peter's and the disciples' minds, the confession of Christ on the one hand and the announcement of a suffering Son of Man on the other created a total dissonance, an impossible possibility. The popular conception of the Messiah in Jesus' time was that this Anointed One would destroy God's enemies by the word of his mouth, deliver Jerusalem from the Gentiles, gather the faithful from dispersion, and rule in justice and glory.[29] And the popular notion of the Son of Man is—according to Jewish Scriptures (Dan. 7)—an apocalyptic figure who would descend from heaven to destroy evil kingdoms and establish the reign of God.[30] The idea of a suffering, rejected, and dying Son of Man—missing the point that he would rise after three days?—was just incomprehensible.

The question arises: Why could the disciples not comprehend Jesus' person and mission? The answer emerges from a close reading of the other two passion announcements. After announcing his passion, death, and resurrection in 9:31, the narrator clearly tells us, "But they did not understand the saying, and were afraid to ask him" (9:32). They therefore sensed some danger in the announcement, but could not actually comprehend its meaning. The reasons for the disciples' closed minds are hidden in the following few verses.

The disciples were not open to the meaning of Jesus' passion, because they were talking along the road about who among themselves were the greatest (9:34). The same self-interested power paradigm that led to a dissonance between "You are the Christ" and "suffering Son of Man," or between following Jesus in his glory and carrying a cross (quite literally), now emerges: instead of being childlike, being the last, and being everybody's servant (9:35–37), they were arguing over who was the biggest, the ruler, the first.[31]

This inward focus on retention of power is reinforced when John[32] proudly announces that they have seen someone driving out demons in Jesus' name, but did not allow him to continue. The reason, given twice, is not that the exorcism has been unsuccessful,[33] but rather "because he was not following us" (9:38). Jesus opens up their enclosed, sectarian mind-set,[34] and explains that who is not against us is for us (9:40), and that even the smallest gift for the sake of Christ (a cup of water) will be rewarded (9:41).

The paradigm of power and glory is revealed most clearly in the third passion announcement: Jesus explains in the greatest detail thus far what suffering and death await him in Jerusalem (10:33–34). James and John—as if no word about suffering was ever mentioned[35]—clearly expect a crowning, glorious future in which they wish to secretly secure their stake: "Grant us to sit, one at your right hand and one at your left, ἐν τῇ δόξῃ σου ("... in your glory," 10:37). That the other ten also hoped for some glory is apparent from their upset reaction when they hear about the request from James and John (10:41).[36]

This is followed by yet another attempt by Jesus to release them from the paradigm of power, dominion, and being "great men" with authority, and instead to understand that in God's kingdom the order is turned entirely upside down. To be the first, you must be everyone's slave (10:44).[37] He ends this passage by reinforcing his passion announcements and self-identification: "For[38] the Son of Man also came not to be served but to serve, and to give his life as a ransom (λύτρον)[39] for many" (10:45).[40]

In a brilliant ironic twist, the narrator inserts the healing of the blind Bartimaeus here. Jesus asks him exactly the same question as he asked from James and John: "What do you want me to do for you?" (cf. 10:51 and 10:36). The disciples asked for glory, the blind man for sight; the disciples were obstructing the way, Bartimaeus "followed him on the way" (10:52).

The entry into Jerusalem that follows here is—in line with the struggle of identity thus far—a confusing event. The readers know Jesus enters to suffer and die, and that his kingdom is from a different order. But he nevertheless enters with the symbolism of a king: riding a colt on which no one has sat (Gen. 49:11; Zech. 9:9); clothes and branches are spread before him as for a royal inauguration (2 Kgs. 9:13). The mainly Jewish crowds are swept away in nationalistic fervor: "Hosanna! Blessed is he who comes in the name of the Lord![41] Blessed is the kingdom of our father David that is coming! Hosanna in the highest!" (11:9–10).[42]

The rest of the Gospel emphasizes the failure of the Twelve to understand the significance of the events and their inability to support their Master in his ordeal. It reinforces the tragic truth set out from the beginning: those closest to Jesus do not know. Judas is shown to be the traitor (14:18ff.), Peter is warned that he would deny Jesus three times (14:27–31), and in the garden the disciples are found sleeping three times, failing Jesus' request to stay awake with him (14:32–42). After Judas's betrayal, Jesus is captured by people sent out by the high priests, scribes, and elders—echoing the exact actors of his passion announcements. The end of the discipleship journey—apart from Peter who still follows from afar and denies Jesus—is but a terse sentence: "And they all forsook him and fled" (14:50).

The identity question prevails even unto the cross. Jesus is crucified under the ironic title "the King of the Jews." The high priests and law scholars ironically acknowledge his messianic status: "Let the Christ, the King of Israel, come down now from the cross that we can see and believe!" (15:32). When Jesus calls out in Aramaic (*Eloi, Eloi, . . .*) some—in line with earlier speculation—mishear him as appealing to Elijah[43] for help.

The question "Who do you say I am?" remains urgent right up to the end. Our hope might be set on the women. At least they followed up to the end and are present at the cross. The news of the resurrection is later told to Mary Magdalene, Mary the mother of James, and Salome. They are asked by the young man in white clothes to go and tell the others to meet Jesus in Galilee. The original text of the Gospel, however, ends in disappointment: "And they said nothing to anyone, for they were afraid" (16:8).

We saw earlier that—contrary to expectation—the unclean spirits knew Jesus. When everyone else was struggling to understand, they confessed, "You are the Son of God" (3:11). At the end, it is left to the Roman soldier, an officer over a hundred men, who had no other exposure to Jesus but his witness of the crucifixion,[44] to say, ἀληθῶς οὗτος ὁ ἄνθρωπος υἱὸς θεοῦ ἦν ("Truly, this man was the Son of God," 15:39).[45] What no one could fully comprehend during Jesus' life and ministry becomes possible through his death.

This exposition may aid us in understanding two interesting remarks in the first encounter between Jesus and Peter after the latter made his confession. The one is the command to keep quiet, and the other is the reference that Peter is a "Satan."

Jesus' strong insistence that they should tell no one that he is the Christ has become known in scholarship as the messianic secret.[46] It is a complex theme recurring in contradictory modes in the narrative: Sometimes someone is urged to go and tell (e.g., the man from Gadara in 5:19), but generally people who are healed are asked not to tell (e.g., 1:44; 5:43; 7:35; and 8:26).

If one reads the identity question of the Markan narrative as playing itself out in the tension between two radically opposing paradigms (reminiscent of Luther's theologies of glory and the cross), the insistence not to tell anyone about the Christ in 8:30 is explained: Jesus is well aware of the nationalistic and self-indulgent misinterpretation of his mission. He understands that his disciples are following him because of their expectation for dominion and glory. This type of Christ is dangerous: "Do not tell others about him."

The problem does not lie in the words of the confession; Jesus is indeed the Christ. The problem—as we saw earlier—lies in the interpretation of this Christ, and the consequences it has for the practical choices made by the disciples. They were dogmatically correct, but were still standing in God's way: closing out others in a sectarian mind-set, struggling to be the most important, involved in secret politicking for positions of glory, and clearly overestimating their own religious loyalties to Christ.

Seemingly orthodox statements are shattered by heterodox attitudes and actions. Theology is constitutively verified or falsified through ethics.

By rebuking Jesus for his passion announcement, Peter is acting naturally. He tries to defend his prevailing paradigm of Christ. His mind is thinking like the minds of people, and he cannot think the way God thinks. He wants to avoid the cross; he wants to save himself. That is equal to being Satan (8:33). By opposing God's will for his Messiah, Peter and the disciples "are acting as spokesmen of God's ultimate enemy" in Peter's role of taking away the word of God (see Mark 4:15).[47] What we see here are "incompatible ideologies" at work, where our human perspective is incapable of grasping divine purpose.[48]

History teaches us that it is when this paradigm of power becomes institutionalized and moves beyond individual notions of Christ for the sake of oneself and one's own in-group that we find the deadly combination of nationalistic politics and the Christian religion. The most dramatic twentieth-century examples are National Socialism in Germany and apartheid theology in South Africa.

Both linked a people (*Volk*), a specific land, and God in an ideological triangle in which the church and ordinary people confessed Christ in an orthodox manner, while dehumanizing others in their narrow pursuit of privilege, power, and racial self-glorification. You could kill in the Name of the One you confess. By God's grace, the alternative truth, the rejection of ideological faith, was also spoken in both countries as represented by Barmen (1934) and Belhar (1982/86). An emerging twenty-first-century example is the preemptive wars initiated by the United States, exhibiting in some respects the same ideological structure of a Christian God identified with Western political values and the protection of American interests and security.

Over against this Satanic temptation to seek power, influence, and glory stands the utterly foolish paradigm of the cross.

IS THERE HOPE FOR LIBERATION FROM AN IDEOLOGICAL FAITH?

The urgent question that now arises is whether there is hope. Is there a possibility that Peter and the disciples can indeed come to an understanding of who Jesus is and shape their lives accordingly? In the context of prevailing Christian ideologies, is there an expectation that those caught up in a paradigm of power, legitimized by theology and supported by political and military means, can indeed turn around?

The story of Peter (as representative of the disciples, and for that matter all followers of Christ) gives us the clue: conversion to a radically new insight is possible through divine intervention.

First, Peter's religious self-confidence had to be shattered by a practical realization that he—despite his good messianic intentions—had been betraying Christ. A simple maid in the house of the high priest and a cock that crows twice are the instruments[49] of shaking the ideological foundations of Peter's faith. (It is again ironic that Peter denies knowledge of Jesus while confessing and protesting all along that he does!) In a fleeting moment he realizes who he really is: a follower and defender, but at the same time a traitor, of Christ. The narrator tells of the effect: "And he broke down and wept" (14:72).[50]

The readers, and the later addition to the ending of the Markan Gospel (16:9–20), know the second part of the radical conversion: the destruction of the previous religious edifice, the revelation of the true self, and the breaking down of all spiritual self-confidence make room for a fresh meeting—this time with the resurrected Christ.[51] Again Jesus reprimands them for their hardness of heart and disbelief,[52] but then—in a gesture of radical grace and acceptance—He empowers them, the very ones who did not understand and at first did not believe, to go into the world, and "preach the gospel to the whole creation" (16:15). Because they then knew the whole gospel, they understood for the first time that the suffering Son of Man is indeed the resurrected Christ.

In the words of Michael Welker, "Reformed theology must engage in a variety of ways in the effort to renew a theology of the word of God, and above all, *it must make clear that the church of Christ lives in the presence of the risen Christ.*"[53] We have the promise that—no matter our past—the risen Christ will work with us and confirm our message by the signs that attend it (Mark 16:19).

While we follow Christ in his command, let us be aware of the ever-present danger of new ideological faiths: the rise of Islamic and Christian fundamentalism in the Middle East, Africa, and the United States; the link between neoliberal capitalism and a prosperity gospel; and the rapid growth of spiritualities that utilize the mass media to turn the Christian gospel into anthropocentric and pleasing entertainment.

"Who is Jesus Christ for us today?" (Bonhoeffer) might be the most important question to answer.

NOTES

1. To track the traditions of "biblical theology," see the well-known effort by Brevard Childs to discuss developments of biblical theology from Irenaeus to Calvin in *Biblical Theology of the Old and New Testaments: Theological Reflection on the Christian Bible* (Minneapolis: Fortress, 1993), 30–52; outline of the current models (11–29); explain the split between biblical theology and systematic theology in J. P. Gabler's famous 1787 speech; and put forward his own proposal of theology that takes the canon as Christian Bible seriously and that does not shy away from systematic theological reflection. For an analysis of Welker's own approach up to the late 1990s, see Bernd Oberdorfer, "Biblisch-realistische Theologie: Methodologische Ueberlegungen zu einem dogmatischen Programm," in *Resonanzen: Theologische Beiträge: Michael Welker zum 50 Geburtstag*, ed. Sigrid Brandt and Bernd Oberdorfer (Wuppertal: Foedus-Verlag, 1998), 63–83, and for Welker's most recent thoughts, distinguishing himself from others like Ebeling, see his unpublished paper (forthcoming chapter in a book on biblical theology) given in Princeton, New Jersey, on January 24, 2007 (Michael Welker, "What Is Biblical Theology?" unpublished paper, Princeton, N.J.: Center of Theological Inquiry, January 24, 2007).
2. Michael Welker, in "Das vierfache Gewicht der Schrift: Die missverständliche Rede vom 'Schriftprinzip' und die Programmformel 'Biblische theologie,'" in "*Das Gott eine grosse Barmherzighkeit habe.*" *Konkrete Theologie in der Verschränkung von Glaube und Leben: Festschrift für Gunda-Schneider* (Leipzig: Evangelische Verlaganstalt), 9–27, refers to the fourfold weight of Scripture in an attempt to clarify the *sola scriptura* idea of the Reformers, and to clarify other concomitant authority formulae. He speaks of historical, cultural, canonical, and theological weight.
3. Michael Welker, "The Task of Biblical Theology and the Authority of Scripture," in *Theology in the Service of the Church: Festschrift for Thomas Gillespie,* ed. Wallace Alston (Grand Rapids: Eerdmans, 2000), 232–41.
4. Michael Welker, *Creation and Reality* (Minneapolis: Fortress, 1999), 3.
5. Michael Welker, "Travail and Mission: Theology Reformed According to God's Word at the Beginning of the Third Millennium," in *Toward the*

Future of Reformed Theology: Tasks, Topics, and Traditions, ed. David Willis and Michael Welker (Grand Rapids: Eerdmans, 1999), 138–39.

6. Welker, *Creation and Reality,* 4; Welker, "Travail and Mission," 142.

7. Welker, "Travail and Mission," 143.

8. Ibid., 141–42.

9. The contextual comments are added in the notes for two reasons: to allow the Markan narrative to proceed uninterrupted, and to allow for other appropriations beyond the South African context. I can imagine a German, Latin American or U.S. reader who might find illumination from the text quite differently from what is presented here.

10. "There can be hardly any doubt that religion and nationalism were the main ideological forces that impacted on the Afrikaners during the twentieth century. The two were interrelated." The exact relationship between the two is a matter of debate, however. For a discussion, see Hermann Giliomee, "The Weakness of Some: The Dutch Reformed Church and White Supremacy," *Scriptura* 83 (2003): 221–26. Giliomee is a foremost South African historian who recently published a major and widely acclaimed work, *The Afrikaners: Biography of a People* (Charlottesville, Va.: University of Virginia Press, 2003).

11. With reference to O'Brien's distinction between a "holy nationalism" and limited self-understanding as a "holy people," Giliomee gives strong evidence that, unlike Germany under National Socialism, Afrikaners never claimed an exclusive right to God's favor, though there was a strong sense of God's providential hand in their history ("Weakness of Some," 224).

12. For a short summary of these theological currents, see Piet Naudé, "From Pluralism to Ideology: The Roots of Apartheid Theology in Abraham Kuyper, Gustav Warneck, and Theological Pietism," *Scriptura* 88 (2005): 161–73. For a more elaborate account, see the excellent essays in Johann Kinghorn, ed., *Die NG Kerk en apartheid* (Johannesburg: Macmillan, 1986); and for a classical historical overview, read John W. de Gruchy and Steve de Gruchy, *The Church Struggle in South Africa: 25th Anniversary Edition* (London: SCM Press, 2004).

13. See Willie Jonker's seminal essay on Barth, "Some Remarks on the Interpretation of Karl Barth," *Nederduitse Gereformeerde Teologiese Tydskrif* 29 (1988): 29–40, and the thorough analysis (with extensive literature) of Barth's significance for understanding justice—also in South Africa—by Dirk J. Smit, ". . . The Doing of the Little Righteousness: On Justice in Barth's View of the Christian Life," in *Loving God with Our Minds: The Pastor as Theologian: Essays in Honor of Wallace M. Alston,* ed. Michael Welker and Cynthia A. Jarvis (Grand Rapids: Eerdmans, 2004), 120–45.

14. Nobody did more than John de Gruchy to appropriate Bonhoeffer's insights for the church in South Africa. See specifically his essays in John W. de Gruchy, *Bonhoeffer and South Africa: Theology in Dialogue* (Grand Rapids: Eerdmans, 1984). Under the able leadership of Dirk Smit, then professor of dogmatics at Western Cape, young scholars like Russel Botman and Johan Botha wrote theses on Bonhoeffer and played an important part in the Confessing Church movement in South Africa.

15. The academic and popular work by internationally acclaimed scholars like Ferdinand Deist (OT) and Bernard Lategan (NT) played an enormous role to reclaim the Bible for an antiapartheid reading.

16. Under the leadership of people like Allan Boesak, ABRECSA (Alliance of Black Reformed Christians in Southern Africa), which issued its *Charter and*

Declaration in October 1981, played a major role in reclaiming the Reformed tradition in South Africa to include black members.

17. In the discussion of the Markan text below, some references will be to the original; most English translations will be taken from the RSV, and in some cases I attempt my own translation.

18. The division of the Gospel into a short prologue (1:1–13) followed by two major sections, 1:14–8:30 and 8:31–15:47, is based on clear textual markers and is reinforced by the narrative structure. For the former, with extensive literature, see Francis J. Moloney, *The Gospel of Mark: A Commentary* (Grand Rapids: Eerdmans, 2002), 16–22; and for the latter, see Donald H. Juel, *The Gospel of Mark* (Nashville: Abingdon, 1999), as well as D. Rhoads, J. Dewey, and D. Michie, *Mark as Story: An Introduction to the Narrative of the Gospel,* 2nd ed. (Philadelphia: Fortress, 1999).

19. "The beginning of the gospel of Jesus Christ" with a later addition of "the Son of God."

20. See 4:1–34 for parables of the Sower, Lamp, Seed, and Mustard Seed.

21. The passive use of καρδία πεπωρωμένη creates a difficult problem of interpretation, as it might suggest that the disciples did not choose to misunderstand Jesus, but were mere passive objects of a divine hardening of the hearts. If one reads this passage in the context of Isa. 6:9–10 (already referred to in 4:12), and links it to Jesus' rebuke of their hardness of heart later (8:17) and after his resurrection (16:14), there is no justification for diminishing the disciples' agency and responsibility, just as Yahweh's hardening of Israel's heart in the time of proto-Isaiah was in no way glossing over their own breaking of the covenant. For discussion and literature, see R. T. France, *The Gospel of Mark* (Grand Rapids: Eerdmans, 2002), 273–74.

22. The reason that the bread miracles are singled out by Mark as the signs of Jesus' true identity—more than the other miracles—might, according to Hooker, be because they are reminiscent of the miraculous manna provision during the exodus (see France, *Gospel of Mark,* 273n73).

23. "Are you thus without understanding also?" The *asunetos* has a ring of being dull or foolish to it.

24. This recognition of Jesus by the heathen king is an ironic twist, remarks James R. Edwards, *The Gospel According to Mark* (Grand Rapids: Eerdmans, 2002), 185. Herod holds Jesus in higher regard than his own people in Nazareth! This may be part of the wider irony—see discussion later—that the "lower" the agent (e.g., unclean spirits and Roman officer), the "higher" their knowledge of Jesus. For an extensive study, read J. Camery-Hoggat, *Irony in Mark's Gospel: Text and Subtext* (Cambridge: Cambridge University Press, 1992).

25. What happens here is that "the demon displays a supernatural insight as yet denied to human actors in the story. The reader is expected to note it . . ." (France, *Gospel of Mark,* 10). To call Jesus "holy" is to emphasize the contrast with his "unclean" opponent, and might also refer to Jesus possessing the "Holy Spirit" (1:8) that empowers his messianic ministry.

26. "Jesus' comrades are asked to render a judgment about his remarkable *exousia,* his divine authority, which they have witnessed and experienced. . . . The disciples must move from the status of passive recipients to active participants" (Edwards, *Gospel According to Mark,* 248).

27. Although Peter replies, the context where Jesus addresses the disciples in vv. 30–31 suggests that Peter serves as spokesperson for the disciples. This role of Peter as group representative is repeated in 10:28; 11:21; and 14:37. See France, *Gospel of Mark,* 329.

28. This self-identification (used fourteen times only by Jesus) might be ambiguous, but was in the time of Jesus largely free from the political and military connotations of the Messiah. "Son of Man" is used in three contexts: an apocalyptic context like in Daniel and 1 Enoch (8:38; 13:26; 14:62), authority to forgive sins and rule over the Sabbath, and predominantly, in the context of suffering (nine times, as in all the passion announcements). For the disciples, the apocalyptic connotation would be most in line with their own expectations.

29. See the short but insightful excursus with further literature on "Christ" in Edwards, *Gospel According to Mark*, 249–52.

30. The fact that Jesus calls himself the Son of Man indicates that he will indeed establish the kingdom of God. This is clear from his opening sermon as reported in Mark 1:14. The problem lies in the means to establish the kingdom: not via military or political victory as understood in an apocalyptic framework, but through suffering and resurrection. This reinforces the point: *the title or description of Jesus per se is not the issue, but the interpretation thereof!* For the complex interpretation of the Son of Man in technical literature, and a clear position based on Dan. 7, read Moloney, *Gospel of Mark*, 212–13.

31. What we see here is a juxtaposition "between Jesus' humility and the disciple's desire for distinction and recognition" on the assumption that messiahship entails privilege, not suffering (Edwards, *Gospel According to Mark*, 285).

32. John's solo role here should be read as part of the narrator's skillful suggestion that it is precisely the inner circle of the disciples (how close can you be to Jesus!) that misses the point of the suffering Son of Man. See the role of John and James (10:35ff.) as discussed later.

33. See a similar event with less satisfactory results in Acts 19:13–16. The "protection" of Jesus' name after his resurrection must have been in the forefront of John's mind, though he expresses this in terms of the exclusive disciple group and not so much as concern over Jesus' honor!

34. Ideological faith is by its very nature sectarian. Where the nationalistic interest and pious belief intersect, a strong denominational church (in the negative sense) is the inevitable result. As the tension between "us" (who are right and are not properly understood) and "them" (who are out to discredit us) grows, ecumenical isolation increases. But the isolation in turn is not interpreted as Christian exhortation, but exactly as vindication of the truthfulness of one's own position. It may take years to change. The ecumenical church in the form of the WCC and SACC (Leslie A. Hewson, *Cottlesloe Consultation: The Report of the Consultation among South African Member Churches of the World Council of Churches, 7–14 Dec. 1960 at Cottesloe, Johannesburg* (1961). South African Council of Churches, *Message to the People of South Africa* (Broamfonten, Transvaal: South African Council of Churches, 1968), the Lutheran World Federation (*status confessionis* 1977), and the World Alliance of Reformed Churches (*status confessionis* 1982) all played this ambiguous role in the life of the Afrikaans Dutch Reformed Church. The story of the DRC's ecumenical relations between 1960 and 1990 could be described as a move from willful isolation to reestablishment of ties in full communion. For an overview of critique from the ecumenical church, read Etienne De Villiers, "Kritiek uit die ekumene," in Kinghorn, *Die NG Kerk*, 144–64; for the constructive role of the ecumenical church, read Piet Naudé, "The Theological Coherence Between the Belhar Confession and Some Antecedent Church Witnesses in the Period 1948–1982," *Verbum et ecclesia* 42, no. 1 (2003): 156–79.

35. The heretical nature of self-serving, ideological faith is rarely (if ever) an open denial of orthodoxy. As is clearly the case with John and James here, it is a hermeneutic at work that renders reading the "unacceptable" parts of the gospel impossible, and framing that gospel to fit your own agenda. They just do not hear the explicit "suffering" predictions, but do hear "Son of Man," and that is enough to cling to the apocalyptic notion of a glorious kingdom. To call apartheid a theological heresy was not based on any explicit doctrinal denial by those supporting the system, but the implicit, unsaid "doctrine" that resulted from a racist, pluralist reading of the gospel. See the essays in John de Gruchy and Charles Villa-Vicencio, eds., *Apartheid Is a Heresy* (Cape Town, South Africa: David Philip, 1983).

36. This is the only case in this Gospel where James and John are mentioned separately from the Twelve. One can easily imagine their intention to sideline Peter, the other member of the inner circle. There are only two positions of glory, but three (if not twelve) contenders.

37. "The preeminent virtue of God's kingdom is not power, not even freedom, but service." *Diakonos* is the ordinary Greek word for waiting on tables, and *doulos* was in ancient society the least and the last. That a slave can be first is an absurd paradox (Edwards, *Gospel According to Mark,* 236). Karl Barth, in *Evangelical Theology: An Introduction* (New York: Holt, Rinehart & Winston, 1963), 187–88, beautifully describes theological work as service: "Since theology is called to serve, it must not rule. It must serve both God in his Word . . . and the man loved by God and addressed by God's Word. It may rule neither in relation to God nor in relation to men."

38. The Greek γὰρ must be read as purposive here, introducing service and giving as the very way of the Son of Man.

39. In the Hellenistic and Roman periods *lutron* refers to "transactions between human beings and gods in which sins were forgiven and offenses expiated" (Collins as quoted by Edwards, *Gospel According to Mark,* 328n67).

40. There are indications that Mark draws on the Servant of the Lord from Isa. 53 here. This Servant will give his life as a guilt offering (Isa. 53:10) and bear the iniquities of many (53:11), in the same way that Jesus describes the Son of Man here. For a discussion, and with literature presenting alternatives, see Moloney, *Gospel of Mark,* 213–14.

41. A direct quotation of Ps. 118:25–26 as a referral to pilgrims' entering Jerusalem.

42. For the sake of my specific reading, i.e., to uncover the traits of ideological faith, I am less open to Edwards's suggestion that the crowds did not harbor messianic expectations from Jesus, but merely welcomed him as a pilgrim (*Gospel According to Mark,* 336–37). In line with the narrator's emphasis on "misunderstanding," the shift from "the kingdom of God" (Jesus) to "the kingdom of our father David" (crowds) is highly significant. *This identification of political interests with divine interest is the deepest core of an ideological faith.* That the Markan account of Jesus' entry is significantly "down-scaled" when compared with Matthew and Luke, is true, but this does not detract from the misreading of Jesus' purpose and identity by those present.

43. It was believed that Elijah had been taken to heaven without dying (2 Kgs. 2:11), and that he could return to help the righteous in times of crises.

44. In the Matthean version (27:54), the centurion's confession is a reaction to the signs accompanying Jesus' death, but here the confession is a direct response to the death of Jesus itself. See the good argument by Philip G. Davis, "Mark's Christological Paradox," *Journal for the Study of the New Testament* 35 (1989):

14, that 15:39 should not merely be seen as the climax of the Gospel, but as the governing key to interpret the Gospel as such. What we find is not merely a narrative climax, "but the Christological climax as well."

45. There are no grammatical grounds for the assertion (inter alia by Earl S. Johnson, "Is Mark 15:39 the Key to Mark's Christology?" *Journal for the Study of the New Testament* 31 [1987]: 14), that, because of the absence of a definite article before "Son of God," the centurion only made a general confession about a son of god, i.e., a special person. As Edwards rightly points out, a definite predicate nominative in Koine Greek omits the article when it precedes the verb (*Gospel According to Mark*, 480). What we have here—according to the narrative—is a full confession in line with the intention of the Gospel as set out in 1:1.

46. The modern scholarship on Mark has been set in motion by the groundbreaking work, *Das Messiasgeheimnis in den Evangelien,* by Wilhelm Wrede, in 1901. His enduring legacy is that Mark is a theological work (not a mere biographical account), and that Christology forms the center of that theology. For a discussion of the reaction to Wrede and major viewpoints up to the mid-1960s, read David Aune's instructive article, "The Problem of the Messianic Secret," *Novum Testamentum* 11 (1969): 1–31, specifically 1–8, with discussions on major scholars from Schweitzer to Bultmann. My fairly straightforward explanation of the messianic secret stems from the specific hermeneutical angle from which I chose to read Mark and is perhaps a good illustration of Bultmann's work on presuppositions.

47. France, *Gospel of Mark,* 338.

48. Ibid., 339.

49. Sometimes—God forbid—the "instrument" to destabilize an ideological self is war and destruction to the point of no return. In other cases, one only realizes those moments when you look back. In the South African case, two seemingly simple events that contributed to insight in the ideological faith of Afrikaner Christians were the rejection of mixed marriages on scriptural grounds by leading ethicists like De Villiers and Kinghorn in the late 1970s, and the declaration of apartheid theology as *status confessionis* accompanied by the draft Confession of Belhar by the "coloured" Mission Church in 1982. It still took some time, but these two viewpoints eroded the moral legitimacy of the system in the minds of ordinary white Christians.

50. This happens at an individual level—sometimes like here with Peter—in an instant. In 1930, Bonhoeffer wrote in *Sanctorum Communio: A Theological Study of the Sociology of the Church* (Minneapolis: Fortress, 1998), 118, that ethical responsibility may be assigned not only to individuals, but to the whole people of God. There is something like "ethical collective persons" and collective guilt that may gradually dawn. Chances are slim that self-realization reaches everyone at the some time: "Breaking down and weeping," an expression of guilt and sorrow, is mostly expressed not by all, but vicariously by some on behalf of all—even if they are not each and every one convinced at the time, and even while they fiercely resist and refuse to accept the radically other picture of the collective self. The confession of Willie Jonker on behalf of Afrikaners and the DRC at the ecumenical Rustenburg conference, "Understanding the Church Situation and Obstacles to Christian Witness in South Africa," in *The Road to Rustenburg: The Church Looking Forward to a New South Africa,* ed. Louw Alberts and Frank Chikane (Cape Town, South Africa, 1991), 87–98, as well as the DRC's own confession of guilt in 1990, stand out as crucial markers on the road to proper insight into "Chris-

tian" policies of apartheid. The role of the Truth and Reconciliation Commission—accompanied by many tears and personal confessions—has been described by some as a national catharsis, a deep look inside our own hearts of darkness (Pauw); a view into the skull of our country (Krog).

51. "The good news does not say: Jesus is simply here again! The pre-Easter Jesus of Nazareth is here again! Instead, the good news, the gospel, says: here is the risen and exalted Christ, who is present in a wholly new way." For that reason the gospel is also called the "gospel of the *resurrection*" (Welker, "Travail and Mission," 148, emphasis original).

52. This is quite instructive: Jesus does not gloss over, but in fact reminds them of their past in the very act of commissioning them. Much has been written about historical guilt. Theologically speaking, the only guilt that is both painful and empowering to remember is guilt covered by the grace of God according to his promise in 1 John 1:7–9, and repeated every Sunday after the reading of the law. The recommissioning of the church in South Africa—those who designed and supported apartheid, together with those who fought against the system—can only happen on the basis of remembered grace. In a country ravaged by the AIDS pandemic, violent gender crime, and a growing poverty gap, there is so much that needs to be done theologically and in practice.

53. Welker, "Travail and Mission," 141.

10

Christology and *Diakonia*

JOHN F. HOFFMEYER

One of the many virtues of Michael Welker's theology is his refusal to reduce the rich complexity of the biblical witnesses in favor of tidy systematic formulations. His theology continually returns to the Bible, always expecting to find there a complex realism that can provoke new insights for theological reflection. In Welker's view, systematic theology will always struggle, never wholly successfully, to keep up with the complex and polycentric realism of the biblical traditions. Welker's approach provides vital stimulation for the renewal of Christian doctrine in realistic engagement with a complex, beautiful, and agonizing world.

The doctrinal focus of this volume is Christology. To honor this biblical theologian who has taught me so much, it seemed appropriate to return to a familiar biblical text and to see what new insights it might provide for christological reflection on Christian ministry with and to human beings in need: what the church has often called *diakonia*. Within that general topic, this essay seeks a christological basis for responding to the question with which a 2007 article in the magazine *Sojourners* opens: "How can Christians live out the commands of Matt 25—without the pity?" The author, J. Todd Billings, continues by relating a story:

"I was just at church, and they were praying for the homeless," Larry said, holding the day's belongings in a bag beside him. As the subway screeched to a halt, I heard him quip, "I decided that I should pray for the housed." Larry was sick of handouts, sick of condescension.[1]

Simone Weil would have appreciated Larry's point. In an essay on "Forms of the Implicit Love of God," she observes,

> It is not amazing that a person who has bread gives a piece of it to someone who is famished. What is amazing is that the former be capable of doing it by an action different from that by which one buys an object. Alms, when they are not supernatural, are similar to a purchase. They buy the afflicted person.[2]

Weil recognizes that the customary one-on-one practice of "charity" is demeaning. She looks for deliverance by the introduction of another dimension: the supernatural. My intention in this essay is not to explore Weil's approach by means of the category of the supernatural. Instead, my thesis is that Matthew 25:31–46, the famous story of the sheep and the goats at the great judgment, suggests a richly woven christological pattern in which ministry with and to human beings in need can find orientation.

In advancing this thesis I am not referring to Matthew 25:31–46 simply as a fixed piece of text, but as it has lived and continues to live in its reading, hearing, teaching, and preaching. This emphasis is important for two reasons. The first reason concerns a historical shift in understanding a key part of the text. As a result of this shift, many interpreters today understand the text differently from the way in which Matthew probably intended it, and from the way in which most extant Christian interpretations long understood it. What makes this shift in meaning unusually important is that the meaning that Matthew probably did not intend is so compelling on basic Christian theological grounds that contemporary Christian interpreters may hold to it even while explicitly acknowledging that it is not the meaning most defensible as an exegesis of the text.

The second reason for emphasizing the function of Matthew 25:31–46 in preaching, teaching, reading, and hearing is that the text is so constructed that readers and hearers of the text, by the very act of reading or hearing, seem to confront the impossibility of placing themselves in the position of the persons whom the text holds up as exemplary. Since this second reason is more central to the main thread of this essay's argument, I devote an initial section to the first reason, then return at length to the second reason. Let us start, though, by placing the text before us.

> "When the Human Being[3] comes in his glory, and all the angels with him, then he will sit on the throne of his glory. All the nations will be gathered before him, and he will separate people one from another as a shepherd separates the sheep from the goats, and he will put the sheep at his right hand and the goats at the left. Then the king will say to those at his right

hand, 'Come, you that are blessed by my Father, inherit the kingdom prepared for you from the foundation of the world; for I was hungry and you gave me food, I was thirsty and you gave me something to drink, I was a stranger and you welcomed me, I was naked and you gave me clothing, I was sick and you took care of me, I was in prison and you visited me.' Then the righteous will answer him, 'Lord, when was it that we saw you hungry and gave you food, or thirsty and gave you something to drink? And when was it that we saw you a stranger and welcomed you, or naked and gave you clothing? And when was it that we saw you sick or in prison and visited you?' And the king will answer them, 'Truly I tell you, just as you did it to one of the least of these my brothers and sisters,[4] you did it to me.' Then he will say to those at his left hand, 'You that are accursed, depart from me into the eternal fire prepared for the devil and his angels; for I was hungry and you gave me no food, I was thirsty and you gave me nothing to drink, I was a stranger and you did not welcome me, naked and you did not give me clothing, sick and in prison and you did not visit me.' Then they also will answer, 'Lord, when was it that we saw you hungry or thirsty or a stranger or naked or sick or in prison, and did not take care of you?' Then he will answer them, 'Truly I tell you, just as you did not do it to one of the least of these, you did not do it to me.' And these will go away into eternal punishment, but the righteous into eternal life."

NARROW AND EXPANSIVE INTERPRETATIONS OF "THE LEAST OF THESE"

Sherman Gray's careful survey of the history of interpretation of Matthew 25:31–46 investigates the readings of this passage by some 170 authors prior to the eighteenth century, along with general trends among interpreters of the last three centuries. Gray observes that controversies about the text's interpretation have centered around two phrases: *panta ta ethne* ("all the nations"), which appears in verse 32, and *heni touton ton adelphon mou ton elachiston* ("one of the least of these my brothers and sisters"), which appears in verse 40 and again in shortened form in verse 45. "All the nations" might mean everyone other than Jews or everyone other than Christians. More broadly, it might mean all human beings.[5] The second phrase, "the least of these (my brothers and sisters)" also has both more restrictive interpretations and more expansive ones. Gray's research finds that, with the exception of the twentieth century, the majority—frequently the overwhelming majority—of interpreters have understood "the least of these" more narrowly as only Christians, or even only specific groups of Christians. Gray concludes that "there is hardly support of the view that 'the least' are everyone."[6] Of the two controverted phrases, the latter is much more important for the purposes of this article, so I attend to it at the expense of the former.

Although Gray notes a dramatic growth in the expansive interpretation of "the least of these" in the last century, many scholars still hold to the narrow interpretation. David Garland argues that "brothers" and "little ones" are terms used elsewhere in Matthew to refer to Jesus' disciples. Garland concludes that the "least of these refers to Jesus' followers."[7] Robert Gundry advances these same arguments, along with the claim that the words "the one who receives you receives me," addressed in Matthew 10:40 by Jesus to his disciples, provide a precedent for Jesus identifying with the treatment his disciples receive.[8] Pointing to those same precedents in Matthew referring to disciples, David Cortés-Fuentes holds that "the least of these" refers to "the community of believers, the disciples in every place who, as vulnerable victims of persecution, suffer hunger, thirst, and other calamities related to their testimony."[9]

As noted, the number of those who embrace an expansive interpretation has been on the rise. George Montague argues that "to highlight only those who have been kind to Christian missionaries would be rather anti-climactic in this cosmic finale."[10] Daniel Patte simply says, "There is no reason to limit this identification of the Son of man to the 'disciples' who are in such situations of need."[11] The older commentary of Adolf Schlatter argues more fully:

> We may not say that these brothers are only the disciples or the Christians, for that would be an arbitrary addition to what Jesus says. Admittedly, he promised that whoever receives the little ones in his name or extends a cup with water to one of his disciples, does it unto him. But this saying makes Jesus' grace still greater, because here he is speaking of all nations. Therefore he speaks not of belief in him or of confession to his name, but only of his hunger and of his affliction. He thereby names a service that anyone anywhere can do unto him.[12]

The story of the sheep and the goats has been a beloved text for Latin American liberation theologians. All of their interpretations with which I am familiar adopt an expansive reading of "the least of these." For Jon Sobrino, "'the least of these my brothers and sisters' (Matt 25:40) has a universal extension, irreducible to the followers of Jesus, applying to any human being in need."[13] Sobrino connects this reading to his assumption that the division between Christian and non-Christian is not the fundamental theological division of humanity. The fundamental division of humanity is instead between "those who take life, survival, for granted, and those for whom that is precisely not what they take for granted."[14] For the latter group, the gift of life, symbolized by the action of feeding the hungry, the first of the actions commended in Matthew's judgment scene, is itself good news, wonderful news, even though survival is not all there is to life. For the former group, the gift of life is not in itself news.

Sobrino's approach resonates with that taken by Gustavo Gutiérrez in his discussion of the passage in his lectionary guide *Compartir la Palabra* (*Sharing the Word*). Gutiérrez insists that the "requirements of the Dominion include giving life today: giving something to eat, something to drink, etc." Like Sobrino, he sees the privileged recipients of such action as the "least," those who are overlooked and whose just claims are postponed.[15] Similarly, Xabier Pikaza equates the brothers and sisters of Jesus with "those who are most needy." Citing Pikaza, Juan Luis Segundo says that to confine "the least of these" to Christian disciples "would amount to unduly reducing the universality that is so obvious in all the symbolic elements of the parable."[16]

The narrow and the expansive interpretations come to an intriguing coexistence in Ulrich Luz's massive commentary on Matthew. Luz concludes that Matthew's text does not justify the expansive interpretation of "the least of these." "In all likelihood the evangelist saw in Jesus' needy brothers not every needy human being, but needy disciples."[17] Yet Luz argues in favor of contemporary readers adopting the expansive interpretation because it is so centrally in keeping with the gospel.

The debate between the narrow reading and the expansive one is of great importance. I remember as a college student organizing a weekend retreat for our Christian students' organization, for which the presenters were to be representatives of the (at the time) recently birthed organization Evangelicals for Social Action. The speakers were to share their vision of how actions such as sharing food with hungry persons and visiting persons in prison arose from the core of their Christian faith. I was shocked to learn that some members of the student group were not planning on attending because they were not sure that such actions were part of the Christian mandate. As one of them argued, Matthew 25:31–46 speaks only of meeting the needs of fellow members of the household of Christian faith.

FOLLOWING THE SHEEP:
CHRISTOLOGICAL FORGETFULNESS

Deciding what Matthew originally intended or how the text originally functioned is not essential to this essay. As becomes clear in the course of this essay, whatever the exegetical arguments about the text in its Matthean context, I think that Christians who refuse the theological substance of the expansive interpretation have a fundamentally confused Christology. The quandary that will guide the development of my argument, though, is a dilemma that arises for the narrow interpretation and the expansive one. It is a quandary posed by the text, specifically in the act of hearing or reading the text. Before stating the quandary directly, several preliminary remarks are in order.

The story of the sheep and goats seems to encourage the kinds of action that in Christian terminology often fall under the heading of *diakonia*: feeding people who are hungry, visiting people who are sick or imprisoned, providing clothing for those who lack it. Some Christian traditions call such actions "works of mercy." Other Christian traditions may speak more of "serving the neighbor in need." Whatever the terminology, this final story of Matthew 25 praises such actions. Countless preachers and teachers have used this text to encourage the performance of such actions. There are many other biblical texts that encourage or even command such actions, but these words from Matthew issue an unusually strong motivation for engaging in such actions. The text suggests that, in feeding persons who are hungry, one will encounter Jesus.

Christian action is often framed in a different, though not necessarily contradictory way, as an imitation of Christ. In recent years, at least in the United States, it has been common to see Christians wearing bracelets with the letters WWJD: "What would Jesus do?" The WWJD phenomenon has received its share of theological criticism (such critique is probably unavoidable for any practice that takes on some of the trappings of a fad). Yet at its best the WWJD practice encourages Christians to reflect on how they might act as Christ toward their neighbor, as Martin Luther puts it in his celebrated treatise on *Christian Liberty*: "Hence, as our heavenly Father has in Christ freely come to our aid, we also ought freely to help our neighbor through our body and its works, and each one should become as it were a Christ to the other that we may be Christs to one another and Christ may be the same in all."[18]

This motif in Christian thought is so strong that sometimes Christians appeal to Matthew 25 even as they are emphasizing the imitation of Christ. One example is the organization Action by Christians for the Abolition of Torture (ACAT). The organization was founded in 1974 by two Protestant women in France. In its statement of "ethical foundation," the French chapter of the organization, which now has chapters around the world, cites Matthew 25: "The message of the love of Jesus, notably in relation to those who are least and those who suffer, constitutes the ethical foundation of ACAT."[19] This sentence emphasizes Jesus' love toward "the least of these." From this perspective, the work of ACAT against torture (and against the death penalty) is an *imitatio Christi*, a following of Jesus' example of love for those who suffer and who count for little by the dominant measurements of human society.

At the same time, ACAT's statement of ethical foundation suggests another perspective. ACAT identifies "the Crucified" as "the brother of all who are tortured."[20] Jesus not only offers love to those who suffer and who are "the least." In his own death by the torture of crucifixion, Jesus identifies with all who are tortured.

This second perspective more truly expresses the direction in which the story of the sheep and goats moves. The story does not say that in visiting persons who are imprisoned one is being Christ to one's neighbor. Christ appears on the other side of the encounter. In visiting someone imprisoned, the visitor meets Jesus, the Human Being of Matthew's story, in the inmate. On this basis, it is tempting for preachers and teachers to use the promise of an encounter with Jesus as a way of encouraging Christians to visit persons in prison and provide food for those who lack it. The proximity of the sheep-and-the-goats story to the story of Jesus' last supper with his disciples in the Gospel of Matthew can even suggest reading Matthew 25:31–46 in a sacramental light. Christ comes to us in the eucharistic meal; Christ comes to us in the hungry person whom we feed and the sick person whom we visit.

The emphasis on meeting Christ in the hungry person whom we feed or the imprisoned person whom we visit is a precious one. I hope and pray that Christian theology will more closely and consistently pair the widespread emphasis on the presence of Christ in the Lord's Supper with an emphasis on the presence of Christ in the person who receives needed clothing, food, or visitation. Yet the story of the sheep and the goats does not quite allow Christian preachers simply to say, "Visit persons in prison or feed persons who are hungry, for in so doing you will encounter Jesus." The problem with this admonition is that the "sheep" in the story, the persons who are praised for their *diakonia*, insist that they had no idea that in feeding a hungry person they were feeding Jesus, the Human Being, the king presiding over the great judgment. They did not provide food or clothing in the hope or expectation of encountering Jesus.

Here at last is the quandary toward which I have been arguing. How can any Christian who hears or reads this story today follow in the footsteps of the "sheep"? Now that the words of the king in the story have been pronounced—"Inasmuch as you did it unto one of the least of these my brothers and sisters, you did it unto me"—how can readers and hearers of the text go back to the position of the sheep, who had not yet made that connection? The sheep, after all, are the ones who are praised in the story. They are praised for their actions. There is not even a hint of chiding them for failing to make the connection that the king articulates.

One could assume that readers and hearers of the text have the opportunity to be like the sheep, with the added benefit of seeing the connection that the king makes. As already noted, that connection can serve as prime motivation for being like the sheep: in serving your neighbor, you will encounter Jesus. The difficulty with this approach is that the insight provided by the king does not function as a simple add-on to the sheep's action. The king praises the sheep for what they did "unto one of the least of these." If I go to visit a person in prison because I expect to encounter Christ, am I not in a sense visiting two persons: the prison inmate and Christ? Is there not the danger that I will no longer sim-ply be visiting "one of the least of these," but instead will expect to be visiting Christ, the bearer of divine glory? Is there not the danger that I will no longer be treating the person in prison as a fellow member of a realm of ends, as Immanuel Kant put it, but as a means to my desired end of an encounter with Christ? Is there not the danger that I will not just be visiting a person in prison, but using her or him for the purposes of my desired encounter with Christ?

The preaching, teaching, and appropriation of the story of the sheep and the goats confront an odd challenge. The story promises an encounter with Jesus, the Human Being, in the performance of diaconal works of the type that the text enumerates. The story functions analogously to the invitation and promise of the Lord's Supper: in doing this, you will encounter Christ. But there is a major difference. The classical words of institution for the Eucharist quote Jesus say-ing to "do this in remembrance of me." They admonish those who come to the Communion table to have Christ in mind. The words over the bread and cup explicitly remind participants to expect Christ's presence, to come looking for Christ: "this is my body"; "this is my blood."[21]

By contrast, Matthew 25 emphasizes that the people it praises are not think-ing that their act of feeding hungry people is an encounter with Jesus. The sheep in the story do not think of their visits to persons in prison as encounters with Jesus. Perhaps they engaged in such actions hoping or expecting to encounter Jesus, but there is no mention of such hope or expectation. At any rate they are surprised when they hear that they were visiting or feeding Jesus, the Human Being, the king. The event that turns out to be an encounter with Jesus is not one that they thought of in that way while they were engaged in it, or even after they had engaged in it. The text presents them as simply feeding a person who was hungry or visiting a person who was sick.

Even the revelation that these actions were encounters with Jesus by no means displaces the hungry person who received food or the naked person who received clothing. The story does not say, "You thought you were visiting an imprisoned human being—one of many who are imprisoned—but you were wrong. You were actually visiting me." The encounter with Jesus does not come by Jesus replacing the person in prison or the person who is sick or the person who is hungry. Far from it. The primary description of the action remains feeding "one of the least of these" who is hungry. It is in and through this action, done in engagement with this particular concrete human being, that the encounter with Jesus occurs.

The fact that the encounter with Jesus occurs in and through an action that the agents do not understand as an encounter with Jesus means that, in a sense, those of us who live this side of the king's praise of the sheep can only follow the sheep's good model by forgetting about Jesus. If I share food with a person who is hungry because in so doing I will be sharing food with Christ, then I am not doing what the sheep in the story do. Even if the encounter with Christ were not my motivation for sharing food with the hungry person, but simply the theological framework in which I understood what I was doing, I would still not be doing what the sheep do.

How can any course of action be Christian that entails forgetting about Christ? Christ is at the center not only of the Christian life, but of the cosmos. Christ is the incarnate Word, through whom all things come into being, and apart from whom not one thing comes into being (John 1:2). Christ is the Son of God, in whom all things, seen and unseen, in heaven and on earth, are created (Col. 1:16).

Play a bit with the image of a center. A center is what it is only in relation to that which it centers. The center of a circle has its centrality in relation to the circle. In the case of a circle simply as a geometric figure, the center is not even part of the circle. If asked to trace a circle, one does not include the center in the drawing.

In his lectures on Christology—translated into English under the title *Christ the Center!*—Dietrich Bonhoeffer[22] insists on the essentially relational constitution of the person of Christ.

> Christ is Christ not as Christ for himself, but in his relation to me. His being Christ is his being *pro me*. This being *pro me* is not to be understood as an effect originating from him, nor as an accident [i.e., of a substance];

rather it is to be understood as the essence, the being of the person himself. The very core of the person is the *pro me*. This being *pro me* of Christ is not a historical or an ontic statement, but an ontological one. That is, Christ can never be thought in his being in itself, but only in his relation to me.[23]

Bonhoeffer is not content to interpret Christ's being for me as something that Christ happens to choose. The *pro me* character of Christ is not merely an important orientation of a person who might be imagined otherwise. The *pro me* character belongs to Christ's ontological constitution.

The emphasis on Christ *pro me* in Bonhoeffer's christological thinking matures into the reflection in his prison writings on Jesus as "the human being for others." In his "Sketch of a Work," Bonhoeffer states "that Jesus only 'exists for others.'" Faith is participation in this being of Jesus for others.[24] The being of Jesus Christ as center is not discretely self-contained. To be drawn to the center that is Jesus Christ is to be drawn to the others for whom Jesus exists.

In the language of physical forces, one might think of Christ as a dynamic center exercising both a centripetal and a centrifugal force. There is both a movement of being drawn to the center and a movement of being propelled away from the center. Christians are drawn to Christ as the Word and Wisdom of God made flesh. Yet because Jesus is a center whose being is for others, to be drawn into that center is simultaneously to be drawn out to the other for whom Jesus exists. One can imagine a religious movement in toward the center without the movement out toward the others, but that movement would not be a movement toward Jesus Christ.

One of the most popular nonfiction books, religious or otherwise, in recent years in the United States has been Rick Warren's *The Purpose Driven Life*. The book opens with the sentence: "It's not about you."[25] Warren offers a religious critique of self-absorbed individualism. Warren tells his reader in so many words: you can never discover your true purpose as long as your life revolves around yourself. This is certainly an important truth. But Christian theology must hasten to add a second truth, without which the claim that "it's not about you" is also untrue. The gospel declares that for the triune God, "It is about you." If we say that God and not any creature is at the heart of the universe, the gospel insists that God has bound God's own heart to us. If we say with Schleiermacher that each human creature and the entire cosmos is "sheerly dependent" upon God, we need also to say that this God refuses to be God without us. As Ingolf Dalferth puts it, the unconditional love of the triune God is so important for us not because it could be without us, while we could not be without it, but because the divine love "treats our finite life as so infinitely important for it, that it binds its own being to our act of free recognition. With every one of us God's own self is at stake." The resurrection of the crucified Christ by the power of the Spirit is God's act of self-determination "not to actualize God's own being without us or at our expense."[26]

Bonhoeffer is plowing a parallel furrow when he describes Jesus as "the human being for others" or when he insists that being *pro me* belongs to Christ's essence. His goal is not to dissolve Christology. He is not saying that, since Christ's essence is *pro me*, individual human beings should make their *me* the focus of their lives. He is not saying that Christology is just another way of describing the imperative to stand with other human beings in their need.

The specific problem arises in the Christian preaching, teaching, and appropriation of the story of the sheep and the goats. How can the story's Christian hearers properly respond to it? In one sense the path taken by the sheep is no longer an option for us. The story has already made the christological connection in our hearing. Having heard the story, we cannot say that in feeding a hungry person, we had no idea that we were feeding Christ. At the same time, the Matthean judgment scene precludes the possibility of saying, "Let's just devote ourselves to serving human beings in need. This stuff about Jesus and transcendence is beside the point."

Matthew's story enjoins us to forget Christ for christological reasons. More precisely, Matthew enjoins an encounter with Christ in "the least of these" that entails a christological forgetfulness, which is both a forgetting of Christology and a christological forgetting. Following the example of the sheep in the story precludes looking beyond the concrete hungry person in search of Jesus. Such looking beyond smuggles in the assumption that Jesus is ultimately located elsewhere, that Jesus is just making an appearance in the person suffering from hunger. The text does not say, "You did it unto me, disguised as one of the least of these my brothers and sisters." Christ does not "really" look like someone or something else (e.g., a heavenly emperor who "out-emperors" all earthly emperors, as in some depictions of Christus Pantocrator), so that the hungry person is a misleading incognito. The text does not say, "You did it unto me, by using the least of these my brothers and sisters as occasions to serve me spiritually." Persons who are hungry or imprisoned or sick are not means to some more elevated end. They are not vehicles whose value lies in carrying their "benefactors" to an encounter with Christ.

The judgment scene of Matthew 25 enjoins forgetting Christ, in the sense that Christ cannot serve as an extrinsic motive for loving persons in need. Love springing from an extrinsic motive is, to that extent, not love. As José Ignacio González Faus observes in discussing Matthew 25, "It would be a falsification of brotherly love if for it we needed commandments and reasons extrinsic to the human being himself."[27] At the same time, the story of the sheep and the goats rejects taking Christ as an extrinsic motive, because it depicts the encounter with Jesus as happening only in and through focus on and care for human beings in need, without giving a second thought to an additional presence, a Jesus who lurks in the spiritual background.

In her much-admired essay "Reflections on the Right Use of School Studies with a View to the Love of God," Simone Weil emphasizes the importance of seeing the human being in front of you. She goes so far as to say that persons suffering affliction "do not need anything else in this world other than human beings capable of giving them their attention."[28] Truly attending to another human means not seeing her as an abstraction, not losing sight of her unique "who-ness" and "there-ness." Weil warns against two differing forms of such abstraction. One is to let the person who is hungry or imprisoned become simply an exemplar of a category, such as "the needy." For Weil, the love of our neighbor has its fullness in "knowing that the afflicted person exists, not as a unit in a collection, not as an exemplar of the social category labeled 'afflicted,' but as a human being, exactly like us."[29] The other form of abstraction is the one that has occupied us more in this article: abstracting from the concrete human being by using her or him as an occasion for having an encounter with God. As Weil writes, "There are times when, as we look at creatures, we must not think explicitly of the Creator. . . . There are times when thinking of God separates us from Him."[30]

The tension of this final line from Weil echoes the creative tension of Matthew 25. The story of the sheep and the goats may push hearers to forget Christ, but it does so for christological reasons. The encounter with Jesus occurs precisely in forgetfulness of Christ: "When did we see you hungry?" This is not an optional place of encounter. All those judged in the story encountered Jesus unawares. The members of one group gave their attention to those whom they encountered, treating them as "human beings, exactly like us." The members of the other group denied basic human solidarity to those whom they encountered. Those are the only two options presented in the story. There is no third possibility, in which people would be able to meet Jesus and knowingly serve him, in abstraction from human beings in need.

At the same time, the story is not a moral appeal for basic human solidarity for which Jesus would be superfluous. The Jesus who is encountered in what I am calling the forgetfulness of Christ is the king who sits in judgment over "all the nations." The point is not that human solidarity is not enough unless we add a religious dimension to it. The point is that Jesus is constitutive of human solidarity in its humanity and humaneness. This perspective receives strong support from the Council of Chalcedon, if one takes the Chalcedonian definition of Jesus as *vere homo* and *vere Deus* not as combining in one person two preexistently understood natures, but as revealing who God is and who human beings are truly created to be. Paul's conception of Christ as the ultimate Adam (*ho eschatos Adam*—1 Cor. 15:45) in Romans 5:12–21 and 1 Corinthians 15:21–23, 45–49 offers profound possibilities for convergence around this point.

A remarkable rumination on the relation of Christology and human solidarity against the backdrop of Matthew 25 can be found in an address given in 2004 by the Italian theologian Paola Ricca for the thirtieth anniversary of the organization ACAT, mentioned above.[31] Ricca is reflecting upon the question of what is specifically Christian about ACAT's work against torture. He makes the point, too often left implicit or even unnoticed, that Christians are disciples of a person who was tortured. Turning to Matthew 25, Ricca says that "we are called . . . to discern in each tortured human being the features of Jesus whipped and ridiculed." Ricca suggests adding to Matthew 25: "I was tortured and you gave me help and relief."[32]

This is a powerful reading of Matthew 25, but one that does not yet confront the sheep's lack of christological awareness in their ministry to persons in need. The charge to discern the features of the tortured Jesus in each tortured human being, as powerful and as welcome as it is, leaves open a small space of abstraction. It leaves open the possibility that we look too quickly "through" the features of the tortured person before us to see the tortured features of Jesus.

The continuation of Ricca's argument introduces a new feature, a striking move away from such abstraction. Ricca's reflections at this point merit quotation at length:

> What is specifically Christian about ACAT is that communion with Jesus, around which all Christian existence turns, brings with it communion with every tortured human being. For Jesus never comes alone. He is accompanied. One cannot have him without having, along with him, his company, his community. Jesus is with his company before being with us. The tortured person precedes us into the community of Jesus. The tortured person is already there, the traveling companion of Jesus. The issue is thus not simply to see in the tortured other the features of Jesus, but to understand how the bond between Jesus and the tortured person affects our bond with Jesus, to understand that, as Church, to be the body of Christ means being one body with tortured humanity, carrying in a way the stigmata of the Cross in its own body.[33]

The danger of "diaconal abstraction," of looking through, beyond, and in some sense away from the tortured person to see the features of the tortured Jesus, disappears in this new set of formulations. One cannot use "the least of these" as means to the end of an encounter with Jesus, because Jesus "never comes alone." Jesus is always accompanied: by those who are tortured, those who are hungry, those who are sick, those who are imprisoned. If, however subtly, one seeks to leave them behind and to gaze upon Jesus, then it turns out that one has also left Jesus behind.

The story of the sheep and the goats cuts short the temptation to look beyond "the least of these" to see Jesus. It cuts short this temptation not because it seeks to undermine the transcendence of Christ. What is at issue is the nature of that transcendence. Bonhoeffer famously suggested a reconceptualization of transcendence in his prison writings. He rejected the idea that "genuine transcendence" lies in "our relation to God" as the "highest, most powerful, and best being conceivable." The true experience of transcendence is Jesus' "being for others." For that reason "God is beyond in the middle of our life."[34] Nazi executioners cut short Bonhoeffer's opportunity to develop this line of thought more fully. Many later theologians have taken inspiration and guidance from Bonhoeffer's suggestive thoughts. For example, José Ignacio González Faus follows Bonhoeffer in describing Jesus' transcendence as his "being for others" and sees the story of the sheep and the goats as containing an overcoming of "the eternal antinomy between immanence and transcendence."[35] Others have set out on different paths, yet ones that share with Bonhoeffer both the insistence on transcendence and the refusal to define transcendence as the opposite of immanence.[36]

A fuller reconsideration of transcendence would be necessary for a proper articulation of what I have been calling christological forgetfulness in the light of

Matthew 25:31–46. Such an articulation and reconsideration require talking of the Spirit. Here I can only take baby steps in that direction. In so doing I am not undertaking a transition from Christology to pneumatology. Christian theology can only distinguish, never separate the two. Christology must be pneumatological, and pneumatology must be christological. Michael Welker has opened up important perspectives for the mutual explication of Christ and Spirit with his appropriation of Niklas Luhmann's category of "resonance." For Welker, the Spirit is "Christ's domain of resonance." In this use "'domain of resonance' refers to a centered multiplicity of relations of resonance that, once one moves beyond their shared centering, can be independent of each other."[37] It is by the Spirit that Christ is encountered in the person who is hungry, or thirsty, or tortured. Among themselves these persons constitute not only a multiplicity, but a breathtaking diversity. In that diversity they are not an unrelated plurality. In and by the Spirit they all resonate Christ.

Rowan Williams is moving in a direction similar to Welker's when he writes: "To identify Word and Spirit as simply two stages of a single process of divine communication somewhat misses the point of the necessary distinction between the event that defines the field and the terms of the interpretive enterprise, and the enterprise itself."[38] We have no uninterpreted access to Jesus. The attribution to Jesus of the title "Christ" is itself a central instance of Spirit-led interpretation. There is no Christ who is separably "out there" somewhere, seated on a spiritual throne to which we could have unmediated access. According to Matthew 25, "the least of these" hold privileged places in the enterprise of interpretation defined by Christ. "The least of these" are particular human beings, with particular names and faces, who are hungry, who are imprisoned, who are sick, who lack protection and shelter. In their particularity they each specify, they each embody Christ. None of these specifications exhaustively presents Christ for all times and places. For that matter, neither does Jesus of Nazareth as a first-century itinerant teacher. The reason for this is not that some unincarnate divine Christ hovers in reserve above Jesus. Rather the reason is that Christ is disseminated forward in the Spirit's process of christological interpretation. Each particular interpretation, in its deployment of signs in the act of interpretation, is simultaneously the process of further dissemination. "Jesus never comes alone. He is accompanied." Christ as a solitary figure, without dissemination, would be an exhaustive specification that would render the Spirit's interpretation of the incarnate Word unnecessary.

CONCLUSION

How do the christological reflections of this essay help address the question with which we began: "How can Christians live out the commands of Matthew 25—without the pity?" In one sense, the term "commands" can easily set discussion on the wrong path. Quickly the focus comes to rest on persons who have resources to do something—"feed the hungry"—and the command that they do it, that they share their resources. On one side are the givers, the feeders, those with resources, the agents, the providers. On the other side are the recipients, those who are fed, those who lack resources, the victims, those who need to be provided for. Or, as in the example quoted at the outset, on one side are those who offer prayers for "them"; on the other side are "them," the prayed for. Under these circumstances, a transaction infected with pity is inevitable.

In this essay I have sought to explore a different perspective, opened up by the story of the sheep and the goats. In this perspective, christological transcendence, the transcendent Christ, is bodily present in the person who is hungry, sick, imprisoned, or tortured. Each such person is a sacrament. Far from being simply a victim, a recipient with nothing to offer, she bestows the presence of Christ, the Human Being, the ultimate Adam. On this basis relationships can unfold that are not experienced as one way. Many kinds of giving and receiving can interact in supplying content to these relationships: one person may give money, food, shelter, some conversation, laughter. The other person may give a story, a drawing, political insight, human presence, a smile, a tear, a challenging argument. Whatever the specifics, such relationships breathe an air made fresher by the dissipation of pity.

NOTES

1. J. Todd Billings, "On Giving and Receiving," *Sojourners* 36 (April 2007): 48.
2. "Il n'est pas étonnant qu'un homme qui a du pain en donne un morceau à un affamé. Ce qui est étonnant, c'est qu'il soit capable de le faire par un geste différent de celui par lequel on achète un object. L'aumône, quand elle n'est pas surnaturelle, est semblable à une opération d'achat. Elle achète le malheureux," from Simone Weil, "Formes de l'Amour implicite de Dieu," in *Attente de Dieu*, preface by J.-M. Perrin (Paris: Fayard, 1966), 133–34, my translation; English: Simone Weil, "Forms of the Implicit Love of God," in *Waiting for God*, trans. Emma Craufurd, with an introduction by Leslie A. Fiedler (New York: Harper and Row, 1966), 147.
3. On this translation of *ho huios tou anthropou*, see Walter Wink, *The Human Being: Jesus and the Enigma of the Son of the Man* (Minneapolis: Fortress, 2002).
4. Since there is no reason to think that the referent here is exclusively male, *adelphoi* can unproblematically refer to a mixed-gender group.
5. Sherman W. Gray, *The Least of My Brothers: Matthew 25:31–46, a History of Interpretation*, Society of Biblical Literature Dissertation Series (Atlanta: Scholars Press, 1989), 8–9.
6. Ibid., 357.
7. David E. Garland, *Reading Matthew: A Literary and Theological Commentary on the First Gospel* (New York: Crossroad, 1993), 243.
8. Robert H. Gundry, *Matthew: A Commentary on His Handbook for a Mixed Church under Persecution*, 2nd ed. (Grand Rapids: Eerdmans, 1994), 514.
9. "La comunidad de creyentes, los discípulos en todo lugar que sufren como víctimas vulnerables de la persecución, el hambre, la sed, y otras calamidades

relacionadas con su testimonio," from David Cortés-Fuentes, *Mateo, Conozca su Biblia* (Minneapolis: Augsburg Fortress, 2006), 161.

10. George T. Montague, *Companion God: A Cross-Cultural Commentary on the Gospel of Matthew* (Mahwah, N.J.: Paulist, 1989), 282.

11. Daniel Patte, *The Gospel According to Matthew: A Structural Commentary on Matthew's Faith* (Philadelphia: Fortress, 1987), 352n28.

12. "Wir dürfen nicht sagen, diese Brüder Jesu seien nur die Jünger oder die Christenheit; denn das wäre ein eigenmächtiger Zusatz zu Jesu Wort. Er hat allerdings verheißen, daß, wer um seines Namens willen die Kleinen aufnehme oder einem Jünger den Becher mit Wasser reiche, es ihm tue. Aber unser Wort macht Jesu Gnade noch größer, weil er hier von allen Völkern spricht. Darum redet er nicht vom Glauben an ihn und vom Bekenntnis zu seinem Namen, sondern nur von seinem Hunger und seiner Not und nennt damit einen Dienst, den ihm jedermann überall tun kann," from Adolf Schlatter, *Das Evangelium nach Matthäus, ausgelegt für Bibelleser,* Schlatters Erläuterungen zum Neuen Testament (Stuttgart: Calwer, 1947), 376–77.

13. "'Los más pequeños de mis hermanos' (Mt 25,40) tiene una extensión universal, no reducible a los seguidores de Jesús, sino a cualquier hombre en necesidad," from Jon Sobrino, *Jesús en América Latina: Su significado para la fe y la cristología,* 2nd ed., Presencia teológica (Santander: Sal Terrae, 1982), 148.

14. "Aquellos que ya dan por supuesta la vida, el sobrevivir, y aquellos que, precisamente, eso es lo que no dan por supuesto," from Jon Sobrino, *Jesucristo liberador: Lectura histórica-teológica de Jesús de Nazaret* (San Salvador: UCA Editores, 1991), 153.

15. "Las exigencias del Reino llevan a dar vida hoy: dar de comer, de beber, etc."; "los 'más pequeños' y postergados," from Gustavo Gutiérrez, *Compartir la Palabra* (San Salvador: UCA Editores, 1998), 372.

16. "Los más necesitados"; "equivaldría a reducir, de manera indebida, la universalidad tan patente en todos los elementos simbólicos de la parábola," from Juan Luis Segundo, *Historia y actualidad: Sinópticos y Pablo,* vol. II/1 of *El hombre de hoy ante Jesús de Nazaret* (Madrid: Ediciones Cristiandad, 1982), 194n16.

17. "Der Evangelist hat in Jesu notleidenden Brüdern aller Wahrscheinlichkeit nach nicht jeden notleidenden Menschen, sondern notleidende Jünger gesehen," from Ulrich Luz, *Das Evangelium Matthäus (Mt 18–25),* Evangelisch-Katholischer Kommentar zum Neuen Testament I/3 (Zurich: Benziger, 1997), 542.

18. "Ideo sicut pater coelestis nobis in Christo gratis auxiliatus est, ita et nos debemus gratis per corpus et opera eius proximo nostro auxiliari et unusquisque alteri Christus quidam fieri, ut simus mutuum Christi et Christus idem in omnibus, hoc est, vere Christiani," from Martin Luther, "Tractatus de Libertate Christiana," in *Werke: Kritische Gesamtausgabe* (Weimar: Hermann Böhlaus Nachfolger, 1897), 66, 25–28; English: Martin Luther, *Christian Liberty,* trans. W. A. Lambert, rev. Harold J. Grimm (Philadelphia: Fortress, 1985), 30–31.

19. "Le message d'amour de Jésus, notamment vis-à-vis des plus petits et de ceux qui souffrent, constitue le fondement éthique de l'ACAT (Matthieu 25, 35–40)," n.p. (cited April 6, 2007). Online: http://www.acat.asso.fr/.

20. "Le Crucifié"; "le frère de tous les torturés" (ibid.).

21. This much is true regardless of whether one thinks of the "is" in these sentences as literal or symbolic. That is, whether Christ's presence is "real" or "merely spiritual" or however else different strands of Christianity may describe it, my point is simply that the celebration of the Supper explicitly adverts to communication with Christ in such a way that it would be odd for communicants

afterward to say, as the sheep in the story do, that they had no idea that they were engaging with Christ.

22. The published lectures are Eberhard Bethge's reconstruction from notes taken by Bonhoeffer's students.

23. "Christus ist Christus nicht als Christus für sich, sondern in seiner Bezogenheit auf mich. Sein Christus-Sein ist sein pro-me-Sein. Dieses pro-me-Sein will wiederum nicht verstanden sein als eine Wirkung, die von ihm ausgeht, oder als ein Akzidens; sondern es will verstanden sein als das Wesen, als das Sein der Person selbst. Der Personkern selbst ist das pro me. Dieses pro-me-Sein Christi ist keine historische oder ontische Aussage, sondern eine ontologische. D. h. Christus kann nie in seinem an-sich-Sein gedacht werden, sondern nur in seiner Bezogenheit auf mich," from Dietrich Bonhoeffer, "Christologie: Vorlesung ," in *Theologie–Gemeinde: Vorlesungen–Briefe–Gespräche, 1927 bis 1944,* vol. 3 of *Gesammelte Schriften,* ed. Eberhard Bethge (Munich: Chr. Kaiser, 1960), 182; English translation adapted from Dietrich Bonhoeffer, *Christ the Center,* trans. Edwin H. Robertson (New York: Harper and Row, 1978), 47.

24. "Der Mensch für andere"; "daß Jesus nur 'für andere da ist'"; "Glaube ist das Teilnehmen an diesem Sein Jesu," from Dietrich Bonhoeffer, *Widerstand und Ergebung: Briefe und Aufzeichnungen aus der Haft,* new ed., ed. Eberhard Bethge (Munich: Chr. Kaiser, 1977), 414, my translation; English: Dietrich Bonhoeffer, *Letters and Papers from Prison,* ed. Eberhard Bethge, trans. Reginald Fuller (New York: Macmillan, 1966), 237–38.

25. Rick Warren, *The Purpose Driven Life: What on Earth Am I Here For?* (Grand Rapids: Zondervan, 2002), 17.

26. Ingolf U. Dalferth describes the triune God "als unbedingte Liebe, die nicht etwa ihre unendliche Wichtigkeit für uns unabweisbar zur Geltung bringt, weil sie zwar ohne uns, wir aber nicht ohne sie sein könnten, sondern die gerade umgekehrt unser endliches Leben für sich so unendlich wichtig nimmt, daß sie ihr eigenes Sein an die freie Anerkennung durch uns bindet. Mit jedem von uns steht Gott selbst auf dem Spiel, weil er sich in der Auferweckung des Gekreuzigten dazu bestimmt hat, sein eigenes Sein nicht ohne uns oder auf unsere Kosten . . . zu verwirklichen" in *Der auferweckte Gekreuzigte: Zur Grammatik der Christologie* (Tübingen: Mohr Siebeck, 1994), 160.

27. "Sería una falsificación del amor al hermano, si necesitáramos para ello razones extrínsecas al hombre mismo y mandamientos," from José Ignacio González Faus, *La humanidad nueva: Ensayo de Cristología,* 9th ed., Presencia teológica (Santander: Sal Terrae, 1984), 597.

28. "Les malheureux n'ont pas besoin d'autre chose en ce monde que d'hommes capables de faire attention à eux," from Simone Weil, "Réflexions sur le bon usage des études scolaires en vue de l'Amour de Dieu," in *Attente de Dieu,* preface by J.-M. Perrin (Paris: Fayard, 1966), 96; English translation adapted from Simone Weil, "Reflections on the Right Use of School Studies with a View to the Love of God," in *Waiting for God,* trans. Emma Craufurd, with an introduction by Leslie A. Fiedler (New York: Harper and Row, 1966), 114.

29. "C'est savoir que le malheureux existe, non pas comme unité dans une collection, non pas comme un exemplaire de la catégorie sociale étiquetée 'malheureux,' mais en tant qu'homme, exactement semblable à nous," from Weil, "Réflexions sur le bon usage," 97; English translation adapted from Weil, "Right Use of School Studies," 115.

30. "Il y a des moments où en regardant les créatures il ne faut pas penser explicitement au Créateur. . . . Il y a des moments où penser à Dieu nous sépare

de Lui," from Weil, "L'Amour implicite de Dieu," 138; English translation adapted from Weil, "Implicit Love of God," 151.

31. A transcription of the address is posted on the Web site of the French chapter of ACAT at http://www.acat.asso.fr/courrier/annee_2005/Courrier_260/Ricca_260.htm (cited April 8, 2007). The transcription was posted without being reviewed by Professor Ricca.

32. "Nous sommes appelés à . . . discerner dans chaque humain torturé les traits de Jésus fouetté et raillé"; "J'ai été torturé, et vous m'avez secouru et soulagé" (ibid., 3).

33. "La spécificité chrétienne de l'ACAT est que la communion avec Jésus, sur qui toute existence chrétienne est axée, entraîne la communion avec chaque humain torturé. Car Jésus ne vient jamais seul. Il est accompagné. On ne peut pas l'avoir sans avoir, avec lui, sa compagnie, sa communauté. Jésus est avec lui avant d'être avec nous. Le torturé nous précède dans la communauté de Jésus. Le torturé est déjà là, compagnon de route de Jésus. Il ne s'agit donc pas seulement de voir dans l'autre torturé les traits de Jésus, mais de comprendre combien le lien entre Jésus et le torturé affecte notre lien avec Jésus, de comprendre qu'être, comme Église, le corps du Christ veut dire faire corps avec l'humanité torturée, porter en quelque sorte les stigmates de la Croix en son propre corps" (ibid.).

34. "Unser Verhältnis zu Gott ist kein 'religiöses' zu einem denkbar höchsten, mächstigsten, besten Wesen—dies ist keine echte Transzendenz"; "Das 'Für-andere-Dasein' Jesu ist die Transzendenzerfahrung!"; "Gott ist mitten im unsern Leben jenseits," from Bonhoeffer, *Widerstand und Ergebung*, 414, 308, my translation; English: Bonhoeffer, *Letters and Papers*, 237–38, 166.

35. "La eterna antinomia entre inmanencia y trascendencia," from González Faus, *La humanidad nueva*, 597.

36. Especially promising for reflection in conjunction with Matt. 25:31–46 are the thoughts on transcendence and fleshly embodiment in Mayra Rivera Rivera, "Ethical Desires: Towards a Theology of Relational Transcendence," in *Toward a Theology of Eros: Transfiguring Passion at the Limits of Discipline*, ed. Virginia Burrus and Catherine Keller (New York: Fordham University Press, 2006). For an important insistence upon the historicity of transcendence, see Ignacio Ellacuría, "Historicidad de la salvación cristiana," in *Escritos teológicos,* Colección Teología Latinoamericana 25 (San Salvador: UCA Editores, 2000), 535–96.

37. "Unter Resonanz*bereich* ist eine zentrierte Vielzahl von Resonanzverhältnissen zu verstehen, die über die gemeinsame Zentrierung hinaus voneinander unabhängig sein können," from Michael Welker, *Gottes Geist: Theologie des Heiligen Geistes* (Neukirchen-Vluyn: Neukirchener, 1992), 289, 288; English translation: Michael Welker, *God the Spirit*, trans. John F. Hoffmeyer (Minneapolis: Fortress, 1994), 314, 313.

38. Rowan Williams, "Trinity and Revelation," in *On Christian Theology*, Challenges in Contemporary Theology (Oxford: Blackwell, 2000), 144.

11

Children, the Image of God, and Christology

*Theological Anthropology
in Solidarity with Children*

MARCIA J. BUNGE

Over the past ten years, scholars in a number of disciplines have turned their attention to children and childhood. Important studies on childhood are now emerging not only in those fields typically devoted to children, such as education and child psychology, but also in history, law, literature, philosophy, sociology, and anthropology. This burgeoning new interdisciplinary area of Childhood Studies is challenging many assumptions about children and opening new lines of intellectual inquiry in a variety of disciplines.[1]

Christian theologians and ethicists are also contributing to the emerging area of Childhood Studies. Like scholars in other disciplines, they are finding that the lens of the child—just like the lens of gender, race, or class—sheds new light on and sometimes challenges a discipline's existing ideas, practices, and methods. The particular lens of the child is helping theologians to reexamine their own presuppositions about children and childhood, to expose neglected or distorted elements of the Christian tradition regarding children, and to reevaluate central Christian beliefs and practices with attention to children.

As a result, Christian theologians and ethicists are beginning to articulate both theologies of childhood and child theologies. This distinction is just emerging among some Christian theologians, ethicists, and practitioners.[2] Theologies of childhood, on the one hand, primarily provide sophisticated understandings of children and childhood and our obligations to children themselves. On the other hand, child theologies reexamine not only conceptions of children and obligations to them but also fundamental doctrines and practices of the church. Drawing on analogies to feminist, black, and liberation theologies, child theologies have as their task not only to strengthen the commitment to and understanding of a group that has often been voiceless, marginalized, or oppressed—children— but also to reinterpret Christian theology and practice as a whole.[3]

One of the areas that must be reexamined both in developing theologies of childhood and child theologies is theological anthropology. Although all human beings on earth once were or are now children, almost all work in the area of theological anthropology both in the past and today has explored the human condition with reference to adults alone. In general, Christian theologians have not provided sound theological understandings of the human condition that take into account both the development and the full humanity of children.

The aim of this essay is to offer the modest beginnings of a biblically informed Christian theological anthropology that takes into account the dignity and complexity of children as well as adults. More particularly, it uses the lens of the child to revisit some of the central themes of Christian theological anthropology, drawing implications for our views and treatment of children and for theological understandings of human nature in general. The essay begins by outlining a biblically informed view of the image of God and its implications for our understanding of the dignity and full humanity of all human beings, including children. It then explores how a theological anthropology that takes seriously the development and full humanity of children might be strengthened and informed by the doctrine of the incarnation and by Christ's own ministry and teaching, including his action of placing a child "in the midst" of a theological argument about the greatness in the kingdom of heaven.

By using the lens of the child to revisit central elements of theological anthropology, this essay contributes to a theology of childhood and to theological understandings of the human condition. It provides a complex and biblically informed view of children and childhood that challenges common and often narrow conceptions of children in contemporary culture and the church. As it outlines a more comprehensive theological understanding of children, the essay, at the same time, challenges reductionistic theologies of human nature in general. In this sense, it serves the developing areas of theologies of childhood and child theologies, generating new questions not only about children but also about theological anthropology in general.

CHILDREN ARE HUMAN BEINGS: THE IMAGE OF GOD AND THE FULL HUMANITY OF ALL CHILDREN

Almost every Christian theological understanding of human nature lifts up the importance of human beings created in the image of God. The biblical passages that support this claim come primarily from the Priestly writer in chapters 1 and 5 of Genesis:

> Then God said, "Let us make humankind in our image, according to our likeness, and let them have dominion over the fish of the sea, and over the birds of the air, and over the cattle, and over all the wild animals of the earth, and over every creeping thing that creeps upon the earth." So God created humankind in his image, in the image of God he created them; male and female he created them. God blessed them, and God said to them, "Be fruitful and multiply, and fill the earth and subdue it; and have dominion over the fish of the sea and over the birds of the air and over every living thing that moves upon the earth." (Gen. 1:26–28)

> When God created humankind, he made them in the likeness of God. Male and female he created them, and he blessed them and named them "Humankind" when they were created. (Gen. 5:1b–2)

The notion that human beings are created in the image of God is also mentioned in Genesis 9:6: "Whoever sheds the blood of a human, by a human shall that person's blood be shed; for in his own image God made humankind."[4]

Although Christian theologians cite these passages and affirm that human beings are made in the image of God, they have variously defined the exact meaning of this claim. As Hall suggests, theologians have tended to define "image of God" in either substantialist or relational terms.[5] Although these categories are certainly not exhaustive, they do help sort out some of the basic approaches theologians have taken to interpreting the meaning of the image of God. Substantialists tend to define the image of God primarily in terms of some kind of physical, emotional, intellectual, or spiritual attribute or endowment, such as physical appearance, rationality, immortality, or free will. Throughout the history of Christianity, theologians have, for example, proposed that the image of God is revealed primarily in the seemingly unique quality of human reason or rationality. This is what distinguishes them from other animals and is the basis for their dominion over them. Yet many other qualities have been proposed, including the outward appearance of human beings, their immortal soul, their ability to make moral decisions, or their ability to love others.[6]

Relationalists conceive of the image of God more as "an inclination or proclivity occurring within the relationship."[7] Hall and others have tended to support relational understandings of the image of God for a number of reasons, and they outline in various ways the specific and distinctive relationships that human beings are to have with God, others, and the created world. For example, Hall claims that "relationship is the essence" of a human being's "nature and vocation."[8] For Hall, all central biblical notions, such as love, justice, and righteousness, are relational. For him, human beings, who are made in the image of God, are to live in a right relationship with God that expresses itself in right relationships with all other creatures. Building on Calvin, Hall says that the vocation of human beings is to respond to God in such a way that "God may be able to behold himself in [us] as in a mirror."[9]

Contemporary theologians and biblical scholars who emphasize the relational meaning of "image of God," including Michael Welker, have been especially helpful in outlining more clearly the specific relationship of dominion that human beings have toward the rest of creation. They have examined the Hebrew word *radah*, "to have dominion," in relation to its parallel, *kabash,* "to subdue," trying to clarify the kind of relationship the biblical texts outline between human beings and other living creatures. They have persuasively shown that dominion in the biblical sense cannot be equated with exploitation. Rather, as Welker has shown, although the biblical texts do depict human beings as having primacy over other animals, "The spread of human beings is inseparably tied to the [care-taking] maintenance of the community of solidarity with the animals."[10] In line with Welker, biblical scholar Sibley Towner also says that the "image of God" is a relational term that describes humanity's relationship with God, other human beings, and creation, and that the biblical notion of dominion is not to be equated with exploitation but rather understood in the sense of justice and right rule.[11] In his book *The Liberating Image: The* Imago Dei *in Genesis 1*,[12] J. Richard Middleton emphasizes that the biblical notion of the "image of God" and "dominion" challenged social stratification and common notions of kingship in other ancient Near Eastern cultures, for the biblical texts affirm that all human beings (not just kings, the rich, or the elite) bear the *imago Dei*, and consequently they all bear the responsibility of "ruling" with justice and "having dominion" over the earth. For Middleton, understanding the *imago Dei* this way leads to "an ethic characterized fundamentally by power with rather than power over."[13]

Despite the helpful nuances they have given to what it means for human beings to be made in the image of God and to have dominion over other creatures, and amid the various substantist and relational understandings of the image of God, both contemporary and classical theologians have tended to think of the image of God only in relation to adults. The neglect of including children into discussions of the image of God is all the more strange because one of the ways of speaking about "image" and "likeness" in the Bible is not so much in terms of male/female relationships, as contemporary theologians often empha-size, but rather child/parent relationships. The Hebrew for "image" (*selem*) is sometimes connected to the Hebrew for "likeness" (*demut*), and both terms are used in speaking about child/parent relationships. For example, Genesis 5:3 uses these terms in speaking about Adam and Seth: "When Adam had lived one hun-dred thirty years, he became the father of a son in his likeness (*demut*), according to his image (*selem*), and named him Seth."

Since all human beings are made in the image of God, as theologians and the biblical texts affirm, we must recognize and affirm in any theological anthropology that children, too, are made in the image of God. As made in God's image, chil-dren, like all adults, are fully human. The biblical texts affirm that "humankind" is made in the image of God. It is a universal category. Thus, all human beings— regardless of gender, race, social status, cultural context, and country—regardless, too, of age—are made in the image of God from the beginning of their lives.

The notion that children are fully human and made in the image of God has often been neglected in Christianity, and children have been referred to as "animals," "beasts," "pre-rational," "pre-adults," "almost human," "not quite human," or "on their way to becoming human." However, some theologians have emphasized the full humanity of children, including infants. For example, Cyprian, the third-century bishop of Carthage, argues that children and adults are equally images of God. In his letter, "To Fidus: On the Baptism of Infants," for example, he claims,

> Moreover, belief in divine Scripture declares to us, that among all, whether infants or those who are older, there is the same equality of the divine gift. . . . All [human beings] are like and equal, since they have once been made by God; and our age may have a difference in the increase of our bodies, according to the world, but not according to God.[14]

For Cyprian, all human beings are made by God. "For what is wanting," he wonders, to one "who has once been formed in the womb by the hand of God?"

The twentieth-century Catholic theologian Karl Rahner also powerfully affirms the full humanity of children. Although he writes very little directly about children, his short essay on "Ideas for a Theology of Childhood" (1966) articulates the beginnings of a robust and complex theology of childhood and affirms children's full humanity and integrity.[15] In this extended but important quotation from this essay, Rahner asserts the full humanity and uniqueness of each child and their immediate relationship with God:

> First and foremost the child is [*a human being*]. Probably there is no religion and no philosophic anthropology which insists so manifestly and so upon this point as one of its basic presuppositions as does Christianity; the point namely that the child is already [a human being], that right from the beginning he is already in possession of that value and those depths which are implied in the name of [a human being]. It is not simply that he gradually grows into a [person]. He *is* a [person]. As his personal history unfolds he merely realizes what he already *is*. . . . The child is the [person] whom God has called by a name of *his own*, who is fresh and unique in each individual instance, never merely a "case," a particular application in the concrete of a general idea, *always* having a personal value of his own and therefore worthy to endure for ever. . . . The child is the [human being] who is, right from the first, the partner of God; he who opens his eyes only to keep that vision before him in which an incomprehensible mystery is regarding him; he who cannot halt at any point in his course because infinity is calling him; who can love the smallest thing because for him it is always filled with the all; he who does not feel the ineffable as lethal to him, because he experiences the fact that when he entrusts himself to it without reserve he falls into the inconceivable depths of love and blessedness . . . This is how Christianity views [the human being] and it sees all this already present in the child. And for this reason it protects the child while it is still in its mother's womb. It takes pains to ensure that the sources of life are not poured away upon the trifles of the lowlands of mere

lust and desire. It has reverence for the child, for the child is [a human being]. . . . The child is a [human being] *right at the very outset.*[16]

Jewish theologian Martin Buber also lifts up the uniqueness and creative potential of each human being and how their characteristics are present right from the start of each human life as an expression of the image of God.

> In every hour the human race begins. We forget this too easily in face of the massive fact of past life, of so-called world history, of the fact that each child is born with a given disposition of world historical origin, that is, inherited from the riches of the whole human race, and also born into a given situation of world historical origin, that is, produced from the riches of the world's events. This fact must not obscure the other no less important fact that in spite of everything, in this as in every hour, what has not been invades the structure of what is, with ten thousand countenances, of which not one has been seen before, with ten thousand souls still undeveloped but ready to develop—a creative event if ever there was one, newness rising up, primal potential might. This potentiality, streaming unconquered, however much of it is squandered, is the reality *child:* this phenomenon of uniqueness, which is more than just begetting and birth, this grace of beginning again and ever again.[17]

We could cite other examples, yet it is enough to affirm at this point that any theological claims about human beings as made in the image of God should include claims about children. Like adults, children, too, are human beings from the start. They are worthy of dignity and respect. They are also, from the start, in relationship to God, to other human beings, and to other creatures. God is fully present to them—just as God is present to adults. Like adults, they are full members of the community. We are accountable to them—just as we are to other adults. Like each adult, each child is created in his or her own uniqueness, and a child's creativity is also a reflection of the creativity of God. We are to build relationships with children in line with the image of God—relationships of love, justice, peace, reconciliation, and forgiveness. We do not have dominion over children. Rather, they also share, with adults, dominion over other creatures. And whatever dominion they have over other creatures is certainly not to be understood in terms of exploitation but rather in lines with God's concern for and care of all creation.

JESUS BECAME A CHILD: THE INCARNATION, THEOLOGICAL ANTHROPOLOGY, AND CHILDREN

In addition to building on the concept of the image of God, many forms of classical and contemporary theological anthropology also incorporate attention to the doctrine of the incarnation and the belief that Jesus Christ became a human being. Although there are diverse forms of Christianity that have denied Jesus' full humanity as well as his divinity, from the early church councils to denominational statements today, most Christians confess that Jesus Christ, although God, was also a human being. The Council of Chalcedon, for example, stated that Jesus Christ had two natures: one human and one divine. More recently, Vatican II's *Gaudium et Spes* (22) continued to affirm Jesus' full humanity, claiming: "Human nature as [Jesus] assumed it was not annulled. . . . He worked with human hands, he thought with a human mind, he acted by human choice, and loved with a human heart." Certain forms of Christianity today do reject Jesus' divine nature, yet continue to affirm that he was a human being.

Such affirmations of Jesus' humanity are often used to provide further grounds for affirming the dignity and value of all human beings. Christianity, like Judaism, certainly affirms that human beings are created by God, and they are made in the image of God. They are worthy of dignity and respect. The doctrine of the incarnation supports and deepens these claims. Since Jesus himself was a human being, since God chose to reveal Godself through this particular human being of Jesus Christ, since God chose to identify with humanity by becoming a human being, since God chose to speak in and through the form of a human being, . . . for these and other reasons, the dignity and worth of each human being is in some way heightened.

Within the Roman Catholic Church, for example, *Gaudium et Spes* (22) claims that since Jesus assumed human nature, human beings are also raised to a "dignity beyond compare." Such affirmations lead, as the American Catholic theologian Elizabeth Johnson recognizes, to a very strong sense in the Roman Catholic Church of the "dignity of every human being precisely as human, and to a very strong social teaching with regard to human rights. The church's social teaching is not based only on simple humanism, but on a deep christological motif: God has so identified with our humanity that each of us as human beings has been lifted to a dignity beyond compare."[18] As Johnson claims, renewed Catholic reflection on Jesus' humanity, sparked by the thinking of Karl Rahner and expressed in recent Catholic teachings, has led to "a new appreciation of the incomparable dignity of every human being."[19]

While acknowledging that Jesus was a human being, theologians today and in the past sometimes neglect to affirm that Jesus was also an infant and grew up as a child or to draw implications of the incarnation for our attitudes and treatment of children. In other words, the "heightened" worth and dignity of human beings, which is affirmed in the incarnation, is not always applied to children themselves. Even forms of narrative theology that focus on Jesus' own life story, mining the Scripture for what they have to say about the story of Jesus in history, often neglect or place very little attention on Jesus' birth or childhood and on the implications of this part of his story for the story of faith communities today. They focus on Jesus' adult activities. Even Johnson, cited earlier, or other contemporary feminist theologians who have emphasized so forcefully the dignity of all human beings based on the incarnation and include attention to the full humanity of women, often neglect to emphasize the full humanity of children. They also often view the story of Jesus beginning with his adult ministry. For Johnson, for example, Jesus' story includes his "ministry, death, and resurrection," and his ministry in turn comprises "three elements: his preaching, characteristic way of behaving, and manner of relating to God."[20]

Yet Jesus' story clearly includes his birth and childhood, and the Gospels of Luke and Matthew both include birth narratives. Luke also includes the story of Jesus as a boy of twelve, going to Jerusalem for the festival of Passover and growing in wisdom:

> The child grew and became strong, filled with wisdom; and the favor of God was upon him. Now every year his parents went to Jerusalem for the festival of the Passover. And when he was twelve years old, they went up as usual for the festival. . . . And Jesus increased in wisdom and in years, and in divine and human favor. (Luke 2:40–42, 52)

If we keep in mind these and other passages regarding Jesus' birth and childhood, and if we revisit the incarnation with the lens of the child, then any theological anthropology that builds on elements of the incarnation must include attention to children as well as adults. More specifically, these passages remind us that any value that we claim for adults based on Christ's incarnation must also be applied to children. The dignity of every human being emphasized in the incarnation is present also in infants and children. Birth and childhood themselves are also given a kind of heightened dignity and value—for Christ became a child. Furthermore, just as the church builds on insights of the incarnation to develop strong social teachings with regard to human rights, the church must also develop strong social teaching with regard to children's rights. In the incarnation we also see the vulnerability of Jesus himself, and we are reminded of the vulnerability of all children. As Pope John Paul II stated,

> In what happened to the Child of Bethlehem you can *recognize what happens to children throughout the world.* It is true that a child represents the joy not only of its parents but also the joy of the Church and the whole of society. But it is also true that in our days, unfortunately, many children in different parts of the world are suffering and being threatened: they are hungry and poor, they are dying from diseases and malnutrition, they are the victims of war, they are abandoned by their parents and condemned to remain without a home, without the warmth of a family of their own, they suffer many forms of violence and arrogance from grown-ups. How can we not care, when we see the suffering of so many children, especially when this suffering is in some way caused by grown-ups?[21]

JESUS' MINISTRY AND TEACHING: JESUS WELCOMES CHILDREN, HEALS THEM, AND PUTS A CHILD IN THE MIDST OF A THEOLOGICAL ARGUMENT ABOUT THE KINGDOM OF HEAVEN

Even if we do focus solely on Jesus' adult ministry and teaching for insights into theological anthropology, we find insights not only into adults but also into children. The New Testament presents children and childhood in striking and even radical ways, and children playing a significant role in Jesus' ministry and teaching. Children and childhood are not a matter of insignificance for Jesus. The Gospels especially turn upside-down common assumptions held in Jesus' time and our own regarding children, including the assumption that their primary role is to learn from and to obey adults. In contrast, the Gospels depict children taking on a number of roles. They prophesy and praise God. They share their food with others. Jesus speaks of them as models of faith and representatives of himself. "Unless you change and become like children, you will never enter the kingdom of heaven," Jesus warns. "Whoever becomes humble like this child is the greatest in the kingdom of heaven. Whoever welcomes one such child in my name welcomes me" (Matt. 18:3–5). Viewing children as models for adults or vehicles of revelation does not mean that they are creatures who are near angels, closer to God, or more spiritual than adults. However, these passages and others do challenge adults to be receptive to the lessons and wisdom that children offer them, to honor children's questions and insights, and to recognize that children can positively influence the community and the moral and spiritual lives of adults.

Although there is much to mine from Jesus' ministry and teaching for theologies of childhood and for theological anthropologies in general, this essay lifts up three significant elements.

First, Jesus blesses, embraces, touches, welcomes, and heals children as well as adults. All four Gospels give accounts of Jesus healing children, and those healed include both Gentile and Jewish children. For example, he heals an epileptic child (Matt. 17:14–20; Mark 9:14–29; Luke 9:37–43). He also heals the daughter of Jairus, a leader of the synagogue (Mark 5:22–43; Matt. 9:18–26; Luke 8:40–56). Jesus takes her "by the hand" and says to her, "Little girl, get up!" (Mark 5:42). He heals the daughter of a Canaanite woman (Matt. 15:21–28; Mark 7:24–30). He also heals the son of a Gentile military officer in Capernaum (John 4:46–53).

Second, Jesus also directly places a child in the midst of a theological argument about the kingdom of heaven. This event is mentioned in all three Synoptic Gospels (Matt. 18:1–5; Mark 9:33–37; Luke 9:46–48):

> At that time the disciples came to Jesus and asked, "Who is the greatest in the kingdom of heaven?" He called a child, whom he put among them, and said, "Truly I tell you, unless you change and become like children, you will never enter the kingdom of heaven. Whoever becomes humble like this child is the greatest in the kingdom of heaven. Whoever welcomes one such child in my name welcomes me." (Matt. 18:1–5)

In Matthew 18 and its parallel passages, Jesus does not place the child in the midst of the disciples in order to heal him or her, as in the previously mentioned texts. In these passages, there is no sign that this child was helped or healed. Rather, in this case Jesus put the child in the middle of an argument with his disciples about the greatness of the kingdom of God. As those involved in the Child Theology

Movement often say, in this particular passage, the child is a "clue to," "sign of," or "guide to" the nature of the kingdom of God and the way into it.[22]

Third, Jesus also warns and rebukes those who turn away or despise children or who put a stumbling block in their way. Matthew 18:6–7 states,

> "If any of you put a stumbling block before one of these little ones who believe in me, it would be better for you if a great millstone were fastened around your neck and you were drowned in the depth of the sea. Woe to the world because of stumbling blocks! Occasions for stumbling are bound to come, but woe to the one by whom the stumbling block comes!"

"These little ones" are part of his horizon, part of his concern, part of his ministry:

> "Take care that you do not despise one of these little ones; for, I tell you, in heaven their angels continually see the face of my Father in heaven. What do you think? If a shepherd has a hundred sheep, and one of them has gone astray, does he not leave the ninety-nine on the mountains and go in search of the one that went astray? And if he finds it, truly I tell you, he rejoices over it more than over the ninety-nine that never went astray. So it is not the will of your Father in heaven that one of these little ones should be lost." (Matt. 18:10–14)

Although these three elements of Jesus' ministry and teaching have been widely interpreted and reinterpreted, they all indicate children and childhood are central to his message, his actions, and even to Jesus' own self-identity. Jesus includes children in his healing ministry. He is surrounded by children; he embraces, touches, and heals them. He directly rebukes those who reject them. Furthermore, he links "becoming like a child" to entering the kingdom. And he links "welcoming children" to welcoming himself.

IMPLICATIONS OF PLACING A CHILD IN THE MIDST OF CHRISTIAN THEOLOGICAL ANTHROPOLOGY

Despite the limited scope of this particular essay, the implications for our attitudes to and treatment of children that follow from a rereading of just three elements that inform Christian theological anthropology are far-reaching. For example, if the church kept in mind that the image of God applies to children as well as adults and that Jesus healed and embraced children as well as adults in his own ministry, then the church might more readily treat all children, regardless of age, race, class, or gender, with more dignity and respect. The church would no longer tolerate or ignore the abuse or harsh treatment of children, including abuse that occurs within the church itself. Furthermore, the church's approach to human rights and social justice issues would include more attention to children. The church would become a stronger and more creative advocate for children and do more to address the host of challenges that children around the world face today, such as poverty, inadequate schooling, or lack of health care. It would also expand its discussion of contemporary ethical issues, such as environmental problems, economic injustices, and consumerism to include attention to the impact of such problems in the lives of children.

If the church recognized that Jesus lifted up children as representatives of himself and models for entering the kingdom of God, then the church would also strengthen spiritual formation and religious education programs, restructuring them in ways that not only cultivate children's growing moral capacities and responsibilities but also honor their questions and insights. Such programs would recognize the importance of teaching children the faith as well as the role of children in the spiritual maturation of parents and other adults.

Turning attention to themes central to Christian theological anthropology through the lens of the child sheds new light, however, not only on our attitudes to and treatment of children but also on larger themes of Christian faith and practice. Focusing on the image of God with the lens of the child sharply reveals its radical breadth. "It also helps emphasize the importance of interpreting biblical notions of 'likeness' and 'image' not only in terms of God-human, adult-adult, or male-female relationships—which is often the case today—but also in terms of the complex and dynamic relationships that are highlighted throughout the Bible between God and children, adults and children, children and children, and parents and children."[23]

Focusing on the incarnation through this lens also opens up new perspectives on the biblical concept of wisdom. The Gospel of Luke testifies that Jesus was filled with wisdom as a child and that he "increased in wisdom." Other biblical texts depict wisdom in connection not only to Jesus or to a female figure but also to children and children at play. For example, the prophet Zechariah includes the image of children at play in his vision of a restored Zion. At a future time, when Jerusalem is restored as a faithful city, "the streets of the city shall be full of boys and girls playing in its streets" (Zech. 8:5). In Proverbs, divine wisdom, often portrayed solely as a woman, is also depicted as a child who is playing, delighting, and growing:[24]

> When [God] established the heavens, I [Wisdom] was there,
>   When he circumscribed the surface of the deep,
> When he secured the skies above,
>   When he stabilized the spring of the deep,
> When he assigned the sea its limit,
>   Lest the waters transgress his command,
> When he carved out the foundations of the earth,
>   *I was beside him growing up,*
> And I was his delight day by day,
>   Playing before him always,
> Playing in his inhabited world,
>   And delighting in the human race.
>   (Prov. 8:27–31, William Brown's trans.)

As Brown notes, such imagery highlights the "primacy of play when it comes to the sapiential way of life. The authority that wisdom embodies is not 'grave' but creative, and playfully so."[25]

CONCLUSION

This essay has explored just three areas that inform Christian theological anthropology, and certainly much more could and must be mined from the tradition for a solid theological anthropology that takes into account the development and full humanity of children. Most Christians confess that human beings are made in the image of God yet also sinful, for example, and their understanding of human nature also incorporates and reflects a certain understanding of sin and responsibility. If we take into account children and childhood as we reflect on human sin, then we are bound to expand, deepen, and perhaps even shift our assumptions about sin, and we will be compelled to ask new questions about many related issues and concepts, such as selfhood, moral agency, conscience, free will, innocence, embodiment, and sexuality. Furthermore, as we mine the biblical texts, the tradition, and wisdom from other disciplines for insights into children and human nature in general, our assumptions about children will also change. Instead of viewing children primarily as either sinful or innocent, as Christian theologians have tended to do today and in the past, we will discover and must hold in tension many of the insightful and almost paradoxical notions of children found in the Bible and the Christian tradition: as developing creatures in need of instruction, yet as fully human beings made in the image of God; as sinful beings and symbols of immature faith, yet as vehicles of revelation and models of faith; as gifts of God and sources of joy, yet as orphans and strangers in need of justice and compassion.[26]

Indeed, those within the Christian community who are offering fruitful directions in theologies of childhood and child theologies are building upon and exploring a number of elements of the tradition that could positively inform a robust theological anthropology, and they are incorporating a wide range of questions, sources, and approaches into their theologies. Bonnie Miller-McLemore, for example, incorporates insights from feminism, pyschology, and the Christian tradition to provide a strong theological understanding of children and to prompt a renewed conception of the care of children as a religious practice and community discipline.[27] John Wall draws on theological and philosophical ethics to develop a social ethics of child rearing that takes into account multiple levels of social responsibility to children.[28] Paul Parvis and Kathleen Marshall explore the concept of children's rights and parental authority with the help of biblical sources, social policy research, and historical, philosophical, and legal perspectives on rights.[29] Jürgen Moltmann integrates biblical texts with philosophical sources, such as the work of Ernst Bloch or Hannah Arendt, to rethink the concept of hope.[30] Dawn DeVries takes seriously children's perspectives as a source for theological reflection as she reinterprets doctrines of salvation and eschatology.[31] Kristin Herzog calls for a theology of childhood that builds on the Bible as well as images of and ideas about children from many world religions.[32] In his discussion of human dignity and child labor, Deusdedit R. K. Nkurunziza incorporates insights from the Bible, Karl Rahner, and traditional African cultures.[33] As Christian theologians continue to use the lens of the child to reexamine Christian faith and practice in a number of areas, and as they build upon the work being carried out in the area of theologies of childhood and child theologies, all of us—regardless of our religious commitments—are challenged to reevaluate our own views of and commitments to children. Furthermore, placing children "in the midst" of serious theological reflection also generates new thinking about how we all, in some way, share much in common—regardless of our age or status—with "these little ones."

NOTES

1. For a review of some of the recent studies, see Scott Heller, "The Meaning of Children Becomes a Focal Point for Scholars," *Chronicle of Higher Education* (August 7, 1998): 14–15.

2. For an introduction to this distinction and to literature on children and childhood in the areas of religious studies, theology. and ethics, see Marcia J. Bunge, "The Child, Religion, and the Academy: Developing Robust Theological and Religious Understandings of Children and Childhood," in *Journal of Religion* 86, no. 4 (October 2007): 549–79.

3. The term "child theology" was first coined by Keith J. White, Haddon Willmer, and John Collier, leaders of the Child Theology Movement (see their Web site for more information: www.childtheology.org). Although they take a certain approach to reexamining Christian faith and practice, the term can and has been used more generally to refer to a variety of approaches.

4. This text links an apparently early law against murder with one of the three *imago Dei* passages attributed to the late Priestly source. The fact suggests that the "image" concept may have had a history prior to its elevation to fundamental status by P. See J. Maxwell Miller, "In the 'Image' and 'Likeness' of God," *Journal of Biblical Literature* 91 (1972): 289–304.

5. Douglas John Hall, *Imaging God: Dominion as Stewardship* (Grand Rapids: Eerdmans, 1986).

6. See W. Sibley Towner for an excellent discussion of the image of God and a survey of its many interpretations, "Clones of God: Genesis 1:26–28 and the Image of God in the Hebrew Bible," *Interpretation* 59, no. 4 (October 2005): 341–56.

7. Hall, *Imaging God,* 98.

8. Ibid., 107.

9. Citing T. F. Torrance, *Calvin's Doctrine of Man* (Grand Rapids: Eerdmans, 1957), 91.

10. Michael Welker, "Creation and the Image of God: Their Understanding in Christian Tradition and the Biblical Grounds," *Journal of Ecumenical Studies* 34 (1997): 447.

11. Towner, "Clones of God," 341–56.

12. J. Richard Middleton, *The Liberating Image: The* Imago Dei *in Genesis 1* (Grand Rapids: Brazos, 2005).

13. Ibid., 297.

14. "To Fidus: On the Baptism of Infants," in *The Ante-Nicene Fathers: The Writings of the Fathers Down to A.D. 325*, vol. 5 (Peabody, Mass.: Hendrickson, 1994), 354.

15. See Rahner's "Gedanken zu einer theologie der Kindheit," in *Schriften zur Theologie* 8 (Einsiedeln: Benziger Verlag, 1966), 313–29; trans. by David Bourke as "Ideas for a Theology of Childhood," in *Theological Investigations*, vol. 8 (London: Darton, Longman & Todd, 1971), 33–50. For an excellent discussion of Rahner's views on children and childhood, see Mary Ann Hinsdale, "'Infinite Openness to the Infinite': Karl Rahner's Contribution to Modern Catholic Thought on the Child," in *The Child in Christian Thought*, ed. Marcia J. Bunge (Grand Rapids: Eerdmans, 2001), 406–45.

16. Rahner, "Ideas for a Theology of Childhood," 33–50. Translation slightly revised in brackets.

17. Martin Buber, "Education," in *Between Man and Man* (New York: Macmillan, 1966), 83.

18. Elizabeth A. Johnson, *Consider Jesus: Waves of Renewal in Christology* (New York: Crossroad, 1990), 32.

19. Ibid., 33.

20. Ibid., 51.

21. Pope John Paul II, "Letter of the Pope John Paul II to Children in the Year of the Family," http://childrenoftheeucharist-waf.org/html/letter.htm.

22. See the CTM Web site; see also Haddon Willmer, "Experimenting Together: One Way of Doing Child Theology" (London: Child Theology Movement Limited, 2007).

23. W. Sibley Towner, "Children as Human Beings: Genesis 1:26–28 and the Image of God in the Hebrew Bible," in *The Child in the Bible*, ed. Marcia J. Bunge, Terence Fretheim, and Beverly Gaventa (Grand Rapids: Eerdmans, 2008), 307–23.

24. William Brown, "To Discipline without Destruction: The Multifaceted Profile of the Child in Proverbs," in Bunge, Fretheim, and Gaventa, *The Child in the Bible*, 63–81.

25. Ibid., 79.

26. See Bunge, "Child, Religion, and the Academy," for a further discussion of these paradoxical notions and their significance for theologies of childhood.

27. Bonnie J. Miller-McLemore, *Let the Children Come: Reimagining Childhood from a Christian Perspective* (San Francisco: Jossey-Bass, 2003).

28. John Wall, "The Christian Ethics of Children: Emerging Questions and Possibilities," *Journal of Lutheran Ethics* 4 (January 2004) at http://archive.elca.org/jle/article.asp?k=167; Wall, "Animals and Innocents: Theological Reflections on the Meaning and Purpose of Child-Rearing," *Theology Today* 59, no. 4 (2003): 559–82; Wall, "Fallen Angels: A Contemporary Christian Ethical Ontology of Children," *International Journal of Practical Theology* 7, no. 2 (Fall 2004): 160–84; and Wall, "'Let the Little Children Come': Child Rearing as Challenge to Contemporary Christian Ethics," *Horizons* 31, no. 1 (Spring 2004): 64–87.

29. Kathleen Marshall and Paul Parvis, *Honouring Children: The Human Rights of the Child in Christian Perspective* (Edinburgh: Saint Andrew Press, 2004).

30. Jürgen Moltmann, "Child and Childhood as Metaphors of Hope," *Theology Today* 56, no. 4 (2000): 592–603.

31. Dawn DeVries, "Toward a Theology of Childhood," *Interpretation* 55, no. 2 (April 2001): 161–73.
32. Kristin Herzog, *Children and Our Global Future: Theological and Social Challenges* (Cleveland: Pilgrim, 2005).
33. Deusdedit R. K. Nkurunziza, "African Theology of Childhood in Relation to Child Labour," *African Ecclesial Review* 46, no. 2 (2004): 121–38.

PART IV
GROWING INTO
HIS LIKENESS
The Eschatological Presence
of Christ in Human Lives

12

"On earth as it is in heaven"

Eschatology and the Ethics of Forgiveness

ANDREAS SCHUELE

Simple as it may sound at first, the request for forgiveness, "And forgive us our debts, as we also have forgiven our debtors" (Matt. 6:12), assumes a central role in the Lord's Prayer in terms of both the literary composition and the theology of the prayer. As Ulrich Luz has shown in a structural analysis, the request for forgiveness is the core element of the Lord's Prayer, while the Lord's Prayer itself takes the center position of the Sermon on the Mount.[1] Thus, it is safe to say that the Sermon on the Mount, as Matthew presents it, evolves around the notion of forgiveness. Since the Gospel of Matthew has often been charged with "legalism" or "legalist perfectionism"[2] ("For I tell you, unless your righteousness exceeds that of the scribes and Pharisees, you will never enter the kingdom of heaven" [Matt. 5:20]), it is often too easily overlooked that this Gospel also reserves a prominent place for the language of forgiveness.

This, of course, begs the question of what Matthew means by "forgiveness" here and elsewhere in the Gospel, and how it figures into his larger theological scheme.[3] The Lord's Prayer itself does not provide much of a context, but simply suggests that forgiveness is something that we need just as much as we need our daily bread and deliverance from evil. Striking here and in most other places in Matthew is the fact that forgiveness includes two distinct relationships—the one between God and humans and the one between human beings themselves. The univocal use of language as well as the propositional phrase "as we forgive . . ." suggest that there is some intrinsic nexus between divine and human forgiveness. But what exactly is this nexus, and how does it affect what Matthew means by forgiveness?

A first guess would be that there is a conditional relationship, which is in fact what, immediately following the Lord's Prayer, Matthew 6:14–15 suggests:[4] "For if you forgive others their trespasses, your heavenly Father will also forgive you; but if you do not forgive others, neither will your Father forgive your trespasses." Taken by itself, this passage could support the charge of legalism against Matthew, since it makes God's inclination to forgive dependent upon humans forgiving each other[5] (cf. also Mark 11:25; Luke 6:37).[6] However, reading further into the Gospel of Matthew, one finds the exact opposite scenario in the parable of the Unforgiving Servant (Matt. 18:24–35). There, it is the experience of God's unexpected and undeserved forgiveness that is envisioned as shaping the ways in which humans interact—or ought to interact—with one another.[7]

Consequently, rather than trying to identify the terms and condition under which God grants forgiveness and whether or not this presupposes any effort on the part of humankind, a more promising approach could be to follow the prayer's own understanding of how the divine and the human spheres are correlated. As has been frequently noted, Matthew 6:12 has a close structural parallel in another verse of the Lord's Prayer: "Your will be done, on earth as it is in heaven" (Matt. 6:10). This is the rendering that one finds in all of the major English translations. However, if one translates this verse closer to the original Greek, the word order is changed and with it the thrust of the argument: "Your will be done—as in heaven so also on earth." Paraphrasing this to make better sense in English, the verse then reads as follows: "Your will be done—as it already is in heaven, so it shall be on earth." In Matthew's cosmology, "heaven" denotes that sphere in which the kingdom of God has already been realized to its fullest extent, whereas this is not the case yet "on earth." It seems that Matthew employs this cosmological dualism to emphasize the expansive dynamic of God's kingdom, which eventually is meant to encompass all of reality.

If one applies the cosmological hermeneutic that is expressed in the opening sequence of the Lord's Prayer also to the petition for forgiveness, its particular thrust becomes clearer: forgiveness already is at work and shapes life where God reigns and where his will is done. For this to become reality on earth as well it is imperative that humans come to forgive each other in the same way God forgives them. This implies a number of crucial insights about the nature of Matthew's understanding of God's kingdom:

1. First of all, the symbol of the "kingdom" presupposes that it is God's very own nature to be forgiving, and not just one of his possible modes of acting toward humankind. The fact that, as the Lord's Prayer suggests, the kingdom of God is based on mutual forgiveness among those who live in it would hardly make any sense if this did not also say something about the king himself.

2. However, for this kingdom to become reality it is not enough that God himself is forgiving—as if God's kingdom was characterized primarily by one-on-one relationships between God and individuals. God's forgiveness would be solely a matter of individual spiritual experience and potentially devoid of any social impact if it did not also model and mold the ways in which humans relate to one another.

3. As such, forgiveness seems to figure into Matthew's larger eschatological vision: in the kingdom of God, people will live fully out of justice, mercy, and faith—according to Matthew, the three distinct qualities of the "law" (Matt. 23:23).[8] This, and not the corrupted forms of how the law is realized in the here and now, will establish the kind of righteousness that characterizes life in the kingdom of God. It seems that Matthew understands forgiveness as that which paves the way for this new righteousness to take its place in human life. Because human beings in the here and now fall short of living up to the eschatological qualities of the law, sin, guilt, and indifference toward one's neighbor are the consequences. Interestingly enough, according to Matthew, intensified efforts to improve one's moral conduct are only one aspect of what this situation calls for. It is not within the power of humans to eliminate sin and suffering from the world. What human beings can do, however, is what the Lord's Prayer suggests: ask God for forgiveness and forgive one's neighbor. The kingdom of God has its own momentum and dynamic to permeate the world beyond human influence.[9] Nonetheless, forgiveness can be characterized as a form of acknowledging the nearness of this kingdom, as a way of reaching out for it, and also as the readiness to receive it.[10] It is worth noticing that Matthew's ethic is not geared simply toward a top-down implementation of eschatological values. Rather, it is an ethic that captures and highlights how human value systems change when the kingdom of God is expected as an immanent reality.

4. If the above conclusions are sound, it becomes clear why forgiveness is an essential key to understanding Matthew's Christology. According to Matthew, Jesus embodies both the kingdom of God in its directedness from "heaven to earth" and the human reality that embraces the coming of this kingdom. Thus Jesus' ministry is characterized by the forgiveness of sins as that which, using Pauline terminology, could be called the firstfruits of the approaching kingdom of God. One crucial text in this regard is Matthew 9:2–7 (par. Mark 2:1–12; Luke 5:17–26), the healing of the paralytic. The scribes take issue with Jesus' forgiving sins and charge him with blasphemy. Matthew leaves out the explanation that the scribes give in Mark 2:7: "Who can forgive sins but God alone?" As we shall see shortly, this charge has its basis in the fact that in the Old Testament the characteristic term for "forgive"—סלח (*sālaḥ*)—occurs exclusively with God as the grammatical subject. From the scribes' perspective, by claiming that he has the power to forgive sins, Jesus puts himself in the place of God. This should not be quickly dismissed as a mean-spirited assault against Jesus. On the contrary, the fact that the scribes challenge Jesus proves the point that forgiveness is no small, or as Jesus himself phrases it, "easy" thing (Matt. 9:5).

It is a powerful reality that effectively changes the lives of individuals and their social settings. There seems to be agreement between Jesus and the scribes that, wherever this reality occurs, the kingdom of God has arrived on earth. But this precisely begs the question of Jesus' role in the arrival of this kingdom. Is he "simply" the messenger or prophet who announces the coming of the kingdom? Or, on the other end of the spectrum, is he the one who, endowed with divine authority, brings this kingdom down from heaven to earth? However one might answer this question, it seems that Jesus' relationship to the kingdom of God is the key issue that determines his exceptional—eschatological—identity and also the character of his ministry. Put in different terms, reading Matthew, the kingdom of God—not Jesus' christological titles—presents itself as the key symbol around which the literary and theological texture of this Gospel materializes.

In the following part of this essay, I seek to substantiate this tentative characterization of how the language of forgiveness figures into the Gospel of Matthew by looking at some of the literary traditions that precede Matthew. This will include first texts from the Hebrew Bible, but then also documents from Qumran, especially the hymnic poetry of the *Hodayot* (1QH). What I want to show is that Matthew's notion of forgiveness—and for the sake of brevity this essay focuses on this Gospel in particular—emerges from his intertextual conversation with these other traditions. To be sure, my claim is not—as the *Religionsgeschichtliche Schule* might have it—that there is a forward-driving development in the intellectual history of the concept of forgiveness that starts in the early Second Temple period and culminates in the New Testament. The claim is, however, that during this period the notion of forgiveness played a productive role in the religious discourse of early Judaism and that Matthew's framing of his account of Jesus' identity and ministry participates in this discourse.

OLD TESTAMENT TRADITIONS[11]

In the Old Testament, the Hebrew term סלח (*sālaḥ*) "forgive" is one of two verbs that is used exclusively with God as the grammatical subject. Only God can "forgive," just as only God can "create" (*bārā*, ברא). To be sure, there are words and idioms in Hebrew that also give expression to the language of forgiveness among human beings. It is striking, however, that the Old Testament reserves one particular word for divine forgiveness, thus setting this concept apart from the human moral sphere. For our purposes it may suffice to give only a brief summary of how *sālaḥ* is used in Old Testament traditions.

It seems that, originally, *sālaḥ* was a technical term for "forgiveness" that had its primary setting in life in the temple cult and the sacrificial system. Twelve out of the forty-six references for *sālaḥ* are found in the ritual texts of Leviticus 4–5 and Numbers 15:25–28. These texts provide instructions for various types of sin offerings. Important in this respect is that this particular offering becomes necessary to redeem sins that were committed unintentionally. Cases that require a sin offering include incidences such as someone coming into contact with something unclean or someone failing to report a felony that he or she has witnessed. Most of the time, however, the texts put the need for such a sacrifice in rather general terms:

> If anyone of the ordinary people among you sins unintentionally in doing any one of the things that by the LORD's commandments ought not to be done and incurs guilt, when the sin that you have committed is made known to you, you shall bring a female goat without blemish as your offering, for the sin that you have committed . . . and the priest shall make atonement on your behalf, and you shall be forgiven. (Lev. 4:27–31)

Sin offerings, atonement, and forgiveness are not so much part of what we would call civil or criminal law; rather, they are the means to maintain the covenantal relationship between God and his people. According to the priestly view, as laid out in Leviticus and related texts of the Pentateuch, human beings constantly and unavoidably transgress the boundaries by which God has established natural and social order. This requires that God himself provide the means to mend the relationship between himself and his people whenever it threatens to fall apart. Order, as understood by the priests in ancient Israel, is a dynamic and at the same time extremely fragile concept. Once established, it relies on divine as well as human attention to remain stable, which allows one to understand forgiveness as one of God's ways to keep the world in balance.

Looking at the religious history of ancient Israel, it seems that, apart from its cultic setting, the concept of forgiveness played an important role in the exilic and early postexilic periods, when the biblical authors faced the reality that God's covenant with Israel was broken and that God had not forgiven the sins of his people.[12] The books of Jeremiah and Ezekiel in particular give us some insight that until the very last years before the temple was destroyed and parts of the Judean population were exiled, there was still confidence among Judean aristocrats and priests that YHWH would turn the fortune of his people around and rescue them "at the last minute" from the Babylonians. One gets the impression that it was not in the worldview of most preexilic Judeans to imagine that YHWH would let them fall victim to their own iniquities. During and after the exile, however, this became the single most important theological and political issue with which the biblical authors had to grapple. Lamentations summarizes the issue in simple but poignant words: "We have transgressed and rebelled, and you have not forgiven. You have wrapped yourself with anger and pursued us, killing without pity; you have wrapped yourself with a cloud so that no prayer can pass through" (Lam. 3:42–44).

It is worth noting that Lamentations expresses the consequences of God's not-forgiving by using the image of God "screening" himself off from his people. The language is intriguing here: the Hebrew term (sākak, סכך) "wrap, cover" plays an important role in the Sinai pericope, where Moses receives instructions for building the tabernacle (Exod. 25:20–22; 26:31–36). There, it is the wings of the cherubim and the veil put up in front of the Holy of Holies that separate the ark of the covenant, God's dwelling place on earth, from those parts of the tabernacle to which the priests have access. The idea is that, although YHWH resides in a restricted place, this area is not isolated from the human world. Sacrifices and prayer get through to him, thus allowing for fellowship between God and his people. Lamentations seems to refer to this cultic notion of God's presence. But whereas God remains accessible in Exodus, Lamentations envisions God's anger as a veil so "thick" that nothing passes through it anymore.

As one of their dominant themes, the postexilic authors of the Old Testament grapple with the reality of the Babylonian exile as a symbol of God's anger and Israel's inability to keep the covenant with God. Their answers of what a new relationship between God and Israel might look like—if there was ever going to be such a relationship again—show a great deal of diversity. However, there are a number of "focal points" that center the inner-biblical discussion about the religious identity of postexilic Judaism—and the notion of forgiveness is certainly one such focal point. In a nutshell, the burning issue at stake was whether there could be forgiveness for Israel beyond the reality of the broken covenant. To summarize a fairly complex picture that presents itself to the reader in texts such as 1 Kings 8:33–34, 46–50; Isaiah 55:3–7; Jeremiah 31:33–34; and Exodus 34:6–9, one can distinguish three different approaches:

1. The notion of forgiveness is woven into Jeremiah's prophecy of a new covenant.[13] According to Jeremiah 31:33–34, this covenant means two things: that God will forgive the sins of the past and that he will inscribe the Torah on Israel's heart, so that it will never again fall back into the sinful existence of their past:

> But this is the covenant that I will make with the house of Israel after those days, says the LORD: I will put my law within them, and I will write it on their hearts; and I will be their God, and they shall be my people. No longer shall they teach one another, or say to each other, "Know the LORD," for they shall all know me, from the least of them to the greatest, says the LORD; for I will forgive their iniquity, and remember their sin no more.

The idea of the Torah inscribed on Israel's heart suggests that Israel's will and God's law will be in perfect harmony with each other. By the same token, this idea means that there won't be a need for forgiveness anymore, because in the world of the new covenant there won't be sins that need to be forgiven anymore. Jeremiah's vision has often and perhaps rightly been suspected of a highly charged and overly optimistic vision of the future relationship between God and his people that could hardly ever pass the litmus test of reality. It is interesting, therefore, that other accounts of a new or renewed covenant in the Hebrew Bible take a more realistic stand and, consequently, arrive at a different understanding of the nature and need for divine forgiveness (discussed below).

2. According to Solomon's temple prayer that models the genre of postexilic penitential prayer,[14] God listens to the cry of those who approach him with a contrite heart and who are willing to turn away from their sinful ways:

"If they sin against you—for there is no one who does not sin—and you
are angry with them and give them to an enemy, so that they are carried
away captive to the land of the enemy, far off or near; yet if they come to
their senses in the land to which they have been taken captive, and repent,
and plead with you in the land of their captors, saying, 'We have sinned,
and have done wrong; we have acted wickedly'; if they repent with all their
heart and soul in the land of their enemies, who took them captive, and
pray to you toward their land, which you gave to their ancestors, the city
that you have chosen, and the house that I have built for your name; then
hear in heaven your dwelling place their prayer and their plea, maintain
their cause and forgive your people who have sinned against you, and all
their transgressions that they have committed against you; and grant them
compassion in the sight of their captors, so that they may have compassion
on them." (1 Kgs. 8:46–50)

Unlike the cultic notion of forgiveness in Leviticus, Solomon's prayer does not
talk about specific kinds or types of sins that require forgiveness; rather, the term
"sin" here is used in the broadest sense possible: Israel will always prove itself
unable to live up to being God's people. It will always transgress the boundaries
of the covenant and thus provoke God's anger and punishment. The one thing
that Israel can do, however, is acknowledge their sin and repent, and this, according to 1 Kings 8, will be sufficient reason for God to have mercy and forgive.

3. The Sinai pericope shares the kind of "covenantal realism" that lies at the
heart of the temple prayer. However, Exodus 34 goes even one step further:
God's forgiveness has to be entirely unconditional if it's supposed to make a
difference in God's relationship with Israel at all. It cannot even build on Israel's
repentance as 1 Kings 8 suggests. This radicalized view of the covenant in Exodus 34:6–9 is presented in form of a dialogue between God and Moses. God
introduces himself to Moses with the so-called grace formula:

The LORD passed before him, and proclaimed, "The LORD, the LORD, a God
merciful and gracious, slow to anger, and abounding in steadfast love and
faithfulness, keeping steadfast love for the thousandth generation, forgiving
iniquity and transgression and sin, yet by no means clearing the guilty, but
visiting the iniquity of the parents upon the children and the children's children, to the third and the fourth generation." (Exod. 34:6–7)

It has often been observed that the grace formula presents God in almost self-
contradictory terms: he forgives sin but he also visits the parents' sins on their
descendants. This much seems clear, however: despite its abundance, there are
limits to God's graciousness; God is slow to anger, but once his anger has been
kindled, he will hold responsible even those who did not themselves commit
sin. Note that when the text speaks of forgiveness here, it does not use the root
sālah but rather a different idiom, that of "lifting up (=taking away) sin." Moses'
response to God's self-revelation reads as follows: "He said, 'If now I have found
favor in your sight, O Lord, I pray, let the Lord go with us. Although[15] this
is a stiff-necked people, pardon our iniquity and our sin, and take us for your
inheritance'" (Exod. 34:9).

At first glance, Moses' request seems pointless, because he asks for something—forgiveness—that has already been granted. However, the way this request is phrased suggests in fact that Moses changes the preconditions of the covenant: Israel is a *stubborn* people; in other words, it will not only be unable to live up to God's expectations, it will even refuse to do so. That is the reality to which God's forgiveness and mercy have to respond if there is to be a "covenant" at all.[16] God has to accept Israel despite its imperfections and its notorious inclination to resist the divine will. The fact that, in Exodus 34:10, God grants the covenant under these terms suggests that the notion of forgiveness that is articulated in Exodus 34:9 is the one that the text in its present form seeks to highlight: There is no reason and no particular motivation for God's forgiveness other than his will to accept Israel for what it is. Forgiveness, in this view, does not have a rationale behind it. It does not presuppose anything and it does not expect anything, which means that there is no other reason for God to be forgiving than the fact that this is his nature. Consequently, forgiveness is never presented as a pedagogical tool that God uses for the betterment of Israel. It is one of the remarkable, although not always sufficiently emphasized, peculiarities of the pentateuchal narratives from Genesis to Deuteronomy that they hardly ever idealize God's people—not the patriarchs and the matriarchs in Genesis and also not the Mosaic Israel in the books that follow. It is never envisioned that the covenant with God will make Israel a better people. As a matter of fact, assuming that the Pentateuch received its final shape for the most part under the impression of the Babylonian exile and the restoration after the exile, it is reasonable to conclude that it is precisely the point of the Pentateuch to give a realistic rather than an idealistic account of who Israel is—and also of who God is.

Summarizing our brief walk through some Old Testament traditions, it is evident that these texts feature a multilayered and also controversial discourse. In the Second Temple period, the notion of forgiveness sparked Israel's thinking about its own history and identity and also about God. To risk a value judgment, this inner-biblical discourse displays its most intriguing facets where it (1) describes God's nature as forgiving, without making this dependent on whether humankind is able or at all willing to reciprocate the experience of being forgiven, and where it (2) grapples with fact that human beings live in the presence of this God, but that this will not necessarily change human nature. The tension between texts such as Exodus 34:9 and Jeremiah 31:31–34 marks the two poles around which the biblical discourse evolves: whereas Jeremiah 31 does in fact expect a rather dramatic change in human nature, Exodus 34 seems to be thoroughly skeptical of any such expectation. It is important to be aware that the Hebrew Bible does not try to redeem this tension or find some sort of a compromise between the different positions. The theological discourse about divine forgiveness and its consequences is essentially open, thus inviting further conversation beyond the boundaries of the Hebrew canon.

As we shall see in the following, the theological discourse about forgiveness in the texts from Khirbet Qumran and in the New Testament show a marked eschatological awareness. Building on the understanding of God as unconditionally forgiving, these traditions raise the question of what this means at a time when people thought of themselves as living at the "end of days" or at least at the brink of a dramatic change in the course of human history.

THE *HODAYOT* OF QUMRAN

As one would expect, the Hebrew term *sālaḥ* occurs with notable frequency in those texts from Qumran that are concerned with cultic and ritual issues. Especially in the "Rule of the Community" (1QS), in the Temple Scroll (11Q19), and in 4QMMT one finds *halakhic* discussion about the proper performance and meaning of the sin offering. Just as in Leviticus, the notion of forgiveness figures largely into this discussion. A detailed account of *sālaḥ* in these texts cannot be provided here; only one characteristic difference to Leviticus may be mentioned: the regulations concerning the *yom kippur*, the great "day of atonement," in Leviticus 16 do not include (as one might expect against the backdrop of Lev. 4–5) forgiveness as the final piece of the ritual process. The prescriptions of the ritual culminate in a statement that this is how he [Aaron] "shall make atonement for the sanctuary, and he shall make atonement for the tent of meeting and for the altar, and he shall make atonement for the priests and for all the people of the assembly" (Lev. 16:33). If one compares this with the Temple Scroll, the characteristic difference is that in 11Q19 XXVI, 9–10, not only atoning purification but also forgiveness of sins is the purpose of the *yom kippur* ritual: "It is the sin offering for the assembly and he [the High Priest] atones with it for all the people of the assembly, *and they shall be forgiven*" (emphasis added).

Apart from this *halakhic* discourse where the Qumran texts, although differing in detail, remain within the linguistic framework that the canonical Scriptures provide, the language of forgiveness takes a new form in the poetic texts of the *Hodayot*. The *Hodayot* are a collection of prayers that have parallels with the biblical psalms, especially psalms of thanksgiving, confessions of trust, and hymns.[17] They present themselves as prayers of a particular individual—the "teacher" or "instructor"—but there is reason to assume that they were prayer literature that circulated in the entire community.[18] They present some of the central theological themes and convictions of the Qumran people, such as God's special election of a small group among Israel, double predestination, and an elaborate concept of God's Holy Spirit and of all the other (created) spirits that fill the cosmos.

The root *sālaḥ* occurs fourteen times in the *Hodayot*: once as a participle (1QH^a VI, 23–24: "You are . . . *forgiving* those who turn away from offense, and punishing the iniquity of the wicked") and thirteen times in form of the noun סליחה "forgiveness." Note that the phrase in which this noun regularly occurs is רב סליחה, *rob sᵉlīḥā* "abundant in forgiveness" as a characterization of God's way of acting toward those who have found favor before him:

> "[For] I [kn]ow that shortly you will raise a survivor among your people, a
> remnant in your inheritance. You will purify them to cleanse them of guilt.
> For all their deeds are in your truth and in your kindness you judge them
> with a multitude of compassion and an abundance of forgiveness." (1QH[a]
> XIV, 7–9)

In this passage the Qumran people reflect on their own status in a time that
they understood as facing God's impending final judgment. It seems clear that
the "survivor" (and "remnant") whom God will cleanse from their sins are the
Qumranites themselves. In some way, the language is reminiscent of the grace
formula in Exodus 34:6–7. However, it is also different, precisely because in
Exodus 34 God is not called "abundant in forgiveness." This phrase has no
direct parallel in the Old Testament and thus seems to be specific to the Qumran texts.[19] The *Hodayot* combine the grace formula with the cultic notion of
forgiveness: it is God's nature to be forgiving, and this shows in the way he
cleanses his chosen ones from their iniquities. Nonetheless, God's forgiveness
does not seem to eliminate his other characteristic as a wrathful God who does
not withhold punishment for those who are not included among the elect. As we
have seen, this double nature of God also plays a controversial role in Exodus 34.
There, however, the text arrives at the conclusion that only unconditional forgiveness can be the basis for a covenantal relationship with God. The Qumran
position, on the other hand, seems to intentionally hold up the tension between
divine forgiveness and divine punishment. One reason for this may be found
in the different cultural and historical circumstances of both traditions: Exodus
34 received its final shape after the Babylonian exile, when the key theological
question of the time was how a new beginning between God and Israel was possible at all and how this new covenant could be secured against Israel's notorious inclination to violate it. The Qumran authors, on the other hand, were not
interested anymore in the future extension of the covenant. In their view, the
world was sinking into moral depravity and impurity. History had arrived at its
end, and the end point was marked by a radical separation between light and
darkness, good and evil.[20] The Qumran people did not put hope in this world
anymore, and the symbol of God's wrath seems to give expression to their expectation of the impending end. Nonetheless, in the midst of all the decay, God had
granted those who had remained faithful shelter from the world that was falling
apart around them. The *Hodayot* are written from this "inside" perspective of
having found the God who is "abundant in forgiveness." This may explain why
these poems combine harsh and even cruel judgments about the wicked with
tender and intimate images of a merciful God:[21]

> Your wholesome watch has saved my soul, with my steps there is an abun-
> dance of forgiveness and a multitude of [compass]ion when you judge me,
> until old age you take care of me. For you are father to all the [son]s of
> your truth. . . . You rejoice in them like her who loves her child, and like
> a wet-nurse you take care of all your creatures on your lap. (1QH[a] XVII,
> 33–36)

In the Qumran view, God's forgiveness is not found by living in this world but by separating oneself from it. It is not always entirely clear if any human being can actively turn away from his or her evil path (as, for example, 1 Kgs. 8 envisions it) and seek the God of mercy, or if this remains a privilege of those whom God has chosen. Although the Qumran texts show a marked tendency toward predestinarianism, there is no discernable systematic concept of either single or double predestination. And this may not even have been a point of concern, since the authors undoubtedly counted themselves among those who had in fact moved beyond the depravity of the world and found the forgiving God. The language of the *Hodayot* is descriptive rather than prescriptive, thus reflecting on the experience of the Qumran people as those whom God spared: "All the sons of your truth you bring to forgiveness in your presence, you purify them from their offenses by the greatness of your goodness, and by the abundance of your compassion, to make them stand in your presence for eternity to eternity" (1QHª XV, 29–32). The key word in this passage is "in your presence" or, in a different translation, "before you." In a world filled with injustice and impurity, a world at the brink of a cosmic disaster, God's nearness provided that rescuing island where the faithful could prevail—and the Qumran people certainly considered their community as that space where God was near and where he showed his kindness and compassion. In this scenario, the term "forgiveness" describes all of God's activity that makes one able and worthy to stand in his presence and, consequently, to be elevated above the world around oneself.

One can summarize the particular concept of forgiveness in Qumran as driven by an interest to stick to the insight that it is God's nature to be forgiving, as the Hebrew Bible, especially Exodus 34:6–10 and Isaiah 55:7, suggests. However, this conviction had to be held up in a world that did not support the notion that God was present among his people at all anymore. As a consequence, finding the forgiving God and understanding his intentions toward the world is one of the foremost theological tasks that the Qumran authors put before themselves. In another text, 4QInstruction, which seems to draw out some of the theological lines of the *Hodayot*, one finds the idea that God introduces the faithful to the "mystery of existence."[22] Although it is never really explained what this mystery of existence is, it at least seems clear that it includes knowledge of God that the ways of the dying world would not betray.

RETURNING TO MATTHEW

There is consensus among historians and exegetes that some of the closest parallels between Qumran and the New Testament occur in the reports about the mission of John the Baptist.[23] Whether John himself was at some point of his life a member of the Qumran community need not concern us here. Interesting is the fact that, according to Mark and Luke, the purpose of John's baptism was repentance and the forgiveness of sins: "John the baptizer appeared in the wilderness, proclaiming a baptism of repentance for the forgiveness of sins" (Mark 1:4; Luke 3:3). Note that the Greek here uses the peculiar phrase βάπτισμα μετανοίας εἰς ἄφεσιν ἁμαρτιῶν. The preposition εἰς expresses a sense of direction: a baptism of repentance that is "leading into" the forgiveness of sins.

This resonates perfectly with the notion of a "return" (שׁוּב) to God as a precondition for forgiveness in Solomon's temple prayer, and it also concurs with the eschatological reinterpretation of this line of tradition in Qumran: now, at the end of history, was the moment to find one's way back to God and seek his forgiveness for one's iniquities. Unlike the Qumran way, however, John's teaching of repentance does not require withdrawal from the world, but rather a radical change of one's moral and religious conduct in the world.

Interestingly enough, in Matthew's expanded report of John's appearance at the Jordan, the term "forgiveness" is missing:

> "Repent, for the kingdom of heaven has come near." This is the one of whom the prophet Isaiah spoke when he said, "The voice of one crying out in the wilderness: 'Prepare the way of the Lord, make his paths straight.'" . . . Then the people of Jerusalem and all Judea were going out to him, and all the region along the Jordan, and they were baptized by him in the river Jordan, confessing their sins. But when he saw many Pharisees and Sadducees coming for baptism, he said to them, "You brood of vipers! Who warned you to flee from the wrath to come? Bear fruit worthy of repentance." (Matt. 3:2–8)

Compared with Mark and Luke, it is quite surprising that, on the one hand, Matthew emphasizes John's message of repentance by reporting that the people did in fact come to confess their sins but that, on the other hand, Matthew does not seem to be equally explicit about the purpose of baptism and repentance with regard to divine forgiveness.

However—and this takes us back to our initial observations—Matthew's interest lies in the transformation of human life that occurs when the kingdom of heaven approaches "life on earth."[24] As a consequence, the effect of repentance cannot be limited to the clearing of past sins but needs to result in what Matthew calls the "fruit of repentance." This again points to the intriguing tension that seems to be so characteristic of Matthew's theology in general: there is the kingdom of God that will transform life as we know it in an eschatological event that only God himself can bring about. As such it comes unexpectedly and unpredictably—like a thief in the night (Matt. 24:43–44; cf. also 1 Thess. 5:2). Nonetheless, there is a way in which human beings respond to the impending presence of this kingdom by changing or, more adequately, adjusting their lives to this presence.[25]

If one approaches the Sermon on the Mount from this angle, its instructions can be understood as depicting the "fruit of repentance" that follows from one's baptismal pledges. This also puts the notion of forgiveness into a perspective that, as we have outlined above, stands at the center of the sermon. What distinguishes the notion of forgiveness and makes it a hinge of Matthew's gospel message is the fact that it can be characterized as both the "fruit of repentance" and at the same time as God's way of interacting with the human sphere. By employing the notion of forgiveness, the Lord's Prayer creates an intimate nexus between divine and human acting. Establishing a connection between the divine and the human spheres by way of univocal language is not uncommon in Matthew. One also finds it with regard to the notion of "righteousness" that leads Matthew to exhort his audience to be "perfect," because the heavenly Father himself is perfect (Matt. 5:48). This is not unlike the fourth Gospel's notion of love that works in a similar way to highlight a quality of living and acting that unites God and humans. However, the idea that human beings are supposed to be righteous, because God is righteous, and that they ought to love God and their neighbor, because they are also recipients of the same love, is already deeply rooted in the Old Testament. The forgiveness of sins, on the other hand, was reserved for God alone,[26] which explains why Matthew draws attention to the strongly negative response that Jesus receives from the religious authorities of his time (Matt. 9:2–7).

Obviously we cannot know for sure if Jesus was the first who used the language of forgiveness univocally for God and humans.[27] But one gets the impression that Matthew—perhaps more so than the other Synoptic Gospels—seems to have been quite aware that this very sentence "forgive us our debts, as we forgive our debtors" crossed a boundary that may not have been crossed before.[28] Forgiveness among humans becomes an eschatological value, because here a divine reality is transformed into a human reality—or, to use the Lord's Prayer's own language, it means that God's will is done in heaven and on earth. This also explains Jesus' counterintuitive claim that there cannot be limits to forgiveness and that, no matter how many times we or our neighbor are in need of being forgiven, it shall be granted. If forgiveness is a divine attribute, then it is not for humans to put any limits to its efficacy. And yet, Matthew and Luke seem to differ on whether or not there should be any preconditions that have to be met, before forgiveness can be granted. According to Luke 17:3–4, the act of repentance is such a precondition:

> "Be on your guard! If another disciple sins, you must rebuke the offender, and if there is repentance, you must forgive. And if the same person sins against you seven times a day, and turns back to you seven times and says, 'I repent,' you must forgive."

This follows a line of tradition that one can trace from Solomon's temple prayer all the way down to the Qumran texts. Matthew, on the other hand, puts a characteristically different spin on the same issue (Matt. 18:21–22):

> Then Peter came and said to him, "Lord, if another member of the church sins against me, how often should I forgive? As many as seven times?" Jesus said to him, "Not seven times, but, I tell you, seventy-seven times."

Matthew does not spell out the conditions that have to be met before forgiveness can be granted. What follows in Matthew is the parable of the Unforgiving
Servant, where the bottom line is that human beings should forgive one another,
because they live out of God's forgiveness.[29] It is not covenantal thinking that
guides the theological imagination at this point but rather the idea that human
forgiveness follows the divine model and, as such, cannot and must not be limited or withheld.[30]

One of the major differences between the eschatology of the *Hodayot* and
Matthew seems to lie precisely in the ethical dimension of forgiveness. Whereas
the *Hodayot* depict divine forgiveness as something that shelters the faithful from
a decadent and dying world, Matthew understands it as a power that changes
the world of those who live in it. This difference may have to do with the fact
that Matthew's eschatology, despite its many facets, depicts the life, death, and
resurrection of Christ as a turning point in human history, rather than as its
endpoint. To be sure, especially the last of Jesus' five speeches that structure the
Gospel of Matthew (Matt. 23–25) has an unmistakably apocalyptic overtone,
envisioning the near end of history as a time of division between the righteous
and the wicked ("the sheep and the goats," Matt. 25:32). Here in particular one
realizes close parallels with the dualistic worldview also found in Qumran. However, woven into the expectation of the immediate end is an eschatology that
focuses on how the present world will be transformed rather than terminated. It
is this side of Matthew's theological scheme in which forgiveness plays a crucial
role. The world past the eschatological event of Jesus' first coming gains a new
ethical orientation, because the kingdom of heaven now lays its claim upon
every aspect of life on earth. Thus it is all the more important that in the Lord's
Prayer, with its emphasis on the expectation of God's kingdom to arrive on earth
("your kingdom come, your will be done on earth as it already is in heaven"), the
one human activity that is mentioned is forgiveness. Matthew was certainly not
of the opinion that there was anything that human beings could do to accelerate
the arrival of this kingdom or, conversely, to prevent it from coming. But this
seems to be precisely the reason that Matthew is interested in how humans can
and should live toward the arrival of this kingdom.

If we now summarize our walk through some of the biblical and extrabiblical
traditions that draw on the notion of forgiveness as a source for their respective theologies, we can identify especially two formative stages: the exilic and
postexilic periods when, after the end of the monarchic history of Israel and the
destruction of the first temple, the biblical authors had to reconsider all the key
concepts of their previous theology: God's covenant with Israel, God's presence
on earth, and the human inability to live up to this presence in their lives. Here
the biblical discourse zeroes in on the limits or unlimitedness of divine forgiveness. Several centuries later and under the influence of an increased eschatological awareness that characterizes both the Qumran literature and the New
Testament, this discourse addresses a new challenge—namely, how one is supposed to live a faithful and ethically truthful life at the brink of a new eon. And

here it is Matthew in particular who, in his version of the Lord's Prayer, interprets the qualitative difference between God's kingdom and human reality as a gap that needs to be filled. It has often been observed that this is where the concept of superior righteousness (Matt. 5:20) figures into Matthew's theological scheme. This essay has attempted to show that an account of Matthew's concept of righteousness would not be complete without the notion that stands at the very center of the Sermon on the Mount and the Lord's Prayer: forgiveness.

NOTES

1. Ulrich Luz, *Matthew 1–7* (Minneapolis: Augsburg Fortress, 2007), 173.
2. For a recent overview of the discussion about Matthew's relationship to Judaism, see Boris Repschinski, "'For He Will Save His People from Their Sins' (Matthew 1:21): A Christology for Christian Jews," *Catholic Biblical Quarterly* 68, no. 2. (April 2006): 248–50.
3. One problem in this regard is the semantic range of the term ὀφείλημα. It refers to something that is owed, a "debt" (cf. also Rom. 4:4). This suggests that the concept of forgiveness in the Lord's Prayer has a very narrow focus: it is not about "sins" as defined in the law codes of Leviticus and Deuteronomy but rather about "debts" that, for whatever reason, cannot be repaid but need to be canceled. As Hans Dieter Betz suggests, Matthew redefines the concept of sin in terms of (legal) obligations: "Remarkably, the fifth petition employs this business language to interpret what otherwise would be called 'sins' and 'forgiveness of sins.' Accordingly, sins are not treated as transgressions of legal, moral, or ritual codes, the way sins are usually understood. Rather, sins are taken to be instances of injustice in the sense of obligations outstanding and not met. Since human life as a whole consists of an interconnected web of obligations, the totality of all unredeemed obligations constitutes human sinfulness" (*The Sermon on the Mount: A Commentary on the Sermon on the Mount, Including the Sermon on the Plain Matthew 5:3–7:27 and Luke 6:20–49*, Hermeneia [Minneapolis: Fortress, 1995], 402). This means, by the same token, that Matthew also sees the relationship with God as characterized in terms of mutual obligations. While Betz's interpretation highlights an essential characteristic of Matthew's concept of forgiveness, this should not be limited to the idea of a debt being canceled. In Matt. 6:14, a verse that elaborates on the fifth petition of the Lord's Prayer (see below), one finds the term παράπτωμα "transgression," which is one of the terms that the Septuagint uses for "sin." Also, when Jesus heals the paralytic (Matt. 9:2–7), this can hardly be subsumed under the category of a "debt" needing to be forgiven.
4. For a discussion of the relationship between Matt. 6:12 and 6:14–15, see Betz, *Sermon on the Mount*, 425–26. Betz himself argues that vv. 14–15 "precede v. 12 logically in that the principle is presupposed in its application. If the petitioners of v. 12a expect that their prayers will be answered, their expectation is conditional upon their own readiness to forgive (12b)."
5. Luz, *Matthew*, 327: "Thus with this statement the evangelist emphasizes precisely the part of the Lord's Prayer where human activity was most directly involved. In contrast to the logion leading into the Lord's Prayer (vv. 7–9), which emphasizes God's nearness, this logion that brings the Lord's Prayer to a close is designed to secure the relationship between prayer and action."

6. Matt. 6:14–15 has a close parallel in Sir. 28:2: "Forgive your neighbor the wrong he has done, and then your sins will be pardoned when you pray" (for references to rabbinic texts, see Luz, *Matthew*, 322).

7. To what extent one should or should not read God into the role of the king in Matt. 18:24–35 has been the subject of controversial debates that cannot be properly reviewed here. On the methodological and theological issues of this parable, cf. especially Christian Dietzfelbinger, "Das Gleichnis von der erlassenen Schuld. Eine theologische Untersuchung zu Matthäus 18, 23–35," *Evangelische Theologie* 32, no. 5 (Sept. to Oct. 1972): 437–51.

8. For a systematic account of the law as a dynamic nexus of "justice, mercy, and knowledge of God," cf. Michael Welker in a number of his publications. As Michael's former assistant, I take the liberty to say that the pertinent passage in his book *God the Spirit* (Minneapolis: Fortress, 1994), 108–24, is arguably the most thoughtful and enlightening account of the meaning of the law in contemporary Protestant theology.

9. One of the main exegetical issues with the interpretation of the Lord's Prayer has been the relationship between its ethical and its eschatological dimensions. Thus, the question has been if the Lord's Prayer envisions a future reality or the breakthrough of God's kingdom in everyday life. A synopsis of the arguments for both lines of interpretation has been provided by Gerhard Theissen and Annette Merz, *The Historical Jesus: A Comprehensive Guide* (Minneapolis: Fortress, 1996), 262–64. I agree with Theissen's and Merz's assessment that the two types of exegesis should be combined (262), and it seems to be especially the request for forgiveness that calls for such a combination: human beings should forgive each other in the present; this is, however, more than just an ethical imperative, because the basis for this claim is the eschatological reality of God's reign: "The end time is seen in the light of the ethical will of God, and everyday life is illuminated by the light of an eschatological liberation from disaster. But both these things happen in a prayer which is addressed to God. In the last resort future and present are combined in the understanding of God" (263).

10. Matt. 6:33 uses the language of "longing for"/"striving" with regard to how human beings should relate to the approaching heavenly kingdom.

11. For a fuller account of the notion of forgiveness in Old Testament traditions, see Andreas Schüle, "An der Grenze von Schuld und Vergebung: סלח im Alten Testament," in "*. . . der seine Lust hat am Wort des Herrn!" Festschrift für Ernst Jenni zum 80. Geburtstag,* ed. Jörg Luchsinger, Hans-Peter Mathys, and Markus Saur (Münster: Ugarit-Verlag, 2007), 309–29.

12. Ibid., 315–27.

13. Ibid., 322–24.

14. For an overview of current research on penitential prayer, see Samuel E. Balentine, "I Was Ready to Be Sought Out by Those Who Did Not Ask," in *Seeking the Favor of God,* ed. Mark J. Boda, Daniel K. Falk, and Rodney A. Werline (Atlanta: Society of Biblical Literature, 2006), 11–16; Mark J. Boda, "Form Criticism in Transition: Penitential Prayer and Lament, *Sitz im Leben* and Form," in *Seeking the Favor of God,* 190.

15. For a discussion of כי cf. R. W. L. Moberly, *At the Mountain of God: Story and Theology in Exodus 32–34* (Sheffield: JSOT Press, 1983), 89–90.

16. Schüle, "An der Grenze von Schuld und Vergebung," 324–27.

17. Interesting is the fact that one genre that defines the biblical Psalter to a major extent is completely absent from the *Hodayot*: the songs of lament.

18. The rhetorical function of the "I" of the leader for the shaping of a sectarian identity in Qumran has been analyzed by Carol A. Newsom, *The Self as Symbolic Space: Constructing Identity and Community at Qumran* (Leiden: Brill, 2004), 287–300.

19. As a matter of fact, the noun סליחה occurs in the Hebrew Bible only once, in Ps. 130:4.

20. For the scenario of the "end" at Qumran, see J. J. Collins, "The Expectation of the End in the Dead Sea Scrolls," in *Eschatology, Messianism, and the Dead Sea Scrolls,* ed. Craig A. Evans and Peter W. Flint (Grand Rapids: Eerdmans, 1997), 74–90.

21. Cf. Julie A. Hughes, *Scriptural Allusions and Exegesis in the Hodayot* (Leiden: Brill, 2006), 105–18.

22. J. J. Collins, "The Mysteries of God: Creation and Eschatology in 4QInstruction and the Wisdom of Solomon," in *Wisdom and Apocalypticism in the Dead Sea Scrolls and in the Biblical Tradition,* ed. F. García Martínez (Leuven: University Press, 2003), 287–305.

23. See the overview article by James H. Charlesworth, "John the Baptizer and the Dead Sea Scrolls," in *The Bible and the Dead Sea Scrolls: The Second Princeton Symposium on Judaism and Christian Origins,* vol. 3, ed. James H. Charlesworth (Waco, Tex.: Baylor University Press, 2006), 1–35.

24. In his inaugural address at the University of Heidelberg, Michael Welker, "The Reign of God," *Theology Today* 49/4 (1993): 500–512, offers a beautiful exploration of transformation language in New Testament tradition. He uses theories of "emergent realities" to describe, from a systematic point of view, what the New Testament expresses in spatial terms when it talks about the "nearness" of God's kingdom.

25. A number of Matthew's parables about the kingdom of heaven are actually parables about the right way of expecting it or living toward it; for example, the parables of the Wedding Banquet (Matt. 22:1–14) and of the Ten Bridesmaids (Matt. 25:1–13).

26. Luz, *Matthew,* 322, notes: "The unusual thing about this petition is the subordinate clause. Although the idea that divine forgiveness is associated with human forgiveness is widespread in Judaism, in my opinion there is no case where human action is taken into a central prayer text in this way." The problem with this assessment is that one needs to distinguish quite carefully between the different ways in which divine and human forgiveness are "associated" with one another. In Sir. 28:2, one of the texts that Luz refers to and that show close parallels with Matt. 6:12, human moral behavior is a precondition for receiving the forgiveness of sins that only God can grant ("Forgive your neighbor the wrong he has done, and then your sins will be pardoned when you pray"). The issue that this text addresses is how one finds forgiveness with God (cf. Matt. 6:14), which is in keeping with practically all of the Old Testament references that we have reviewed above. The "unusual thing" about the subordinate clause in Matt. 6:12, "as we also have forgiven our debtors," is that it does not specify any such preconditions. Rather, it puts divine and human forgiveness on the same qualitative level.

27. This also points to a linguistic problem: Jesus' first language was Aramaic, and the Gospel stories were written in Greek. Thus, the question arises to what extent the notion of סלח can be presupposed as a background even in these other languages. At least this much is clear: the standard rendering of סלח in the LXX is ἀφίημι (although there are exceptions, especially when

the LXX aims at a more idiomatic Greek), which is also the term that is used in Matthew, including the nominal phrase ἄφεσις ἁμαρτιῶν "forgiveness of sins."

28. For a comparison between the Lord's Prayer and rabbinic texts, see J. Massyngberde Ford, "The Forgiveness Clause in the Matthean Form of the Our Father," *Zeitschrift für die neutestamentliche Wissenschaft und die Kunde der älteren Kirche* 59 (1968): 127–31.

29. Welker, *Reign of God,* 504, summarizes the experience articulated in Matt. 18:23–35 as follows: "Entry into the reign of God is no less marked by experiences of mercy received, of forgiveness or of payment beyond our own expectations."

30. This does not mean, however, that Matthew would reject the idea of communal discipline. Right before 18:21–35, Matthew addresses the issue of how a member who had wronged the community should be properly rebuked and even expelled, if that person remained unreasonable.

13

"We Once Knew Him from a Human Point of View"

PAUL D. HANSON

While Shia and Sunni Muslims battle over which of them preserves the authentic succession of the prophet Mohammad, Christians argue over the legitimate path to discovering the real Jesus. While it may seem odd for a student of the Hebrew Bible/Old Testament to enter a discussion located within the domain of New Testament specialists, this essay arises out of the conviction that a discussion that has focused primarily on a Greco-Roman intellectual environment and on the growth of traditions about Jesus after his death may benefit from a more concerted look at a Jewish context and at traditions belonging to his own religious tradition.[1] While organizing the diverse approaches to the problem of the historical Jesus inevitably involves oversimplification, the following threefold distinction will be made: (1) historical-critical, (2) disinterested, (3) historical-theological.

We begin with the historical-critical approach, inasmuch as it has dominated the media coverage of the problem of the historical Jesus and has tended to frame the question for scholars, the media, and laity alike. While it could be argued that we should retain the common designation "the Quest for the Historical Jesus," reference to the historical-critical approach not only avoids the confusion raised by distinctions in the literature between the quest, the new quest, and now, the third quest, but it points to the ideological starting point of all phases of "the quest."

That starting point is the approach to biblical research that grew out of the Enlightenment. With the ascendancy of reason as the legitimate instrument for the pursuit of knowledge in all fields of study, appeals to revelation or any other avenue of cognition not considered in keeping with the rules of scientific research were repudiated by those applying historical-critical methods to the literature of the Bible. The goal was to recover whatever historical facts interrogation of the texts could yield. And the interrogators approached their task with the confidence that not only did the recorded data have to withstand the usual tests of reliability of the witnesses and corroborating evidence from other ancient sources but also the test of modern experience—that is, if a modern analogy could not be cited, the reported event could not be credited with facticity.[2]

After Hermann Samuel Reimarus (1694–1768) had initiated the application of the historical-critical method to the New Testament Gospels by denying the historicity of the miracles, a virtual stream of books dedicated to recovering the historical Jesus followed.[3] Though differing in details, they presented a Jesus that closely matched the ethical and cultural norms of the time, in effect, one who would have been welcomed in the liberal faculties of philosophy and theology in Germany and England, or for that matter, at Thomas Jefferson's dinner table in Monticello. But the civil discussion with a liberal-minded Jesus ended abruptly with the publication of Albert Schweitzer's *The Quest of the Historical Jesus* in 1906, in which he depicted a fiery prophet announcing God's imminent judgment on a wicked generation and calling those who would hear to repent and follow his way of this-world renunciation. In my own reflections on the issue of the historical Jesus, I am indebted to Schweitzer's scathing critique of the life of Jesus scholarship and to his historiographic principle that can be described thus: A figure from the past must be interpreted within his or her native context rather than being forced into a world of the interpreter's making (be it a nineteenth-century liberal-rationalism or a twentieth–twenty-first-century construction based on a hybrid consisting of Hellenistic philosophy and contemporary social-scientific models). At the same time, I find less than helpful his next step.

The next step taken by Schweitzer ironically folds his theological program into that of his liberal contemporaries. Having declared the apocalyptic message of Jesus quite irrelevant to citizens of his modern world, he focuses on basic ethical elements in Jesus' preaching that become the foundation of his lifelong program of serving humanity, "the Fatherhood of God and the Brotherhood of Man." While it would be foolhearted to pass judgment on the ethical significance of contributions that after all won him a Nobel Peace Prize, I do not find in Schweitzer's New Testament theology a way forward in the contemporary debate over the historical Jesus.

Upon graduation from college in 1961, I spent a year as a Fulbright scholar at the Universität Heidelberg in Germany, and since that institution has served as the academic home of our esteemed colleague Michael Welker, a personal reminiscence seems appropriate. Upon my arrival, theological students were actively discussing Günter Bornkamm's *Jesus of Nazareth*, but at the time I little realized that a new, chastened quest was under way. It was a quest that would contribute subtleties lacking in the earlier quest (and as history would prove, in the later quest), specifically in the lines of continuity Bornkamm perceived between the eschatological teaching of Jesus and the resurrection faith of the post-Easter church. During the same semester that I was listening to Bornkamm's lectures in the crowded *Alte Aula*, I was studying the parables of Jesus in a small pro-seminar taught by Ferdinand Hahn. Only years later did it become apparent to me that in reading Joachim Jeremias's *Parables of Jesus* I was being tutored in a reading of the Gospels that was sensitive to the Jewish world of Jesus, a world categorically closer to the historical Jesus than the world of Cynic teachers or peasant revolutionaries. The renewal of the quest initiated by Jeremias and Bornkamm, indebted to be sure to the groundbreaking work of Rudolf Bultmann, was a stage of research rich in theological promise.

This brings us to the so-called third quest, which unlike its predecessors is largely an American phenomenon. If the participants in the first quest pursued their task with the positivist's assurance that their historical-critical approach, purged of superstition and supernaturalism and relying on reason alone, was able to recover the historical facts of Jesus' life, one strand in the third quest represented by Robert Funk, John Dominic Crossan, and others associated with the Jesus Seminar, while acknowledging the incompleteness of the evidence provided by the New Testament and other early Christian texts and the tentativeness of every reconstruction, energetically advances its portraits of the historical Jesus by application of a new method.[4] The starting point is the collection of Jesus sayings and small number of episodes (both from the New Testament Gospels and noncanonical writings) voted by the Jesus Seminar to be authentic. Since both the narrative sequences found in the canonical Gospels and the traditions recorded in the Pauline letters are set aside as later, ideologically driven creations, a model enabling the individual scholar to integrate the disaggregated words and deeds into an intelligible whole must be found outside of the biblical writings. The solution is found by recourse to social-scientific method that provides an ideal type into which the scattered data can be fit to produce a plausible picture of the historical Jesus. In comparison to the nineteenth-century quest, what one encounters is a historical-critical method modified by introduction of a social-scientific dimension, but the results, in producing a Jesus reflecting the worldview of the various authors, is essentially the same. The impasse encountered is thus reminiscent of the age of Strauss and Renan.

This brings us to the question of why so many scholars using the same method on the same materials have ended with such wildly divergent portraits of Jesus. To list only a few that have emerged: Jesus as romantic visionary (Renan), as eschatological prophet (Schweitzer, Wright), as wicked priest from Qumran (Thiering), as husband of Mary Magdalene (Spong), as revolutionary zealot (S. F. G. Brandon), as agrarian reformer (Yoder), as revitalized movement founder and charismatic

(Borg), as gay magician (Smith), as cynic sage (Downing), as peasant thaumaturge (Crossan), as peasant poet (Bailey), and as guru of oceanic bliss (Mitchell).[5]

Needless to say, even a brief survey of the many reconstructions of the historical Jesus that have arisen out of the third quest would be beyond the scope of this essay. We therefore focus on one author as representative of the group of scholars who (1) identify the authentic data for the historical Jesus with the sayings receiving an affirmative vote from the Jesus Seminar; (2) exclude the eschatological/apocalyptic dimensions as products of the post-70 era; (3) find in the narrative accounts of the four Gospels—such as the passion/resurrection narratives—the propaganda of the early church; (4) in the search for authentic Jesus sayings consider noncanonical gospels alongside Matthew, Mark, Luke (and John); and (5) derive from social anthropology and comparative religion focusing on Hellenistic/Roman culture an ideal type (e.g., Cynic teacher or peasant miracle worker) that serves as the principle into which the purported authentic data is fit to create an intelligible whole.

While scholars like Burton Mack and Marcus Borg, with their portraits of Jesus the Cynic teacher, could serve as our representative of the third quest, the enormous popularity of John Dominic Crossan's publications make him an even more appropriate choice. Written in a lively style and with the passion of one called to rescue Christianity from the disrepute brought upon it by its authoritarian teachers, past and present, his books are directed especially to those torn between the secular worldview that purportedly is identical with modernity and the allegedly passé doctrines of the traditional church.[6]

Crossan's methodology might be compared to that of a Near Eastern archaeologist of an earlier generation. Beginning with the canonical text, Crossan digs through multiple layers of interpretation with the aim of reaching the earliest stratum. Unlike archaeologists currently in the field, the archaeologist of our analogy has scant interest in Crusader or Mamaluke strata, and he calls in excavation equipment to clear his site of medieval remains so as to enable him to get to the evidence he considers significant, that of more ancient civilizations. Even here, though, the analogy is inadequate in one respect: while the archaeologist's attitude toward later strata is one of disinterest, Crossan, in a manner similar to Robert Funk,[7] holds a decidedly hostile attitude toward those who deposited the later layers of tradition on top of Jesus' words—namely, the churchly interpreters who not only distorted the picture of the real historical Jesus, but transformed him into a warrant for hierarchical ecclesial structures and christological teachings that have deleterious effects down to the present day, such as gender discrimination, alliance of the church with political and economic forces that oppress the poor, imperialism, and homophobia. Guided by his conviction that "early is true," however, Crossan's efforts are rewarded with the discovery of a historical Jesus who stands in solidarity with peasants of all times and places in their opposition to tradents, like Paul and the writers of the Gospel narratives, who use their positions of authority to secure their definition of truth against rival movements.

This is a message that has tremendous appeal to those who have become alienated from the structures of their churches and whose acceptance of a secular/naturalist view of reality has invalidated a priori the truth claims of the New Testament regarding the salvific role of Jesus in relation to a sinful humanity and an endangered world. When I read the letters from readers with which Crossan introduces the chapters in *Who Is Jesus?*[8] I am reminded of the marketing style of modern televangelists: We find heart-stirring testimonials of thoughtfully honest folks praising the scholar who has rescued the truth of Jesus for them alongside criticisms of traditionalists hopelessly imprisoned in their unexamined orthodoxies.

Moving from analogy and impression to a more analytic critique of Crossan's methodology, we shall begin with the most important insight that has arisen out of two centuries of hermeneutical reflection, namely, the importance of fore-knowledge (*Vorverständnis*) in any interpretative endeavor. In the case of interpreting the New Testament, aspects of the interpreter's fore-knowledge that are in play include worldview (e.g., naturalism or theism), judgment as to what counts as evidence (e.g., the Jesus words declared authentic by the Jesus Seminar [which systematically excluded certain categories of sayings, such as those expressing an eschatological dimension] or a wider range of New Testament materials), choice of an interpretive framework within which to create a comprehensive/comprehensible picture of the subject being studied (e.g., Cynic teacher or prophet in the tradition of the prophets of the Old Testament), and an attitude toward the interpretive traditions that shaped the New Testament pictures of Jesus (e.g., negative or sympathetic). In the case of Crossan, a naturalistic view of the world privileges reason as the most appropriate tool for interrogating the New Testament writings, which equates early with true and late with distortion and measures evidence against the test of modern analogy. The evidence that this method yields is an aggregate of sayings and deeds that do not manifest inner connections or a pattern of meaning and thereby require the introduction of an ideal type into which they can be fit so as to produce a comprehensible picture of the historical Jesus. Not surprisingly, the fore-knowledge of the interpreter plays a major role in selecting which ideal type is deemed appropriate. The wide range of candidates nominated by the questers, whether in the nineteenth century or our own time, has discredited in the minds of many the legitimacy of the whole endeavor of searching for the historical Jesus. But it could also raise the question of whether the cultural context within which the ideal type has been sought is the appropriate one. Is, for example, the Cynic philosopher of Athens or Rome an appropriate type for understanding Jesus? When Marcus Borg, for example, arrives at the contrast between Jesus' "politics of compassion" as opposed to the "politics of holiness" of his (Jewish!) adversaries, one versed in the history of Second Temple Jewish religion may question the usefulness, not to mention validity, of such a comparison. For now, I shall leave these questions suspended, pausing briefly to mention a distinctly different position that has been chosen by certain scholars regarding the historical Jesus question, and then turning to describe what I regard to be a suitable approach.

In identifying three approaches that have been taken to the question of the historical Jesus, I named the second "disinterested." It is an inadequate designation, and involves the clustering together of representatives of a very diverse group who, however, share the one characteristic of attributing to history of Jesus research little or no importance, since theological meaning resides in the New Testament writings in their received form.

The fore-understandings that inform the specific theologies of those we place in this cluster vary from a doctrine of biblical inerrancy to an existentialist hermeneutics to a traditionalism predicated on a high view of the teaching authority of the church (e.g., the Magisterium in the Roman Catholic confession). The reason that recovery of a historical Jesus beneath the surface of the biblical narrative is unimportant for inerrantists and traditionalists is obvious. However, it may be less obvious why a scholar like Rudolf Bultmann, universally known for his form-critical analysis of the Synoptic Gospels, can be placed in this category. The reason lies in his view that not only is it impossible to recover the historical Jesus, but such recovery is intrinsically of no theological value. What the one addressed by the gospel encounters is the post-Easter message of the risen Christ, which when translated from its ancient mythological trappings into the modern existentialist philosophy of Martin Heidegger is an invitation to accept God's gift of authentic humanity through identification with the living Christ. What follows then should come as no surprise: the Gospel most discredited by those searching for the historical Jesus regains a level of respect it had not enjoyed since the seventeenth and eighteenth centuries. For Bultmann, the theologically richest Gospel is the Gospel of John!

We now have set the stage to ask whether—besides (and between) the approach that proposes to utilize the Enlightenment's gift to biblical studies called historical criticism to recover the real Jesus and the approach that, for widely diverse reasons, categorically strips the historical Jesus research of any theological significance—there is a third way?

I believe there is, and I designate this approach "historical-theological." How does such an approach differ methodologically from the other two?

First, in relation to the option that attributes no theological value to historical Jesus research, the historical-theological approach assumes that what can be known of the historical Jesus is theologically significant, and for a reason that is intrinsic to biblical faith in both Testaments: in contrast to the great mythopoeic religions of antiquity, the faith of the biblical communities through their many generations arose through experiencing a God encountered in the stuff of their historical existence, a theologumenon captured by the epithet *Immanuel*, God with us.

Proponents of a historical-theological approach therefore share with the Jesus Seminar questers an interest in gaining knowledge of the historical Jesus, but that is where the commonality ends, for everything from their fore-understanding to the methodological principles guiding their research stands in stark contrast to the approach we illustrated by reference to John Dominic Crossan.

First of all, the secular naturalism that underlies the historical-critical method is rejected as an inadequate basis for understanding the message of the New Testament and discerning the source of that message in the words and deeds of Jesus of Nazareth. Not only is its view of a closed universe unbiblical; it is also a view deemed to be impoverished and woefully inadequate conceptually in dealing with the most profound aspects of existence. Immersion in the world of the biblical writers thus fuses with contemporary experience of the mystery at the heart of contemporary life in creating an openness to the entry into human experience of the divine Spirit, specifically, of the Spirit of the living Christ.

This fore-understanding shapes the historical method that guides the search for the historical Jesus. The simple route of categorical rejection of all data that do not meet the naturalist test or the criterion of modern analogy or the arbitrary declaration that themes eschatological must be attributed to later interpreters seeking to transform the peasant teacher Jesus into the mythical figure of Christ is regarded as a route that will lead to something other than the "real" Jesus. A more textured understanding of history that includes the openness of human experience to divine presence does not impose an indiscriminate acceptance of all biblical data as describing the historical Jesus. A criteriology capable of discerning historical Jesus sayings and deeds is essential, though it can only be illustrated in what follows.[9]

A further difference has to do with the relation of the historical Jesus to the traditions reflecting the meaning and significance of the post-Easter experiences of Jesus. Here the positivist-rationalist formula *early = true // late = falsification* will be rejected as historiographically discredited and philosophically naive. Historiographically, an aetiological explanation of the combined second- and third-generation Christian witness to Jesus Christ as Savior is in my judgment impossible if one predicates as a source a Cynic teacher. How could a Cynic teacher, teaching moral platitudes like myriad teachers before and after, become commonly proclaimed within widely dispersed communities as God's chosen Messiah? Only a deep vitriol toward the classical teachings of the church is capable of producing the incredible conclusion that the evidence for the historical Jesus is limited to the *logia* and other scattered data recovered by the Jesus Seminar and that all else is the product of deliberate, calculated distortion and deception by power-hungry leaders like Paul and the Gospel writers.

Finally, resorting to the world of Hellenist thought and culture to find the ideal type enabling reassembly of the disaggregated Jesus sayings into a comprehensible whole remains unconvincing, and specifically from the very social-scientific and comparative-religions perspective invoked by the seekers. The problem is this: though the "ideal type" as a heuristic category suffers from distinct limitations (the most influential figures in human history were complex and not reducible to a stereotype), insofar as the category can be applied to shed some light on a historical figure, is it not common sense to derive that type from that figure's own culture and religious tradition? That is what we shall now seek to do as the first step in sketching our understanding of a historical-theological approach to the historical Jesus.

The apostle Paul extended the good news originating with Jesus to all nations. Among the boundaries transcended was this: neither Jew nor Greek.[10] While there is evidence that Jesus did not see the new era of divine righteousness confined to the Jews (e.g., the narrative of the Samaritan woman), it is clear that it was to the tribes of Israel that he devoted his attention. Paul's border-shattering formula notwithstanding, it is clear that he is aware of an early stage of history when even Christ was known from a human point of view[11] and, from that point of view, he was deeply and authentically Jewish.[12] Some major proponents of the third quest also ascribe a particular cultural localization for Jesus, but, ironically, they opt for the other side of Paul's polarity: Jesus, the Cynic teacher or the wandering peasant miracle worker, seems more at home in the Greco-Roman world than in the Jewish countryside![13]

Since the apostle Paul is not a villain in my theological understanding, I have no difficulty following his historical approach to locating Jesus religiously and culturally. And Paul was not alone. Throughout the New Testament, the nature of Jesus' ministry and the significance of his life were sought through close scrutiny of Jewish Scripture and within the context of the Jewish traditions within which he was raised. It seems reasonable to believe that Jesus himself understood his role on the basis of his own religious and cultural traditions.

In considering the religious and political situation into which Jesus was born, the apocryphal work the *Psalms of Solomon* offers valuable evidence. Arising out of the stinging experience of Pompey's conquest of Jerusalem in 63 BCE, it combines condemnation of the Hasmoneans for their perfidy and responsibility for the disgrace that had fallen upon the Jewish people with an announcement of God's imminent sending of a king of the Jews, an anointed one, a messiah, who would restore the nation to the glory of the Solomonic Age.

As the series of self-proclaimed messiahs who arose in the Herodian Period indicates, the world in which Jesus lived was one rife with expectation, a situation providing political movements like the Zealots and terrorists like the sicarii with the opportunity to draw large segments of the subjugated Jewish populace into their revolts against Rome.

It is evident that Jesus refused to be identified with such revolutionary movements. Yet the fact that he was killed by the Romans requires an explanation.

Here the most plausible route is to take seriously the well-attested New Testament tradition that associates Jesus with the biblical Hebrew prophets. What are the central characteristics of this indigenous "ideal type," the Hebrew prophet?

Though varying in the manner in which they related their message to the political powers of their times,[14] the prophets share this view of the context within which they carry out their vocation: they represent the imperium of God as the only legitimate ruling authority in the universe. Earthly rulers, whether native or foreign, were legitimate in the exercise of penultimate authority only to the degree that they served the purposes of the divine imperium. The purposes of that imperium were described in the Torah. The cornerstone of the Torah, in turn, was the First Commandment, which limited worship to one God. Therefore, in the judgment of the prophets, the most egregious of all sins was the imperial claim to divinity.[15] On this basis Elijah, Hosea, Amos, Isaiah, and Jeremiah spoke with one voice in condemning the attempted usurpation of God's ruling authority by human rulers. Beginning with the biblical writings and further developed in the legends of the prophets, the tradition developed that the prophets suffered at the hands of ruthless impostors they denounced, and that their suffering often culminated in death at the hands of those desperately clinging to the reins of earthly power.[16]

The second characteristic of the biblical Hebrew prophet is the opposite side of their judgment on earthly regimes that repudiate God's imperium. It is the announcement of the ultimate victory of God's reign over all rival principalities. The phrase that captures this theme is "kingdom of God," and it is constituted by the announcement of the restoration of universal justice, mercy, and peace that will accompany God's appointment of his anointed one (*messiah*) as king. Like the theme of the persecution of the prophets, the theme of eschatological restoration runs through the entire history of Hebrew prophecy.[17]

Given the fact that the Hebrew prophets shaped their indictment of the rich and politically powerful of their time in terms of an assault on God's legitimate reign and accompanied that message with an announcement of the reign of God that would restore justice and peace on earth, it seems far-fetched to depict Jesus, who like John condemns the abuse of power and announces the advent of God's kingdom of righteousness, as a Cynic preacher reciting moral aphorisms, whose simple humane message became corrupted by later intrusion of the eschatological themes of universal judgment and the restoration of faithful Israel. Such a move involves a complete break with Jewish tradition and yields what one would expect once interpretation has turned its back on Jesus' own religious tradition by deconstructing the Jewish matrix of his career and reconstructing it on the basis of an ideal type taken from a different culture.

By drawing attention to Jesus' roots in Hebrew prophecy, and pointing specifically to the theme of suffering and death of the prophet and the eschatological theme of messianic restoration, we could be credited with providing the basis for interpreting the historical Jesus as a Jewish martyr while leaving the theme of suffering on behalf of others and divine vindication in the resurrection to be explained as post-Easter inventions of despairing disciples. To do so would be to leave out an important datum, the so-called Servant Songs of Isaiah 42; 49; 50; and 52–53. Themselves instances of the ongoing interpretation and reapplication of the atonement theme of Leviticus 17–18, they reach a dramatic climax in ascribing to the death of the innocent faithful servant of God atoning significance (Isa. 53:10–11) and announcing God's vindication of the one who willingly offered his life for the sins of others (Isa. 53:10–12). The history of interpretation of this remarkable passage has also left its imprint, from Daniel 11:33–36 and 12:2–3 to the letters of the apostle Paul to the New Testament Gospels.

In seeking to gain a historical understanding of Jesus in light of the prophetic tradition indigenous to his own religious heritage, we recognize a prophetic figure addressing the despair of a community subjugated to an imperial power led by a self-proclaimed divine savior and looking to God for deliverance. In keeping with the prophets before him, he proclaims that the imposter kingdom is under the judgment of the true ruler of the universe, who through his anointed one will inaugurate a long-awaited reign of righteousness and peace. From the history of the prophets, Jesus is well aware that his message will incur the wrath of the deified Roman emperor and all of his clients and collaborators, even those among his fellow religionists. But he refuses to unsheathe his sword to join the cause of the Zealots, trusting instead in the ultimate victory of the kingdom of his God. Even when it has become evident that the likely result of his denunciation of idolatry will be his death, he derives assurance from Scripture that the servant of God who is faithful even unto death will be an instrument of God's redemption and will be vindicated in the day when justice and peace are permanently established.

The apostle Paul writes as one who has received the testimony of those who followed Jesus and walked in the path of the one who embodied God's compassion and courage in all that he said and did. Likewise he received the joyous news that the one who was crucified by the Romans was vindicated in keeping with the tradition and appeared to assure his followers that he could never again be cut off from them. Though they too could expect to suffer at the hands of those who refused to submit to God's reign, his Spirit would be with them to sustain their trust in the ultimate victory of God's kingdom through all trials.

The basic pattern of meaning that the apostle Paul worked out in his letters underlies as well the several narrative construals provided by the Gospels. As redaction criticism has shown, each of the Gospels is shaped by a particular theological perspective, but amid the emphases and embellishments and interpretations found in each, the basic pattern remains consistent: With prophetic courage, Jesus denounces those who flaunt their positions of power to oppress and exploit the weak and the poor and unmasks them as agents of the powers of darkness that attack God's reign of compassionate justice. Confident of the ultimate victory of truth over falsehood, Jesus expresses God's love and healing power in his every word and deed. In the tradition of the prophets before him, however, he is bitterly opposed by those whose rule he declares illegitimate and doomed, but even their final resort to execution fails as God vindicates his mission in the resurrection. Consistent with his divine compassion, Jesus promised his followers that his Spirit would never leave them. The validity of that promise was experienced in a special way every time those followers ate the bread and drank the wine that renewed his presence with them.

It remains to describe how the unbroken line of continuity from the Hebrew prophets to the historical Jesus to Jesus Christ of Paul's epistles and the Gospels continues in the community life of the church today. We shall focus on one narrative, the Lord's Supper.

Anyone resisting the false comfort of Cartesian certainty must admit that every effort to reconstruct an event in the life of a historical figure like Jesus must be content with categories like plausibility or probability. I believe that the following description of the Last Supper passes that test.

Read within the context of Jesus' Jewish religious heritage, the account in Mark 14:22–25[18] of the supper that Jesus shared with his disciples on the eve of his death is imbued with a high degree of verisimilitude that is best explained in terms of a living narrative tradition tracing back to the experience of the disciples with their Lord. Beginning with a blessing over the food and followed by the breaking of the bread and sharing the cup of wine follows Jewish custom. Relating the wine to his blood in anticipation of the imminent suffering and death that was by then clearly visible draws deeply upon Jewish atonement ritual; placing this ritual language within the overarching concept of covenant established what the disciples were experiencing and would experience in the trials of the next days squarely within the context of Israel's history of relationship with God. Finally, Jesus' naming his next opportunity to drink "this fruit of the vine" as "that day when I drink it new with you in my Father's kingdom" fits precisely the eschatological kingdom theme that we have traced back to the biblical prophets, which theme commonly was portrayed through the image of banquet.[19] Not for the first time, but with an intensity of meaning that would leave its imprint on his disciples and on the generations of the church to follow, Jesus celebrated a common meal with those gathered around him in anticipation of the messianic banquet to come.[20]

Corroborating the historicity of the account of the Last Supper is the important fact that when Paul transmits the words Jesus spoke "on the night when he was betrayed," he describes his role as that of a link in a tradition that he had received: "For I received from the Lord what I also handed on to you . . ." Already in Paul's generation, which is to say merely two decades after Jesus' death, the cup and the bread had become symbols of the sacramental unity they experienced "in the blood of Christ" and "in the body of Christ" (1 Cor. 10:16). And it was a unity that carried with it a profound moral quality, as indicated by the apostle's outrage upon hearing that in gathering "to eat the Lord's supper . . . one goes hungry and another becomes drunk" (1 Cor. 11:20–21). When one encounters such shaping of teaching and tradition by the second generation of followers, it is hard to understand the accusations of subversion of original social reform and deception and exploitation of the poor by the emerging elite leadership of the church. One could develop this point further by contrasting the concept of sin in Crossan's Jesus in terms of faulty social structures requiring human efforts at change with Paul's understanding of Jesus as one treating sin as a deep-seated corruption in which humans are being destroyed along with all the rest of creation and requiring death to the order dominated by principalities and powers so as to prepare for new birth to God's eschatological order of šalom (Rom. 6:5–11; 8:18–39). The former program is well served by a peasant wonder worker or Cynic philosopher; the latter condition looks to one anointed by God to suffer and die for the fallen world and then through resurrection to lead the way to new life for individuals and communities as well as the entirety of creation. Paul's theology, far from detracting from Jesus' call to reform, grasps the radical, universal scope of that call and draws those responding in faith into the body that continues God's redemptive work in the world.[21]

Our description of continuity between the historical Jesus and the understanding of Jesus' reality in the second and third generations of Christians manifests aspects of our fore-understanding that will be of utmost importance when we make our final move of describing the meaning of Jesus within the church today. We spoke of Jesus' roots in the prophetic tradition's testimony to God's universal imperium, of his both holding up that kingdom as the standard against which all human institutions were to be judged and embodying the justice and mercy of God's reign in his every word and act; of his awareness of treading a path toward opposition, suffering, and death at the hands of this world's leaders; and finally of his confidence in the ultimate victory of the mission to which God had called him. For his followers, the resurrection not only assured them of that ultimate victory, but it granted the further assurance of Christ's presence as they continued God's work of reconciliation and redemption.

Christ's Spirit remains with the church today, not only as an example to be followed, but as the living presence into which we are drawn, the body of Christ in the world for the world. We belittle the work in which God has been engaged in the lives of the Hebrew prophets, in John the Baptist, and in Jesus of Nazareth if we do not see underlying their social and political reform a more fundamental work in which reality on the most fundamental level is being reordered toward God's eschatological reign of universal justice, mercy, and peace. Reform of political, social, economic, and ecclesiastical structures is not dismissed as irrelevant but takes on a new urgency by being related to the deeper movement of which such reform is a part, the growth of God's kingdom of righteousness that eschews compromising alliances and glitzy announcements of premature victories and perceives good news only where individuals and groups that were dead to sin are raised to life and thereby become participants in God's new creation.

So what does the one subscribing to the historical-theological approach do with the historical Jesus research? Let us begin with the popular media, which is the best marketer of historical Jesus books. Any biblical scholar at a recognized university or seminary is familiar with the telephone call I received recently: "Hello, this is NN. I'm calling from Copenhagen. Would you be so kind as to comment on the recent reports that Jesus' tomb has been discovered? What implications does that discovery have for Christian faith?" In the five minutes I felt justified to commit to this inquiry, I try to lay down some principles of historical research: "Does the evidence offer any reliable witness to the particular Jeshua central to Christian faith? Are you aware of the fact that Jeshua was a very common name at that time? Etc., etc." Books on the historical Jesus, no matter how shoddy their methodology, are guaranteed good sales if they play to this kind of popular curiosity. But its yield for history and theology is nil.

Now more seriously: if simple historiographic considerations dismiss as irrelevant the popular reports of Roman Age tombs with Jesus names and bones or no bones, what would represent an archaeological (i.e., historical) discovery that would be theologically significant? This would be: "Archaeologists at a hitherto unexcavated site in Upper Egypt have discovered in a library of what appears to be a monastic community an account of the Last Supper. It reports that Jesus, on the eve of his death, gathered his disciples together for supper, at which he blessed the menu consisting of the roasted flesh of the babies of the Roman occupation and blood that had been ritually drained from their arteries." In subsequent months, further reports appeared in the media of third-century Christian texts discovered in sites near Rome describing liturgies centered around sacramental infanticide and ingestion of the flesh of babies snatched from Roman families.[22]

Such reports as these would require disciplined historical research on the part of Christian scholars, for if they on the basis of rigorous standards of research proved to be reliable, the implications for Christian faith would have to be considered with all seriousness.

As we have seen in our examination of the evidence of the historical Jesus, a vastly different pattern emerges. Specifically in the case of the Last Supper, we find the most credible interpretive context in the traditions of the Hebrew Bible, and they revolve around atonement and life, not cruelty and death. The same life-redeeming meaning resides within Mark's narrative of the Last Supper, and its authenticity is corroborated by Paul, who, moreover, ties its significance securely to the lofty moral ideal that discrimination between rich and poor stands in contradiction to the central sacrament of the Christian faith.

In the regular celebration of Christ's gifts, those gathered in Christ's name renew the solidarity with their Lord that constitutes their unity and the essential meaning of their corporate life as the extension of God's reconciling work in the world. Even as baptism commemorates their death to the world and new birth as members of God's redeemed creation, so this supper creates in them "the mind of Christ" and sets them on the path of obedience to God and love for one another.

Clearly, this interpretation of the Lord's Supper shatters the limits with which it would be circumscribed by a secular/naturalistic reading. For those committed to the rationalistic fore-understanding of the higher critical method, it will be dismissed as submission to the mythology introduced by Paul and the Gospel writers to lead unsuspecting followers away from the practical teachings of peasant Jesus and into the bondage of dogma and hierarchy. In a culture within which secularism has pervaded all institutions, it is not surprising thus to find among biblical scholars striving to demonstrate their modernity another kind of submission, submission to a worldview that excludes transcendence and to a historiography that, with all of its qualifications, still preserves one of the principles of positivism, namely, early is true and late is false.

Some of those who reject such reductionism as an impoverishment of Christian faith make a move with which I am uncomfortable, namely, conceding "the academy" to secular/naturalistic methodology and seeking to keep alive a theological understanding of the classics of the Christian tradition within "the church." This move suffers from the myopia that views as normative the history of the university from the Enlightment to the present, forgetting that in earlier eras a far more nuanced understanding of reality prevailed, forgetting as well that the methodology of the questers by no means goes unchallenged in many university departments of religion and philosophy today.

In the academy and in the church alike, it is important that Christian scholars make their case that a methodology is called for in every area of study that is appropriate to its object of study. In the case of the Bible, an approach is called for that is capable of grasping the essential reality that brings coherence to the whole. That reality cannot be understood by focusing exclusively on a highly subjective reconstruction of the historical Jesus that cuts him off from the tradition that preserves and transmits and interprets his central role in the biblical drama reaching from creation to fall to redemption.

In the final analysis, the discussion returns to the question of fore-understanding, and in the case of the historical-theological approach fore-understanding includes the belief that the chain of tradition from Jesus of Nazareth to Paul to the Gospel writers to the present gathering of Christians around the bread and wine is a tradition guided by God through the abiding presence of the Spirit of Christ. This in no way excludes critical attention to aspects of the tradition that compromise or contradict the central gospel message of obedience and compassion, but that critique occurs within and not outside of the *regula fidei*, and thus differs sharply from the approach that would resolve tensions within the tradition by simply chopping off everything except the hypothetical earliest history.

The choice one makes between the options of historical-critical and historical-theological profoundly influences one's view of the role of Christians in the world today. While the role envisioned by the scholar projecting Jesus the Cynic teacher is the humanistic role of summoning humans to programs of social, political, and economic reform (an admirable effort comparable to the best of similar efforts by other humanistic groups), the role of those recognizing the guiding presence of Christ's Spirit in the church's ongoing interpretation of and incorporation into the central reality of Jesus Christ is the role of the body of Christ serving as ambassadors of a new creation through acts of advocacy for the poor, denunciation of false gods, and peacemaking in troubled parts of the world. To this belongs a dimension that shatters the closed universe of secular modernity, for as in the life of Jesus, so too in the life of the church, concrete acts of compassion and justice here and now are in unbroken continuity with proclamation of God's eschatological reign as history's and creation's final goal. The hope and yearning that derive from this vision are what makes the church's presence in the world distinct from secular agencies.

In the usual flow of narrative structure, we have arrived at the fitting point for a triumphal conclusion. Or, in adherence to the genre of the scholarly essay, we should now summarize how our argument has trumped opposing positions. Unfortunately, an obstacle stands in the way of such closure: the church's repeated failure to perceive the world with the mind of Christ and to conduct its life as the body of Christ has blemished its credibility and contributed to the popularity of the very ones who promise to free modern humans of churchly clutter and offer them the "real" Jesus. If to end with confession rather than triumph offers scant intellectual satisfaction, an arresting image from the church's portrait of Jesus may be instructive, the image of his dying words expressing abandonment, the image of brokenness longing for fulfillment. And longing is the work of the Spirit,[23] the Spirit of Christ that is at work in us even today, even in our brokenness.[24]

NOTES

1. Michael Welker is both a dear friend and an esteemed theologian whose prolific writings have been a source of enrichment for my own scholarship. It was a great honor to be asked to write an essay for a festschrift in honor of Michael's sixtieth birthday. But what does an Old Testament theologian contribute to the topic of Christology? The answer arises out of my growing sense over the years that the historical Jesus that has been constructed by certain participants in the "third quest" has looked more like a Greek than a Jew. This essay contains both a critique of that stream in the quest and my own reflections on "Christ from a human point of view" (2 Cor. 5:16), that is, the historical Jesus.

2. Especially influential was Troeltsch's insistence that Christianity, like any other religious phenomenon, had to be subjected to scientific historical analysis if it was to be taken seriously by modern thinkers. Excluded from investigation into the historical Jesus were references to transcendence or appeals to categories such as revelation or the doctrinal authority of the church. See Ernst Troeltsch, *Der Historismus und seine Probleme* (Tübingen: C. B. Mohr, 1922). The most emphatic rejection of this notion of "scientific" historiography came from Karl Barth: "We must open our eyes and see this quite particular history: God becomes man, the Word was made flesh, it lived in the midst of men. . . . One must clearly either accept this 'myth' as history itself, and call all the other histories myth, or otherwise refuse the Christian 'myth' and remain with the human notion of history" (*The Faith of the Church: A Commentary on the Apostles' Creed According to Calvin's Catechism* [New York: Meridian Books, 1958], 98).

3. The classic expression of this genre was reached by David Friedrich Strauss's *Leben Jesu* (1835–36).

4. In focusing on one strand of the third quest, I am mindful of passing over the important works of John Meier, N. T. Wright, E. P. Sanders, and Ben F. Meyer, authors with whom I hold much in common and to whose thought I am deeply indebted.

5. Luke Timothy Johnson, "The Humanity of Jesus," in *The Jesus Controversy: Perspectives in Conflict*, ed. John Dominic Crossan, Luke Timothy Johnson, and Werner H. Kelber (Harrisburg, Pa.: Trinity, 1999), 53ff.

6. For a recent critique of Crossan's position, see Shawn Kelley, *Radicalizing Jesus: Race, Ideology, and the Formation of Modern Biblical Scholarship* (London: Routledge, 2002). See also Elisabeth Schüssler Fiorenza, *Jesus and the Politics of Interpretation* (New York: Continuum, 2000).

7. Robert W Funk, *Honest to Jesus: Jesus for a New Millennium* (San Francisco: Harper, 1996).

8. John Dominic Crossan and Richard G. Watts, *Who Is Jesus? Answers to Your Questions about the Historical Jesus* (Louisville, Ky.: Westminster John Knox, 1999).

9. Cf. Norman Perrin, *Rediscovering the Teaching of Jesus* (London: SCM Press, 1967), and John P. Meier, *A Marginal Jew: Rethinking the Historical Jesus* (New York: Doubleday, 2001).

10. Gal. 3:28; Rom. 10:12.

11. 2 Cor. 5:16.

12. Rom. 9:4–5.

13. See Susannah Heschel, *Abraham Geiger and the Jewish Jesus* (Chicago: University of Chicago Press, 1998).

14. Robert Wilson, *Prophecy and Society in Ancient Israel* (Philadelphia: Fortress, 1980).

15. Isa. 14:12–20; Dan. 7–8.

16. Odil Hannes Steck, *Israel und das gewaltsame Geschick der Propheten: Untersuchungen zur Überlieferung des deuteronomistischen Geschichtsbildes im Alten Testament, Späjudentum und Urchristentum* (Neukirchen-Vluyn: Neukirchener Verlag, 1967).

17. Amos 9:11–15; Isa. 2:2–4; 9:1–6; 11:1–9; Jer. 33:14–16; Ezek. 34:17–22; Dan. 7:13–14.

18. The Synoptic parallels are Matt. 26:26–29 and Luke 22:14–20.

19. The parallel account in the *Didache* is similarly imbued with Jewish Scripture and tradition.

20. Cf. Helmut Koester, "The Memory of Jesus' Death and the Worship of the Risen Lord," *Harvard Theological Review* 91, no. 4 (1998): 335–50. Koester concludes, "In the earliest understanding of the continuity with the historical Jesus, neither the report of Jesus' miracles nor the transmission of his sayings were constitutive. Rather, the new understanding of the significance of Jesus' celebration of common meals in anticipation of the 'messianic banquet' and the story of his suffering and death provided the constitutive elements for the self-definition of the community as a new nation and its claims to eschatological fulfillment of the hopes of all people."

21. Johnson, "Humanity," 67, includes in his criticism of Borg and Crossan, "Their reduction of religious sensibility to the level of political position, which represents an impoverished view of reality, not to mention traditional Christianity, which has based itself on the conviction that Jesus was less about the rearrangement of the structures of society than the transformation of the very structures of existence." Another fine contribution to the historical Jesus debate, both in terms of critique and substantive argument, is Ben F. Meyer's *The Aims of Jesus* (Eugene, Ore.: Pickwick, 2002).

22. I am patterning my test case on charges of cannibalism that actually were brought against early Christians.

23. Rom. 8:22–23.

24. In the course of writing this essay, I have benefited enormously from the suggestions and insights of professors Laura Nasrallah, Daniel Harrington, SJ, and Paul Gavrillyuk.

14

Personhood and Bodily Resurrection

CHRISTOPH SCHWÖBEL

"It is true: the Lord has risen; he has appeared to Simon" (Luke 24:34). The message with which, according to Luke's account, the disciples returning from Emmaus are welcomed by the eleven who had remained in Jerusalem expresses in a condensed form the core of the Christian message through the centuries. The resurrection of Jesus and his appearance to his followers is the central truth claim on which the Christian understanding of reality rests. It vindicates Jesus' message of the present coming of the kingdom of God in which God's history with Israel culminates and that opens the saving relationship of the God of Israel to believers of all nations. Belief in the resurrection of Jesus validates their trust in the faithfulness of God the Creator to his creation, by proclaiming the faithfulness of God to Jesus who lived his life in utmost trust in the God he calls Father, even though his obedience to God the Father leads him to the death on the cross. From the perspective of the resurrection of Jesus, the scandalous injustice of the cross is disclosed as the victory of God's justice over every form of injustice. On the basis of the Easter revelation, Christians, from the group that Luke describes as welcoming their friends on their return from Emmaus with the gospel of the resurrection until today, have believed that the victory of God's justice also includes God's victory over death and gives a firm foundation to their hope of being raised from the dead. The statement that Jesus was raised from the dead on the third day and belief in the resurrection of the flesh have therefore been an integral part of Christian creeds from their earliest formulation, inextricably connected to the Christian church's proclamation of the gospel, its practice of baptism, and its celebration of the Lord's Supper.

Even before Luke's account of the sharing of the Easter message among the disciples in Jerusalem, the connection between believing in the resurrection of Jesus and believing in our own resurrection has been boldly, and with inescapable logic, pinpointed by Paul in his discussion of those who seemed to deny the resurrection of the dead in Corinth:

> Now if this is what we proclaim, that Christ was raised from the dead, how can some of you say there is no resurrection of the dead? If there is no resurrection, then Christ was not raised; and if Christ was not raised, then our gospel is null and void, and so too is our faith; and we turn out to have given false evidence about God, because we bore witness he raised Christ to life, whereas, if the dead are not raised, he did not raise him. (1 Cor. 15:12–15, author's trans.)

The logic is, indeed, impeccable: "For if the dead are not raised, it follows that Christ was not raised" (v. 16). The force of this conclusion affects the whole scheme of Christian faith: "your faith has nothing to it and you are still in the old state of sin" (v. 17). In Paul's argument, nothing remains of Christian faith once the crucial connection between the resurrection of the dead and the resurrection of Christ proves to be invalid. Therefore, everything depends on whether Christians, then in Corinth and today, can share Paul's bold statement, "But the truth is, Christ was raised to life—the firstfruits of the harvest to come." (v. 20).

Throughout the history of Christian life and thought, Christians have attempted to grapple with the problems posed by the connection that Paul, asserting the ultimate significance of the Easter revelation, makes central to their faith. Since Christian faith is—as we have been reminded time and again— "faith seeking understanding," the problem is not settled once and for all. Every generation of believers, every believer, has to make a new attempt at understanding what he or she believes and so work again through the problems that have exercised both the most brilliant minds in the history of Christian thought and every ordinary believer in the church.[1] One of the central problems that occurs in the Christian doctrine of God, in Christology as well as in the Christian understanding of what it means to be human, is the connection between the understanding of personhood and bodily resurrection. Because the question of how this connection should be understood from the perspective of Christian faith comprises dimensions of the central connected doctrines of God and Christ and of the understanding of the human, it concerns the intelligibility of the whole Christian vision of reality.

The following sketch is intended to point out some of the dimensions that are significant in understanding the problems that are involved in this connection and to explore possibilities of their resolution. We can offer not much more than a provisional sketch of the questions and a preliminary outline of how they could be answered. However, this only confirms that the attempt at understanding, even if one finds orientation for one's faith in Scripture and in the creeds of the church, has to start again in every individual life and in every generation, although it will remain open-ended and incomplete, awaiting the full disclosure of truth in the kingdom of God.

THE RESURRECTION DILEMMA

Even at the most peremptory glance it becomes clear that the understanding of persons is in many ways crucial to the understanding of the resurrection and vice versa. Many aspects are focused on the question of identity and the continuity of persons in death and resurrection. In order to show that the question of the relationship between personhood and resurrection does not seem meaningful on some accounts of personhood and in some versions of resurrection, it suffices to pick out two opposing views of continuity and discontinuity.

If persons possess a substantial immaterial and immortal core identity that is only contingently related to the possession of a body, this implies a kind of personal continuity through death and resurrection that makes the resurrection immaterial for the question of personal identity. The message "the Lord is risen" would not carry much significance since the personal identity of the crucified Lord would not have been threatened by death in any case, and the acquisition of a new body could hardly count as having a primary soteriological significance. It would in any case not concern the question of personal identity if the possession of a body is only contingently related to personal identity. On such a view, the proclamation of the resurrection of Christ could hardly be gospel.

Conversely, if the resurrection is understood as a totally new creation, including no continuity with my personal identity *ante mortem*, it would also be quite unclear why this should be good news to me now. Too much discontinuity destroys the gospel of the resurrection just as much as too much continuity. One can call this the resurrection dilemma. If the one who is raised is not me but another person (total discontinuity), there would not be much to hope for for me. If the one who is raised is simply the old me again, or at least my core identity, as I am now or as I will be at the moment of my death (total continuity), there would not be much to hope for either. The extravagant claim that the early Christians made on the basis of the resurrection of Jesus as the foundation of their hope for their own resurrection could have been based neither on a view of total continuity (as the prolongation of an immaterial and immortal core identity through death) nor on a view of total discontinuity (as the new creation of another identity after death). What is needed is a view of personhood in which continuity and discontinuity are somehow mediated in such a way that there is enough continuity to give me something to hope and enough discontinuity to give me something to hope for, to expect with the certainty of faith a new life that is discontinuous with all that is now frustrating the fulfillment of my personal destiny that is still my personal life. The metaphorical use of the language of rising—and the effort Paul undertakes to explain the relationship between a "physical body" and a "spiritual body" in 1 Corinthians 15 by the use of various more or less fitting analogies for something that by definition must display greater dissimilarity than similarity—points to such a mediation between continuity and discontinuity with regard to the relationship of person and body.

In this essay we look at the question from two different angles: We shall, first of all, sketch a number of ways in which personhood has been understood, contrasting approaches that take their starting point from the understanding of finite persons with a theological approach that starts from the understanding of the divine persons in the doctrine of the Trinity. Second, we shall briefly explore the theological meaning of matter and its significance for embodied personhood. Third, we shall see how the two lines of approach intersect in the understanding of bodily resurrection and try to relate them to ways in which the embodiment of persons can be understood in order to prepare the way for a sketch for the basic outlines of an understanding of bodily resurrection. The concluding section merely hints at the significance that this understanding of bodily resurrection has for the understanding of the church and its life in the celebration of sacraments and the proclamation of the gospel. This essay is therefore nothing more than a thumbnail sketch indicating avenues of further conversations and argument.

PERSONS

The history of the concept of person is complex and shows that the concept combines already in antiquity influences from a variety of contexts: the theater (dramatis personae), the law, the status of human beings in social relationships (from the family to the state), and grammar (first person, second person, etc., in the conjugation of a verb). The theological and philosophical use of the concept in Christianity shows from early on a variety of adaptations of these diverse contextual uses to God and humans in their relationship and to humans in their various relationships. The common use of the term "person" in everyday language in the context of a variety of situations of communication and interaction retains the multidimensional richness of person-language.

We speak of persons in order to distinguish somebody from something and combine a variety of dimensions in one concept. The concept of person in this way invokes:

- The question of personal identity
- The question of personal continuity through time and at different places

- The question of personal dignity: person is a *nomen dignitatis*
- The question of personal responsibility in interpersonal relationships
- The question of personal accountability for our actions before others
- The question of personal rights and duties

In all these different dimensions the concept of person is never used as a purely descriptive concept but always as a concept that combines descriptive, ascriptive, and prescriptive functions. To describe somebody as a person implies ascribing a status to him or her which, in turn, prescribes certain forms of interaction and forbids others. The ontology of the person is therefore one in which questions of fact and value are inextricably connected. This does not only concern the ones who are referred to and related to as persons but also those who relate to them. Any definition of what it means to be a person must in some sense do justice to the multidimensional character of the understanding of a person.

In the history of Western thought, the concept of the person has been discussed predominantly in three major paradigms.

1. The first is the definition of "person" in the paradigm of substance metaphysics that has its locus classicus in Boethius's definition of the person as the individual substance of reasonable nature ("naturae rationabilis individua substantia").[2] This definition which Boethius intended to apply to the Trinitarian personhood of God and to the person of Christ as well as to created persons, focuses on two significant emphases. In order to be a person, one must have such a degree of specific, relative independence that one can be a term in a relationship as a specific individual which can be identified, distinguished, and related to by others. "Substance" indicates here that in relating to this person we relate to an element of reality that cannot be substituted or replaced, which is not a place holder for something or somebody else. Ontologically, we have touched rock bottom, although the substance of personhood is a class that has numerous elements. Particular personhood is a combination of substantial attributes shared by many others. "Of a rational nature" can be interpreted in such a sense that this individual substance is capable of relationships with other entities who also possess a nature capable of rationality. The way a person relates to other reality and, perhaps more importantly, is related to, is determined by the reasonable nature to which it belongs. It was not Boethius's aim to distinguish degrees of rationality and only count those beings as persons who achieve a certain degree of rationality. Rather, he wanted to specify the particular ontological stratum to which persons belong and which make them capable of reciprocal relations with other persons, be they created or uncreated persons.

The great achievement of the understanding of person in the paradigm of substance metaphysics is to understand persons as individual entities who have a specific, unique identity and to interpret this identity substantially so that it is irreplaceable by other entities. One obvious implication is that this understanding of personhood clearly intended to exclude the understanding of persons as "masks," social roles or functions, that can be filled by many individuals. Much of the medieval discussion is devoted to improving this particular definition in close interaction between Trinitarian, christological, and anthropological reflections. However, the way in which this understanding of persons is to be related to belief in the bodily resurrection, Christ's and ours, is not immediately clear. If the individual substance of a reasonable nature is, also in the case of created persons, understood as an immaterial and immortal substance, our embodied existence neither seems to contribute to personal identity, since mortal bodies can only be contingently related to such an immaterial substantial core. What does this make of faith in the bodily resurrection?

2. The second major paradigm is the understanding of the person in the context of a metaphysics of consciousness. John Locke's definition of the person can serve as an exemplary case of defining "person" in this paradigm. He defined a person as "a thinking intelligent Being, that has reason and reflection, and can consider it self as it self, the same thinking thing in different times and places; which it does only by that consciousness, which is in separable from thinking, and as it seems to me essential to it: It being impossible for any one to perceive, without perceiving, that he does perceive."[3] In this definition the Boethian understanding of "rationabilis natura" is significantly expanded. Boethius's understanding "of a reasonable nature" in the framework of substance metaphysics merely indicated membership of a specific class of beings and thereby specified the kind of relationships that can be maintained by the beings of that class. Locke, however, first of all adds reflection to reason and explains it as the conscious self-relation of persons since they can consider themselves as themselves. Second, Locke connects "reflection" with continuity in different times and places. Descartes's *res cogitans*, the "thinking thing," thus acquires continuity only in conscious self-relation. Personal continuity thus means being conscious of oneself in different times and places. The identical continuum in all spatial and temporal changes is thus the conscious self-relation of the person. It is only logical that Locke draws the conclusion, "*Personal Identity* consists not in the Identity of Substance, but in . . . the Identity of *consciousness*."[4] However, self-consciousness is bound to time. In order to guarantee the continuity of consciousness we must identify at a later point of time with those actions that we performed at an earlier point of time. In this way the identification with one's deeds enables continuity of consciousness and thus responsibility.

However, Locke is aware that self-interest and the care for happiness to avoid misery may distort this continuity because they may lead us to identify with different aspects of the past. Here, for Locke a theological element becomes inevitable. If the unity of consciousness is constituted through self-identification from the future, it must have a fixed reference point in order to avoid the dissolution of identity in disconnected moments of consciousness. The ground of unity is therefore the last judgment that decides over eternal torment or bliss and therefore provides an absolute reference point for our temporal self-identification in consciousness. "And therefore conformable to this, the Apostle tells us, that at the Great Day, when every one shall *receive according to his doings, the secrets of all Hearts shall be laid open* [2 Cor. 5:10 and 1 Cor. 14:25]. The Sentence shall be justified by the consciousness all Persons shall have, that they *themselves* in what Bodies soever they appear, or what Substances soever that consciousness adheres to, are the *same*, that committed those Actions, and deserve Punishment for them."[5] The replacement of a substantial identity antecedent to the moral or religious qualification of human persons by the subjective process of self-identification in consciousness seems complete: "For whatever Substance there is, however framed, without consciousness there is no Person."[6]

The achievement of understanding personal identity as the identity of consciousness is to focus on the fact that all our relations to what is different from us are accompanied by reflection so that the conscious self-relation becomes the place where all our other relationships are reflected. Our relationships thereby acquire a reflective transparency and consciousness becomes the seat of responsibility. However, the question with which much later philosophy after the age of Locke and Kant grappled was whether this reflexivity is constituted by our active conscious life or whether it is constituted for us. A personal identity that is constituted by us remains vulnerable—as the critique of Hume directed against Locke's position aptly demonstrated.[7] With regard to the question of identity and bodily resurrection we may merely note that it becomes difficult to maintain the significance of a material body before or after the resurrection for the question of identity, since consciousness alone defines a person. As Locke himself noted, it does not matter at all for people in the Last Judgment "in soever Bodies they appear."

3. The third major paradigm for understanding persons is the paradigm of social relationships. Over against the paradigm of substance metaphysics and the paradigm of subjective consciousness, theories in this paradigm neither presuppose substantial identity nor the continuity of consciousness but understand personal identity as being constituted in personal relationships. The many variations in which this view is expounded all have the advantage of showing how personal identity is formed in social interaction or through interpersonal communication, both in informal relationships and in institutional forms of interaction. For all its descriptive strength in being able to show in which ways persons relate to one another passively and actively, in reciprocity and spontaneity, these theories have one major flaw. If our personal identity is constructed in acts of social interaction and by modes of communicative acknowledgment, it can also be deconstructed in this way. An identity that is only socially affirmed can also be socially denied. The heaven of dialogical personalists is Sartre's hell: *L'enfer c'est les autres.* For all its advantages for analyzing concretely the shaping of personal identity through time in social relationships and their patterns of reciprocity in symmetry and asymmetry, once this process is understood as the constitution of personal identity it poses the most serious threat to personal identity, because there is no antecedent substantial identity that may be understood as the seat of human dignity and no continuity of consciousness that could provide a secure fortress against the destructiveness of social relationships once they no longer affirm but deny personal identity. The attractiveness of this third paradigm and

its descriptive strengths can help very little to alleviate its fundamental flaw. With regard to the personal identity of the risen Christ, the ascription of reality to the resurrection appearances relying on this view of the constitution of personal identity alone could quickly turn fact into fiction, and vice versa.

In recent years a number of attempts have been made to develop an understanding of what it means to be a person in the context of Trinitarian theology. In a way, reflection on the ontological status of personhood returns to its origins in the understanding of the tripersonal God. The direction in which reflection proceeds is thus reversed. Instead of starting by human personality and proceeding to divine personality in the time-honored manner of R. J. Illingworth, these new attempts start again from divine personhood and proceed to define human persons in relation with divine persons.[8]

The most consistent attempt to define personhood along the lines of Trinitarian thought has been made by John Zizioulas, who draws on a particular interpretation of the ontology of the person in the Cappadocian Fathers.[9] Zizioulas sharply distinguishes between the "what" question and the "who" question. The "what" question always defines persons in terms of the general characteristics belonging to a common nature or substance. The "who" question points to the ultimacy of personal particularity. "Personhood is not about qualities or capacities of any kind: biological, social or moral. Personhood is about hypostasis, i.e. the claim to *uniqueness* in the absolute sense of the term, and this cannot be guaranteed by reference to sex or function or role, or even cultivated consciousness of the 'self' and its psychological experience, since all of these can be *classified*, thus representing qualities shared by more than one being."[10] This, however, is possible only with regard to the persons of the divine Trinity since their personhood is not dependent on an underlying nature, but on their relationship with one another. "In God it is possible for the particular to be ontologically ultimate because *relationship is permanent and unbreakable.* Because the Father, the Son and the Spirit are always together, the particular beings are bearers of the totality of nature and thus no contradiction between the 'one' and the 'many' can arise."[11] As persons in communion, the Father, the Son, and the Spirit are persons in an ultimate sense, not depending on qualities of an underlying nature, but solely on their relationship to one another.

This, however, only applies to the persons of the Trinity in the strict sense. Created persons always depend on an underlying nature. Their claim to uniqueness can only be fulfilled in their relationship to the triune God. This, Zizioulas points out, can only be mediated christologically, since the person of Christ does not depend on the natures, neither the divine nor the human. The doctrine of the hypostatic union states the opposite: "In Christ the general exists only in and through the particular; the particular is thus raised to ontological primacy. The 'Who' of Christ is the Son. In Him the two natures give their qualities to the identity without making the identity depend in the primary ontological sense, on these qualities."[12] The personal identity of created persons depend on their participation—by grace and not by nature—in the communion of the triune God which is grounded in the person of Christ and mediated in baptism: "This 'new birth,' which is the essence of Baptism, is nothing but the acquisition of an identity not dependent on the qualities of nature but freely raising nature to a hypostatic existence identical with that which emerges from the Father-Son relationship."[13] However, even this personal identity which a created person receives in baptism will not be realized fully until the eschaton: "When death ceases to be 'natural,' humanity will experience the true ontology of the person."[14]

This approach to define personhood on the basis of the Trinitarian persons and establish human personhood mediated in the person of Christ through sacramental participation in the Trinitarian life of God is not confined to an ontology based on the Cappadocian ontology of being as communion. A similar approach can be developed from the depiction of the Trinity as relationship of love in Richard of St. Victor,[15] the doctrine of the Trinity of Duns Scotus,[16] or even from Luther's Trinitarian theology. Three elements are characteristic for this Trinitarian understanding of "persons":

- The persons of Father, Son, and Spirit are to be understood as hypostatic identities constituted by their reciprocal real and internal relations so that personhood is seen as ontologically and logically primitive. Although the divine persons are constituted in communicative relations, this constitution nevertheless leads to an incommunicable existence of divine nature (*divinae naturae incommunicabilis existentia*). It follows: *Persona non est relatio.*
- The unity of Father, Son, and Spirit is to be understood as relational unity in which the unity of the divine *ousia* is actualized.
- Created personhood is freely granted by relationship to the Trinitarian persons. The advantage of such a Trinitarian view of personal being is that it can account for the absolute uniqueness of persons which Boethius tried to establish, but without making persons dependent on a "nature," which both Boethius's notion of "substance" and of "nature" implies. It can express the unbreakable, eternal continuity of personhood that the Lockean conception was at pains to establish, and it can understand relationality in such a way that it constitutes personal particularity without threatening it with destruction.

Created personal identity can be understood as unique in virtue of its relationship to the divine persons in communion. In this way, personal identity as the irreplaceable and nontransferable existence in relation to others can be understood as being continually granted and upheld by the Trinitarian God—and not by the underlying human nature or the continuity of self-consciousness. The relationship of personal identity to the transcendent Trinitarian God constitutes personal dignity.

This Trinitarian view of being a person can either be developed in weak version, exploring the conceptual possibilities provided by Trinitarian theology (concepts such as hypostasis, *koinonia* as relational unity, and perichoresis) in order to illuminate human personal being, or it can be developed in strong version, which defends the thesis: our personal being is rooted in the relationship of the tripersonal God to us.

The strong version, however, needs to be spelled out in the relationship of the triune God to created persons in the divine economy. Such an account would have to comprise a number of related points in outlining the formation of human persons:

- As *imago Dei* human beings are called to be persons in communion, imaging the Trinitarian persons in communion. The personal identity of created persons is rooted in their relationship to the triune God and destined to find its fulfillment in communion with the triune God (creation).

- Human beings are alienated from God as the ground of their being and their personal identity by attempting to find the ground of their personal identity in themselves (sin): self-relation becomes *incurvatio in seipsum*.

- God actualizes the destiny of created persons to find their personal and communal identity in communion with God through his promises to Israel and the covenant with Israel, which is extended to include people from all nations in Christ. In Christ through the Spirit the communion with God the Father is open to all believers in Christ in the power of the Spirit. The re-creation of created personal identity is gained through participation in Christ in whom God has reconciled the world to himself (reconciliation).

- By being reconciled to God in Christ through the Spirit, human persons are brought on the way toward the fulfillment of their destiny to be persons in communion with God and with God's reconciled creation in the kingdom of God: for humans, personal identity in communion is an eschatological concept. The call to *be* persons is realized by *becoming* persons. The actualization of human personal identity involves the judgment over sin as the separation of the person from the effects of attempting to achieve personal identity apart from God (eschatological fulfillment).

The formation of created personhood is in this way framed by the self-actualization of the immanent Trinity in the Trinitarian economy, which actualizes the created destiny of humans to *be* persons by enabling them to *become* persons in communion with the triune God and so with the whole of God's reconciled creation.

EMBODIED PERSONS

We now have to turn to the other track of trying to understand the connection between personal identity and bodily resurrection by reflecting on the theological significance of embodiment. A body can be defined in a variety of ways—for example, by its simple extension in space (Descartes's impoverished concept of everything that is not *res cogitans* as *res extensa*), a biological organism in constant interaction with its physical environment, and as a social entity. Animate bodies are subject to physical, chemical, and biological processes that are governed by regularities connecting the individual body in its individuality to the general structures of the material cosmos. These processes encompass growth and decay; they are never value-neutral since they can result in sickness or health and ultimately lead to death.

For human persons as embodied beings, the body is both their connection to all other forms of life and the medium of their relationships to other persons and to themselves. The body is the medium of personal relationality; it provides the medium for our communicative availability to others. Our bodily being therefore is the basis for our being-there-for-others. This also includes the self-relation, which for created persons always seems to be one of embodied consciousness and experience. The bodily form of our relationships includes both our vulnerability and our lovability. Social forms of personal interaction are attempts to deal with these aspects of our bodily relational existence. Our bodies witness to our history and in the realm of embodied nature they come closest to expressing our personal identity as our identifiability for others in embodied forms of communication. If one follows the view of biblical anthropology, the affective center of the human person, the heart, is the interface between material, mental, and spiritual dimensions of our embodied personal existence and the point where our relations to God, to other people, and to nonpersonal nature intersect within our embodied selves.

Why then does matter matter—theologically? God's history with the world is a history of God's creative, redemptive, and perfecting engagement with matter. We can summarize this again schematically:

- In creation God freely creates a material universe in order to be in communion with a material creation. Nevertheless, from a Christian perspective the matter of creation is not to be interpreted materialistically: its structure and its life are both externally constituted. Its order is ordained by the divine Logos and its life enabled by the divine Spirit, who is also the ground and the medium of creation's capacity to respond to the Creator by the very act of life.
- The history of God's engagement with Israel in the covenant comprises Israel's embodied existence, which, although it is based on Israel's relationship to God, is expressed in the material conditions of historical

life. Therefore, material questions like the promise of the land and the concern for Israel's integrity and corporeal (material, social, and historical) continuity can be of primary theological importance. The relationship with Israel is exercised within the regularities granted by God the Creator to the material creation as a reliable field of action for God's human creatures because its regularities are disclosed in the material world to humans (wisdom). The theological significance of the this-worldly relationship of God with his people in his material creation contrasts Israel's faith sharply with the otherworldly preoccupation of, for instance, the Egyptian religion with the realm of the dead as the place where justice and salvation can only be fully experienced.

- In the incarnation, which builds upon the material and historical significance of God's relationship to Israel, matter is sanctified by the assumption of a material human nature by God the Son in the hypostatic union. In Christ, human nature is, in union with the divine nature, enhypostatized in the person of the Son. The embodied forms of interaction in a material world become the means for the communication of God's salvation: in embodied forms of communication, in healing and the sharing of meals. In Christ—that is the pervasive emphasis of the New Testament and the point of convergence of its diverse traditions—the eschatological destiny of the world is fulfilled. The embodied forms of communication, the sharing of meals, and the healing ministry of Jesus thereby become pointers to the inclusion of material reality in the eschatological perfection of the community of the creator with his creation. The ontological point of the miracles is to emphasize that Christ as the incarnate Lord participates in the Lordship of the Creator over his creation.

- The resurrection is understood as an event in the material world, and its significance is disclosed in the material world. The ascension depicts the incorporation of the risen and transformed body of Christ into the eternal life of God.

- In the bodily preaching of the word and by the sacraments of baptism and the Lord's Supper, each including matter as a means of communion and communication, as instruments of the self-giving presence of the risen Lord, the ongoing relationship of believers with the risen Lord is proclaimed and celebrated and the goal of all creation to be in communion with God is witnessed.

- Believers participate in Christ's death and resurrection, which begins already here in their material existence: "if the Spirit of him who raised Jesus from the dead dwells within you, the God who raised Jesus from the dead will also give new life to your material bodies through his indwelling Spirit" (Rom. 8:11). God's Spirit, which is the presence of the transforming power of Christ's resurrection, counteracts the tendency of the body to find its orientation in the "flesh" in the self-referential fulfillment of matter apart from the Spirit which brings certain death.

- The whole material creation—the hope for creation grounded in the resurrection of Christ—will be brought from a state of frustration under the shackles of mortality to a state of fulfillment characterized by freedom "so that the creation itself will be liberated from its bondage to decay and brought into the glorious freedom of the children of God" (Rom. 8:21).

Matter matters theologically because, as Luther says of us, God's material creatures: "For He created us in order so that He might redeem and sanctify us."[17] The point is that the actualization of the will of the Trinitarian God to be in communion with his creation in the divine economy becomes part of God's identity so that God is not who God is unless he is the one "who brought you out of Egypt, out of the land of slavery" (Exod. 20:1) or the one "who raised Jesus our Lord from the dead" (Rom. 4:24). God's engagement with matter is part of his eternal self-determination so that his faithfulness to his material creation is his faithfulness to his own self-determination, which includes being determined by his creation. Matter matters theologically because without matter there would be no theology of *this* God who lets his identity be defined by his engagement with the stuff of creation. This, however, has important implications for our understanding of matter. On this understanding of God, matter is not self-subsistent. It has its subsistence in the will of God its creator. Because of that, matter is exposed to the powers of death and decay once it denies its dependence on God's will. If matter has no subsistence of its own, it is ontologically intrinsically discontinuous so that its continuity is granted through God's creative, preserving, and perfecting relationship to matter. This is why theology matters to matter in the most literal sense.

BODILY RESURRECTION

The background of the understanding of the reality of the resurrection in the New Testament is the reality of the death of Jesus on the cross. The reality of Jesus' real death has been maintained in Christianity throughout its history in the face of all temptations to treat Jesus' death only as an apparent death, that he somehow survived his own death. No, the witnesses insist, Jesus really died, he experienced the fate of material creation when it is cut off from its source of life in God. The reality of Jesus' death had been experienced by Jesus' disciples as the ultimate falsification of Jesus' message of the coming of God's reign in his person and so as the failure of their own investment in the truth of that message so that they flew from the place where the catastrophe occurred (Mark 14:50). Against this background, the message with which the eleven who had remained in Jerusalem welcomed the disciples returning from Emmaus and their encounter with the one they had recognized as their Lord could not be more astonishing: "It is true: the Lord has risen; he has appeared to Simon" (Luke 24:34). Much of the discussion of the earliest witness to the resurrection has centered on the alternative of understanding it either as an event that has objectivity apart from the way it is received or as the beginning of faith, which sees the subjective transforming experience of the message of the resurrection as its crucial point. The first view stresses the importance of the bodily resurrection, the other focuses on the transforming new insight that the disciples gained and which transformed their lives from the experience of failure to the joy of proclaiming the gospel. The first view loses its point, if the resurrection of Jesus is simply the return of a dead man, even if that could be substantiated by historical proofs. Bodily resurrection into the old order of things that leaves the question of the reality of salvation still open could not have become the cornerstone of the rapidly developing Christian belief. Similarly, the creation of faith can only have a transforming power if it does not only offer a new interpretation of reality but can be connected to experience in such a way that the new outlook on reality can already be experienced as real. Just providing a better interpretation of the fact that all mortals have to die could not be experienced as a liberation for those "who all their lives were held in slavery by their fear of death" (Heb. 2:15).

The understanding of the resurrection of Christ must therefore combine the emphasis on Jesus being really raised from the dead with the experience that the new order of reality has been inaugurated amid the old. If one looks a little more closely at the early Christian testimonies to the resurrection, one can see that the resurrection of Christ is seen as an eschatological disclosure event. It is not simply an event in the historical sequence of the old order of the world but the turning point from the old to the new eon. Therefore, the resurrection must be seen against the background of apocalyptic beliefs that the resurrection is the ultimate breakthrough of God's righteousness which grants eternal life. If the resurrection that was hoped for as the ultimate establishment of God's righteousness that cannot be canceled by death has occurred, as it is revealed by God in the disclosure experience of the crucified Jesus as the risen Christ, then the discontinuity of the mortality of created life is taken up into the continuity of God's created life and appears in the light of the glory of God. The continuity of God's creative life takes up the discontinuity of created life that has no self-subsistent continuity, and this is made certain in the fact that the risen Christ bears the scars of the dead Jesus and the light of the knowledge of God appears in the face of Christ (2 Cor. 4:6). The statements about Jesus' resurrection are therefore, first of all, theological statements about the eschatological actualization of God's creative will to establish communion with his creation by taking it up into his glory and so transforming its mortality by participation in God's eternal life. On the basis of the disclosure experience of the resurrection, these theological statements provide, second, the basis for the christological statements that the personal identity of Jesus is his relationship to God the Father in the Spirit so that in the unity of this personal, hypostatic identity his humanity, crucified and risen, participates in the eternal life of God. These christological statements provide, third, the basis for anthropological statements concerning our participation in the eternal life of God by participating by faith in the power of the Spirit as God's sons and daughters in the relationship of Jesus as the Son to God the Father. God's eschatological action in the resurrection of Jesus as God's own vindication of his faithfulness to his creation therefore provides the pattern for the relationship of continuity and discontinuity of personal identity in including the discontinuity of death into the continuity of God's eternal life.

The point of the disclosure experience of Jesus' resurrection is that the continuity of his personal identity which transcends the discontinuity of death and which is rooted, as later dogma specifies, in his relationship to God the Father in the Spirit, is disclosed in the material order of creation. The disclosure experience of the risen Christ therefore includes his bodily identifiability for his disciples as being included in his participation in the glory of God. The personal identity of Christ is revealed in the material identifiability of his body. Faith in the risen Christ is therefore epistemologically knowledge by acquaintance, and this provides the basis for all knowledge by description. The disclosure experience reveals Christ in his spiritual body, which is the transformation of his natural body in the communion of God's eternal life to those whose experience is still bound to the capacities of their natural bodies. The body of the risen Christ is therefore the exemplification of the resurrection body Paul is at pains to describe in the dialectics of continuity and discontinuity: "The body that is sown is perishable, it is raised imperishable; it is sown in dishonor, it is raised in glory; it is sown in weakness, it is raised in power; it is sown a natural body, it is raised a spiritual body" (1 Cor. 15:42–44).

The resurrection dilemma with which we started finds its resolution in the way the continuity of God's creative action envelops the discontinuity of death. Death can be understood as the end of all our active relationships, including our relation to ourselves, to others, and to God. In this way death is the total surrender of relational being into the hands of the Creator from whom we have received it in the first place. Death is the moment of total discontinuity of all active relationships of our embodied life and so discloses the absolute dependence on God maintaining his active, life-giving relationship to us, in this way preserving our identity. Continuity lies only in the faithfulness of the Creator upholding his relationship to us. The only continuity we can hope for is neither substantial continuity nor the continuity of consciousness, but only the relational continuity of our absolute dependence on God the Creator.

In the resurrection—that is, the hope of our resurrection based on faith in the resurrection of Christ—continuity is not established along a linear trajectory from the past through the present into the future. It is established from the eschaton to incorporate the past, including the material relationality of our bodily existence, in a transformed, spiritual way and so grants us a specious present in which our material existence is no longer defined by the shackles of mortality but by the overcoming of death in Christ in which we participate bodily in the Spirit.

THE ECCLESIAL CONTEXT OF BEING A PERSON

The bodily resurrection of Jesus which is experienced in the eschatological disclosure event of his resurrection as the foundation of the Easter faith of the Christian church implies that Christ is alive and remains bodily available to us in the body of Christ, the church. The bodily resurrection of Christ is thus the foundation of the real presence of the risen Lord in the word of the gospel and in the celebration of the sacraments. Word and sacraments are the instruments of Christ's bodily availability to those who believe in his resurrection as the ultimate promise of God the Creator to his material creation—*ubi et quando visum est Deo*. From the perspective of Christian faith, participation in the body of Christ through the bodily word of the gospel and the visible words of the sacraments is therefore the foundation of our personal identity. In baptism we participate in the death of Christ and thus participate in his resurrection (Rom. 6:3–14). Our personal identity is therefore no longer defined by its relationships to ourselves or to the material world but by the relationship to the triune God which gives a new pattern to our relationship to ourselves and to the material world, since both are no longer the ground for our identity-definition. In the Lord's Supper we participate in the ongoing communion with the risen Lord, who makes his presence bodily available to us in the bread and the cup and thus continues his table fellowship with sinners so that they receive the promise of eternal life. This testifies to God's faithfulness to his material creation by sanctifying it as the material instrument of communicating his grace. Through the encounter with the word of the gospel as the word of the living God and in celebrating the sacraments as the bodily availability of Christ in the communion of his body, knowledge of Christ is now, as it was for the first witnesses of the resurrection, knowledge by acquaintance as the basis for all dogmatic knowledge by description.

NOTES

1. Michael Welker, to whom these reflections are offered as birthday greetings, has devoted much of his considerable energy to organizing theological conversations on the resurrection across the boundaries of the disciplines, both in the United States and in Europe. See (among numerous other publications) Hans-Joachim Eckstein and Michael Welker, eds., *Die Wirklichkeit der Auferstehung* (Neukirchener: Neukirchen-Verlag, 2002); Ted Peters, Robert Russell, and Michael Welker, eds., *Resurrection: Theological and Scientific Assessments* (Grand Rapids: Eerdmans, 2002). The considerations in this brief essay continue conversations on numerous occasions on this topic while we were colleagues together at Heidelberg.
2. Boethius provides this definition in the beginning of *Contra Eutychen* III. The full quotation reads: "Quocirca si persona in solis substantiis est atque in his rationabilibus substantiaque omnis natura est nec in universalibus sed in individuis constat, reperta personae est definitio," from *The Theological Tractates*, ed. H. F. Stewart and E. K. Rand (Cambridge, Mass.: Harvard University

Press, 1962), 84. Roughly this can be translated as follows: "Hence, if person is only in substances and only in reasonable ones and if every substance is a nature and consists not in universals but in individuals, the definition of person has been found: 'the individual substance of a reasonable nature.'" For a detailed analysis of Boethius's concept of the person see Corinna Schlapkohl, *Persona est naturae rationabilis substantia. Boethius und die Debatte über den Personbegriff* (Marburg: Elwert, 1999).

3. John Locke, *An Essay Concerning Human Understanding*, edited with a foreword by Peter H. Nidditch (Oxford: Oxford University Press, 1975), book 2, chap. 27, §9, 335.
4. Ibid.
5. Ibid., §26, 347.
6. Ibid., §23, 344.
7. Hume abolishes the concept of substance by interpreting substances as conventional associations of ideas so that "what we call a mind, is nothing but a heap or collection of different perceptions, united together by certain relations, and suppos'd, tho' falsely, to be endow'd with a perfect simplicity and identity," from David Hume, *A Treatise of Human Nature*, ed. L. A. Selby-Bigge (Oxford: Oxford University Press, 1973 [1888]), book 1, part 4, sect. 2, 207.
8. The title of the book Colin Gunton and I edited some years ago therefore alluded to R. J. Illingworth's *Personality—Human and Divine* (London: Macmillan, 1894), while changing the sequence of the Divine and the human. See Christoph Schwöbel and Colin E. Gunton, eds., *Persons, Divine and Human* (Edinburgh: T&T Clark, 1991).
9. On his interpretation of the Cappadocian doctrine of the Trinity, see this brief account: "The Doctrine of the Trinity: The Significance of the Cappadocian Contribution," in *Trinitarian Theology Today: Essay on Divine Being and Act*, ed. Christoph Schwöbel (Edinburgh: T&T Clark, 1995), 44–60.
10. J. D. Zizioulas, "On Being a Person. Towards an Ontology of Personhood," in *Persons, Divine and Human*, ed. Christoph Schwöbel and Colin E. Gunton (Edinburgh: T&T Clark, 1991), 33–46.
11. Ibid., 41.
12. Ibid., 43.
13. Ibid.
14. Ibid., 44.
15. Cf. Markus Mühling, *Gott ist Liebe. Studien zum Verständnis der Liebe als Modell des trinitarischen Redens von Gott*, 2nd ed. (Marburg: Elwert, 2005), 144–80.
16. Eilert Herms has shown in his comprehensive article, "Person IV. Dogmatisch," in *Religion in Geschichte und Gegenwart*, ed. K. Galling, vol. 6 (Tübingen: Mohr Siebeck, 2007), 1123–26, that Duns Scotus found a way of asserting both singularity and relatedness in the person and comes to the conclusion: "nulla erit perfecta persona nisi divina" (3 Sent. 1.1.3 Nr. 10; cf. 1125).
17. Martin Luther, "Large Catechism," in *Luther's Primary Works Together with His Shorter and Larger Catechisms* (London: Hodder and Stoughton, 1896), 107.

15

From Easter to Parousia

TED PETERS

We Christians today live between the times, *zwischen den Zeiten*, as the early-twentieth-century neo-orthodox theologians said frequently. We live between the Easter resurrection of yesterday and the advent of the new creation tomorrow. What we want to say christologically about the historical Jesus finds itself inextricably linked to what we want to say eschatologically about God's promise for our future. The significance of what happened to Jesus cannot be decided until the future to which he is inextricably connected comes to pass.

Both continuity and discontinuity imbue our thoughts about the divinely promised future. On the one hand, God promises fulfillment, and fulfillment implies continuity with our past and present yearnings. On the other hand, God promises something new, a transformation (Isa. 43:19: "I am about to do a new thing").

Michael Welker incorporates this double future into his concept of eschatological complementarity. "On the one hand, the reign of God is pictured as an emergent reality in which—in multifarious experiences and acts of love, care, and forgiveness—a new reality latently breaks through, endangered and clouded from all sides, visible only to eyes of faith. On the other hand, the reign of God comes fully only at the complete theophany at the end of time."[1] The Easter resurrection of Jesus anticipates proleptically the coming reign of God in the new creation. Between the times, when we Christians engage in love, care, and forgiveness, then that future arrives ahead of time. It becomes present in our own time.

In what follows I plan to depict this double future as an interconnectedness between Easter and the Parousia. With the term "Easter,"[2] I refer to the event of Jesus' resurrection from the tomb. This is a historical event in two senses. First, Jesus' resurrection took place in our past, our history. Second, this event is subject to historical investigation. What distinguishes the Easter event theologically is its inextricable tie to what is coming in the future, namely, the eschatological new creation to be ushered in by the Parousia.

The word "parousia" (παρουσία) in the New Testament means something like "arrival." In common Christian parlance this idea has come to be called Christ's second coming. Regarding the Pauline use of the term, N. T. Wright remarks, "The word *parousia* itself is not an Old Testament word, but seems to be borrowed from the language of the court, of princes and emperors. It is what happens when a king is making a state visit to a city, or indeed returning to Rome after a journey or battle. He appears, and is thus 'present,' as opposed to 'absent,' in his royal pomp. . . . Paul keeps the anti-pagan emphasis fully in play: what counts it's the *parousia* not of Caesar, but of Jesus."[3]

The central historical question is: did resurrection really happen as the Easter accounts say it did? In order to get at this question, the move from Scripture to history will begin with a slightly different question: what must have happened to explain the rise of the early church and the writing of the Bible as we have it? When we turn from these historical questions to the theological question, we ask: did it really happen as an eschatological event, as a prolepsis of the Parousia?

To pursue such questions, we must begin with the Christian symbols of Easter and the Parousia as we have inherited them from the Bible, symbols that already guide and direct today's Christians toward the fulfilled life.[4] The stories of Jesus' exit from the tomb and post-Easter appearances as we find them in the Bible come shrink-wrapped in the Parousia package, complete with understandings of Jesus as the Son of God and savior of the world, and they come with existential understandings of what this means for our daily life. To ask the historical question and to ask the theological question is to explicate abstractly the more concrete symbolic meaning that has already inspired faithful living for two millennia.

REVELATION AND ILLUMINATION

What we today have received from our past is a tradition (*paradosis*) of symbolic meaning. The symbols surrounding the person of Jesus Christ and the symbols pointing to God's eschatological promise of transformation provide the context of meaning for living the Christian life. If we think of the events in the life of Jesus of Nazareth as reported in Scripture as the revelation, then we can think of the message of the Bible with all of its evocative images as illumination. The biblical symbols illuminate our everyday experience. They provide the context for seeing our lives as meaningful in relation to Easter and the Parousia.

To use Michael Welker's vocabulary, such symbolic self-understanding is itself a revelation for us that opens up new realities for living. "Centered on God's name, centered on Christ's person, we have a different knowledge and experience of ourselves and of the realities in which we live. We are transformed by revelation. Revelation grounds and opens up a new force field of experience, action, and interaction, of which we become a part."[5] Or, more specifically, eschatological symbols elicit a fullness of life. "Eschatological symbols and symbol systems indeed focus on possible experiences and a reality that should not be ignored or even given up by the sciences. I should like to name this reality the *reality of the fullness of life* understood as both individual and communal life 'in God.'"[6] Welker interprets eschatological symbols of God's promised future as eliciting if not validating today's experience of fullness, of fulfillment.

However, the fullness of life or even perfection of life is something we experience in the moment in only a fragmentary way. We get fullness in fragments, but they are authentic fragments. The fullness of life or even perfection of life we embody today is dependent upon the truth of tomorrow, the eschatological fulfillment. "Perfection is not an original state to which creation is bidden to return," writes John Zizioulas, "but a πέρος which summons from ahead. . . . The truth of history lies in the future, and this is to be understood in an ontological sense: history is true, despite change and decay, not just because it is a movement *towards* an end, but mainly because it is a movement *from* the end, since it is the end that gives it meaning."[7] The future Parousia retroactively defines the past, gives meaning and even being to the past.

The impact of christological and eschatological symbols is that they place us meaningfully between yesterday's Easter and tomorrow's Parousia. Even more can be said. The promised arrival of Christ in the so-called second coming can be experienced now, ahead of time, in lives characterized by love, care, and forgiveness. Just as Easter was a prolepsis of Parousia, so a Spirit-inspired life can also be experienced as the proleptic presence of tomorrow's reality. "The Spirit of Christ acts as a power that . . . persistently works toward the universal establishment of justice, mercy, and knowledge of God," writes Welker.[8] Or, again with still heavier emphasis on prolepsis, "Eternal life that finds its form in Christ's life presses for its anticipation already here on this earth. It presses for the new creation to become present already under the conditions of the old, vanishing creation."[9]

IS CHRIST NECESSARY FOR SALVATION?

If eschatological salvation is yet future, then we might ask whether there is an inextricable link with historical happenings many years ago in Jerusalem. We might ask: Is the historical Jesus Christ an essential component to salvation? Or, does Jesus Christ point to a salvation that is detachable from Christology?

We can get at this question by asking, what salvific effect resulted from Jesus' death on the cross? Pauline scholar David Brondos says, none. "It is not *Jesus' death* that redeems believers, as if they were saved by an *event*, but *Jesus himself*, or rather, God through his Son, Jesus. Here Jesus' death does not 'effect' anything or produce some type of change in the situation of believers or humanity as a whole."[10] The agent of redemption, according to Brondos's interpretation of Paul, is God. And, further, redemption was not accomplished in its final form in the past on Calvary. Rather, it is still future, and this future redemption is anticipated in Jesus' Easter resurrection. "Humanity and human nature in general remain exactly as they were before Christ's coming. . . .What has changed is that the future deliverance from sin, death, and evil is now a certainty through Christ for believers, who will be freed from their present condition so as to participate in the new world to come."[11] Salvation here is not divorced completely from Christology, to be sure, but the significance of the events surrounding the historical Jesus is made dependent upon the salvific work of God yet to be accomplished in the future.

The question can be further illustrated by comparing Schubert Ogden with S. Mark Heim. For Ogden, Jesus Christ does not constitute salvation; rather, he represents (re-presents) the salvific or unbounded love of the everlasting God who is always and everywhere saving the world. The fundamental existential question universally asked by human beings has to do with who we are in relationship to God. We may or may not be aware of our asking this question, yet it is fundamental to human existing. The historical Jesus represents this existential quest and God's unbounded love. The general or universal human condition is that we live in relationship to a loving God. God is the "ever-present ground and end of all created things."[12] What Jesus Christ does is make explicit what is always implicitly true about the human relationship with the divine. "Jesus is the decisive re-presentation of God." Jesus also re-presents "the meaning of ultimate reality for us that is always already presented implicitly in our very existence."[13]

With this as his christological background, Ogden asks whether there is necessarily only one true religion or are there many? Because this soteriology is basically a revelational soteriology, in principle many revelations of what is always true about God are possible. The revelation in Jesus Christ does not constitute God's saving work; rather, it constitutes only the symbols for articulating God's independent saving love. Other religious traditions could provide their own symbolic representations of this same unbounded love of God.[14]

The problem with Ogden's position, complains S. Mark Heim, is that it eliminates a constitutive role for Jesus Christ either in God's love or in the content of salvation. "I believe that Jesus Christ is in fact constitutive of salvation. . . . Christ is one who comes *from* the triune life but also one who brings human life into its fullest participation in the triune life. Christ is not extrinsic to the love of God, not only a representation of it, but also the working of it. Christ is in such unity with God that communion with God involves a fundamental relation with Christ."[15]

The eschatological symbols within which the events of Jesus' death and resurrection come to articulation are universal symbols. They apply to the entire
scope of world history from creation to eschaton, from alpha to omega. They are
universal symbols regardless of whether they are believed or not; they apply even
if not believed by members of contemporary contiguous religious traditions or
by ancient Romans who consciously rejected the Christian claim. The Christian
claim is that Jesus' Easter resurrection is the trigger that fires the cannon announcing the advent of the consummate new creation. Yesterday's Easter and tomorrow's Parousia constitute a single comprehensive divine action that redeems the
world. Christological symbols do not point to what God is otherwise doing everywhere and always; rather, they point to a specific intrahistorical and eschatological
combination of events that together make up the one salvation story.

"NO" TO EASTER AND "NO" TO PAROUSIA:
JOHN DOMINIC CROSSAN

What we have just said would be disavowed by Jesus Seminar scholar John
Dominic Crossan. Crossan's historical judgments negate the biblical claim that
Jesus was raised by God from the dead on the first Easter. Crossan understands
his work to be that of a historian stepping up to meet the need to "give an accu-
rate but impartial account of the historical Jesus as distinct from the confessional
Christ."[16] Based upon canonical and extracanonical texts, Crossan reconstructs
a historical Jesus without Easter and, thereby, without Parousia.

Crossan's method locates the historical Jesus where three independent vectors
cross: cross-cultural anthropology, Greco-Roman and especially Jewish history,
plus literary or textual criticism.[17] The third, the textual criticism vector, reveals
that the primary biblical texts are structured according to three successive levels:
first, retention of original or historical Jesus materials; second, the transmission
or development of those materials; and, third, redaction that includes creation of
wholly new or fictional materials.[18] The composition of the canonical text of the
Bible, which includes all three levels, says Crossan, is due to deliberate theological or confessional interpretations of Jesus. These confessional redactors believed
that Jesus was raised from the dead, so they superimposed this belief upon the
history they were reporting. If we take away this layer of confessional redaction,
we will be able to reconstruct the historical Jesus.

Who, then, was the actual historical Jesus? The historical Jesus Crossan con-
structs looks like this: "The historical Jesus was a *peasant Jewish Cynic*. . . . His
strategy, implicitly for himself and explicitly for his followers, was the combination of *free healing and common eating*, a religious and economic egalitarianism
that negated alike and at once the hierarchical and patronal normalcies of Jewish
religion and Roman power."[19] The Jesus behind the Bible is not the Jesus of
Easter and the Parousia; rather, he is the Jesus of social equality and threats to
social hierarchy.

A key plank in Crossan's platform is that Jesus engaged in open commensality—that is, dining at table in an egalitarian and antihierarchical fashion. Jesus advocated "an open commensality, an eating together without using table as a miniature map of society's vertical discriminations and lateral separations."[20] This turned out to be politically disruptive. "Open commensality is the symbol and embodiment of radical egalitarianism, of an absolute equality of people that denies the validity of any discrimination between them and negates the necessity of any hierarchy among them."[21] After removing the transmissional and redactional levels of biblical text, Crossan finds a rural Jewish cynic with a message of social equality that upsets the existing hierarchical worldview.

This Jewish cynic replaces the Easter Christ, for Crossan. This historian cannot find a resurrected Christ, largely because of an assumption that he takes to his historical investigation. "I do not think anyone, anywhere, at any time brings dead people back to life."[22] Now, if the alleged Easter event is a reported miracle that could not have happened as it is reported, then what might its theological or confessional purpose be? Crossan answers that the Easter story functions to confer leadership and authority. At the redactional level, the biblical writers were countering the historical Jesus' original egalitarianism by establishing a hierarchy. The problem with the apparition accounts of the resurrected Jesus is that they conferred individual authority on individual persons and, thereby, justified for the developing church its clerical hierarchy. From Scripture onward, a male priest presides at the eucharistic table and the women serve. Jesus' original egalitarianism has disappeared. In sum, the resurrection redaction cancels out the previous egalitarianism of the historical Jesus.

Should we think of the Easter story as a lie told by the confessional redactors? Well, not exactly, says Crossan. Crossan prefers to avoid using the word "lie." Rather, he says the *words and deeds* of Jesus were updated to speak to new situations and problems, new communities and crises. They were adopted, they were adapted, they were invented, they were created."[23] What eventually developed over time from the adoption and adaptation process is a resurrection community of believers who intend to continue beyond Jesus' death what he embodied while still alive. Crossan places Jesus' postresurrection appearance story in Luke 24:13–33 in the representative role. "Resurrected life and risen vision appear as offered shelter and shared meal. Resurrection is not enough. You will need Scripture and Eucharist, tradition and table, community and justice; otherwise, divine presence remains unrecognized and human eyes remain unopened."[24] Evidently, the Emmaus appearance reinforces egalitarian commensality, whereas the other resurrection reports support a late-developing church hierarchy.

Crossan builds his historical case on a foundation of biblical accounts and the symbolic experience of the Christian community, especially the symbolism of the Eucharist. From these he abstracts to construct a historical Jesus devoid of an Easter resurrection yet still engaged in hosting a meal. Crossan's emphasis is on an egalitarian and not a hierarchical meal.

I would like to pose two critical questions to Crossan. First, why is Crossan's reconstructed historical Jesus divorced from the message of salvation? Why does he see it necessary to divorce common commensality from the Eucharist which anticipates the eschatological kingdom, a connection apparent in the Emmaus appearance? Why is Crossan reluctant to connect commensality with a "foretaste of the feast to come"? These seem to be inextricably bound together in the biblical text from which Crossan abstracts his slimmed-down and trimmed-down historical Jesus. The Jesus of the Bible is already inextricably tied to the message of salvation, so the burden of proof lies with one who wishes to cut the tie.

This leads to the second question, having to do with cutting the historical Jesus away from the third or redactive level of interpretation. Why does Crossan reverse causal logic? He argues that the confessional bias of the written biblical tradition superimposed a theology of resurrection upon a history without a resurrection. What we should be asking is this: From whence did these writers get their confessional bias? What precipitated it? Could it have been experiences with Jesus' Easter resurrection?[25]

"YES" TO EASTER AND "YES" TO PAROUSIA: N. T. WRIGHT

The answer to such questions offered by the bishop of Durham, N. T. Wright, is just the opposite to that of Crossan.[26] For Wright, the historian is perfectly right in saying that Jesus rose from the dead on Easter, and, further, that this original Easter event can be understood theologically only as the advent of the final reign of God, the new creation.

The argument for the historicity of Jesus' resurrection is constructed on the observation: the church exists. Easter, with its accompanying promise of the Parousia, explains why the church exists. "The *only* possible reason why early Christianity began and took the shape it did is that the tomb really was empty and that people really did meet Jesus, alive again. . . . The best historical explanation for all these phenomena is that Jesus was indeed bodily raised from the dead."[27] Easter is the explanation. "The combination of empty tomb and appearances of the living Jesus forms a set of circumstances which is itself *both necessary and sufficient* for the rise of early Christian belief. Without these phenomena, we cannot explain why this belief came into existence, and took the shape it did. With them, we can explain it exactly and precisely."[28]

Wright and Crossan do not agree on this. Whereas Crossan sees the Synoptic and Johannine resurrection accounts as late, at the third level, Wright sees them as early, at the first level. Whereas Crossan declares them fictional additions, Wright grants them historical status. Wright writes, "Crossan traces the origins of resurrection stories themselves to an educated, middle-class scribal movement which developed away from the pure, early peasant roots of Jesus himself. . . . The resurrection narratives are thus declared worthless as history: they are projected politics, and the politics (what is more) of the wrong sort of people, the wicked educated scribes instead of the noble virtuous peasants. . . . It looks as though Crossan is saying it can't be done when he means that it shouldn't be."[29] Wright finds Crossan's arguments unsatisfactory.

As we saw earlier, Crossan begins his historical investigation with the assumption that nobody has or ever will rise from the dead. Wright acknowledges that this was also the assumption made by New Testament reporters of the Easter event, but that assumption was overturned by what actually happened. "*The fact that dead people do not ordinarily rise is itself part of early Christian belief,* not an objection to it. The early Christians insisted that what had happened to Jesus was precisely something new; was, indeed, the start of a whole new mode of existence, a new creation."[30] What happened on Easter seems to have overturned the widespread assumption that dead people remain dead.

We have a methodological issue at stake here. Crossan's assumption has become a nonnegotiable when evaluating the historical evidence. Crossan appears to be applying Ernst Troeltsch's principle of analogy—that is, because he has himself not observed a dead person rising, he argues, by analogy, that it is not plausible to argue that Jesus or anybody else could have risen in the past. Wright, in contrast to Crossan, will allow the historical evidence to override this use of analogy. "It is precisely the uniqueness of the rise of the early church that forces us to say: never mind analogies, what happened?"[31]

When inquiring about the political significance of Jesus, Wright and Crossan draw similar conclusions. They both agree that humanly constructed hierarchies and systems of domination are antithetical to the kingdom of God as taught by Jesus. The two scholars differ, however, on where they locate the basis for this political implication. Crossan locates it in commensality, in the affirmation of peasant egalitarianism during Jesus' own lifetime that was continued by his disciples following his death. Wright, in contrast, locates the political significance in the Easter resurrection. The reality of resurrection of the body means that rulers cannot use the threat of death to enforce their dominion. The resurrection is testimony that God will overthrow the bullies and dictators of human oppression.

> No wonder the Herods, the Caesars and the Sadducees of this world, ancient and modern, were and are eager to rule out all possibility of actual resurrection. They are, after all, staking a counter-claim on the real world. It is the real world that the tyrants and bullies (including intellectual and cultural tyrants and bullies) try to rule by force, only to discover that in order to do so they have to quash all rumors of resurrection, rumors that would imply that their greatest weapons, death and deconstruction, are not after all omnipotent.[32]

To describe ecclesiology within Pauline theology, N. T. Wright appeals to what he calls "inaugurated eschatology"—that is, "a sense that God's ultimate future has come forwards into the middle of history, so that the church is living within—indeed, as constituted precisely by living simultaneously within!—God's new world and the present one. The age to come has already arrived with Jesus; but it will be consummated in the future. The church must order its life and witness, its holiness and love, along that axis."[33] We in the church are sandwiched between Easter and the Parousia.

PAROUSIA AND PROLEPSIS

What does resurrection look like? Wright believes he knows how to answer this when explicating the Pauline corpus. "Jesus' resurrection indicated not just *that* something extraordinary had come to pass, but *what that extraordinary thing was*: the anticipation, breaking in to the scene of ongoing history, of the ultimate End. Inaugurated eschatology, framed, explained and given depth by the reworking of monotheism and election, is one of the most central and characteristic notes of Paul's whole theology."[34]

Wright, while offering an exposition of what the early church believed, says we can expect a bodily resurrection, first for Jesus and then for the rest of us.

> Early Christianity was a "resurrection" movement through and through, and that, indeed, it stated much more precisely what exactly "resurrection" involved (it meant going through death and out into a new kind of bodily existence beyond, and it was happening in two stages, with Jesus first and everyone else later); second, that though the literal "resurrection" of which the early Christians spoke remained firmly in the future, it colored and gave shape to present Christian living as well.[35]

Where Wright uses "inaugurated eschatology," I would prefer to use "prolepsis." The term "prolepsis" indicates that Jesus' Easter resurrection embodies ahead of time the promised future new creation. Today, your and my anticipation of new creation affects present living, and this too brings up the issue of prolepsis. Wright uses this term, though not often. "The heart and center of it all, then, is the defeat of death in the future, based on the proleptic defeat inflicted in the resurrection of Jesus himself; or, to put it another way, it is the final completion of the 'age to come,' which was inaugurated, in the midst of the 'present evil age,' through the Messiah's death and resurrection."[36] With prolepsis, we are understanding the Easter resurrection of Jesus as a prefiguration of the advent of the eschatological new creation. This is a theological judgment, already present in the New Testament. It is built right into the meaning of the history of Jesus.

Once Wright has rendered his historical judgment—Easter gave rise to a church that remembers Easter—Wright proceeds to tease out theological implications. He recognizes the need to move beyond the strictly historical judgment regarding what the early church believed and why they believed it. What comes next is the question: what does this mean? What is its theological meaning? To move from history to theology, Wright recaptures the hermeneutical distinction between referent and meaning. By "referent" he refers to the historical judgment that Jesus rose bodily from the dead. By "meaning" he draws out its significance, namely, Jesus is the Son of God. "The resurrection, in other words, declares that Jesus really is God's Son: not only in the sense that he is the Messiah, though Paul certainly intends that here, not only in the sense that he is the world's true lord, though Paul intends that too, but also in the sense that he is the one in whom the living God, Israel's God, has become personally present in the world, has become one of the human creatures that were made from the beginning in the image of this same God."[37]

A hermeneutical matter is worth identifying here. Is Wright working with the assumption that the historian can begin with the referent (historical fact) and then add the meaning (theological interpretation)? It appears that way, although not quite. To draw the issue out further, we might ask: do we have access to the referent independently of the meaning? Do we have the luxury of pouring theological meaning on top of a historical event like sugar over cornflakes? No, we do not, because our only access to the referent is through a text already filled with the taste of meaning. Or, to put it another way, the only Easter resurrection of Jesus we know is the eschatological event described in the Bible.

Even if we ask, "Did it happen?" we still need to ask, "What is the *it* that happened?" The *it* is Easter. Built right into the definition of Easter is the proleptic or anticipatory embodiment in Jesus' person of the eschatological kingdom of God as the destiny of the world. The Parousia is not something added to Easter; it constitutes Easter.

If we ask both scholars the same question—how do you explain the rise or the birth of the Christian church?—they give quite different answers. John Dominic Crossan answers, "The birth of Christianity is the interaction between the historical Jesus and his first companions and the continuation of that relationship despite his execution."[38] N. T. Wright answers, "The proposal that Jesus was bodily raised from the dead possesses unrivaled power to explain the historical data at the heart of early Christianity." [39] For Crossan, Jesus was executed and remained dead, while his followers provided continuity between the preexecuted Jesus and the birth of the early church. For Wright, the executed Jesus rose bodily from the dead, and this historical fact accounts for the rise of faith in the early church. It also gives us reason to place our hope in the promised Parousia.

"YES" ON EASTER AND "YES" ON PAROUSIA: JÜRGEN MOLTMANN AND WOLFHART PANNENBERG

The power and energy of the theology of hope as it emerged in the 1960s derived from this connection between Easter and the Parousia. "The resurrection has set in motion an eschatologically determined process of history, whose goal is the annihilation of death in the victory of the life of the resurrection, and which ends in that righteousness in which God receives in all things his due and the creature thereby finds its salvation," wrote Jürgen Moltmann.[40] In this view, a Christianity based solely on commensality without resurrection would not suffice. "Christianity stands or falls with the reality of the raising of Jesus from the dead by God. In the New Testament there is no faith that does not start *a priori* with the resurrection of Jesus."[41] Moltmann further emphasizes that the historical event of the past Easter will not suffice by itself; it must be attached to the promised eschatological transformation. "If Christ has been raised *from* the dead, then he takes on proleptic and representative significance *for* all the dead. . . . The two sides necessarily belong together: there is no resurrection of the dead without the new earth in which death will be no more."[42]

As I indicated previously, my preferred term for linking Easter and Parousia is prolepsis, used here by Moltmann and developed more fully by Wolfhart Pannenberg. The Pannenberg of the 1960s emphasized the prerealization of the eschatological promise. "The ministry of Jesus shared with prophecy the character of an anticipation, but not only as in prophecy and apocalyptic in the sense of mere pre-*cognition*, but, so to say, as a pre-*realization* of the future, as its proleptic dawning."[43]

At the originary symbolic level as we find it in the New Testament accounts, Jesus' Easter resurrection is the dawning of the general or universal resurrection previously anticipated in apocalyptic prophecies.[44] Whether Jewish listeners to Jesus believed or disbelieved in the apocalyptic vision of resurrection, they understood it, and they could understand why what happened to Jesus on Easter would be interpreted within this horizon. Jesus' resurrection is the "first fruits" of those having "fallen asleep" (1 Cor. 15:20). What was expected for all of us has already happened individually to the person of Jesus. "Jesus' expectation of the speedy realization of the eschatological reality did not simply fail. It was fulfilled, and thus confirmed, though only in his own person. . . .The general human destiny has occurred in Jesus—if he *really was* resurrected from the dead."[45]

Pannenberg actually makes his theological assertion contingent upon a historical one: "If he *really* was resurrected from the dead." Theological commitment is dependent upon historicity of the founding event, Jesus' personal resurrection. Faith is dependent on history. Faith, even though it is a subjective appropriation of Christian belief, is not reducible to its subjective character; it requires grounding in the objective realm of fact. This means, among other things, that a historical judgment against the authenticity of the biblical claim regarding Jesus' resurrection would undermine Christian belief. "Now let us assume that the historical question concerning the resurrection of Jesus has been decided positively, then the meaning of this event as God's final revelation is not something that must be added to it; rather, this is the original meaning inherent in that event within its own context of history and tradition."[46]

Curiously, in this perspective, what happened in the past is dependent on what will happen in the future, which in turn makes theological explications based upon historical judgments hypothetical. This should not be surprising. In principle, all faith commitments are hypothetical, contingent upon their confirmation by God. "Anticipation therefore always involves hypothesis."[47] So, it is necessary for the systematic theologian to proceed with the explication of the meaning of Jesus' resurrection while incorporating the probable status of its historical foundation. Both this referent and the meaning of this historical event are contingent upon their eschatological confirmation or disconfirmation.

Can we actually say that the past is dependent on the future? Can we say that to understand Easter we must begin with the Parousia? Can we say Christology is dependent on eschatology? Pannenberg would answer "yes" by arguing that the proleptic events surrounding the historical Jesus and the eschatological event of new creation are a single reality, a single act by an eternal God with a temporal world:

> The coming again of Christ will be the completion of the work of the Spirit that began in the incarnation and with the resurrection of Jesus. From the standpoint of eternity we have here one and the same event because the incarnation is already the inbreaking of the future of God, the entry of eternity into time. For us, however, confession of the incarnation has its basis in Jesus' resurrection, and only at his return will debate concerning the reality of the Easter event be at an end and will that reality definitively and publicly come into force, for the resurrection of Jesus is a proleptic manifestation of the reality of the new, eschatological life of salvation in Jesus himself.[48]

Only in the future will we know the past for certain.

ANTICIPATING THE FUTURE NOW

Based upon the biblical witness to Jesus' resurrection, we can now anticipate our eschatological future in at least three ways. First, we can use our imaginations to construct a picture of what deliverance and salvation might look like. "The New Testament invites us, then, to *imagine* a new world as a beautiful, healing community; to envisage it as a world vibrant with life and energy, incorruptible, beyond the reach of death and decay; to hold it in our mind's eye as a world reborn, set free from the slavery of corruption, free to be truly what it was made to be."[49]

Second, by imagining a new and better world, we can use this constructed picture to guide moral activity. Ethics begins with a vision of a better world, then seeks to actualize or realize that vision. Proleptic ethics seeks to make real today what we expect God will deliver tomorrow. "God's future had already broken into the present in Jesus, and the church's task consisted not least of *implementing* that achievement and thus *anticipating* that future."[50]

Third, when celebrating the sacraments we expand our vision of reality to gain a foretaste of the feast that is yet to come. The final future is not here yet, so we cannot perceive it with our senses. Yet the sacraments can bridge the realm of present sense with anticipated future.

Michael Welker's sacramental theology is relevant here. Welker contends that biblical testimonies to witnessing the resurrected Jesus shock us into perceiving the limits of our present view of reality. The tension between the corporeal or physical presence of the resurrected Jesus and the apparitional or trans-physical dimensions lead Welker to say, "Testimonies to the resurrection emphasize that the resurrection reality is more than a merely natural event."[51] On the one hand, this earthly being is, like all of us, limited in space and time; yet, mysteriously, the one who has overcome death "can and does reveal himself in many locations at the same time."[52] Moving from the biblical witness to the sacrament of the altar—what Welker calls "the Supper"—the same expanded view of reality applies. "The Supper centers on a complex, sensuous process in which the risen and exalted Christ becomes present. . . . At the same time the limits of merely sensuous experience are consciously noted."[53]

This dimension of appearance, combined with the sensuous experience of bread and wine, means that the historical and the future Christ can be present each time the sacrament is celebrated. "The celebration of the Supper takes place in communion with the past, present, and future church of Christ. . . . The celebration of the Supper ties together in communion the living and the dead and the not yet born. . . . The New Testament conceptions compel us to grasp the onset of Christ's reign not in one particular time and world, but in all times and all worlds."[54]

NOTES

1. Michael Welker, "Theological Realism and Eschatological Symbol Systems," in *Resurrection: Theological and Scientific Assessments,* ed. Ted Peters, Robert John Russell, and Michael Welker (Grand Rapids: Eerdmans, 2002), 40.
2. Our liturgical remembrance of the resurrection of Jesus has garnered the name Easter, *Ostern,* having to do with what is east. A variety of theories attempt to explain this association. "Im 8.Jh. hat Beda Venerabilis O. auf die angelsächsische Morgengöttin Eostra zurückgeführt, die ahd. Ostara heißt. Honorius von Autun (12.Jh.) leitet O. von Osten ab (Sonnenaufgang im Osten als Symbol für den Auferstandenen)." More recent theories associate the term "Easter" or "Ostern" with water pouring, perhaps a pre-Christian form of baptism. Georg Kraus recommends we let the differing theories sit beside one another without resolution, in "Ostern," in *Religion in Geschichte und Gegenwart,* ed. Hans Dieter Betz, Don S. Browning, Bernd Janowski, and Eberhard Jüngel, 4th ed., vol. 6 (Tübingen: Mohr Siebeck, 1998–2005), 727.
3. N. T. Wright, *Paul: Fresh Perspectives* (London: SPCK, 2005), 142.
4. Symbols give rise to concepts. Symbolic language functions as primary discourse, whereas theological language operates at the level of secondary discourse. Biblical discourse is symbolic speech—that is, the Bible's metaphors, images, stories, visions, and speculations are multivalent. Symbols give rise to multiple directions for meaning, and each direction is determined by the hermeneutics of the interpreter. Theological discourse is reflective discourse—that is, it interprets biblical language in such a way as to construct a system of concepts. These concepts are hypothetical descriptions of reality. It is important for the theologian to keep in mind that his or her conceptual construction constitutes one of many possible levels of interpretation of the

single set of biblical symbols. See Ted Peters, *God—The World's Future,* 2nd ed. (Minneapolis: Fortress, 2000), chap. 2.

5. Michael Welker, *Creation and Reality,* trans. John F. Hoffmeyer (Minneapolis: Fortress, 1999), 31.

6. Welker, "Theological Realism and Eschatological Symbol Systems," 34.

7. John D. Zizioulas, *Being as Communion* (Crestwood, N.Y.: St. Vladimir's Seminary Press, 1993), 96.

8. Michael Welker, *God the Spirit,* trans. John F. Hoffmeyer (Minneapolis: Fortress, 1996), 221.

9. Michael Welker, "Resurrection and Eternal Life: The Canonic Memory of the Resurrected Christ, His Reality, and His Glory," in *The End of the World and the Ends of God,* ed. John Polkinghorne and Michael Welker (Harrisburg, Pa.: Trinity, 2000), 290.

10. David A. Brondos, *Paul on the Cross: Reconstructing the Apostle's Story of Redemption* (Minneapolis: Fortress, 2006), 76.

11. Ibid., 192.

12. Schubert M. Ogden, *Christ without Myth* (New York: Harper, 1961), 153.

13. Schubert M. Ogden, *The Point of Christology* (New York: Harper, 1982), 82.

14. Schubert M. Ogden, *Is There Only One True Religion or Are There Many?* (Dallas: Southern Methodist University Press, 1992), 98.

15. S. Mark Heim, *The Depth of the Riches: A Trinitarian Theology of Religious Ends* (Grand Rapids: Eerdmans, 2001), 52.

16. John Dominic Crossan, *Jesus: A Revolutionary Biography* (San Francisco: Harper, 1994), xi.

17. Ibid., xi–xii. See also Crossan, *The Birth of Christianity* (San Francisco: Harper, 1998), x.

18. Crossan, *Jesus,* xiii, 83, 145.

19. Ibid., 198 (italics in original); see also John Dominic Crossan, *The Historical Jesus: The Life of a Mediterranean Jewish Peasant* (San Francisco: Harper, 1991), 421.

20. Crossan, *Jesus,* 69.

21. Ibid., 71.

22. Ibid., 95.

23. Crossan, *Birth of Christianity,* 524 (italics in original).

24. Ibid., xi.

25. Both Günther Bornkam and Luke Timothy Johnson begin with what the early church in the Scriptures reports and then ask the right question: what happened to Jesus to precipitate this report? What did Jesus do that accounts for the rise of faith in his resurrection? See Günther Bornkam, *Jesus of Nazareth* (New York: Harper, 1960), 183, and Luke Timothy Johnson, *The Real Jesus: The Misguided Quest for the Historical Jesus and the Truth of the Traditional Gospels* (San Francisco: Harper, 1996), 50. This seems warranted, because biblical critics are largely in agreement that the pre-Pauline story in the opening verses of 1 Cor. 15 (*paradosis*) of Jesus that includes his resurrection may have begun almost immediately. "This tradition, we can be entirely confident, was *formulated as tradition within months of Jesus' death,*" writes James D. G. Dunn in, *Christianity in the Making,* vol. 1, *Jesus Remembered* (Grand Rapids: Eerdmans, 2003), 855 (italics in original). Even Gerd Lüdemann would concur: "*the formation of the appearance traditions mentioned in I Cor. 15:3–8 falls into the time between 30 and 33 CE,*" in *The Resurrection of Jesus,* trans. John Bowden (Minneapolis: Fortress, 1994), 38 (italics in original). In sum, what

Crossan calls a later redactional confession of Jesus' resurrection seems in fact to be the earliest stratum of Christian tradition.

26. See Robert B. Stewart, ed., *The Resurrection of Jesus: John Dominic Crossan and N. T. Wright in Dialogue* (Minneapolis: Fortress, 2006).

27. N. T. Wright, *Christian Origins and the Question of God*, vol. 3, *The Resurrection of the Son of God* (Minneapolis: Fortress, 2003), 8 (italics in original).

28. Ibid., 696 (italics in original).

29. Ibid., 19.

30. Ibid., 712 (italics in original).

31. Ibid., 18. For a thorough critique of the Troeltschian overuse of the principle of analogy in historical research, see Wolfhart Pannenberg, *Basic Questions in Theology*, vol. I (Minneapolis: Fortress, 1970–1971), 38–53.

32. Wright, *Resurrection*, 737.

33. Wright, *Paul*, 57.

34. Ibid., 136 (italics in original).

35. Wright, *Resurrection*, 210.

36. Ibid., 336. Brondos fears that Wright comes too close to imposing the "participation" model of atonement on his exegesis of Paul. Brondos denies that the New Testament teaches any notion that the human race participates mystically or ontologically in the events of Jesus' death and resurrection. "N. T. Wright ascribes to Paul the idea that Jesus 'sums up his people in himself' as an 'incorporative Messiah' but makes no effort to define how this should be understood," from *Paul on the Cross*, 158.

37. Wright, *Resurrection.*, 733.

38. Crossan, *Birth*, xxi.

39. Wright, *Resurrection*, 718.

40. Jürgen Moltmann, *Theology of Hope* (New York: Harper, 1967), 163.

41. Ibid., 165.

42. Jürgen Moltmann, *The Coming of God: Christian Eschatology*, trans. Margaret Kohl (Minneapolis: Fortress, 1996), 69 (italics in original).

43. Wolfhart Pannenberg, "Focal Essay: The Revelation of God in Jesus of Nazareth," in *New Frontiers in Theology*, vol. 3, *Theology as History*, ed. James M. Robinson and John B. Cobb Jr. (New York: Harper, 1967), 112–13 (italics in original).

44. For Pannenberg, the very explication of the early apostolic witness in the Bible leads one to ask about the precipitating historical cause for the apostolic faith in the resurrection. "The history of early Christianity seemed to show that a certain event, the event of Jesus' resurrection, was the precondition for that step from implication to explication," from Wolfhart Pannenberg, "An Intellectual Pilgrimage," *Dialog* 45, no. 2 (Summer 2006): 189.

45. Pannenberg, "Focal Essay," 114 (italics in original).

46. Ibid., 128.

47. Wolfhart Pannenberg, *Theology and the Philosophy of Science*, trans. Francis McDonagh (Philadelphia: Westminster, 1976), 310. "The truth of the Christian tradition can function only as a hypothesis in any theology which proceeds scientifically" (261). On the provisionality of dogma, see Pannenberg, "What Is a Dogmatic Statement?" in *Basic Questions*, 1:181–210.

48. Wolfhart Pannenberg, *Systematic Theology*, trans. Geoffrey W. Bromily, vol. 3 (Grand Rapids: Eerdmans, 1991–1998), 627. See Ted Peters, "Clarity of the Part versus Meaning of the Whole," in *Beginning with the End: God, Science, and Wolfhart Pannenberg*, ed. Carol Rausch Albright and Joel Haugen (Chicago: Open Court, 1997), 289–302.

49. N. T. Wright, *Evil and the Justice of God* (London: SPCK, 2006), 76.
50. Ibid., 65 (italics in original).
51. Michael Welker, *What Happens in Holy Communion?* trans. John Hoffmeyer (London: SPCK, 2000), 15.
52. Ibid.
53. Ibid., 18.
54. Ibid., 117.

Contributors

Marcia J. Bunge is Professor of Humanities and Theology and Director of the Child in Religion Program at Christ College, Valparaiso University, Valparaiso, Indiana.

Sarah Coakley is the Norris-Hulse Professor of Divinity and Fellow of New Hall at Cambridge University, Cambridge, United Kingdom.

Thomas W. Gillespie is Professor Emeritus of New Testament at Princeton Theological Seminary, Princeton, New Jersey.

Paul D. Hanson is the Florence Corliss Lamont Professor of Divinity at Harvard Divinity School, Cambridge, Massachusetts.

John F. Hoffmeyer is Associate Professor of Systematic Theology at the Lutheran Theological Seminary at Philadelphia, Philadelphia, Pennsylvania.

Catherine Keller is Professor of Constructive Theology in the Theological School at Drew University, Madison, New Jersey.

Peter Lampe is Professor of New Testament at the University of Heidelberg, Heidelberg, Germany.

Patrick D. Miller is Professor Emeritus of Old Testament at Princeton Theological Seminary, Princeton, New Jersey.

Piet J. Naudé is Professor of Ethics in the Nelson Mandela Metropolitan University Business School, University of Port Elizabeth, Port Elizabeth, South Africa.

Ted Peters is Professor of Systematic Theology and Director of the Institute for Theology and Ethics at the Pacific Lutheran Theological Seminary, Berkeley, California.

John Polkinghorne is Professor Emeritus of Mathematical Physics at Cambridge University, Cambridge, United Kingdom.

Andreas Kurt Schuele is the Aubrey Lee Brooks Professor of Biblical Theology at Union Theological Seminary and Presbyterian School of Christian Education, Richmond, Virginia.

William Schweiker is the Director of the Martin Marty Center and the Edward L. Ryerson Distinguished Service Professor of Theological Ethics in the Divinity School, University of Chicago, Chicago, Illinois.

Christoph Schwöbel is Professor of Systematic Theology and Director of the Institut für Hermeneutik und Dialog der Kulturen at the University of Tübingen, Germany.

Dirk Smit is Professor of Systematic Theology at the University of Stellenbosch, Matie-
land, South Africa.
Günter Thomas is Professor of Systematic Theology and Theological Ethics at the Ruhr
Universität, Bochum, Germany.

Index